SHI'A MINORITIES IN THE CONTEMPORARY WORLD

Alternative Histories: Narratives from the Middle East and Mediterranean

Series Editor: Sargon Donabed

This series provides a forum for exchange on a myriad of alternative histories of marginalised communities and individuals in the Near and Middle East and Mediterranean, and those of Middle Eastern or Mediterranean heritage. It also highlights thematic issues relating to various native peoples and their narratives and – with particular contemporary relevance – explore encounters with the notion of 'other' within societies. Often moving beyond the conventional state-centred and dominant monolithic approach, or reinterpreting previously accepted stories, books in the series examine and explain themes from inter-communal relations, environment, health and society, and explore ethnic, communal, racial, linguistic and religious developments, in addition to geopolitics.

Editorial Advisory Board

Professor Ali Banuazizi
Dr Aryo Makko
Professor Laura Robson
Professor Paul Rowe
Professor Hannibal Travis

Books in the Series (Published and Forthcoming)

Sayfo: An Account of the Assyrian Genocide
'Abd al-Masih Nu'man of Qarabash
translated and annotated by Michael Abdalla and Łukasz Kiczko

Tunisia's Andalusians: The Cultural Identity of a North African Minority
Marta Dominguez Diaz

Palestinian Citizens of Israel: A History Through Fiction, 1948–2010
Manar Makhoul

Armenians Beyond Diaspora: Making Lebanon their Own
Tsolin Nalbantian

The Art of Minorities: Cultural Representation in Museums of the Middle East and North Africa
Edited by Virginie Rey

Shi'a Minorities in the Contemporary World: Migration, Transnationalism and Multilocality
Edited by Oliver Scharbrodt and Yafa Shanneik

Protestants, Gender and the Arab Renaissance in Late Ottoman Syria
Deanna Ferree Womack

edinburghuniversitypress.com/series/ahnme

SHI'A MINORITIES IN THE CONTEMPORARY WORLD

MIGRATION, TRANSNATIONALISM AND MULTILOCALITY

Edited by Oliver Scharbrodt
and Yafa Shanneik

EDINBURGH
University Press

Edinburgh University Press is one of the leading university presses in the UK. We publish academic books and journals in our selected subject areas across the humanities and social sciences, combining cutting-edge scholarship with high editorial and production values to produce academic works of lasting importance. For more information visit our website: edinburghuniversitypress.com

© editorial matter and organisation Oliver Scharbrodt and Yafa Shanneik, 2020, 2022
© the chapters their several authors, 2020, 2022

Edinburgh University Press Ltd
The Tun – Holyrood Road
12 (2f) Jackson's Entry
Edinburgh EH8 8PJ

First published in hardback by Edinburgh University Press 2020

Typeset in 11/15 Adobe Garamond by
Servis Filmsetting Ltd, Stockport, Cheshire,

A CIP record for this book is available from the British Library

ISBN 978 1 4744 3037 1 (hardback)
ISBN 978 1 4744 3038 8 (paperback)
ISBN 978 1 4744 3039 5 (webready PDF)
ISBN 978 1 4744 3040 1 (epub)

The right of the contributors to be identified as authors of this work has been asserted in accordance with the Copyright, Designs and Patents Act 1988 and the Copyright and Related Rights Regulations 2003 (SI No. 2498).

CONTENTS

List of Figures viii
Acknowledgements ix
The Contributors x
Glossary xv

Introduction

1 'My Homeland is Husayn': Transnationalism and Multilocality in Shi'a Contexts 3
   Oliver Scharbrodt and Yafa Shanneik

Part I Localising Global Shi'a Minority Spaces

2 Performing Shi'ism between Java and Qom: Education and Rituals 33
   Chiara Formichi

3 *Mi corazón late Husayn:* Identity, Politics and Religion in a Shi'a Community in Buenos Aires 46
   Mari-Sol García Somoza and Mayra Soledad Valcarcel

4 Bektashism as a Model and Metaphor for 'Balkan Islam' 73
Piro Rexhepi

5 Living Najaf in London: Diaspora, Identity and the Sectarianisation of the Iraqi-Shi'a Subject 96
Emanuelle Degli Esposti

Part II Transnational Shi'a Trajectories

6 Global Networks, Local Concerns: Investigating the Impact of Emerging Technologies on Shi'a Religious Leaders and Constituencies 123
Robert J. Riggs

7 'Still We Long for Zaynab': South Asian Shi'ites and Transnational Homelands under Attack 142
Noor Zehra Zaidi

8 From a Marginalised Religious Community in Iran to a Government-sanctioned Public Interest Foundation in Paris – Remarks on the 'Ostad Elahi Foundation' 163
Roswitha Badry

Part III 'Alid Piety and the Fluidity of Sectarian Boundaries

9 Ideas in Motion: The Transmission of Shi'a Knowledge in Sri Lanka 185
Arun Rasiah

10 Limits of Sectarianism: Shi'ism and *ahl al-bayt* Islam among Turkish Migrant Communities in Germany 209
Benjamin Weineck

11 'For 'Ali is Our Ancestor': Cham *Sayyids*' Shi'a Trajectories from Cambodia to Iran 227
Emiko Stock

Epilogue

12 Shi'a Cosmopolitanisms and Conversions   257
    Mara A. Leichtman

Notes   281
Index   310

FIGURES

5.1	Iraqi institutions in London by political/religious affiliation	101
5.2	Map showing the main religious institutions in the 'Shi'a triangle' of northwest London	102
5.3	ICARE Facebook post depicting Iraqi soldier from the PMF militia	109
10.1	Website of *Oniki İmam Yolu*	218
11.1	'Ali Hanaphiah (and his doubles)	234
11.2	From Zayn Al-'Abidin to Nosavan	238
11.3	Repetitive Zayn Al-'Abidins	242
11.4	Wali Songo (Part I)	245
11.5	Wali Songo (Part II)	245

ACKNOWLEDGEMENTS

This volume is one of three publications that came out of a conference organised at the University of Chester in May 2016. The conference provided a unique platform to bring researchers from a variety of disciplines together who work on Shi'a minorities in non-Muslim contexts. The conference concluded the project '"Karbala in London": Transnational Twelver Shia Networks between Britain and the Middle East' that investigated Twelver Shi'a organisations and communities based in London. The project was funded by a research grant of the Gerda Henkel Foundation. We would like to thank the Gerda Henkel Foundation for providing the funding for the project and this publication and for making the conference in Chester possible.

In particular, we owe thanks to the contributors to this volume for their patience in the longer than expected journey of putting this volume together. We are also grateful to Nicola Ramsey and Kirsty Woods at Edinburgh University Press for their support for this book project.

The Editors
Birmingham, July 2019

CONTRIBUTORS

Roswitha Badry is Professor of Islamic Studies at the University of Freiburg, Germany. Her publications and research interests centre on the history of the MENA-region since the nineteenth century, the continued influence of classical ideas in contemporary discourses, Shi'a Islam, gender issues, (auto-)biographies of religious scholars and intellectuals, and contemporary Arabic literature.

Emanuelle Degli Esposti is Research and Outreach Associate at the Centre of Islamic Studies, University of Cambridge, where she is investigating intra-communal antagonism and identity politics. In particular, her work makes use of theories in critical discourse analysis and psychoanalysis to theorise the production of in- and out-group boundaries relating to Sunni-Shi'a sectarianism, especially at the level of everyday practices. She holds a PhD in Politics and International Studies and an MSc in Middle East Politics from SOAS, University of London, and an MA and BA in Philosophy and Modern Languages from the University of Oxford. Her doctoral research drew on the case study of the Iraqi Shi'a diaspora to develop an alternative framework for conceptualising sectarianism as the unconscious of identity formation.

Beyond academia, Emanuelle Degli Esposti also delivers security and risk analysis on Europe and the Middle East for a range of private-sector clients, as well as having professional experience in consultancy and journalism. In 2011, she founded *The Arab Review*, an online journal showcasing arts, culture and politics from the Middle East.

Chiara Formichi is Associate Professor in Southeast Asian Studies at Cornell University. Her work focuses on Islam as a lived religion and as a political ideology in twentieth-century Indonesia and Southeast Asia more broadly. As such, her interests lie at the disciplinary intersection between Islamic Studies, History and Area Studies, methodologically resting on archival research as well as ethnography. Thematically, her research has addressed the role of Islam in politics, the status of Muslim minorities, the shaping of Indonesia's socio-political modernity, and the history of Islam in Asia.

Mari-Sol García Somoza graduated in Sociology from the University of Buenos Aires. She holds an MA in Social and Human Sciences from the EHESS, France. She is currently a PhD candidate at the UBA-Paris Descartes University. Her doctoral thesis is entitled 'From Fatima to Evita: Identities, Involvement Spaces and Religious Sociabilities of Muslim Women in Argentina'. She is a Lecturer in Culture and Hispanic Civilisation in France. She is a member of the editorial board for the CEIL-CONICET journal *Sociedad y Religión* and for the ACSRM/UFRGS journal *Ciencias Sociais e Religião*. She is also a member of the Centre for Cultural Anthropology, Paris Descartes University and of CEIL-CONICET's Society, Culture and Religion Programme. She was a member of the Steering Committee of the MERCOSUR Association of Social Scientists of Religion 2015–18.

Mara A. Leichtman is Associate Professor of Anthropology and Muslim Studies at Michigan State University. Her research highlights the interconnections among religion, migration, politics and economic development. She is the author of *Shi'i Cosmopolitanisms in Africa: Lebanese Migration and Religious Conversion in Senegal* (2015). She also edited (with Dorothea Schulz) a special issue of *City and Society* on *Muslim Cosmopolitanism:*

Movement, Identity, and Contemporary Reconfigurations (2012) and (with Mamadou Diouf) the book *New Perspectives on Islam in Senegal: Conversion, Migration, Wealth, Power, and Femininity* (2009). Her articles have appeared in the *British Journal of Middle Eastern Studies, Anthropological Quarterly, Contemporary Islam, Oxford Islamic Studies Online, International Journal of Middle East Studies, Journal of Religion in Africa* and *Ethnic and Racial Studies*. She was a visiting Fulbright Scholar at the American University of Kuwait (2016–17) where she launched a new research project that examines Islamic humanitarianism in the Gulf directed to global economic development in Africa.

Arun Rasiah is Associate Professor of Liberal Studies at Holy Names University in Oakland, California. His research on the transmission of knowledge in the Muslim world traces the movement of ideas, the development of formal education, and practices of informal learning in several contexts. Currently, he is a Visiting Fellow at the Oxford Centre for Islamic Studies where he is working on a project entitled 'The Pedagogy of Malcolm X: Teaching Decolonisation'.

Piro Rexhepi is an Assistant Professor of Global Studies at Northampton Community College. He holds a PhD in Politics from the University of Strathclyde and was a post-doctoral research fellow at the Max Planck Institute for the Study of Religious and Ethnic Diversity. His interdisciplinary research covers the politics of sexuality, religion and de/coloniality in the Balkans and has been published in *Interventions: International Journal of Postcolonial Studies, Ethnic and Racial Studies, East European Quarterly, Big Data & Society* as well as local and international media such as *The Guardian, Critical Muslims, Balkanist* and *Desde el Margen*.

Robert J. Riggs is a specialist in contemporary Shi'ism, focusing on its emergence as a complex of local and transnational movements. He serves as Associate Professor of Religion and Politics at the University of Bridgeport in Connecticut, where he teaches courses on Islamic history and religion, on comparative monotheisms and the history of Muslim–Christian–Jewish relations, on the political economy of the MENA region, and on Islam and

Democracy, among others. He focuses in his research on the influence of contemporary Shi'a religious authorities based in Lebanon, Iraq and Iran over local and transnational Shi'a religious movements. His forthcoming book, *Shiascapes: The Changing Face of Contemporary Arab Shi'ism*, examines the contemporary histories of Shi'a communities in Iran, Iraq, Lebanon and their diasporas in Europe and the US. Robert Riggs also serves as a regular commentator on the Middle East for a variety of news outlets, such as *CTV News* and *Al-Jazeera*.

Oliver Scharbrodt is Professor of Islamic Studies at the University of Birmingham. His research expertise covers the intellectual history of modern Islam, Shi'ism, Sufism and Muslim minorities in Europe. Oliver Scharbrodt is the author of *Islam and the Baha'i Faith: A Comparative Study of Muhammad 'Abduh and 'Abdul-Baha 'Abbas* (2008) and co-author of *Muslims in Ireland: Past and Present* (Edinburgh University Press, 2015). Currently, he is the principal investigator of an ERC-funded project investigating the transformation of clerical authority in Twelver Shi'ism since the late 1950s.

Yafa Shanneik is Lecturer in Islamic Studies at the University of Birmingham. She researches the dynamics and trajectories of gender in Islam within the context of contemporary diasporic and transnational Muslim women's spaces. She works on Sunni and Shi'a women communities in Europe and their transnational links to the Middle East. She also has a particular research interest in the authority and leadership of Muslim women and the changing nature of women's participation in religious practices in Europe and the Middle East. She has published several articles on gender and Islam and migrant identities in Europe such as: 'Remembering Karbala in the Diaspora: Religious Rituals among Iraqi Shii Women in Ireland' (*Religion*, 2015) and 'Religion and Diasporic Dwelling: Algerian Muslim Women in Ireland' (*Religion and Gender*, 2012).

Emiko Stock received Masters in Khmer Studies from INALCO (National Institute of Oriental Languages and Civilizations) and in Anthropology from Nanterre University, both in Paris, before joining the Department of Anthropology at Cornell University as a graduate student. In Phnom Penh, she studied archaeology at the Royal University of Fine Arts while working various jobs, primarily as a fixer-interpreter. Her ethnographic work in Cambodia and Iran is conducted as a videographer and historiographer. She is a Postdoctoral Fellow in the Asian Studies Program at Hamilton College starting Autumn 2019 where she teaches digital film production.

Mayra Soledad Valcarcel graduated in Anthropological Sciences from the University of Buenos Aires (UBA). She is currently PhD candidate of the National Scientific and Technical Research Council (CONICET) at the Interdisciplinary Institute of Gender Studies (IIEGE, FILO: UBA) at the University of Buenos Aires, researching on Muslim women in Argentina.

Benjamin Weineck is director of a research group at the Department for the Study of Religion at Bayreuth University, Germany. His research group addresses questions of religious differentiation, sectarianism or sectarian indifference among Muslims (mostly Shiʻa and Alevi) in the European diaspora and in the respective countries of origin (with a focus on Turkey, the Ottoman Empire and Iran). He is the editor, together with Johannes Zimmermann, of *Alevism between Standardisation and Plurality: Negotiating Texts, Sources and Cultural Heritage* (2018). In addition, he has published various articles concerning historical as well as contemporary aspects of Alevi and Shiʻa Islam. His monograph on the history of the Kızılbaş-Alevis in the Ottoman Empire, sixteenth to eighteenth century, is currently in preparation.

Noor Zehra Zaidi is Assistant Professor of History at the University of Maryland, Baltimore. Her research expertise covers sectarianism in the modern Middle East, modern Shiʻa communities, pilgrimage and gender. She completed her PhD in 2015 at the University of Pennsylvania with a dissertation entitled 'Making Spaces Sacred: The Sayyeda Zaynab and Bibi Pak Daman Shrines and the Construction of Modern Shiʻa Identity', which explores the evolution of pilgrimage to two female shrines in Syria and Pakistan. She is currently working on a new manuscript on sites of sectarianisation in Saddam Hussein's Baathist Iraq, which explores prisons, shrines, homes and visual space as sites of memory-making and the construction of an identity of resistance amongst the Shiʻa Muslim community of Iraq.

GLOSSARY

ahl al-bayt/ al al-bayt – family of the Prophet and his descendants, particularly venerated in all Shi'a traditions and Sufism.

ahl al-kisa' – lit. 'people of the cloak': according to a *hadith*, Muhammad gathered one morning his daughter Fatima, his cousin and son-in-law 'Ali and their children Hasan and Husayn under a cloak and referred to them as his *ahl al-bayt*.

ahl-e haqq – lit. 'people of the truth': religious group found in western Iran and northeastern Iraq with esoteric teachings and origins in Shi'a *ghulat* traditions which include the belief in divine incarnation and metempsychosis; also referred to as Yaresan.

akhlaq – Arabic for manners, ethics or morals.

akhund – Persian reference to lower-ranking Shi'a clerics which is used in Iran, Azerbaijan, Afghanistan and Pakistan; can have derogatory connotations. See also *mullah*.

Alawite/Nusayri – esoteric movement with links to Shi'ism; present in Syria, Lebanon and Arabic-speaking communities in the Turkish province of Hatay. Not to be confused with Alevis who are of Eastern Anatolian origin.

Alevi – movement with roots dating back to the twelfth century, often esoteric in nature and with links to Shi'ism; today especially strong among Turks and Kurds of Eastern Anatolian origin.

Arba'in – Shi'a religious observance, forty days after the day of 'Ashura', to commemorate the death of Husayn ibn 'Ali (third Shi'a Imam).

ashik – lit. 'lover': term used for lay followers of the Bektashi order.

'Ashura' – festival on the tenth of Muharram (first month of the Islamic calendar) marking the death of Husayn ibn 'Ali (third Shi'a Imam) at the battle of Karbala in 680 CE; a central Shi'a religious observance.

ayatollah – from *ayat allah* (lit. 'sign of God'): title of senior Shi'a cleric who is entitled to perform *ijtihad*.

baba – lit. 'father': denotes the head of a local Bektashi order. The term *dede-baba* (lit. 'grandfather') is used for the highest spiritual authority in the Bektashi order.

Bektashi – a Sufi order with Ottoman roots; marginalised during the mid-nineteenth century Ottoman reforms and banned with other Sufi orders by the Turkish Republic in the 1920s; Bektashi beliefs contain strong Shi'a elements.

Bohra – also Dawoodi Bohra, see Ismaili.

da'wa – Islamic term for missionary or proselytising activities.

dervish – a common term for a Sufi.

du'a al-kumayl – supplication which Shi'ites believe 'Ali ibn Abi Talib dictated to his companion Kumayl ibn Ziyad; usually recited by Shi'ites on Thursday nights.

fiqh – the discipline of Islamic jurisprudence.

ghadir khumm – pond located half way between Mecca and Medina where Prophet Muhammad gave his final sermon after his farewell pilgrimage; Shi'ites believe that at the event of *ghadir khumm* Muhammad appointed 'Ali ibn Abi Talib as his successor.

ghulat – lit. 'extremists' or 'exaggerators': derogatory term used in Shi'a heresiography for all Shi'a groups who exaggerate the status of the Shi'a Imams by assigning divinity to them or holding 'extremist' views such as the belief in metempsychosis that deviate from Twelver Shi'a 'orthodoxy'.

hawza 'ilmiyya – term used in reference to Shi'a seminary institutions for the training of clerics; the shrine cities of Najaf in Iraq and Qom in Iran host the most important ones.

husayniyya – centre of learning and devotion in Shi'ism; used in particular for rituals during 'Ashura'.

ijtihad – independent reasoning, the cleric's ability to arrive at legal judgements. The license to perform *ijtihad* is central to being a senior Shi'a cleric, a *mujtahid* or ayatollah.

Ismaili – denomination within Twelver Shi'ism that follows a different line of succession than Twelver Shi'ites; Nizari-Ismailis are the largest group with Aga Khan IV (b. 1939) as their forty-ninth and current Imam. Dawoodi Bohras believe the Imam is in occultation and is represented by a designated deputy.

Ja'fari – in reference to the sixth Shi'a Imam Ja'far Al-Sadiq, name of the Twelver Shi'a school of law (*madhhab*); the term *caferi* is used in modern Turkey to refer to Turkish Twelver Shi'ites.

kalam – term used for Islamic theology.

Khoja – mercantile community of Gujarati origin with strong presence in East Africa and historically engaged in trade across the Indian Ocean; Khojas can be Ismailis or Twelver Shi'ites. As part of the Africanisation policies in the early 1970s, many Khojas moved from East Africa to Great Britain and North America.

khums – lit. 'one fifth': religious tithe Shi'ites need to pay to senior clerics, *maraji' al-taqlid*, usually 20 per cent on any profit or surplus income to be paid annually.

khutba – sermon given at a mosque, regularly given on the occasion of the Friday midday prayer.

latam – also known in Persian as *sine-zani* or *matam* in South Asia; central Shi'a ritual including rhythmic breast-beating to express sorrow and grief for the martyrdom of Imam Husayn and the suffering of the *ahl al-bayt* more generally. Usually performed during 'Ashura'.

maqtal – a narration of the martyrdom of Imam Husayn or other members of the *ahl al-bayt*.

marja' al-taqlid (pl. *maraji'*) – lit. 'source of emulation': title of most senior clerics in Twelver Shi'ism whom lay Shi'ites must chose to follow. As an institution, also referred to as *marja'iyya*.

masjid – Arabic for mosque.

maulud – birthday of the Prophet Muhammad. Important holiday in certain Islamic traditions, in particular Sufi and Shi'a, but rejected as heretical practice by modern Salafis.

mujtahid – a cleric who is entitled to perform *ijtihad*; prerequisite to become a *marja' al-taqlid*.

mullah – Persian name of low-ranking cleric.

nesip – level of initiation in the Bektashi order.

Al-Sahifa Al-Sajjadiyya – book of supplications attributed to the fourth Imam 'Abi ibn Husayn Zayn Al-'Abidin.

sayyid – also *seyyid*: title of descendant of Prophet Muhammad.

sepoy – Indian soldiers who served under British or other European orders.

takfir – declaring a Muslim to be an unbeliever.

taqiyya – pious dissimulation: the permission, and at times obligation, of Shi'ites to hide their religious identity when facing danger, harm or death.

tariqa – Arabic word for Sufi order.

tawassul – seeking intercession of the Imams on the Day of Judgement.

ta'ziya – in Persian *ta'zieh*, *ta'ziyeh*: passion plays and dramatic performance of the events during 'Ashura' leading to the martyrdom of Imam Husayn.

tekke – a Sufi meeting place (Turkish).

turba – piece of clay made out of soil, preferably from Karbala; used during the ritual prayer by Shi'ites.

turbeh – a small mausoleum built over the grave of a Muslim saint, especially under the Ottomans.

'ulama' – plural of Arabic *'alim*: used to refer to the learned class or scholars in Islam.

wakil (pl. *wukala'*) – representative of a *marja' al-taqlid* who communicates between a *marja'* and his followers and collects religious tithes on his behalf.

wilayat al-faqih – in Persian *velayet-e faqih* – lit. 'guardianship of the jurisconsult': term used to denote Ayatollah Khomeini's understanding that only a cleric can be head of an Islamic state. The concept serves as ideological foundation for the political system of the Islamic Republic of Iran after the 1979 revolution.

Zaydi – branch of Shi'ism following a different line of succession of Imams than Twelver Shi'ites; in terms of their legal and ritual practices and their views on the Imamate, closer to Sunni Islam.

ziyara – or *ziyarat*: pilgrimage to the shrines of the Twelve Imams or other members of the *ahl al-bayt*.

INTRODUCTION

1

'MY HOMELAND IS HUSAYN': TRANSNATIONALISM AND MULTILOCALITY IN SHI'A CONTEXTS

Oliver Scharbrodt and Yafa Shanneik

Introduction

This volume engages with questions of migration, diaspora, transnationalism and multilocality in relation to Shi'ism by focusing on the presence of Shi'a communities in Muslim minority contexts. Significant research has been produced on Shi'a minorities in the so-called Muslim world (Monsutti *et al.* 2007; Mervin 2010; Ridgeon 2012). The aim of this volume is to shift the focus to Shi'a presences in non-Muslim societal contexts where Shi'ites constitute 'a minority within a minority' (Sachedina 1994: 3) that has emerged in the process of migration, through conversion or both. The volume thereby makes important contributions to research on Shi'a communities in unexplored contexts, adding to the growing body of research on Shi'ites in Europe (Shanneik *et al.* 2017; Scharbrodt *et al.* 2019) and North America (Walbridge 1996; Takim 2009) and providing novel insights into Shi'a communities in South America, South Asia and South East Asia (Formichi and Feener 2015). By concentrating on Shi'a spaces in Muslim minority contexts, the volume opens up comparative perspectives on Shi'a minority presences in diverse geographical areas outside of the so-called Muslim world. Thereby, the volume further illustrates the heterogeneity of 'Shi'a worlds' (Mervin 2010: 9) and contributes to 'de-centring Shi'ism' (Clarke and Künkler 2018) by shifting the focus not just outside of the Middle East but outside Muslim majority countries. Public and academic narratives on Shi'ism are further widened by extending the scope of this volume to Shi'a groups outside of Twelver Shi'ism, investigating Bektashis in the Balkans, the Ahl-e Haqq from Iran and Alevis of Turkish background in Germany.

The volume contributes to recent debates on diasporic religion by presenting the case study of Shi'ites as a minority within a minority and the challenges and opportunities such a setting entails. In light of geopolitical events in the Middle East post-Arab Spring and their global repercussions, the contributions in this volume equally question simplistic notions of Sunni–Shi'a sectarianism and discourses that suggest a global politicisation of sectarian identities. While the reality of such processes cannot be dismissed, the contributions in this volume – based on extensive ethnographic research in a variety of contexts – interrogate crude suggestions of an Iranian alignment of global Shi'a communities and of clear-cut sectarian boundaries between Sunnis and Shi'ites.

Global Shi'a Trajectories

The historical background of the formation of Shi'ism is the question of succession of Muhammad and the struggles in the early Islamic community over its leadership that ensued after his death. While Sunnis accept the way by which the first 'rightly-guided' caliphs from the Companions of the Prophet assumed leadership in early Islam, Shi'ites hold the view that the family of the Prophet (*ahl al-bayt*) possesses a special spiritual and subsequently sociopolitical status within the Islamic community and was designated to lead it. Sunnis argue that Muhammad left the question of his succession open and therefore the emergence of the caliphate was a legitimate process to solve the leadership question. Shi'ites, however, believe that Muhammad explicitly appointed his cousin and son-in-law, the husband of his daughter Fatima, 'Ali ibn Abi Talib as his successor and first Imam (Arabic for 'leader') (Madelung 1996; Ayoub 2003). After him, the Imamate passed onto his eldest son Hasan and then to Hasan's younger brother Husayn. In 680 CE, Husayn launched a revolt when the old Arab Umayyad clan turned the caliphate into dynastic rule – he was killed together with his entourage on the plains of Karbala in southern Iraq, only survived by his female relatives and his son 'Ali who became Imam after him. The events in Karbala, which, according to Shi'a tradition, occurred in the first ten days of the Islamic month of Muharram, are remembered annually in a period called 'Ashura' and have been central in shaping Shi'a collective memories and sectarian identities.

From Husayn onwards, the Imamate passed from father to son in a patrilineal line until the twelfth Imam, Muhammad ibn Hasan, who as a child went into occultation in 874 CE to escape from persecution. According to the Shi'a tradition, he has been in hiding since then and will appear as the Islamic saviour, the Mahdi, at the end of times. Twelver Shi'ites believe in a succession of twelve Imams and constitute the largest denomination within Shi'ism. Other Shi'a groups follow different lines of succession such as the Ismailis. Further splits occurred among the Ismailis in their history. For the Nizari-Ismailis, Aga Khan III (b. 1936) is their forty-ninth and current Imam (Daftary 1992). As part of the wider Shi'a world, one also needs to mention the Zaydis who follow a different line of succession of Imams. Zaydis are particularly strong in Yemen, and although they have been identified with Shi'ism as part of the sectarianisation of geopolitical conflicts in the Middle East and the regional rivalry between Saudi Arabia and Iran, Zaydis are much closer in their legal and ritual practices to Sunni Islam than other forms of Shi'ism, including its Twelver variant (Haider 2014: 103–22). Finally, a number of smaller movements exist within Shi'ism of a more esoteric nature that entertain religious beliefs and practices that mainstream Shi'ism would consider 'heterodox'. The Alevis from Eastern Anatolia, the Alawi-Nusayris in Syria and Lebanon, the Druze in Syria, Lebanon, Israel and Jordan, and the Ahl-e Haqq or Yaresan in western Iran and northeastern Iraq exhibit different historical formations but share certain beliefs that originated in the *ghulat* milieu. *Ghulat* (lit. 'exaggerators' or 'extremists') is a derogatory term in Shi'a heresiography for the followers of the Shi'a Imams and certain movements that exaggerate the position of the Imams by ascribing divinity to them and believing in divine incarnation, reincarnation and metempsychosis (Moosa 1988). To different degrees, the aforementioned movements share these beliefs and managed to survive over centuries – despite their heterodoxy – in remote parts of the Middle East outside the control of imperial powers of the past.

All these different movements in Shi'ism share a strong veneration of the family of the Prophet (*ahl al-bayt*) based on the belief that as his descendants they possess charismatic authority that distinguishes them from ordinary Muslims and has entitled them to be the only legitimate leaders of the Islamic community. More importantly, through their Prophetic descent and as Imams they possess divine knowledge, receive divine inspiration and are the only sources of infallible guidance. This strong veneration of the *ahl al-bayt* crosses over to various Sufi traditions in Islam whose spiritual genealogies, known as *silsila*, often include various Shi'a Imams and go back to 'Ali ibn Abi Talib, the first Imam. This veneration finds its expression in Sufi orders of a Sunni background as well as in Sufi traditions with stronger Shi'a tendencies such as the Ni'matullahis (Lewisohn 1998; Scharbrodt 2010) or the Bektashis whose presence in the Balkans is discussed in this volume.

Shi'ites as a minority presence within Islam are present across the so-called Muslim world; from North Africa to the Middle East, Central and South Asia. Shi'ites constitute national minorities in a variety of Muslim majority countries. While countries such as Lebanon, Saudi Arabia, Kuwait, Yemen, Syria or Pakistan have significant Shi'a minorities, only Iran, Iraq, Azerbaijan and Bahrain have Shi'a majority populations. However, with the exception of Iran where Twelver Shi'ism has shaped the country's social, cultural, economic and political life since the rise of the Safavid dynasty in the early sixteenth century, Shi'ites have been 'functional minorities' (Cole 2002: 173) in Iraq, Azerbaijan and Bahrain. Until 2003, Iraqi Shi'ites have been politically marginalised and disenfranchised under a political elite dominated by Sunnis; the secularist policies in Soviet Azerbaijan and firm state control of the religious sector since the country's independence in 1991 have equally marginalised Shi'ism; in Bahrain, the Shi'a majority lives in a monarchy ruled by a Sunni family closely allied with Saudi Arabia (Matthiesen 2013).

The specific understanding of religious and spiritual authority around the family of the Prophet and the Imams is a salient feature of Shi'ism and its different articulations. Twelver Shi'ism, in particular, developed a specific form of clerical authority that not only distinguishes it from Sunni patterns of religious authority but also contributed to the rise of transnational Shi'a networks. Twelver Shi'ism possesses more formalised structures of religious authority. Every lay Shi'ite needs to follow the religious guidance of a senior cleric and emulate his edicts. These clerics are referred to as grand ayatollah (*ayat allah al-'uzma*) or 'source of emulation' (*marja' al-taqlid*) (Walbridge 2001: 3–13). The more formalised structures of religious authority in Twelver Shi'ism and the location of specific centres of authority have given Shi'a clerical networks a transnational or – prior to the formation of nation states – a trans-local character (Louër 2008; Corboz 2015). The most important seminary institutions (*hawza*) of Twelver Shi'ism are based in the shrine cities of Iraq and Iran, in Najaf and Qom, which also host the most senior clerical authorities of Twelver Shi'ism. Emulating a particular senior cleric not only entails following his religious edicts and teachings but also paying religious taxes (*khums*) to him. As channels of communication between their followers and for the collection of religious taxes, senior clerics run a network of representatives (*wakil*, pl. *wukala'*) who act as their agents in particular localities across the world and as members of a particular clerical network ensure its transnational reach. The most senior and most widely followed cleric in contemporary Twelver Shi'ism is Iranian-born Grand Ayatollah Sayyid 'Ali Sistani (b. 1930) who was trained and is based in Najaf and heads a network spanning the entire globe (Rizvi 2018).

The formation of Shi'a Islamist movements in the latter half of the twentieth century further added to the transnational nature of Twelver Shi'ism. Shi'a Islamist parties in countries like Kuwait, Bahrain or Saudi Arabia were initially offshoots of Iraqi parties such as the *Hizb Al-Da'wa*, which is the most important Shi'a Islamist party in the country, established in 1958 (Jaber 2003, 73–43; Louër 2008, 82–8). Given the leading role clerical authorities played in the formation of these parties in Iraq, their spread to the other Arab Gulf countries was facilitated by existing clerical networks between Iraq and Shi'a communities in the Gulf monarchies (Louër 2008). In Lebanon, the Iranian-born and Iraqi-trained Musa Al-Sadr (b. 1928, disappeared in 1978) not only reflects the cosmopolitan nature of clerical authority in Twelver Shi'ism; when he moved to Lebanon in 1959 he also mobilised the dispersed Shi'a communities with the formation of the Supreme Islamic Shi'a Council in 1969 (Ajami 1986). Such politicisation of marginalised Shi'a communities or minorities in the Middle East responded to the formation of post-colonial nation states in the region and the secular-nationalist or sectarian ideologies underpinning their formation, which either explicitly or implicitly excluded

Shi'ites from the national body or assigned to them a marginalised position. However, such mobilisation in national contexts always contained a transnational dimension as the role of Musa Al-Sadr in Lebanon most aptly illustrates (Shaeri-Eisenlohr 2009).

The transnational dimension of Shi'ism was further extended by global migratory flows after World War II. Shi'a presences have been established in Western Europe and North America as part of wider Muslim immigration and settlement, whether as part of the labour migration of Pakistanis to Britain, South Asians from East Africa to North America or Turkish Alevis to Germany, Belgium and the Netherlands. The oppression and persecution of Iraqi Shi'ites with the rise of the Baath regime from the 1970s onwards, the 1991 Gulf War and the repression of a Shi'a uprising in its aftermath, and sectarian conflicts in Iraq after 2003 have created a large and influential Iraqi Shi'a diaspora, in Britain and North America in particular. The 1979 Islamic Revolution in Iran also created a significant Iranian diaspora in Western Europe and North America whose majority at least is of a Twelver Shi'a background while often exhibiting strong secular if not anti-Islamic attitudes (Gholami 2015). Other less known migration trajectories also exist. There is an important Lebanese diaspora in West Africa which also counts Twelver Shi'ites among its members (Leichtman 2015). Arab migration to South America included Shi'ites, in particular from Lebanon (see García Somoza and Valcarcel, Chapter 3 in this volume).

Conversion is another factor that has led to the globalisation of Shi'ism (Inloes and Takim 2014; Shanneik 2018). Conversions to Twelver Shi'ism of Europeans or North Americans of a Christian or secular background is one factor – very often through an initial exposure and conversion to Sufi or Sunni forms of Islam. Equally, conversions of Sunni Muslims to Twelver Shi'ism can be observed both in minority contexts, such as among Moroccans in Belgium (Lechkar 2017), or among Sunni populations in Africa (Leichtman 2015) or Asia – a phenomenon that this volume discusses with case studies from Sri Lanka, Cambodia and Indonesia. The Islamic Revolution in 1979 triggered interest in Shi'a Islam among politically active Sunni Islamists, often students, who were attracted to the success of the Revolution. The global profile Iran and the political significance Twelver Shi'ism gained after the Revolution also led certain Muslim communities to 'rediscover' their

Shi'a roots, as Stock discusses in relation to Cham Muslims in Cambodia (see Chapter 11).

At the same time, this volume problematises the concept of conversion. Members of communities presented in the volume tend to reject or downplay the notion of conversion by referring to common notions of 'Alid piety shared by Sunnis and Shi'ites or their own Prophetic descent as an implicit 'Shi'a-ness' that was rediscovered, as Stock shows, for example. A further interrogation of the notion of conversion to Shi'ism is provided by Rasiah (Chapter 9) who demonstrates how Shi'i Muslims in Sri Lanka of a Sunni background reject the label 'conversion' in the sense of a radical transformation and prefer to speak about a 're-orientation' from one form of Islam to another, presenting it as being more pristine and authentic and thereby minimising a sense of rupture (see also Leichtman, Chapter 12 in this volume). In all cases, Shi'a 'converts' engage in a discourse of indigeneity presenting Shi'ism not as an alien, transnational phenomenon that entered a country from outside but as having been part and parcel of a particular Muslim society or community, even if unacknowledged.

Shi'ism as a Political Factor: The Islamic Revolution and its Transnational Impact

The Islamic Revolution in Iran of 1979 was a significant watershed event in the recent history of global Shi'ism. It not only created an Islamic state via the revolutionary overthrow of a secular regime but also mobilised Shi'a communities across the region and in the wider Muslim world. Khomeini's political reading of the mandate of a Shi'a cleric, known as the 'guardianship of the jurisconsult' (*wilayat al-faqih*), suggests that the head of an Islamic state needs to be a senior cleric. In its implementation, the Islamic Republic of Iran thereby fuses political and clerical authority (Calder 1982). The success of the Islamic Revolution has made Khomeini's concept appealing to politicised Shi'a activists across the world and has also led to the conversion of Sunni Muslims involved in Islamist activism to Twelver Shi'ism to some degree. At the same time, the concept is highly contested among the Shi'a clerical establishment itself, both outside and inside of Iran, which is sceptical of such a close political involvement of clerical leaders or outrightly rejects such a notion.

The Islamic Revolution turned Iran into a leading state actor within global Shi'ism. This is evident in initial efforts to export the Islamic Revolution to other countries in the Middle East and to provide ideological and logistical support in the political and military mobilisation of Shi'a communities across the region – with Hezbollah being one of most important and successful cases (Norton 2007a). While the policies of the current Supreme Leader of Iran 'Ali Khamenei (b. 1939) do not seek to replicate the Islamic Revolution in other contexts, they are equally meant to secure Iran's regional influence and articulate its hegemonic ambitions in the wider Shi'a world. Such ambitions are more often dictated by strategic geopolitical interests rather than sectarian allegiances, as the close rapport between Iran and the Alawi-Nusayri Assad regime in Syria illustrates. The Alawis in Syria are mostly secular in their religious conduct and adhere to doctrines that are deemed 'heretical' within mainstream Twelver Shi'ism. The contributions in this volume attest to Iranian efforts to extend its influence across Shi'a communities globally but direct their attention to another aspect of Iranian transnational religious activism by focussing on its use of soft power. The global network of educational institutions connected to the Al-Mustafa International University, headquartered in Qom and directly managed by the office of the Supreme Leader of Iran, provides preliminary clerical training and serves as an entry point for international students to the seminaries in Qom (Sakurai 2015). Cultural sections of Iranian embassies equally are present and often support religious, cultural and educational activities of local Shi'a communities across the world (see Formichi, Chapter 2 in this volume).

While Iran is central and one of the most important state actors in global Shi'ism with the relevant resources and clout to extend its soft power, the contributions in this volume equally qualify assumptions of a quasi-automatic ideological alignment of organisations and individuals receiving support from Iran or clerical students who have studied in Qom. As contributions in this volume show (see Formichi, Rasiah and Stock, Chapters 2, 9 and 11), local Shi'a communities often exhibit ambivalent attitudes towards Iranian influence, even though they send students for clerical training to Qom, receive financial support for their activities or attend functions organised by Iranian embassies. Training in Qom does not necessarily lead to an indoctrination in Iran's official ideology of *wilayat al-faqih* and does not turn returning students to local agents of Iran's global soft power, as Rasiah illustrates in the context of Sri Lanka and Stock in relation to Shiʻites in Cambodia. The political and ideological engagement with Iran is more nuanced and diverse, given that clerical authorities in Qom themselves do not entirely subscribe to Khomeini's ideological reading of Twelver Shiʻism. A simplistic connection of religious training in Qom with a political alignment with Iran equally overemphasises political identity formations among Shiʻites in various contexts (Clarke and Künkler 2018: 2–3). The contributions by Rasiah (Sri Lanka), Formichi (Indonesia) and Stock (Cambodia) illustrate that the conversions to Twelver Shiʻism were initiated by the Islamic Revolution in 1979 and its global appeal among politically active Sunni students and intellectuals with an Islamist orientation (Zulkifli 2013). However, these contributions also confirm observations made by Formichi and Feener (2015: 14) that Sunni Muslim student activists and intellectuals engaged more with the philosophical and mystical intellectual heritage of Iranian Twelver Shiʻism than with ideological discourses that emerged in the course of the Islamic Revolution.

The second event in recent history that changed the sectarian dynamics in the Middle East and globally is the toppling of Saddam Hussein in Iraq in 2003. Sectarianism has emerged as a major issue in debates on Sunni–Shiʻa relations since the peak of sectarian violence in Iraq in 2005 and 2006, and in particular in the post-Arab Spring Middle East in which the regional rivalry between Saudi Arabia and Iran and the proxy wars fought between both countries and their allies are read in sectarian terms. These recently unfolding dynamics have led to a proliferation of literature addressing sectarianism in the Middle East, its historical roots and current manifestations. Many contributions of this volume equally address the issue of sectarianism: how Sunni–Shiʻa relations unfold in diverse contexts, how local Shiʻa communities respond to and are affected by the sectarianisation of geopolitical conflicts in the Middle East and demotic processes on the ground that deconstruct neat sectarian categories.

Hashemi and Postel (2017: 1–22) reject the notion of a primordial antagonism between Sunni and Shiʻa Islam, deeply rooted in history and essentially unsurmountable. Instead, they adopt a constructivist approach and argue that recent events in the Middle East suggest a sectarianisation of geopolitical conflicts. Sectarian identities are used by political actors to pursue and achieve certain goals and to mobilise religious groups and communities by appealing to their religious sentiments. For both, a strong link exists between sectarianism and authoritarianism: autocratic rulers in the Middle East use sectarianism to strengthen and perpetuate their power. Existent ethno-religious identities are instrumentalised by socio-political elites and state actors to distract from corruption, socio-economic disparity and intensifying authoritarian rule and to exploit and escalate social cleavages along sectarian lines. Hashemi and Postel's reading of sectarianisation also resonates with Appadurai's (2006) and Geschiere's (2009) analysis of the resurgence of discourses of indigeneity and autochthony. For Appadurai, minorities tend to be invisible and hence not a matter of concern for the majority which intends to retain its power. However, certain processes – such as transnational political mobilisation that threaten existing power relations – can make such minorities 'problematic' (Appadurai 2006: 46). The Islamic Revolution and the Shi'a empowerment in Iraq in 2003 are two such historical developments crucial in creating a transnational communal identity among Shi'a minorities in the Middle East and other parts of the Muslim world. Similarly, Geschiere argues that autochthonous discourses coming from different communities in a state are less the result of historical divisions, which only an autocratic government can keep at bay and hence come to the fore once the state collapses. Such discourses and dynamics – as they have unfolded in Iraq between Sunnis, Shi'ites and Kurds, for example – are a reflection of local and national struggles about who has access to power and resources (Geschiere 2009: 21–3).

The various contributions in the book present a mixed image and show the limits of sectarianism and the importance of contextualising its manifestations. Migration, minority status and diaspora can indeed solidify sectarian identities, as Degli Esposti and Zaidi illustrate in their contributions (Chapters 5 and 7). Formichi, Weineck and Stock (Chapters 2, 10 and 11), on the other hand, highlight the significance of trans-sectarian notions of 'Alid piety and the veneration of the *ahl al-bayt* across the Sunni–Shi'a divide. Rasiah, referring to Sunni–Shi'a relations in Sri Lanka, reveals the porosity of sectarian divisions: while Shi'a converts have been increasingly targeted by Salafi Muslims, they receive support from representatives of other forms of Sunni Islam, in particular from members and leaders of Sufi orders.

Leichtman makes a similar observation about Sunni-Shiʿa relations in Senegal where Shiʿa converts continue to be involved as leading figures in Sunni Sufi orders (see Leichtman, Chapter 12 in this volume). While the contributions illustrate that the sectarianisation of religio-political identities is a reality, it unfolds differently in various contexts and is met with counter-discourses and initiatives that challenge approaches that read the Sunni–Shiʿa divide in the light of the historical denominational differences in Christianity.

Migration, Transnationalism, Diaspora: Multilocal Shiʿa Imaginaries

The volume investigates questions of migration, transnationalism and diaspora in various Shiʿa contexts and therefore resonates with debates in this area, in particular as they pertain to the study of transnational or diasporic religion. In discussing transnational Islam, Bowen (2004) distinguishes different dimensions: the actual movement of Muslims from one location to another as part of global migratory processes that leads to the formation of diasporas. The creation of Shiʿa minority presences in Europe or North America was a part of such processes. Similar to Vertovec's definition of transnationalism (2009: 136), another dimension, identified by Bowen, refers to the networks and interactions occurring between the homeland and the diaspora as part of transnationally operating Islamic networks, organisations and institutions. Given the nature of clerical networks within Twelver Shiʿism, their modus operandi is inherently transnational. The same is true for Shiʿa political organisations that initially extended transnationally across the Middle East and then – in response to state oppression – became exilic and engaged in diasporic politics from Europe or North America.

However, the reduction of transnationalism to the migration of people and the operations and activities of transnational networks does not sufficiently capture the de-territorialising and re-territorialising processes of religions on the move. For Bowen, there is a third dimension to transnational Islam: 'a global public space of normative reference and debate' (2004: 880). It denotes a discursive field of Islamic normativity and legitimacy, involves Muslim actors in Europe or North America who debate the place and nature of Islam within these particular Muslim minority contexts, while retaining reference points to the wider Muslim world and traditional sources and centres of normative authority within Islam: they debate on 'how to become wholly "here" and yet preserve a tradition of orientation towards Islamic institutions located "over there"' (Bowen 2004: 882). Recent contributions to the study of diaspora have emphasised this ideational aspect of diasporic formations. Diaspora has been defined as 'an imagined connection' (Vertovec 2009: 136) with the place of origin or a wider community which can be real but is also imagined in the sense that it purports strong emotive connotations and is based on collective memory. Werbner broadens the meaning of diaspora by arguing that 'diasporic, rather than simply ethnic or religious, is an orientation in time and space – towards a different past or pasts and towards another place or places' (2002: 125).

'My homeland is Husayn (*watani al-husayn*)' is a prominent eulogy on the third Shi'a Imam Husayn, recited during 'Ashura' to commemorate his martyrdom. It articulates an identification with Husayn that transcends territorial boundaries and allegiances and suggests that a Shi'ite's true homeland is not the town where one was born or one's country, but Husayn. While Husayn's shrine in Karbala is an important destination of pilgrimage (*ziyara*) and hence allows Shi'ites to ritually perform their allegiance to Husayn at this physical site, the eulogy moves beyond transnational identifications. The eulogy is 'supralocal' (Tweed 1997: 85) as it pronounces a vertical connection with the transcendental; Husayn as the 'master of martyrs (*sayyid al-shuhada*)' is the ultimate isthmus between God and humanity. As such, the eulogy suggests an ideational and emotive connection to Husayn that not only transcends but defies the limitations of physical spaces and territorial boundaries and unites the Shi'a in their collective memory of his martyrdom. In this sense, the eulogy raises interesting questions on the multilocal sites of Shi'a 'homing desire' (McLoughlin 2010: 225; Brah 1996: 179–80). Home is understood here to be both 'a realm of concrete locality and everyday experience' and 'a more ideational, symbolic or discursive realm' (Stock 2010: 26).

Shi'a presences, as a minority within a minority embedded in particular local and national contexts, entertain multilocal and supra-temporal orientations They are part of transnational networks, engage with global articulations of 'Shia-ness' and as local actors are affected by, respond to and participate in a transnational public sphere of global Shi'ism. Ritual practices, such as reciting eulogies in memory of Imam Husayn, foster a collective memory to create Shi'ite socialities and articulate 'the idea of an alternative, utopian, as well as potentially millenarian and apocalyptic, moral space exceeding the limits of their diasporic location and minority status' (McLoughlin and Zavos 2014: 170–1). In Zaidi's contribution, Shi'ites of South Asian background in North America do not identify with Pakistan, the country of origin of their parents or grand-parents, but articulate a trans- and supra-local identification with the shrine cities in Iraq and Syria as their actual 'spiritual' homeland. In Argentina, Imam Husayn's revolt against the oppressive Umayyad dynasty is framed as an example of anti-imperialist struggle and aligned with leftist post-colonial South American politics, as García Somoza and Valcarcel illustrate in their contribution (Chapter 3). The use of the internet to expand the transnational reach of clerical authorities and facilitate easier and more direct communication between the office of a senior cleric based in the Middle East and his followers around the globe can also destabilise normative discourses and interrogate traditional conceptions of clerical authority, as Riggs points out in his contribution (Chapter 6). For Shi'a converts in Sri Lanka as a minority within a minority in a particularly volatile position, the orientation towards a 'Shi'i International' (Mallat 1993) led by Iran is more pronounced, while the examples of Cambodia and Indonesia in this volume illustrate how Shi'ites in these contexts negotiate between the need to localise Shi'ism and the role of transnational (often Iranian) actors and their influence. 'Decentering Shi'ism' (Clarke and Künkler 2018) can assume various forms as part of demotic processes to create alternative forms of individual and collective Shi'a religiosities and respond to the needs of local communities. Authoritative discourses coming from transnational state and non-state actors are never carbon copied but indigenised, creatively re-interpreted and localised by Shi'a communities in diverse contexts (Leichtman 2015: 236–41). The contributions in this volume further illustrate the salience of ethnographic research in local contexts to uncover such demotic processes.

The 'Perils of Belonging': Being a Minority Within Minority

The case studies included in this volume represent Shi'a communities in a variety of national contexts as 'a minority within a minority'. Hence, some reflections on the question of being a minority are in place. As Appadurai (2006) observes, the ethnic chauvinism inherent in the formation of modern nation states and their ideological underpinnings suggesting ethno-national purity has been further exacerbated through globalisation and the subsequent blurring of territorial and communal boundaries. Minorities within a nation state are thereby seen as problematic, as their presence reveals in particular the majoritarian anxiety of incompleteness: the minority is a constant reminder for the majority of the gap in achieving complete homogeneity. Geschiere, similarly, presents the re-emergences of discourses of autochthony as the 'flip side of globalization' (2009: 1). For him, globalisation and transnational mobility are central factors leading to a renewed pre-occupation with notions of belonging when such notions are destabilised. Equally, the rise of modern nation states based on a sense of shared nationhood leads to the question of who belongs and who does not. As such, Geschiere observes a fundamental tension between globalising forces and transnational movements and the continuing importance of nation state as a regulating force that yields discourses of autochthony (2009: 21–2).

How does this unfold among Shi'a minorities in a double-minority status in this volume? Discourses of autochthony view transnationally connected religious minorities with suspicion as a minority that not only threatens the majority's power and yearning for ethno-national homogeneity but also as a minority that because of its transnational links and foreign connections is not really autochthonous and is potentially controlled by outside powers (Appadurai 2006: 69–72). In research on Shi'a minorities in Sunni majoritarian Middle Eastern contexts, this trope is often articulated with reference to Iranian influence on, if not control of, local Shi'a religious and political actors that are perceived as being the long arm of the Islamic Republic. Their identification with a 'Shi'i International' questions their loyalty to the state and the nation. In response, local Shi'a actors adopted their own discourses of autochthony. Shi'ites of Saudi Arabia present their community as an integral part of Saudi society, having made significant historical and cultural contributions to the Arab peninsula (Ibrahim 2006: 169–76). Shi'ites, by referring to themselves as *baharna*, conceive of themselves as the indigenous inhabitants of Bahrain and the ruling Al-Khalifa clan as outsiders (Matthiesen 2013: 31–2). The Iranian-backed Hezbollah in Lebanon conceives of itself as the 'Islamic resistance' against Israel protecting thereby the whole Lebanese nation (Norton 2007b).

Similarly, the case studies in this volume problematise the perception of a tension between the cosmopolitan formation of Shiʻa minorities and local discourses of autochthony. In line with Leichtman's (2015: 14) observations in the context of Senegal, the examples examined suggest a more complex relationship with global and transnational formations being indigenised. In Argentina, the Iranian Revolution with its leader Khomeini is framed in the context of Latin American anti-imperialist political activism (see Bruckmayr 2018 on similar discourses in Venezuela). The 'foreignness' of Shiʻism is undone by Cham Shiʻites in Cambodia by narratives that suggest that ʻAli, the first Shiʻa Imam and son-in-law of the Prophet Muhammad, migrated to Cambodia, married a local Cham girl and initiated an indigenous line of *sayyids*. As ʻAli was a Shiʻite, they would argue, their own turn towards Shiʻism is nothing but a rediscovery of their obscured Shiʻa roots. Rexhepi in his contribution (Chapter 4) critiques similar efforts by Bektashis in the Balkans to present Bektashism as an indigenous European Islam that is moderate and tolerant and stands in contrast to radical forms of Islam exported from abroad. The Ahl-e Haqq are an example of a movement that transformed from an esoteric group located in remote rural areas of Iran and Iraq to a global movement that taps into cosmopolitan discourses of religious and ethical universalism, appeals to the liberal elite of a globalised world and is endorsed by the French state (see Badry, Chapter 8 in this volume). Hence, the examples illustrate that 'transnationalism neither prevents Shiʻa communities from constructing national identities, nor does it stop them from integrating into the states they resort under' (Mervin 2010: 21). In all these cases, the local and parochial co-exist with the transnational and cosmopolitan (Leichtman 2015: 231; Werbner 2009).

Such discourses can be highly problematic as the place of Islam in 'Western' minority settings illustrates. Shiʻa Muslims need to undertake particular efforts to maintain both an Islamic as well as particular Shiʻa identity in terms of communal activities and practices and public perception and recognition, responding to the rise of Islamophobia more generally and anti-Shiʻa sectarianism more specifically. At the same time, a religiously neutral non-Muslim state can act as arbiter between hostile sectarian groups and protect Shiʻites who face anti-Shiʻa sectarianism, as the case of Sri Lanka demonstrates in this volume. While being 'the other within the other' (Takim 2009: 143) is meant to articulate a sense of double-marginalisation of Shiʻa minorities within a larger Muslim minority, it also offers certain opportunity structures for Shi'ites to demarcate themselves from other radical and violent forms of Islam and to present themselves as the victims of the same global terrorist actors that have been targeted as part of the securitisation of Islam after 9/11 (Scharbrodt 2011). Hence, Shi'a minorities in European minority contexts similarly engage in their own discourses of autochthony to articulate their belonging. By presenting themselves as victims of global terrorism (Degli Esposti 2018; Shanneik 2018) and promoters of social cohesion within the context of the politics of British multiculturalism (Scharbrodt 2018) certain Iraqi Shi'a actors in London articulate their belonging to British society. The Ahl-e Haqq with their headquarters in Paris present themselves as a universalist religious movement promoting peace, spirituality and a global ethos, while the Bektashis turn into role-models of what European Islam should look like.

Hence, the double minority status allows Shi'ites to articulate notions of belonging by distancing themselves from 'suspicious' forms of Islam that are represented as alien and foreign. Rexhepi in his critique of such discourses around Bektashism in the Balkans reveals the problematic nature of such approaches. Such discourses confirm the dichotomy between 'good Muslim' and 'bad Muslim' (Mamdani 2004) and reveal the 'perils of belonging' (Geschiere 2009): they attempt to undo otherness by articulating and identifying with respective national identity markers and implicitly adopt assimilationist agendas of host countries. Such discursive strategies overlook transnational connections and historical and contemporary links to global Shi'a actors, obscure the complex historical formations of certain movements and limit possibilities of Islamic solidary and cooperation beyond politicised sectarian identities (Gholami and Sreberny 2018). That many groups investigated in this volume revert to such an approach reveals the inherent precarious situation of Shi'a minorities within Muslim minority contexts. It is because of their double-marginalisation that they might feel a particular need to prove their belonging to the majority society.

Chapter Overview

The volume includes ten chapters with an epilogue and is divided in three distinct but interrelated thematic parts. The first part, 'Localising Global Shi'a Minority Spaces', investigates Shi'a minority presences in specific local contexts. The four chapters in this part illustrate how transnational institutional networks and reformist discourses are localised in specific contexts, examining Indonesia, Buenos Aires, the Balkans and London.

Chiara Formichi's contribution is the only one in this volume not focusing on Shi'a minorities in a non-Muslim context, by investigating Twelver Shi'ites in Indonesia. Her chapter discusses the role that transnational educational institutions, sponsored by the Islamic Republic of Iran, play in Indonesia and the ambivalent perceptions of Iranian involvement. On the one hand, the Islamic Revolution created a global awareness of Shi'a Islam and initiated the conversion of local Indonesian Muslims to Shi'ism. The presence of Iranian institutions facilitates access to Shi'a literature and scholarships to study in Qom. On the other hand, Indonesian Shi'ites are equally eager to retain a certain independence from Iran in order not to appear as representing the interests of a foreign power in their country. Formichi's chapter also illustrates how local folklore traditions, articulating more a sense of 'Alid piety than a specific Shi'a sectarian orientation, are also attended by representatives from Iran who frame these traditions in Java as local articulations of global Shi'ism.

Shi'a communities in South America are entirely under studied. Therefore, Mari-Sol García Somoza and Mayra Soledad Valcarcel's chapter on Twelver Shi'a communities in Buenos Aires constitutes an important contribution to mapping Shi'a minorities globally. Their chapter begins with an outline of the changing religious demographics of Argentina with the return of democracy in 1983 and the background of Muslim immigration and settlement in the country. Outlining the Shi'a Islamic field and its formation in the city's neighbourhood of Floresta, García Somoza and Soledad Valcarcel discuss how local Shi'a communities relate both to fundamental doctrines of Twelver Shi'ism and the global influence of the Islamic Revolution in Iran and apply them to the local Argentinian context and situate the Revolution in particular within the context of anti-imperialist Latin American political activism.

Piro Rexhepi moves the attention outside of Twelver Shi'ism by investigating Bektashis in the Balkans. Bektashi is a Sufi order with Ottoman roots that exhibits strong Shi'a tendencies. After the fall of Communism in the Balkans in the early 1990s and as part of the region's European integration path, the Islamic heritage present from Ottoman times is often perceived as a liability. One strategy to counter this concern is to present Bektashism as a 'tolerant' and 'moderate' form of Islam that is genuinely European and representative of local Balkan culture, in contrast to Sunni Islam and its connections to global discourses of reformism and political activism. Such notions of Bektashis being 'good' Muslims is further supported by references to Orientalist scholarship of the early twentieth century that separates Bektashism from mainstream Islam. Rexhepi engages in a detailed critique of such discourses and argues for a 'decolonial' approach towards Bektashi and Balkan Islam more generally: a historical archaeology that emphasises the Ottoman roots of the order and its links to Twelver Shi'ism.

The important and influential Iraqi Shi'a diaspora in London is the focus of Emanuelle Degli Esposti's chapter. From the early 1980s, London emerged as one of the major centres of Iraqi Shi'a diasporic politics. Her contribution provides an overview of the Shi'a religious field in London and its main actors and their transnational connectivities and focuses on the discursive formation of an 'Iraqi-Shi'a diasporic subject'. Shifting the attention to the political economy of sectarianism in the diaspora, her chapter investigates the role of London-based charities in fostering and strengthening sectarian discourses both in the diaspora and in Iraq. Similarly, through the public performance of Shi'a identity at the annual processions during 'Ashura' in central London, a discourse of Shi'a victimisation is created presenting Shi'ites as victims of radical forms of Sunnism following the rise of ISIS in Iraq in 2014.

The second part, 'Transnational Shi'a Trajectories', focuses on the transnational dimension of Shi'a minorities. What does transnationalism mean in Shi'a contexts, in what ways does it manifest and how it is articulated? The role of the Internet in transnationalising clerical authority, the articulations of transnational senses of belongings within Shi'a diasporas and the transformation of a Shi'a movement as a consequence of its engagement with global discourses are examined in this section.

Robert J. Riggs covers another important facet of global Shi'ism. With the rise of a global information network in the late twentieth century, powered by the Internet, senior Shi'a clerics have established websites that play a vital role in the maintenance of local constituencies. The use of Internet technology provides greater opportunities for constituency-building and at the same time the potential loss of control over the production and dissemination of knowledge. Riggs discusses the use of websites to expand clerical authority by looking into the web presence of the clerical establishment in Najaf. Thereby, the Internet facilitates the global reach of clerical leaders who can be accessed directly without the traditional intermediary of their representatives. Riggs thereby elucidates the creative ways in which these uniquely situated religious authorities articulate the relationship between the local and the global.

In her chapter, Noor Zehra Zaidi explores the role that pilgrimages to the shrines of the Shi'a Imams and other members of the *ahl al-bayt* play in maintaining transnational and symbolic links to global Shi'ism. The fall of Saddam Hussein in 2003 and the massive pilgrimage industry that has emerged as a consequence created particular connections for young American Shi'ites of South Asian background who consider Iraq as their actual 'spiritual' homeland and not Pakistan, the country of origin of their parents or grand-parents. The precarious contexts in which many of these shrines are situated equally create a sense of anxiety about losing this connection to the shrines. The bombing of the Al-'Askari shrine in Samarra, north of Baghdad, in 2006 and the perceived threat to the shrine of Sayyida Zaynab – Imam Husayn's sister – near Damascus following the rise of ISIS in 2014 further strengthen the emotive connections of American Shi'ites to these places and yield particular articulations of sectarian identities in North America.

Roswitha Badry investigates another trajectory of transnationalisation by discussing the transformation of the Ahl-e Haqq after the move of its leaders and headquarters to Paris. The Ahl-e Haqq (also known as Yaresan) are an esoteric Shi'a group originally based in remote parts of western Iran and northeastern Iraq that underwent significant transformations in the twentieth century. Badry focuses on the reformist branch of the Ahl-e Haqq that was led by Ne'matollah Jayhunabadi (1871–1920) and Nur Ali Elahi (1895–1974) who systematised the teachings of the group and closer aligned it to mainstream Twelver Shi'ism. Nur Ali Elahi's son Bahram Elahi (b. 1931) moved the headquarters of the reformist branch to Paris by establishing the Ostad Elahi Foundation in 2000. In its public representation and activities – which has received support from the French state – any connection to Islam or Shi'ism is omitted: the Ostad Elahi Foundation presents itself as a universalist religious movement promoting peace, spirituality and a global ethos, thereby, as Badry illustrates, obscuring the movement's roots in esoteric Shi'ism.

The final part, "Alid Piety and the Fluidity of Sectarian Boundaries', includes contributions that interrogate simplistic notions of sectarian divisions between Sunnis and Shi'ites. 'Alid piety or the veneration of the *ahl al-bayt* become common denominators connecting Sunni and Shi'a Muslims, create links between different Shi'a groups or – while being a gateway for Sunni conversions to Shi'ism – are used to present the turn to Shi'ism not as a radical rupture but as a continuation of existing religious orientations, albeit differently articulated.

The formation and situation of the Twelver Shi'a community within the Muslim minority of Sri Lanka is discussed in Arun Rasiah's contribution. Being a minority within an already precarious minority in the country requires particular caution on the part of Shi'a converts who often revert to the practice of *taqiyya*, often translated as pious dissimulation to denote the right and at times obligation of Shi'ites to conceal their faith in order to avert danger, harm or death. Shi'ites in Sri Lanka face in particular anti-Shi'a agitation by local Salafis with the support they receive from transnational actors. Equally, Rasiah illustrates how Sri Lankan Shi'ites are part of transnational Shi'a networks linked to Iran but also other parts of South Asia, Pakistan and Afghanistan in particular, and how religious knowledge is transmitted via these networks and localised. While Shi'ites face a Salafi backlash in Sri Lanka, their conversion narratives often reveal a background in Sunni Islamist movements. In addition, Shi'ites forge alliances with traditional forms of Sunni Islam, Sufism in particular, that are equally targeted by Salafis.

A good example of the porosity of sectarian boundaries is provided by Benjamin Weineck in his contribution on Turkish migrants in Germany of Shi'a backgrounds. While the Shi'a religious field in Germany is fairly small and has only recently grown, Alevis from Turkey have had a long presence in Germany. Weineck discusses lines of cooperation between different Shi'a groups – a cooperation based on pragmatic considerations given their limited numbers and few resources in the small diasporic space of Germany. At the same time, Alevis, Twelver Shi'ites and Nusayri-Alawis from Turkey cooperate and hold events together based on the shared orientation towards and veneration of the *ahl al-bayt* that transcends the historical, cultural and doctrinal differences between these movements. At the same time, Weineck observes how certain Alevi movements undertake a rapprochement towards Twelver Shi'ism, adopting some of its legal and ritual practices and following its clerical authorities.

Emiko Stock studies another underexamined Shi'a minority presence by discussing the conversion of Cham Muslims in Cambodia to Shi'a Islam. Many Cham Muslims claim Prophetic descent and are *sayyids* and, hence, argue that their conversion to Shi'ism is not a deviation from traditional understandings of Islam among them but a rediscovery of their latent Shi'a roots. Stock engages in a discussion of the various mythico-historical narratives that circulate among Cham Muslims that create genealogical and spiritual lineages to the *ahl al-bayt* and central figures in the Islamisation of South East Asia. The complex web of narratives that emerges contains ambiguities and contradictions and articulates a particular 'homing desire' among Cham Shi'a Muslims: indigenising Shi'ism in Cambodia and connecting its fairly recent presence in South East Asia with historical trajectories of the spread of Islam in the region.

To conclude the volume, Mara A. Leichtman provides a final discussion of all contributions, focusing on the themes of cosmopolitanism and conversion and bringing in a perspective from the African context which is otherwise missing in the volume. Basing her reflection on theories of cosmopolitanism, Leichtman discusses the various contributions in terms of the different geographical axes they open, not only between the diaspora and its country of origin but also to the two centres of global Shi'ism, Iraq and Iran. These connections can be institutional, financial or educational but equally contain a strong symbolic element, in particular with regards to the shrine cities in Iraq as the actual and newly revived spiritual centre of global Shi'ism. Finally, Leichtman deconstructs the concept of 'conversion' addressed in many contributions, which often demonstrate the fluidity of Shi'a identity constructions and the porosity of sectarian boundaries and defy simplistic narratives of conversion as a complete re-orientation of one's religiosity. At the same time, becoming Shi'a also involves a localising of Shi'ism in a particular context, as most contributions illustrate.

Conclusion

The contributions to this volume provide diverse and multifaceted insights into Shi'a minority presences in a variety of Muslim minority contexts. They explore what it means to be a minority within a minority and discuss the relevance of recent debates on migration, transnationalism, diaspora and multilocality for Shi'a minority spaces. By focusing mostly on the manifestations of Shi'a minority spaces in specific local contexts, based on extensive ethnographic research, the contributions emphasise the salience of local contexts and problematise a number of assumptions that circulate within both public and academic discourses on global Shi'ism:

– Sectarianism and Iranian influence: most of the contributions address this issue and the question of Sunni–Shi'a relations. While they do not negate the global pervasiveness of sectarianism and its impact on local Shi'a communities, they equally illustrate the porosity of sectarian boundaries and areas of cooperation between Sunnis and Shi'ites that qualify any sense of an inherent sectarian animosity. Related to this question is the role of Iran as a major power in global Shi'ism. While Iranian transnational networks play a role in many local Shi'a communities and the reformist discourse that originated in the context of the Islamic Revolution has its local repercussions, their influence is not uncontested and often negotiated and adapted to local needs. In the case studies included in this volume, the Islamic Republic is not the uncontested hegemon of global Shi'ism.
– Conversion: as discussed in Leichtman's contribution to this volume, many chapters also address the issue of conversion while pointing at the limitations of this term in understanding the dynamics of Sunnis who become Shi'ites. Local community converts are reluctant to use the term 'conversion', as its Christian connotations based on the paradigmatic Pauline experience suggest a complete rupture. However, for most of the Shi'a converts discussed in this volume, their turn to Shi'ism did not entail a break with the past but was often perceived as a continuity or rediscovery of religious leanings that were latently present and more openly articulated following their 'conversion'. In many cases, becoming

Shiʿa did not mean turning away from local religious practices of a Sunni character, in particular if they included elements of ʿAlid piety.
- Double-minority status: the impression that being 'a minority within a minority' entails a sense of double-marginalisation for Shiʿa minority spaces is also qualified by the contributions. While the situation of Shiʿa minorities can be precarious, being based in a non-Muslim societal context can offer more freedom and also allows Shiʿa minorities to dissociate themselves from radical and violent expressions of Sunni Islam and to present themselves as 'moderate' Muslims. The contributions equally illustrate how problematic such a discursive positioning of Shiʿa communities can be.
- The local and the global: finally, all contributions illustrate how localised forms of Shiʿa Islam emerge in conversation with global Shiʿism, its various religious, ideological, political and factional tendencies and orientations and how they are translated and contested into a variety of local contexts further demonstrating the diversity of 'Shiʿa worlds' (Mervin 2010: 1). As such the volume makes the case for adopting the perspective of multilocality (McLoughlin and Zavos 2014) to move beyond the potentially limiting approaches of migration, transnationalism and diaspora. A full investigation into Shiʿa minorities needs to take the local context seriously, to understand their embeddedness in nation states, to disentangle their various transnational connectivities and to engage seriously with the demotic constructions of individual and collective religiosities outside of organised religious structures. The collected chapters in this volume make an important contribution to understanding Shiʿa minorities as multilocal phenomena.

References

Ajami, Fouad (1986), *The Vanished Imam: Musa Al-Sadr and the Shia of Lebanon*, Ithaca: Cornell University Press.

Appadurai, Arjun (2006), *The Fear of Small Numbers: An Essay on the Geography of Anger*, Durham: Duke University Press.

Ayoub, Mahmud M. (2003), *The Crisis of Muslim History: Religion and Politics in Early Islam*, Oxford: Oneworld.

Bowen, John R. (2004), 'Beyond migration: Islam as a transnational public space', *Journal of Ethnic and Migration Studies* 30:5, 879–94.

Brah, Avtar (1996), *Cartographies of Diaspora: Contesting Identities*, London: Routledge.
Bruckmayr, Philipp (2018), 'Divergent processes of localization in twenty-first century Shi'ism: the cases of Hezbollah Venezuela and Cambodia's Cham Shi'is', *British Journal of Middle Eastern Studies* 45:1, 18–38.
Calder, Norman (1982), 'Accommodation and revolution in Imami Shi'i jurisprudence: Khumayni and the Classical Tradition', *Middle Eastern Studies* 18:1, 3–20.
Chibli, Mallat (1993), *The Renewal of Islamic Law: Muhammad Baqer as-Sadr, Najaf and the Shi'i International*, Cambridge: Cambridge University Press.
Clarke, Morgan, and M. Künkler (2018), 'De-centring Shi'i Islam', *British Journal of Middle Eastern Studies* 45:1, 1–17.
Cole, Juan R. (2002), *Sacred Space and Holy War: The Politics, Culture and History of Shi'ite Islam*, London: I. B. Tauris.
Corboz, Elvire (2015), *Guardians of Shi'ism: Sacred Authority and Transnational Family Networks*, Edinburgh: Edinburgh University Press.
Daftary, Farhad (1992), *The Isma'ilis: Their History and Doctrines*, Cambridge: Cambridge University Press.
Degli Esposti, Emanuelle (2018), 'The aesthetics of ritual – contested identities and ritual performances in the Iraqi Shi'a diaspora: ritual, performance and identity change', *Politics* 38:1, 68–83.
Formichi, Chiara, and M. Feener (eds) (2015), *Shi'ism in Southeast Asia: 'Alid Piety and Sectarian Constructions*, Oxford: Oxford University Press.
Geschiere, Peter (2009), *The Perils of Belonging: Autochthony, Citizenship, and Exclusion in Africa and Europe*, Chicago: University of Chicago Press.
Gholami, Reza (2015), *Secularism and Identity: Non-Islamiosity in the Iranian Diaspora*, London: Routledge.
Gholami, Reza, and A. Sreberny (2019), 'Integration, class and secularism: the marginalization of Shia identities in the UK Iranian diaspora', *Contemporary Islam*, 13:3, 243–58.
Hashemi, Nader, and D. Postel (2017), 'Introduction: The sectarianization thesis', in N. Hashemi and D. Postel (eds), *Sectarianization: Mapping the New Politics of the Middle East*, Oxford: Oxford University Press, pp. 1–22.
Ibrahim, Fouad (2006), *The Shi'is of Saudi Arabia*, London: Saqi.
Inloes, Amina, and L. Takim (2014), 'Conversion to Twelver Shi'ism among American and Canadian Women', *Studies in Religion/Sciences Religieuses* 43:1, 3–24.

Jaber, Faleh A. (2003), *The Shi'ite Movement in Iraq*, London: Saqi.
Lechkar, Iman (2017), 'Being a "true" Shiite: the poetics of emotions among Belgian-Moroccan Shiites', *Journal of Muslims in Europe* 6:2, 241–59.
Leichtman, Mara A. (2015), *Shi'i Cosmopolitanisms in Africa: Lebanese Migration and Religious Conversion in Senegal*, Bloomington: Indiana University Press.
Lewisohn, Leonard (1998), 'An introduction to modern Persian Sufism, part I: the Nimatullahi Order: persecution, revival and schism', *Bulletin of the School of Oriental and African Studies* 61:3, 437–64.
Louër, Laurence (2008), *Transnational Shia Politics: Religious and Political Networks in the Gulf*, London: Hurst.
Madelung, Wilferd (1996), *The Succession to Muhammad: A Study of the Early Caliphate*, Cambridge: Cambridge University Press.
Mamdani, Mahmoud (2004), *Good Muslim, Bad Muslim: America, the Cold War, and the Roots of Terror*, New York: Pantheon.
Matthiesen, Toby (2013), *Sectarian Gulf: Bahrain, Saudi Arabia, and the Arab Spring that Wasn't*, Stanford: Stanford University Press.
McLoughlin, Seán (2010), 'Muslim travellers: homing desire, the *umma* and British Pakistanis', in K. Knott and S. McLoughlin (eds), *Diasporas: Concepts, Intersections, Identities*, London: Zed Books, pp. 223–9.
McLoughlin, Seán, and J. Zavos (2014), 'Writing religion in British Asian diasporas', in S. McLoughlin, W. Gould, A. J. Kabir and E. Tomalin (eds), *Writing the City in British Asian Diasporas*, London: Routledge, pp. 158–78.
Mervin, Sabrina (ed.) (2010), *The Shia Worlds and Iran*, London: Saqi.
Monsutti, Alessandro, S. Naef and F. Sabahi (eds) (2007), *The Other Shiites: From the Mediterranean to Central Asia*, Bern: Peter Lang.
Moosa, Matti (1988), *Extremist Shiites: The Ghulat Sects*, Syracuse: Syracuse University Press.
Najam, Haider (2014), *Shī'ī Islam: An Introduction*, Cambridge: Cambridge University Press.
Norton, Augustus R. (2007a), *Hezbollah: A Short History*, Princeton: Princeton University Press.
—— (2007b), 'The role of Hezbollah in Lebanese domestic politics', *Italian Journal of International Affairs* 42:4, 475–91.
Ridgeon, Lloyd (ed.) (2012), *Shi'i Islam and Identity: Religion, Politics and Change in the Global Muslim Community*, London: I. B. Tauris.
Rizvi, Sajjad (2018), 'The making of a *marja'*: Sistani and Shi'i religious authority in the contemporary age', *Sociology of Islam* 6:2, 165–89.

Sachedina, Abdulaziz (1994), 'A minority within a minority: the case of the Shi'a in North America', in Y. Y. Haddad and J. Idleman (eds), *Muslim Communities in North America*, New York: State University of New York Press, pp. 3–14.

Sakurai, Keiko (2015), 'Making Qom a centre of Shi'i scholarship: Al-Mustafa International University', in M. Bano and K. Sakurai (eds), *Shaping Global Islamic Discourses: The Role of Al-Azhar, Al-Medina and Al-Mustafa*, Edinburgh: Edinburgh University Press, pp. 41–72.

Scharbrodt, Oliver (2010), 'The *qutb* as special representative of the hidden Imam: the conflation of Shi'i and Sufi *Vilāyat* in the Ni'matullāhī Order', in D. Herman and S. Mervin (eds), *Shi'i Trends and Dynamics in Modern Times (XVIIIth–XXth Centuries)*, Beirut: Orient Institute, pp. 33–50.

——— (2011), 'Shaping the public image of Islam: the Shiis of Ireland as "moderate" Muslims', *Journal of Muslim Minority Affairs* 31:4, 518–33.

——— (2019), 'A minority within a minority?: The complexity and multilocality of transnational Twelver Shia networks in Britain', *Contemporary Islam*, 13:3, 287–305.

Scharbrodt, Oliver, R. Gholami and S. A. Dogra (2019), Special Issue on Shia Muslims in Great Britain, *Contemporary Islam* 13:3.

Shaeri-Eisenlohr, Roshanak (2009), 'Territorializing piety: genealogy, transnationalism, and Shi'ite politics in modern Lebanon', *Comparative Studies in Society and History* 51:3, 533–62.

Shanneik, Yafa (2018), 'Moving into Shi'a Islam: the "process of subjectification" among Shi'a women converts in London', in K. V. Nieuwkerk (ed.), *Moving In and Out of Islam*, Austin: University of Texas Press, pp. 130–51.

Shanneik, Yafa, C. Heinhold, and Z. Ali (eds) (2017), Mapping Shia Muslim communities in Europe: local and transnational dimensions, *Journal of Muslims in Europe* 6:2.

Stock, Femke (2010), 'Home and memory', in K. Knott and S. McLoughlin (eds), *Diasporas: Concepts, Intersections, Identities*, London: Zed Books, pp. 24–8.

Takim, Liyakat (2009), *Shi'ism in America*, New York: New York University Press.

Tweed, Thomas A. (1997), *Our Lady of Exile: Diasporic Religion at a Cuban Catholic Shrine in Miami*, Oxford: Oxford University Press.

Vertovec, Steven (2009), *Transnationalism*, London: Routledge.

Walbridge, Linda S. (1996), *Without Forgetting the Imam: Lebanese Shi'ism in an American Community*, Detroit: Wayne State University Press.

——— (ed.) (2001), *The Most Learned of the Shi'a: The Institution of the Marja' Taqlid*, Oxford: Oxford University Press.

Werbner, Pnina (2002), 'The place which is diaspora: citizenship, religion and gender in the making of chaordic transnationalism', *Journal of Ethnic and Migration Studies* 28:1, 119–33.

——— (ed.) (2009), *Anthropology and the New Cosmopolitanism: Rooted, Feminist and Vernacular Perspectives*, Oxford: Berg.

Zulkifli (2013), *The Struggle of the Shi'is in Indonesia*, Canberra: Australia National University Press.

PART I

LOCALISING GLOBAL SHI'A MINORITY SPACES

2

PERFORMING SHI'ISM BETWEEN JAVA AND QOM: EDUCATION AND RITUALS

Chiara Formichi

Introduction

I met Fatima[1] at a Shi'a educational centre in Yogyakarta, on the Indonesian island of Java, while she was studying international relations at the prestigious Gadjah Mada University.[2] Fatima is now in her late twenties, and her life encapsulates the many facets of Indonesia's Shi'a communities. She grew up in Bengkulu, a small town on the western coast of Sumatra, as her father taught at the local university, and led the Shi'a community there. After completing secondary school, Fatima moved to Pekalongan, in Central Java, to enrol at the Shi'a religious school *pesantren* Al-Hadi.[3] Her brother, also an Al-Hadi alumnus, is now one of the teachers there. A couple of years after we had met, Fatima had moved to Jakarta, where she prepared to further her studies in political sciences at Tehran University. Her sister had by then been admitted to the Jami'at Al-Mustafa in Qom.[4]

In what follows I pull some of the threads hinted at above, each originating in a specific 'place' – understood both as a physical location and as a point on the moral geographies of Shi'a Islam – in order to uncover the relationship between Indonesia's devotees of the *ahl al-bayt* and Iran's role in propagating a set paradigm of rituality. Analysing Shi'a educational institutions and Muharram rituals in Java and Western Sumatra, this contribution shows how although not all of Indonesia Shi'ites[5] feel a connection to the Islamic Republic of Iran, one way or another, the vast majority of Shi'a-inclined institutions feel compelled to display such a connection.

Pekalongan

Aware of my interest in Shi'a Islam, Fatima suggested I visit *pesantren* Al-Hadi, and thanks to her brother's position there, I was welcome to spend time with pupils, teachers and their families. This turned out to be the first stop of a ten-day whirlwind immersion in a network of Shi'a educational centres across Java (itself the first of many Muharram cycles); each centre was connected to the next by kinship, marriage or student–teacher relation, letting surface a tightly knit community.

It is the third night of Muharram, in 1431 AH /2009 CE. I am standing in the courtyard at Al-Hadi, and as I wait to be received, nothing strikes me as any different from the (Sunni) *pesantren*s I have visited before. That assessment was soon to be corrected, as a little girl ran across the yard wearing a yellow Hezbollah shirt; Muharram *maqtal*s called for the death of Israel and the long life of Iran; I was informed, with much pride, that the local publishing house is supported by a Shi'a shaykh from Kuwait; and that as all the teachers – male and female – are alumni of the Shi'a seminaries in Qom, Iran (thus referred to as *qomiyyun*), the curriculum is designed to facilitate pupils' transfer to Qom.

By the time that I met with the school's director, a few months later, I was only slightly taken aback by his style: it was a scorching hot day, and Ustadz Sayyid Ahmad Baragbah – an Indonesian Arab of Prophetic lineage – was wearing the standard *libas* (clerical attire) of Shi'a *'ulama'*, complete with mantel, turban and shawl. After studying Arabic at Yogyakarta's Gadjah Mada University, Ustadz Ahmad had received a scholarship to go to Saudi Arabia. However, as news of the Iranian Revolution reached Indonesia, he opted for transferring to Qom. The details of this transfer are not clear, especially since in those days there were limited diplomatic relations between Indonesia and Iran, and travel could only happen through subtle subterfuges, such as connecting in Singapore, Pakistan, and yet another country.

Conversion happened swiftly, and during a short trip back to Indonesia in 1984 several of his relatives followed his cue. Upon completion of his degree at Qom in 1987, Ustadz Ahmad had turned into a celebrity in his hometown, Pekalongan. Returning from Qom, he had acquired the rank of 'teacher'. In 1989, following his entourage's pressures, he established Al-Hadi as a centre of Shi'a education. Started off with just a handful of pupils, in 1992–3 the school accommodated 150 students.

Al-Hadi was not the first Shi'a *pesantren* to come onto the scene in Java. Already before the Iranian Revolution, between the mid-1960s and late-1970s, East Java had witnessed the mushrooming of several centres. Under the leadership of two members of the Arab diaspora, the Al-Sadiq Foundation opened in 1966 and Pesantren Al-Wafa in 1972. However, the most prestigious place for Shi'a education in Java has always been the Yayasan Pesantren Islam (YAPI) in Bangil and Bondowoso. Even though its name does not evoke any Shi'a connection, YAPI hosts circa 500 pupils coming from across the archipelago to learn about Shi'a Islam. Sayyid Husayn Al-Habshi (1921–94), also an Arab of Prophetic descent, had taught informally for several years before establishing YAPI in 1973. It is claimed that Al-Habshi had had connections with Najafi *'ulama'* in the 1950s–60s, and that at around the same time he had held the leadership of the Arab Twelver Shi'a diaspora community in Java (Zulkifli 2013: 156–80). His offspring, who have retained leadership of the *pesantren*, studied in Qom and married Iranian wives.

Devotion for Muhammad is a characteristic feature of many *sayyids*, most evidently among the Ba 'Alawis. Whether being genealogically part of the *ahl al-bayt* and practising devotion for the five core members of the family should translate into 'switching' to Shi'a *fiqh*, however, is a contentious issue (F. Alatas 1999; I. Alatas 2015). Hence, of key importance to these figures and their communities is the ability to prove that their being Shi'a is not a betrayal of their historical identity. The *sayyids* of Java claim descent from the Prophet via Ahmad b. Isa Al-Muhajir, the fourth son of Imam Ja'far Al-Sadiq. Born in Basra in 820 CE, he had migrated to Hadhramawt, and there, some argue, he followed Ja'fari *fiqh*. 'Wouldn't it be recorded in the books of history if the very son of Al-Sadiq was not a Ja'fari?', argues *Tarikh Hadramawt*, a book I was shown during my visit to YAPI. Or, some add:

'why would Al-Muhajir have settled in the Shi'a enclave if he were not a Shi'ite?' There was, after all, a Shafi'i community in Southern Yemen which would have received him with open arms, had he chosen to join them. One last line of argument suggests that several of the *sayyid*s in Java arrived in the aftermath of Ibn Sa'ud's takeover of Arabia, marking their disagreement with Sunni Islam and *therefore* their Shi'a background.

An additional layer is provided through local stories: a handwritten *do'a* stuck between the pages of a nineteenth-century *maulud* text calling upon the five who 'extinguish the fire of hell', one's childhood memories of lullabies invoking 'the holy five', and another's dietary restriction to not eat fish without scales. Grounding a community's legitimacy on these elements thus provides historical depth and allows for a discourse of reversion vis-à-vis conversion, dispelling claims of Shi'a Islam as a mere consequence of the Iranian Revolution of 1979.

However, there is a strong sense that familial rituals by themselves are not enough, as they might rather be indicative of the 'in-between' zone of 'Alid piety, to borrow Marshall Hodgson's expression. As he argues for the context of ninth-century Iraq, 'Alid loyalism manifested itself in two different ways: some devotees focused on giving to 'Ali and some of his descendants 'an exclusive role in special religious systems', thus giving shape to Shi'ism in its various forms; others instead performed a broader reverence towards the *ahl al-bayt* 'to color in manifold ways the life of Sunni Islam' (Hodgson 1955: 2).[6] These practices, common among many Sunni Muslims in Southeast Asia, are thus perceived as weak sources to prove denominational affiliation to a programmatic and legalistic understanding of Shi'a Islam (which is seen as *opposed* to Sunni Islam). This last layer can only be provided through a conscious commitment to Ja'fari *fiqh* and ritual orthodoxy as promoted by the government apparatus of the Islamic Republic of Iran. There are several other lines, genealogical and intellectual, connecting today's Indonesian Shi'ites to outside sources of legitimation and authority. However, as time passes by, the Islamic Republic of Iran becomes increasingly predominant.

Khomeini's leadership of the Iranian Revolution and his establishment of the Islamic Republic, with its state-driven ritualistic apparatus, provided a double-edged sword to Indonesia's Shi'ites. On the one hand, more Indonesians were exposed to Shi'a literature and doctrines (as we have seen in the case of Ustadz Sayyid Ahmad Baragbah), with those already inclined towards Shi'ism being granted a recognisable source of orthodoxy, and therefore legitimation. On the other hand, that very apparatus and orthodoxy was (and largely is, once again, now) shunned by the Indonesian government as destabilising of domestic harmony (Formichi 2014a).

The primary impact of the 1979 Revolution was the consequent awareness of Shi'a Islam and its activism for Muslims across the world. This phenomenon inserted itself on the revivalist landscape already shaped by the Six-Day War of 1967, Sadat's politics of tolerating Islamist activism in Egypt, the Wahhabi emergence on the global scene, Zia-ul-Haqq's Islamisation of Pakistan, and the Soviet invasion of Afghanistan. Within the specific context of Indonesia, the Iranian Revolution also met with the youth's growing frustration towards the repressive government of General Suharto (1921–2008; president: 1967–98) (Hefner 2000).

Suharto's rule was characterised by a two-pronged approach to Islam: on the one hand, political Islam (as any other form of independent political activism) was seen as a danger to the status quo; on the other hand, though, personal piety was incentivised as a key strategy against Communism. This created the context for mosques to become the one place of congregation, and for religion to become the one language that could be used to articulate discontent. As university-based political organisations were banned in the mid-1970s, it was Islamic circles that absorbed the disaffected youth. Primary locations were the Institute for Technology in Bandung (ITB; and its Salman Mosque) (Rosyad 1995) and the Gadjah Mada University in Yogyakarta (through Jama'ah Shalahuddin) (Karim 2006; Nef 2012).

Bandung

Located in the western region of Java, the land of Sunda, Bandung has been characterised by a deeper commitment to Islam than the rest of the island, and since colonial times the city had a politically active youth. West Java was the point of origin of Islamic reformism in the 1920s and the epicentre of the Darul Islam Islamic State (Negara Islam Indonesia) movement in the 1940s–60s (Formichi 2012). In the same vein, the ITB Institute for Technology was a hub for the Islamic revival in the 1980s–90s (Temby 2010).

Da'wah circles became the main engine behind the nationwide spread of the *usra* (or *tarbiya*) revivalist movement, attracting university students as well as high school pupils. They gathered in mosques, avidly reading Islamist literature in home-made translations from Arabic and English. Like their peers in Egypt and Malaysia, they discussed the works of prominent Muslim intellectuals such as Hasan al-Banna (1906–49), Abu al-A'la Mawdudi (1903–79) and Sayyid Qutb (1906–66) (Latif 2008; Machmudi 2008). However, in our view most interestingly, in Indonesia they also read the works of Murtada Mutahhari (1919–79) and 'Ali Shari'ati (1933–77). No thoughts were given to 'sectarian' allegiances, as political activism was approached through the lens of 'orthodox Islamism' as much as that of third-worldism (van Bruinessen 2002). While the Muslim Brotherhood was unsuccessful in its attempts to obtain political power in Egypt, the Iranian Revolution's victory fed popular fascination.

Eventually finding the *usra* movement's dogmatism and obsession with *takfir* unsatisfactory and limiting, alienating any possibility for intellectual engagement, some of these students were pulled by Mutahhari's contestation of the political establishment and equal commitment to independent thought, religious brotherhood, and metaphysics. It is in this context that Fatima's father, Sadiq,[7] encountered Shi'ism as a young university student in the 1980s.

IJABI, the All-Indonesia Assembly of Ahlul Bait Associations (*Ikatan Jama'ah Ahlul Bayt Indonesia*), was established in 2001 (soon after the fall of the Suharto regime) but its genesis lies in the intellectual environment described above. Jalaluddin Rakhmat, the founder of IJABI, was a former *tarbiya* leader at ITB, who, in the mid-1990s, was inspired by Mutahhari's prioritisation of critical thinking, to the effect that he established the Mutahhari School in Bandung (now a series of schools).

Reflecting the fluid context in which several of IJABI's leaders were formed, the organisation depicts itself as open to 'the lovers of the *ahl al-bayt* regardless of their *madhhab*'.[8] Prioritising *akhlaq* over *fiqh*, IJABI remains inclusive, committed to local forms of Shi'a piety and open to individuals who only 'partially' follow Shi'a rituals. The organisation and its leaders – which include Fatima's father – thus still engage with Shi'ism on the same level of intellectualism and philosophy, rather than directing their interests towards politics and jurisprudence (Rakhmat 2002). However, even though

IJABI often shies away from formalistic ritualism to intentionally distance itself from other communities of devotees, in more recent times the organisation and its members have nonetheless been wary of retaining connections with Iran.

Jalaluddin Rakhmat has personal connections with several ayatollahs who occasionally come to preside at events taking place in Bandung, but he specifically talks of the need to preserve local practices from their 'Iranianisation', rejecting the influence of the Islamic Republic's apparatus; and although he has visited Iran, he has not studied there. His son, who did, was sent to study philosophy in Mashhad, rather than *fiqh* in Qom. Similarly, Sadiq – who never attended a *hawza* seminary school – entertains close relations with the Iranian Embassy in Jakarta, and two of his daughters have studied in Iran, one at Tehran University, and the other at the *hawza* in Qom.

A third figure is emblematic of this contested relationship. Zainal Abidin[9] became involved in the *tarbiya* movement as a high school student in Makassar (Sulawesi), but like Jalaluddin and Sadiq in Bandung, he was attracted to Shi'a philosophical thought, rather than its political embodiment. In 1995, during the Suharto regime, he opened a centre for people interested in learning more about Islamic philosophy and metaphysics. A few years later he moved to Yogyakarta and opened a sister foundation there, while at the same time becoming involved in IJABI.

Yogyakarta

Yogyakarta and Bandung offer very different outlooks in demographic, social and historical terms; but they are both politically important, each in its own way. Whereas Bandung's activism was always characterised by Islam, Yogyakarta played a key role in the anti-colonial revolutionary struggle at the side of Sukarno, the nation's founding father and first president. As a result of this city's commitment to the Republic, Yogyakarta was granted special status, still being ruled by its Sultan; and the city was also awarded funds to establish the first national university. Yogyakarta was and remained extremely secular – or, in Indonesian terms, *pancasila*-ist, referring to the country's founding ideology.[10] Students flocked from across the country, making the city extremely diverse and vibrant, a cultural hub where the traditional arts thrived (for their own sake, but also for tourists' perusal) alongside a lively youth culture, which here was unshackled by religious conservatism (at least until the early 2000s).

Fatima was active at Zainal Abidin's foundation throughout her stay, as she saw it as the only place she could pursue a Shi'a education and perform community rituals in Yogyakarta. The centre is indebted to 'Ali Shari'ati, and is committed to the deepening of its members' knowledge and understanding of Islam. In the spirit of IJABI, the centre retains a rather 'relaxed' approach to ritual – students are not obliged to attend *tawassul* or *do'a kumayl* meetings, nor Muharram evening gathering, or the 'Ashura' congregation. In fact, only a handful of them regularly participate in all these events. This indicates that more often than not, this youth is more interested in philosophical and intellectual explorations and discussions than in the ritual performativity of religion. At the same time, however, the centre has also established connections with other educational institutions with more marked ties to Iran. Most prominent among these, is the Islamic College in Jakarta (established as ICAS in 1999 and a decade later re-named as IC). They co-organise a *pesantren mahasiswa* (a religious school for university students) with courses lasting one or two years; they co-publish the *Mulla Shadra Journal*, described as a 'journal of Islamic philosophy and mysticism'; prominent Iranian scholars visiting the capital travel to Yogyakarta to offer lectures at the foundation (such as Ayatollah Sayyid Muhammad Khamenei, brother of Grand Ayatollah 'Ali Khamenei); and every year a handful of its students receive scholarships to study in Jakarta, from where they might be able to go to Iran, as was the case with Fatima.

Jakarta

The environment in Jakarta is dramatically different, deeply harnessed to the Islamic Republic's effort to spread its orthodoxy and orthopraxy. The rise in Iranian influence emanates out of Jakarta into the 'peripheries', mostly thanks to the activities of the Islamic Cultural Centre (ICC). Established in 1998 by a group of Iranians who wished to improve 'mutual understanding' between Iran and Indonesia, the ICC first made a mark as a centre for the study of the Persian language and then gradually became (1) the go-to place for people who want to further their education in Iran; (2) the hub for returning *qomiyyun*; (3) the source for Shi'a *pesantrens* across the country for material and human resources; and (4) the unofficial cultural centre of the Iranian Embassy. In fact, at its inception the ICC had no ties to the Islamic Republic's political establishment – in 2010 the then-director was clear that he did not wish for the ICC to be co-opted by the Embassy[11] – but since late 2011 a change of leadership has brought the Centre closer to the Embassy. Since then, this political connection has affected the ICC's ritual performativity, as Embassy officials often preside over the Centre's event and performances which now conform to paradigms promoted by the Islamic Republic.

Education in Jakarta is strongly characterised by the influence of Iran. The Islamic College was initially established by a handful of Indonesian Muslim intellectuals in collaboration with Jakarta's Paramadina University, offering undergraduate and graduate degrees in Islamic theology, philosophy and mysticism. In the early 2000s, however, it was transformed into a platform for Indonesians interested in Shi'a philosophy, metaphysics and *fiqh*, to the extent that it has become characterised (meaning both understood and run) as an *Iranian* centre of education. Its teachers are either Iranians or Indonesian *qomiyyun*; its director is chosen by Qom's Jami'at Al-Mustafa; and like its British sister institution, the Islamic College in London, it is funded by an Iran-sponsored charity.

Bengkulu

The last site I wish to explore in this contribution is Bengkulu, western Sumatra, which stands as an example of the impact that closer ties with Iran – in education, political, cultural and ritualistic terms – have on society more broadly.

Initially an important port along the pepper trade route, Bengkulu became infamous at the beginning of the nineteenth century. Described by the British colonial statesman Sir Stamford Raffles (1781–1826) as a malaria-fostering swamp, this small town was turned into a penal colony staffed with South Asian guards and convicts. Today, Bengkulu is famous across the country for the Festival Tabot, which takes place every year during the first ten days of Muharram. During the festival, neighbourhoods compete to craft make-shift coffins of Hasan and Husayn (here called *tabot*, or *tabuik*, an adaptation of the South Asian *tajah*) and cultural entertainment takes various forms, most notably drumming competitions between young boys' groups. On the first day of the month, the ceremony is opened with the collecting of a handful of 'Karbala soil', and on the tenth day, 'Ashura', the *tabots* are taken on a procession, first to visit the grave of Shaykh Burhanuddin, the *sepoy* soldier deemed to have started the ritual in Bengkulu, and then left to float into the sea.[12]

The iconography matches many accounts of Muharram processions in India, and the historical evidence is there to support the fact that Tabot was indeed taken to Sumatra by *sepoy*s and convicts during British rule. As Muharram processions in India were attended by Sunnis and Shi'ites, Muslims and Hindus, Tabot in Sumatra has become a marker of local identity; not just as irrespective of 'sectarian' identities, but – under the close watch of the Suharto regime – as a secular festival.[13] Tabot remained as such from the 1970s throughout the 1990s, but when I visited Bengkulu in December 2011 this was no longer the case. Beside the T-shirts with '*ya Husayn*' in Arabic script, and the occasional drumming group staging *maqtal*-style songs, what struck me was the hosting of a seminar on the Tabot tradition and the inclusion of a *ta'zieh* excerpt performed by an Iranian troupe. All was arranged by local Shi'a communities through the Iranian Embassy, with the sponsorship of Iran's Islamic Culture and Relations Organisations.

The seminar was organised by the chairman of the local branch of IJABI and was held at the local (Sunni) Higher Institute for Islamic Studies (STAIN), with the co-sponsorship of the Embassy of the Islamic Republic of Iran, the Islamic College and the ICC. With lectures offered by the Iranian Ambassador, the ICC director and three Indonesian scholars – trained respectively in Qom, Indonesia and the Netherlands – the seminar addressed the role of *tabot* in enhancing the social, cultural and political consciousness of the *umma*. Local participants argued that Tabot had been transformed beyond recognition, becoming a performance no longer related to the Shi'a commemoration of Husayn's martyrdom, and thus making it irrelevant to discuss its relationship to Shi'a rituals today. On the other hand, the Iranian approach – as expressed by Iran's representatives as well as by the Indonesian *qomiyyun* – stressed their undeniable connections. The Ambassador had set the tone for this in his opening speech:

One of the beauties of this world is its cultural differences. I have noticed differences in Sumatra [compared to Iran], but the ceremony [of Tabot] is very similar, to the point that there's almost no difference . . . these differences are just the result of time. We are sad [for the martyrdom], we remember [the martyrdom], but then each place is different. The essence is the same, but this is packaged in local traditions. The content is still Husayn, its expression reflects culture.

The tension between these two perspectives, one arguing for Tabot as a manifestation of local identity, the other pressing for its connection to Shi'ism and *therefore* Iran, was tangible on stage. That evening, the sequence of drumming groups, who were playing against the sound of the battling rain, was interrupted to fit in the Iranian *ta'ziyeh* troupe which had been included in the Tabot Festival for the first time this year. Shortly after the beginning of the Persian-language *ta'ziyeh*, in a mixture of excitement and fear, the procession that each evening would circle around town visiting specific landmarks suddenly barged in to interrupt the play. Those in the procession frantically danced in the mud to the rhythm of the drums, only to then take over the stage and push aside the three Iranian actors. After several minutes of dancing, shouting, drumming and waving their standards, the procession stormed away accompanied by a crowd that continued chanting '*ya Husayn*' (see also Formichi 2014b).

Concluding Remarks

Through this investigation of 'Alid devotion in Java and Sumatra I have highlighted the 'places' that connect Indonesian devotees of the *ahl al-bayt* to exogenous sources of knowledge and their influence on modes of Shi'a rituality. Most saliently, I have focused on the impact of religious knowledge networks (and financial resources) on the shaping of ritual paradigms. This is important because it offers a window on the multiple realities of Indonesia's Shi'a communities, and the tensions among them. Some see this international connection as necessary for the survival of Indonesia's Shi'a traditions and its communities; the resources – both tangible and intangible – provide legitimation, opportunities and visibility. However, it is the impact of these resources which is shunned by others, who fear that foreign intervention in local religious matters will not only cause the obliteration of local practices in favour of a 'globalised Islam', but will also attract the attention of ultra-conservative Sunni Muslims. Religious extremism has been on the rise in Indonesia for the last decade, and the Shi'ites (together with the Ahmadis and Christians) have been constantly victimised (Formichi 2014a).

References

Alatas, Farid (1999), 'The Tariqat al-Alawiyyah and the emergence of the Shi'i school in Indonesia and Malaysia', *Oriente Moderno* 18:2, 323–39.

Alatas, Ismail Fajrie (2015), 'They are the heirs of the Prophet: discourses on the *Ahl al-Bayt* and religious authority among the Bā 'Alawī in Modern Indonesia', in C. Formichi and M. Feener (eds), *Shi'ism in Southeast Asia: 'Alid Piety and Sectarian Constructions*, Oxford: Oxford University Press, pp. 139–64.

Bruinessen, Martin van (2002), 'Genealogies of Islamic radicalism in post-Suharto Indonesia', *South East Asia Research* 10:2, 117–54.

Denny, F. M. (2017), 'Pesantren', in P. Bearman, T. Bianquis, C. E. Bosworth, E. van Donzel and W. P. Heinrichs (eds), *Encyclopaedia of Islam, 2nd edn*, available at: http://dx.doi.org/10.1163/1573-3912_islam_SIM_6116, last accessed 6 May 2017.

Federspiel, Howard M. (2017), 'Pesantren', in *The Oxford Encyclopedia of the Islamic World*, Oxford Islamic Studies Online, available at: http://www.oxfordislamicstudies.com/article/opr/t236/e0632, last accessed 6 May 2017.

Feener, Michael (2015), "'Alid piety and state-sponsored spectacle: *Tabot* tradition in Bengkulu, Sumatra', in C. Formichi and M. Feener (eds), *Shi'ism in Southeast Asia: 'Alid Piety and Sectarian Constructions*, Oxford: Oxford University Press, pp. 187–202.

Feener, Michael, and C. Formichi (2015), 'Debating "Shi'ism" in the history of Muslim Southeast Asia', in C. Formichi and M. Feener (eds), *Shi'ism in Southeast Asia: 'Alid Piety and Sectarian Constructions*, Oxford: Oxford University Press, pp. 3–16.

Feith, Herbert, and Lance Castles (eds) (1970), *Indonesian Political Thinking, 1945–1965*, Ithaca: Cornell University Press.

Formichi, Chiara (2012), *Islam and the Making of the Nation: Kartosuwiryo and Political Islam in Twentieth Century Indonesia*, Leiden: KITLV Press.

——— (2014a), 'Violence, sectarianism, and the politics of religion: articulations of anti-Shi'a discourses in Indonesia', *Indonesia* 98, 1–27.

——— (2014b), 'Shaping Shi'a identities in contemporary Indonesia between local tradition and foreign orthodoxy', *Die Welt des Islams* 54:2, 212–36.

Formichi, Chiara, and M. Feener (eds) (2015), *Shi'ism in Southeast Asia: 'Alid Piety and Sectarian Constructions*, Oxford: Oxford University Press.

Hefner, Robert W. (2000), *Civil Islam: Muslims and Democratization in Indonesia*. Princeton: Princeton University Press.

Hodgson, Marshall (1955), 'How did the early Shi'a become sectarian?', *Journal of the American Oriental Society* 75:1, 1–13.

Karim, Abdul Gaffar (2006), 'Jamaah Shalahuddin: Islamic student organisation in Indonesia's new order', *The Flinders Journal of History and Politics* 23, 33–56.

Latif, Yudi (2008), *Indonesian Muslim Intelligentsia and Power*, Singapore: Institute of Southeast Asian Studies.

Machmudi, Yon (2008), *Islamising Indonesia: The Rise of Jemaah Tarbiyah and the Prosperous Justice Party (PKS)*, Canberra: Australian National University Press.

Nef, Claudia (2012), 'Living for the Caliphate', PhD dissertation, University of Zurich, Zurich.

Pew Forum (2010) *The Future of the Global Muslim Population*, available at: http://www.pewforum.org/The-Future-of-the-Global-Muslim-Population.aspx, last accessed 16 July 2014.

Rakhmat, Jalaluddin (2002), *Dahulukan akhlak di atas Fikih*, Bandung: Muthahhari Press.

Rosyad, Rifki (1995), *A Quest for True Islam: A Study of the Islamic Resurgence Movement Among the Youth in Bandung, Indonesia*, Canberra: Australian National University Press.

Sakurai, Keiko (2015), 'Making Qom a centre of Shi'i scholarship: Al-Mustafa International University', in M. Bano and K. Sakurai (eds), *Shaping Global Islamic Discourses: The Role of al-Azhar, al-Medina and al-Mustafa*, Edinburgh: Edinburgh University Press, pp. 41–72.

Temby, Quinton (2010), 'Imagining an Islamic state in Indonesia: from Darul Islam to Jemaah Islamiyah', *Indonesia* 89, 1–36.

TEMPO (2012), 'Kang Jalal on Shia in Indonesia', 4 September, available at: http://www.tempo.co/read/news/2012/09/04/055427522, last accessed 16 July 2014.

Zulkifli (2013), *The Struggle of the Shi'is in Indonesia*, Canberra: Australian National University Press.

3

MI CORAZÓN LATE HUSAYN: IDENTITY, POLITICS AND RELIGION IN A SHI'A COMMUNITY IN BUENOS AIRES[1]

Mari-Sol García Somoza and Mayra Soledad Valcarcel

Muslim Political Identities in Diasporic Contexts

The religious field in Argentina today is plural (Mallimaci 2000) and diverse (Frigerio 2007). For all that contemporary Argentine society is in transition towards a more open social fabric, the latest statistical surveys (Mallimaci 2008) reveal that it nevertheless maintains a strong Christian presence within.[2] While Catholicism preserves high levels of institutional hegemony and enjoys certain privileges in its relationship with the state (Esquivel 2010; Mallimaci 2010), difference is less costly than in the past, when state control translated into persecutions and prohibitions of other religious identities distinct from Catholicism (Calvo 2004, 2006; Zanatta and Di Stéfano 2000).

Authors such as Mallimaci (2015) have described a process of transition from Catholic monopoly to religious pluralism. They talk about the shattering of the 'myth of the Argentine Catholic nation'. Mallimaci and Giménez Béliveau (2007) explain that in the Southern Cone of South America religiosity has become hazy. Catholic symbols and rituals are utilised and re-articulated by different religious and lay actors. They also claim that the process of modernisation in this region is heterogeneous and expresses lay and secular tendencies, new forms of collective or individual belief (self-styled believers and nomadic subjects) and even forms of unbelief (2007: 47). These authors emphasise that modernity in Latin America does not necessarily imply a process of secularisation but is characterised by the break-up of the Catholic monopoly (Giménez Béliveau and Esquivel 1996: 117–18; Mallimaci 2001: 22–4) and the pluralisation of the religious field: in other words, the existence of a fluid and fragmentary landscape.

A different vision from the above is suggested by authors like Frigerio and Wynarczyk (2008). In their reading, the analysis of the breakdown of religious monopoly – primarily the Catholic monopoly – accepts or assumes an overly linear transition which loses sight of minority groups' difficulties and negotiations. Diversity and pluralism for them are not synonymous. They recognise the existence of greater religious diversity, or rather, its greater public visibility. This does not, however, imply a real and effective positive assessment of this diversity. They recognise the existence of 'asymmetric tolerances' (2008: 248), which, in Argentina at least, does not imply the same type of relationship or interreligious dialogue between Catholicism and the other Abrahamic traditions as exists with African-American cults, Umbanda or even Evangelical groups. The year 1978 saw the reinstatement of the National Register of Religions through Act 21,745.[3] This body was originally set up in 1946 under the Perón administration to monitor and control non-Catholic faiths. While some religious minorities reject and attack the Register, others see in it a way of achieving or guaranteeing their social legitimacy.

Accordingly, Frigerio (2007) warns us that the fact that more than 75 per cent of the Argentine population recognises itself as Catholic – in other words, identifies Catholicism as its social identity – tells us nothing about the way they experience that identity at a personal level or whether indeed they constitute a collective identity. The author conceives of identity as an emerging, situationally negotiated relationship. He therefore prefers (as do Beckford 2001, 2003; Finke 1997; Iannaccone 1998; Stark and Finke 2000; Stark and Iannaccone 1993; Stark and McCann 1993; Warner 1993) to speak of the existence of religious markets (some more regulated or deregulated than others) in which various formal and informal state and non-state mechanisms control the assets of salvation, belief and religious groupings.

To illustrate, the progressive social deregulation of the religious market does not eliminate the state favouritism enjoyed by the Catholic Church in Argentina as expressed in Article 2 of the Argentine Constitution (Frigerio and Wynarczyk 2008: 249).

For Frigerio and Wynarczyk (2008), who take up Beckford's contributions, what is regulated is not so much credibility – the loss or reduction of the monopoly on the truth – but the differential legitimacy of religious beliefs. Religious pluralism exists when religious diversity is valued morally and politically in a positive way, and ceases to be hierarchical and exclusively nominal in nature. As pointed out by Bokser-Liwerant (2008), secularisation (separation of the sacred and the profane in the private and public spheres respectively) is not synonymous with laicism (the separation of church and state and the latter's subsequent non-denominational nature). As a result, many groups use religion as a vehicle of identitarian, political and civic expression in the public space.

The opening process within the Argentine religious field slowly gathered form and force primarily with the return to democracy in 1983, when a climate of tolerance towards religious, ethnic and cultural minorities began to spread (Bianchi 2004). The growing liberalisation of Argentine society brought change even to the Catholic Church's institutional strategies, paving the way to an internal pluralism and recognising other faiths belonging to the Argentine religious field, especially those from monotheistic traditions. This favoured the growth of visibility[4] and greater participation in the public space of these religious minorities.

If we plot the course of this shift towards the pluralisation of the Argentine religious field, we can see the build-up of relative tolerance towards religious expressions linked to European immigrant groups. Nevertheless, considering the diversity of Catholicism in particular and of the religious field in general not only involves bringing visibility to the breakdown of Catholic predominance, and to the presence of numerous organisations and religious movements, but also to the different displacements, circulations and circuits of beliefs that are made explicit in a plural, mobile, diversified and diverse field (Giménez Béliveau 2006).

The Muslim field in Argentina has since its early days seen the gradual escalation of *visibility production* (García Somoza 2017). Incorporating the categories suggested by Segato (2007), we can understand this change as a process that starts with the production of historical othernesses, which we term *arabidades* (expressions of 'Arabness'), and moves towards the creation of political identities, or *musulmanidades* (expressions of 'Muslimness'). These can be linked in some cases to what certain writers have called the formation of political Islam (Burgat 2016; Roy 1992).

Identity-building based on *arabidad* involves the reproduction of cultural patterns of origin (handed down by forebears and reworked in contexts of rootlessness and diaspora) that put down roots in the country of destination and recreate the image of the 'land left behind' in the new territory. This process does not necessarily imply a return to sources but a constant reworking of the memory of the homeland, the group, and the ethno-cultural and religious traditions. We would therefore suggest that *arabidad* is a form of identity reflecting a *historical otherness* in which the resource of the national is often sought by appealing to 'stories of origin' that serve as a foundation for the national community identity. Among the best-known stories about the Arab and Muslim community is the 'Arab Gaucho'.[5] Therefore, it is also safe to say that *arabidad* is viewed as a form of 'being others' in a national society whose dynamics of interaction between the different sectors are, among other things, defined or determined by the state (Segato 2007).

Musulmanidad, on the other hand, involves a complex construction of Islamic identities informed by the context of symbolic production, and by local and transnational iconography. We therefore talk about political identities in contexts informed by globalisation processes. *Musulmanidades* can be understood in terms of recomposed or reassembled identities (García Somoza 2009): the search here is not for the simple reproduction of ethno-cultural traditions but for the espousal of a transnational religious discourse, re-appropriated and interpreted in local terms. In this constellation, *musulmanidad* calls for national attribution to be reinterpreted in political, ideological and religious terms.

We examine the configuration of a local Muslim subject based on three converging elements (García Somoza 2017): (1) distance (detachment or proximity) from the legitimised national collective identity; (2) discursive and iconic production combining symbols of local national rhetoric with ethnic and religious symbols (García Somoza and Valcarcel 2016), as visualised, for example, in the updated motif of Imam Husayn's martyrdom and his consequent performative expression in the 'Ashura' ritual; and (3) different 'stories of memory' recreating an 'other' that seeks to be acknowledged and affirmed in the 'we', embodied especially in certain stories of origin that validate their place in the national community[6] (*argentinidad*). National identity, ethno-religious identity and stories of memory are the elements that come into play.

From *bilad al-sham* to the Port of Buenos Aires: The Origin and Development of the Shi'a Community in Argentina

The way in which the Shi'a community memory is preserved and handed down will involve not only an identitarian reaffirmation but also a resolute political strategy. The website of the Argentine Islamic Arab Association states that this is: 'because they were sure people who forget their history and turn their back on their traditions inevitably lose awareness of their destiny.'[7] Not forgetting 'its history' and preserving 'its traditions' are part of the exercise of a group's collective memory-building. Remembering[8] involves defining a present identity from a past reinterpreted in present terms to define and guide a community project in the future, and hence the continuity of the group.

Over the past twenty years the various different Argentine Islamic institutions have understood that discursive/counter-discursive strategies and forms of dissemination (through images, icons and symbols) have a direct impact on how socially visible the group is, a not insignificant strategy when it comes to 'forming part of a national membership' (being Argentine) and reaffirming oneself in it, while also reaffirming oneself in the line of believers that belong to the *umma*. The question of identity will give rise to the search for practical and discursive strategies that will shape the group's outward image.

Before we go any further, let us briefly review the history of the Argentine Muslim presence in general to understand what place the At-Tauhid Mosque, and the Floresta Shi'a community in particular, have in the local Islamic field. The presence of Islam in Argentina goes back to the end of the nineteenth century and early twentieth century, with the arrival of immigrants mostly from the current territories of Syria and Lebanon, and to a lesser extent Iraq and Palestine. This region, also known as *bilad al-sham*, included at that time territories of the Ottoman Empire, hence the label *turcos* (Turks) that these populations were given upon arriving in Argentina and was printed on their passports (Akmir 2011).

Though the majority of immigrants from this region professed the Christian faith, within the group there was a small percentage of Muslims who arrived in Argentina between the years 1880–1930, the period that saw the country's highest Arab immigration flows. Later, by around the second half of the twentieth century, there was a succession of smaller waves of immigration after the conflicts in Palestine and Lebanon, when a new generation of Muslims integrated into small communities already installed there.

In the first collective of immigrants – the *turcos* – the appeal to personal identity (Goffman 2006)[9] was outlined in terms of their country of origin rather than their denomination or religious practice. Once they were more settled in Argentina, this gave way to the construction of *arabidad*, which was fostered above all by a group of intellectuals of Arab origin. They turned to the construction of the first stories of origin, thus ensuring that *arabidad* became the primary form of identitarian attribution. Later, the first primarily cultural and social associations would be created in ethno-cultural guise; although there were some *musalla* (small prayer rooms), the religious would generally be confined to the private sphere until the end of the twentieth century, together with a wealth of publications in the press, literature and social studies (Yáser 1997). In this period, Argentina consolidated its place as the largest producer of Arabic press publications on the American continent. This reflected a circulation and large consumption of cultural goods by the Arab collective, placed third numerically, socially, politically and culturally, just behind the Italian and Spanish communities, in first and second positions respectively.

During the first half of the twentieth century the Arab community in general (including Christians, Jews and Muslims) enjoyed an intense public, social and cultural life. Although for Argentine society as a whole they were identified as Syrian/Lebanese, within this 'Arab collective', the 'compatriots' – as they tended to call each other – distinguished each other in terms of region, nationality or native town (Akmir 2011). There was some internal tension imported from the conflicts in those countries, but this was confined to the community's political debates as reported through its press organs.[10] However, the most violent internal ruptures and conflicts manifested in a series of international events that made an impact on local public opinion and primarily intra-communal relations, a process that would give way to the reconfiguration of identities moulded in a new appellation, which we refer to here as *musulmanidades*.

In this context, the religious – especially Islam – was kept to the private sphere, within the intimate family circle.[11] Although some social clubs had been founded, like the Syrian/Lebanese Club, along with other institutions, there were no institutions exclusively for Islamic worship. Indeed, the three mosques of the Autonomous City of Buenos Aires were only built during the period of democratic openness post-1983. Nevertheless, the absence of places of worship did not imply the absence of religious life; on the contrary, this context reflected the way religious life was developing in a time that demanded the hypercorrection and homogenisation of differences for the sake of *national being* (Balibar 1990; Sayad 1999; Segato 2007).

During the 1970s and 1980s a 'revival' or 'born again' movement to Islam, as some authors have termed it (Marty and Scott Appleby 1994), aroused interest among some young people whose religious practice had hitherto been almost imperceptible. The Iranian Revolution of 1979 prompted closer ties to Islam among many young Argentines from Muslim (some even from traditional Sunni families) or Christian families, in this case leaning to a Shi'ism informed by the discourse of resistance to oppressive powers. By this time, Argentina lived under a military dictatorship, which may have reinforced such an ideological-cum-religious tendency. Inspired by the 1979 Revolution, this movement consolidated the institutionalisation of the current Floresta Shi'a community centring on the Argentine Islamic Organisation and its At-Tauhid Mosque, founded in 1983.

In the first half of the twentieth century the members of this sector of Argentina's Muslim population used to meet informally either in their own homes – the majority located in the Buenos Aires boroughs of Flores and Floresta – or in a makeshift hall for social gatherings.[12] The aim of these meetings was not only the strengthening of ethnic solidarities (even by helping compatriots recently arrived in the country to settle in) but also its members' growing concern for raising funds to establish their own community institutions, above all a mosque.

Where fund-raising was concerned, in 1959 the Argentine Islamic Arab

Association (AAIA) was formed as a result of the merger of three institutions in the Floresta Arab Community. These were created in the 1920s and, interconnected yet separate, acted as a focus for the whole community's cultural, social and sporting activity: the Argentine Islamic Arab Cultural, Social, Sporting and Charitable Association; the Argentine Arab Young Persons' Social and Cultural Club; and the 'The Arab Alliance' Cultural, Social and Charitable Association.

These new bodies would likewise be responsible for realising three well-defined aims: namely, the establishment of an Islamic cemetery, the creation of an Arab/Islamic College and the construction of a mosque. These spaces would not only firm up intra-community ties, but would also bring the group continuity, while consolidating the cycles of specifically Islamic religious life and practices. In other words, these places allowed them to keep the group's community memory alive.

In 1961 the Deliberative Council of San Justo District granted the whole Muslim community of Buenos Aires City and Greater Buenos Aires two hectares within the Justo Villegas Municipal Cemetery for the building of an Islamic cemetery, the aim being for the community to perform burials exclusively according to Islamic rites. The cemetery was founded in 1962. It was the first in Argentina and Latin America and has twice been expanded, two hectares being added in 1964 and a further three in 1997.[13]

Around 1971, the Floresta community ordered the laying of the first foundations of what today is known as the Imam 'Ali ibn Abi Talib (P) Argentine Islamic Arab Institute (*Instituto Argentino Árabe Islámico*). The Argentine Islamic Arab Institute, the first Islamic College in Argentina and Latin America, began imparting official teachings in 1972 at the initial levels, later incorporating new classrooms and adding further courses to its prospectus year by year, until by 1974 it catered for all levels of primary education. It was as late as the year 2000 that the College also began offering a complete secondary education, thus becoming the first Islamic secondary school in Latin America. While it has been incorporated into the formal education process – in other words, recognised by the state – extra-curricular subjects such as Islamic education and Arabic language are also taught. As community members are fond of mentioning, this educational institution, '[which] tries to build by integrating into the social fabric of Argentina, is at once a way of showing gratitude and a commitment from the Arab and Islamic community to our country and our Argentine community'.[14]

Within the educational area, the community also has the Argentine Institute of Islamic Culture (IACI), which acts as a body to disseminate Islamic culture. Its various activities include the 2003 seminar 'Sociology, History and Thought of the Muslim World' at the Faculty of Social Sciences of the University of Buenos Aires. This seminar was organised by Sheikh Abdul Karim Paz, Professors Gustavo C. Bize, Ricardo H. S. Elía and Masuma Assad de Paz. According to the seminar's introduction it aimed to present Islam as an age-old culture from its sources and to connect Eastern and Western knowledge, and so 'avoid the numerous barriers that have been erected between the two'.[15]

The At-Tauhid Mosque was founded in 1983, again in the borough of Floresta. Construction began on a small plot of land to which new facilities have been added year by year. The last renovation of the main hall and prayer hall was carried out in 2012–13, and received contributions from several members of the community. Among its activities are Arabic language classes and classes in Islamic culture and religion. It also organises study tours to Iran. It has a newspaper (*El Muecín*), a magazine (*Al Kauzar*, printed in Iran and distributed in Argentina), and distributes books on Islamic culture and religion. Most of its outreach and education materials are funded by religious institutions in Iran. This bears witness to the bond of cooperation and financial support maintained by the At-Tauhid Mosque and the community with the Islamic Republic of Iran.

The mosque is home to the Argentine Muslim Women's Union (UMMA), founded two years later in 1985 by a group of young Muslim women from Argentina and other countries, to become one of the first Islamic women's organisations in South America.[16] The main objectives of UMMA, as stated on its webpage and as reported to us by several of its members, are the spread of Islam and the participation of women in cultural, social and religious activities. The Union is led by the spouse of the mosque's resident imam. Being a small sector of the local Muslim field, both the community comprising the At-Tauhid Mosque and the UMMA group have begun to grow in both numbers of converts and visibility in the public space over the last fifteen years as the result of a series of communicative strategies by their leaders.

The local Muslim field as a whole is currently heterogeneous and dynamic, while encompassing various simple, multiple or mixed affiliations that are liable to change over the years. There is a transit (in terms of circulation) within the Muslim field that is not uniform. Some transit more than others, establishing a variety of links within the local Muslim network (which we term 'multiple affiliations'). Others have exclusive key affiliations with a single institution and/or membership group (which we term 'simple affiliations'). Still others have had a stronger affiliation with one institution or group that dissolves after a time, and shifts to fresh affiliations, dropping the previous one while maintaining links with some of its members, but without keeping up regular activity within the group (this we term 'mixed affiliations') (García Somoza 2017). The members of the Floresta community exercise different types and degrees of participation. The type of participation directly matches their position within the institutional structure. Accordingly, we find individuals who inhabit administrative, organisational or religious roles occupying a close simple kind of membership with the institutional structure, while others circulate – especially during times of celebration like Ramadan – within a network of relations comprising institutions and fairly formal groups. These spaces of interaction may be both Shi'a and Sunni. In the latter case the degree of porosity in the type of participation is due to the fact that these individuals do not hold any particular institutional post, which allows them to circulate more flexibly without being tied to the frameworks of a particular institution. Institutional affiliation displays a given politico-ideological stamp, while also defining the religious identity – *musulmanidad* – of that individual (García Somoza and Valcarcel 2016). It is not the same to belong to 'Alberti, Floresta or Palermo', as Buenos Aires's city mosques are called in the local parlance, 'as to the Sufi tariqa'.

Historical and Mythico-religious Time at a Local Site

As reworked by the 'Floresta group',[17] *musulmanidad* is characterised by 'the Islamic' over 'the Arab' (although sometimes the two dimensions are amalgamated), the fight against the negative image of Islam at local level (against the backdrop of the bomb attack on the Argentine Israelite Mutual Association in 1994)[18] and at global level (with the mediatisation of Islamist terrorism) and conceptualising a political project based on the pursuit of social justice. In this last aspect, there is a movement that refers simultaneously to a historical time (social inequalities) and a mythico-religious time (the Islamic principle of social justice and the idea of the Final Judgement). One interviewee, for example, told us that the constant wars, violence, social inequalities and even the potential for communication throughout the world herald the arrival of the *mahdi* (The Guided One), the expected saviour in Twelver Shi'a Islam:

> In all religions, we believe a Messiah will come. The difference is that for us he's alive and is going to come back. He *is* going to return . . . Once he begins his government, there'll be peace on earth. They say it's forty years. We don't know if it's forty or four hundred. But there will be peace and it will be an Islamic government of course. Then come the imams. And the first to come is Imam Husayn. After that comes the Final Judgement.[19]

Historical otherness is transformed into a political identity of public visibility and discursive negotiation (Segato 2007). In this movement *musulmanidad* constitutes a reconfigured identity (García Somoza 2009; García Somoza and Valcarcel 2016; Valcarcel 2013), which at times seeks to 'de-Arabise' itself (Montenegro 2002). It constitutes a nationalisation of Islam as reflected in the expression 'Argentines of Islamic faith' printed on certain institutions' placards when representing the community at events in the public space; in the growing supply of courses on Islamic culture and learning taught at different institutions around the city of Buenos Aires; or in the fact that the *khutba* in the Floresta mosque is delivered in Spanish rather than Arabic to connect more directly with converts or with worshippers of Arab descent who do not speak the language. There is also the necessary distinction drawn in various different talks and interviews between Arabism and Islam. On other occasions, however, interviewees emphasise their Arab roots (as expressed in their dance, food, customs and ancestry). At one event held during Arab Countries' Culture Week (*Semana de la Cultura de los Países Árabes*)[20] in the city of Buenos Aires in May 2010 one woman from the community stated: 'The *dabke*, the dance of our origins, of our ancestors . . . strikes deep because folk music is the earth.'[21] A few hours earlier that day, at a conference on the Nakba and the conflict in the Middle East, the speakers – whose number included a respected member of the Floresta community – described and praised 'Arab culture as a culture of resistance',[22] choosing to use the Arabic term *muqawwama*.

With the globalisation of Islam (Roy 2002) and the politicisation of identities Muslim actors have set in motion practical and discursive strategies that allow them to respond and align themselves to global Islam, while also redefining and locating its icons, messages and symbols, and adapting them to their own context (García Somoza and Valcarcel 2016; Valcarcel 2014b). This is true, for example, of the utilisation and significance of the hijab within the Floresta community. The hijab becomes a symbol of female *musulmanidad*, making women's identities visible and reconfiguring them. 'The Constitution's telling me about freedom of worship, everyone has a right to profess their religion, and you won't take my identity away because I'm a Muslim',[23] stated the founder and president of the Argentine Muslim Women's Union (UMMA) to the state authorities who refused to allow her to wear the hijab on the photograph for her ID card. After a long battle with the authorities, she won the right to wear it, thus setting a precedent: since 2005 Muslim women in Argentina have been able to obtain their ID cards wearing the hijab. This is how, for many members of the Floresta Shi'a community, *argentinidad* and *arabidad* sustain their socio-cultural identity, whereas Islam allows them to build a collective identity and to establish cognitive, moral and emotional connections among themselves (Frigerio 2007; Polleta and Jasper 2001).

According to this community's own members, the Islamic Revolution in Iran has gained great relevance in this process of identitarian reconfiguration. They point out that it has helped them recover their religious line of thought, as well as becoming a political symbol. In the words of one community member:

> 11 February marks the anniversary of the Islamic Revolution led by Imam Ruhollah Al Khomeini (RA), it was the victory of a people subjugated by an oppressive tyrannical absolutist monarchy put there by the hand of the North American empire after the overthrow of Mohammad Mossadegh by the CIA in 1953.
>
> Thirty-seven years of light and prosperity returned not only to the Iranian people but also to the entire Islamic *umma*, in what can be filed as

the true beginning of the Islamic Awakening . . . But at the same time the luminous Leader embarked upon another struggle: to educate his people, to build a new paradigm full of dignity and honour founded on Islam, on the teachings of the Qur'an, the Prophet Muhammad and his Purified Family (AS). But also as an example for an Islamic world plunged into lethargy and at the mercy of indirect colonialism.

He recovered the oil for his people, virtually made illiteracy vanish, encouraged science (Iran is a nanotechnology leader) fostered the active role and participation of women in society (64% of the university population in Iran is female) and led the Islamic Republic to be a powerful industrialised country and an indisputable touchstone in the Middle East . . .

Today the Islamic Republic of Iran stands as a beacon clear and strong, as a Stoical pillar of anti-imperialist resistance in the region, and vital support for other resistances like the Palestinian and the Lebanese movements, as a loyal ally of Syria in this tragedy, which has also been imposed by the usual suspects.

The Iranian people is out to celebrate thirty-seven years of renewed freedom, demonstrating that the Revolution is alive and well, declaring with their presence in the streets that no 'Colourful Revolution'[24] can overcome a people convinced of its chosen way of life. Health and Victory to the Radiant Islamic Revolution.[25]

Certain points in this statement need highlighting. First, the significance this community places on the Revolution and the phenomenon of 'Islamic awakening', which other groups from the local Muslim collective do not bestow on it. Various Floresta members – especially their leaders – point to the Revolution and the link with the Iranian Muslims arriving in Argentina at that time as a pivotal moment in the 'recovery' of their Islamic identity. This local/international connection is expressed in the construction (financing, formation and dissemination of doctrinal and informative material) of their mosque and the different community actors' journeys to Iran – men and women – to take part in religious training courses or conferences on 'Islamic awakening'.

One of the leading shaykhs at the At-Tauhid Mosque is an Argentinian from a Catholic background and with no Arab descent, who converted to

Islam in his youth and studied theology in Iran, a country where he currently resides with his family, although he periodically travels to Argentina to lead various activities; a man whose 'performance' combines elements of traditional religious authority with those of the charismatic urban leadership typical of the so-called 'new religious groups' or political parties (Sunier 2009). This shaykh delivers the *khutba* in Spanish, marking a clear difference with the city's other mosques, where the leaders are from Arab countries and preach in Arabic. Many of those attending do not understand what is being said and read it afterwards in the translations handed out or downloaded from the institutions' websites.

In this sense, the religious performance of the Shi'a shaykh favours proximity with local community members, as well as participation by converts of non-Arab descent. In the *khutba* at the Ramadan celebrations in 2013 he explained that Islam is a more integral system than capitalism or communism. He spoke of how necessary it was to 'Islamise society' (Valcarcel 2013: 103) and to conceive of Islam as a form of socialisation. While the members of this community have no wish to Islamise Argentine society nor to form a theocratic regime in the country, they praise the Iranian system and consider it important to disseminate its achievements as well as religious moral principles that help improve social coexistence. Their political language is informed by the religious discourse. We can therefore speak of a political use of Islam that transforms it into an expansive democratising force by disputing and breaking the monopoly of traditional religious authority (Eickelman and Salvatore 2002), and so reinforces charismatic political leadership. The existence of a converted shaykh with so much influence in the community and its receptive stance towards those wishing to embrace Islam is a good example of this. Islam becomes a political language that leads to the emergence of a Muslim public sphere where religion, politics and civil life combine (Montenegro 2007).

Second, there is the need to emphasise the status of women in Iranian society. This is a way to reverse not only widespread prejudice about Muslim women but also the image of the country propagated by the media. This image is built on local and international factors: on the one hand, the issue of human rights, in particular with regard to the application of Islamic law and issues relating to sexual minorities; on the other hand, the Argentine Israeli

Mutual Association (AMIA) case and the Memorandum of Understanding between Argentina and Iran.[26] In various different interviews and informal talks community members speak about how painful it was for them to lose the participation of some of the Iranians attending the mosque over allegations regarding the AMIA case. According to statements made by a representative to one local media outlet: 'We suffer all this together with the Jewish community. They for their victims, we for our persecution.'[27] For this reason, they highlight as one of their main objectives the dissemination of 'the true face of Islamic piety to reverse the disinformation dumped daily on the major media, politicised and influenced by the great powers'.[28]

True to this objective, the UMMA, as we mentioned above, was created on 9 February 1985. This organisation has inherited a group of students formed by the wife of an Iranian shaykh resident in Argentina in the 1980s. The UMMA was formed later, presided over by the wife of the Argentine shaykh who embraced Islam, a sociologist of Arab-Muslim descent who also studied theology in Iran. The UMMA strives to tackle stigmatisation and reverse the stereotypes circulating about Muslim women (commonly represented as submissive, oppressed, etc.).[29] Its website broadcasts news about the Islamic world and publishes religious material on the role of Muslim women and sexual/family morality. Its discourse is opposed to the homogenisation, sexual liberalism and objectification of women that, according to them, reigns in Western societies, although at the same time it supports Shi'a temporary marriage (*mut'a*)[30] so as to allow some flexibility or openness in the interaction between men and women. The practice of temporary marriage sparks intense criticism from other sectors of the Muslim population. The members of the Floresta community do, however, recognise that it has to be conducted responsibly and in accordance with religious principles. We see that within the community it works as a way of 'Islamising or sanctifying courtship' in Argentine society (Valcarcel 2013: 114). In the framework of this grammar the use of the hijab, particular among female converts or those who have a prominent institutional role, gains in significance. Not only is it an identitarian symbol but the physical manifestation of an ethical value: modesty (Mahmood 2001; Valcarcel 2014a). In the words of one interviewee:

in this society where the physical is valued, I'm going to have my precaution[31] and I'm going to say: 'Value me for my intellect and for my person. For the way I am.' How do I protect myself? By having modesty which are the tools given to me by God. (Valcarcel 2013: 123–4)

The members of UMMA also collaborate in inter-religious dialogue or meetings such as Women of Monotheistic Faith. They also organise solidarity collections to help children's hospitals or neighbourhood canteens; they take part in setting up and tending to the stand the Argentine Islamic Organisation and the At-Tauhid Mosque has at the Buenos Aires Book Fair; they organise and convene 'female religious celebrations' within the mosque, such as the anniversary of the birthdays of the Prophet's daughter (Fatima) and granddaughter (Zaynab); and, finally, they hold public outreach activities such as the photography exhibition for the International Hijab Day held on 1 February 2016 in Villa Devoto's borough, and another exhibition of Women in the Islamic Revolution, held on 11 February 2016 in the Plaza Irlanda in the Buenos Aires borough of Caballito.

Third, the Islamic Revolution as a political symbol is locally re-articulated and compared with processes gestating in Latin America for the past fifteen years, especially with the presidencies of Hugo Chávez and Evo Morales. The community presents a clear geopolitical alignment in favour of Iran, and Palestinian, Lebanese and Syrian resistance movements. They do not seek to import external conflicts; rather they reinterpret them in local terms. They view these processes as anti-imperialist and anti-Zionist movements that are reconcilable with the imaginary of the 'Great Latin American Homeland'.[32] A few years ago, in a talk to commemorate the Nakba[33] held as part of Arab Countries' Culture Week,[34] one of the community's representatives made a comparison between the Israeli occupation and the colonisation of Latin America, praising the 'resistance of the natives' – both historical and contemporary – here and there. On the other hand, they emphatically condemn the actions of ISIS (the so-called Islamic State operating in Syria and Iraq) and other terrorist groups.[35] They argue that the emergence, financing and proliferation of these groups is the responsibility of the United States, Israel and Saudi Arabia. Some members of the Floresta and José Ingenieros communities[36] consistently demonstrate against such groups and the international policy of those three countries.

The Floresta community not only holds celebrations and religious events – let us remember that the Shi'a calendar of activities is more intense than the Sunni, with the importance they attach to *ahl al-bayt* – but also organises events with clearly political content, such as talks and video screenings on the International Al-Quds Day,[37] or a meeting on 13 February 2015 to commemorate the death of Sheikh Nimr, executed forty days earlier by the Saudi regime. We can see how they join up political and religious dimensions. For them it is a moral and therefore religious duty to fight social injustice. They take up iconic figures from the Shi'a tradition as an example of the struggle against oppressive powers. This strategy serves as a sub-narrative (Wertsch 2002) aligned to the collective memory of the community, updated through female performance, a definite interpretation and form whereby women reconstruct individual and community memories (Shanneik 2015). In this sense, there exists a certain way of politicising the religious and of consecrating the political (Pace 2001, 2006).

The Argentine Islamic Organisation, together with the leaders of the Alawi Community in José Ingenieros (Buenos Aires Province), are the main organisers and provide the speakers at demonstrations held each year in commemoration of the Nakba outside the Israeli Embassy. The shaykhs of At-Tauhid Mosque and José Ingenieros's community make themselves visible wearing their distinctive religious attire. These demonstrations – which take place a few metres from the emblematic Plaza de Mayo – are attended and supported by left-wing parties and the organisations *Quebracho*[38] and *MILES* of the *piquetero* ('picketer') leader, Luis D'Elía. The groups comprise individuals from different sectors of the Arab and Islamic communities. In fact, many women who do not wear the hijab on a daily basis use it on this occasion as an identitarian symbol of resistance. Also present are representatives of FEARAB[39] and FEIRA.[40]

Other religious institutions such as the Islamic Centre are not represented in these demonstrations, although their members do participate independently. On the contrary, institutionally speaking, they prefer to attend interreligious prayers and supplications for peace. According to some Muslims in the Floresta community, this is because other sectors of the Muslim organised field do not wish to be associated with these political groupings. The presence of Luis D'Elía is perhaps one of the greatest sources of tension. D'Elía leads the demonstrations alongside Muslim religious leaders and also attends the Al-Quds Day meetings at the At-Tauhid Mosque. His controversial statements on certain publicly sensitive issues, as well as his political stance, have led to disruptions. This intensified further after certain illegal recordings recently came to light of conversations – supposedly linked to the investigation into the Memorandum of Understanding between Argentina and Iran,[41] and therefore to the AMIA bombing – between D'Elía, a staunch defender of the Kirchnerist administration and Iranian policy, and members of the Floresta community. Another allegation was published in the media in August 2013[42] reporting 'anti-Semitic events in this mosque' in the presence of Luis D'Elía, Esteche and Emilio Pérsico, an ex-Montonero,[43] a *piquetero* leader in the 1990s and leader of the Evita Movement (a pro-Kirchnerist social political group), who was also a civil servant, holding the post of Family Farming Secretary in Cristina Fernández de Kirchner's administration.

We detect that the tensions between this and other sectors in local Muslim communities lie not so much in their religious and/or theological differences but in their (geo-)political and ideological stances. At the international level, we have already highlighted some points, but these cannot be understood at the expense of the local context. This is reflected, for example, in the formation of the Interfaith Network of Young People of the City of Buenos Aires (RIJBA) in 2014. This network, funded by the City Government's Department for Worship, has been presented in various religious institutions in Buenos Aires city. According to one woman from Floresta, when the proposal was put to them, they found it very interesting and elected their youth representatives. However, she pointed out that these representatives were never called up for the activities. The network involves Sunni Muslims and recently a Shi'a woman joined, but she has no institutional links to the Floresta mosque.

According to the explanations provided, although guided tours are conducted through the Network and activities of the At-Tauhid Mosque are promoted, the non-inclusion of the mosque's members is a top-level governmental political decision. Despite the different voices involved and their different versions, it is difficult to determine conclusively what happened between the official announcement to the Network and its later informal 'exclusion'. However, we believe that the community's political stance in national and international arenas, the relationship of its religious leaders with figures such as Luis D'Elía, Fernando Esteche, Emilio Pérsico and others, and tensions with some sectors of the local Jewish community are likely to have been determining factors. We should also remember that the PRO (Republican Proposal), the Buenos Aires government's political party, has in its ranks Rabbi Sergio Bergman, who has had confrontations with Luis D'Elía and been a staunch opponent of the Argentinian-Iranian Memorandum of Understanding.[44] Some sectors of the Jewish community argue that the attack on the AMIA was perpetrated by Iran and Hezbollah, while the Floresta community claims that these allegations are false and support both the policy of Iran and of the Lebanese Hezbollah.

Another example of tensions between the two sectors became visible at an event on 10 September 2010 to celebrate the Eid Al-Fitr of Ramadan at the Islamic Centre of the Argentine Republic (CIRA). An invitation was sent to President Cristina Fernández de Kirchner, who was in office at the time and who months later would embark on an official Middle Eastern tour of Kuwait, Qatar and Turkey.[45] She was accompanied by a commission consisting almost entirely of CIRA members.[46] During the end-of-Ramadan celebrations the President was invited to give a speech at CIRA.[47] On stage there were not only members of the government of the day, such as Foreign Minister, Héctor Timerman, or Secretary for Worship, Ambassador Guillermo Oliveri, but also several leaders of Islamic institutions who gave speeches and other leaders such as shaykhs Abdul Karim Paz and Mohsen Ali of the José Ingenieros Association, who were the only ones not to speak. According to several members of the Floresta and José Ingenieros communities who were in the audience with one of the authors, they remarked on the 'injustice committed' and how their leaders 'had been silenced by CIRA' (García Somoza 2017) not allowing them to deliver a speech not only before the vast majority of Muslim organisations but before CIRA representatives and the President herself.

Although historically the country's Arab-Muslim community has maintained significant links with Peronism, the Shi'a sector (Floresta's At-Tauhid Mosque, the Alawis of José Ingenieros, the mosques in Mar del Plata,

Cañuelas and Tucumán) has been most vocal in its support for the laws and measures implemented during the presidencies of Néstor and Cristina Kirchner between 2003 and 2015. They praise their efforts in the field of human rights and national and international policy. We even see men and women in the Floresta community strongly supporting the figure of Cristina Kirchner. The former president's discursive leadership, presence and ability are widely appreciated. They understand that the measures taken during the Kirchnerist administration favoured national sovereignty and were therefore anti-colonialist or anti-imperialist. Their policy was consequently associated with that of other like-minded international regimes that reflected 'the resistance of the peoples' or 'popular resistance'.

In this respect, we can better understand the last sentence of the statement on the anniversary of the Iranian Revolution: 'declaring with their presence in the streets that no "Colourful Revolution" can overcome a people convinced of its chosen way of life'. A process occurring in another country, albeit with a global impact, has been read in local terms. The 'Colourful Revolution' is a subtle way of referring to Mauricio Macri's office as President of the Argentine Republic since December 2015. This allusion refers to the slogan and aesthetic of Macri's presidential campaign, which relied on the incorporation – alongside the PRO's characteristic yellow – of various colours (representing the diversity of political positions that make up the 'Cambiemos' alliance),[48] the use of balloons and music for dancing at the close of polling, and the use of words like change, peace, dialogue and joy in his speeches and publicity spots.

They understand that this political party represents Argentina's conservative right, which they associate with major media outlets, international capital and the Zionist lobby. They claim that the party has been able to win elections against the candidate for the *Frente para la Victoria* – Front for Victory[49] – by selling 'illusions' or 'coloured mirrors' to the people. They think of both the Kirchnerist administration and the Islamic Revolution as true revolutions in contrast to the imposture of the current Macri government. Their support for and participation in the political group *Musulmanes al Frente* (Muslims Forward), presented at the Buenos Aires headquarters of the Justicialist Party[50] on 25 August 2015 is no coincidence. A member of the Floresta community stated in his speech that Muslims Forward is a 'novel, genuine and authentic' proposal seeking to make a contribution based on 'our thinking and Islamic identity framed within our being Argentine'.[51]

Finally, as we said earlier, the religious is not detached from the political dimension. Demonstrating against certain national and international hegemonic powers is seen as a moral duty for this community. It is derived from the Islamic principle of social justice and expressed as such in a message the UMMA and the At-Tauhid Mosque issued on 11 February 2015 in commemoration of the Islamic Revolution in Iran: '[in] any other Muslim society *taqwa*[52] exists mainly among the poor, the oppressed masses (or whatever their understanding of it may be) but it does not extend to those above [the powerful who dominate and oppress the people]'. Just as they have locally read Argentine national politics in light of the Iranian Islamic Revolution, they apply the figure of Imam Husayn to current local struggles. He is a symbol of resistance against oppressive powers. Every year, as in other parts of the world, they commemorate the events of 'Ashura'. They gather to relate and recall the events in various commemorative rituals.

On the Day of 'Ashura'[53] the members of the Floresta community congregate in the mosque and, after emotional speeches, recite devotional poetry in Arabic. Women wail as men recite eulogies in a circle, flagellating themselves (*latam*)[54] and emulating the suffering and martyrdom of Imam Husayn and his companions. Following tradition, those attending dress in mourning. The women stand on one side of the prayer hall, the men on the other. They share the same space, although they are separated by a screen marking the separation between men and women, but which is open most of the time. The women, many of whom do not wear the hijab on a daily basis, come in the traditional Iranian chador. Some, albeit mainly men and children, wear black t-shirts with the caption in red and white that reads '*Mi corazón late Husayn*': 'My heart beats Husayn'. Many young people wear headbands with inscriptions in Arabic. Once the ceremony is over, they eat, talk and socialise.

At the 2015 commemoration we met some women we had once interviewed. They looked deeply moved and sorrowful. One of them, with tears in her eyes, drew parallels between the martyred figure of Imam Husayn and Jesus, noting how important it was to remember the message associated with these events, just as the community was doing, unlike Christians who take advantage of the Easter weekend to go on holiday. Echoing the speeches made at the event, another woman claimed that those who today form and fund ISIS are the same people Imam Husayn fought against. As we pointed out above, the political and the religious, the national and the international, historical time and mythical time are multidirectional juxtapositions.

Conclusion

Contrary to what the premises of theories of secularisation and modernity argued regarding the retreat of the religious to private spaces, the boundaries between public and private fuse and confuse in equal measure. They reconfigure themselves in a dialogical continuum where actors adopt multiple practical and discursive strategies[55] to redefine such spaces and their boundaries. It is from this perspective, through a cross of political and religious discourses, that we have sought throughout this contribution to develop an analysis of the ways the Arabo-Islamic other is constructed in Argentina, basing our study on the Floresta Shi'a Muslim community. Using documentary sources (local press archives, as well as the community press),[56] field data and interviews with members of the Floresta community[57] we have shed light on the ways *musulmanidades* are constructed: from the analysis of stories of origin, reconstructed memories and the production of images and discursive fabrics woven around the figure of the Other[58] (Todorov 1982, 1989).

The Floresta community redefines its *musulmanidad* in terms of a specific theological line – Twelver Shi'ism – and a political project, inspired by the Islamic Revolution in Iran of 1979, about the pursuit of social justice and the fight against stigmatisation. This identitarian construction project refers simultaneously to a historico-political time (social inequalities, Islamic awakening, 'glocal' contexts) and a mythico-religious time (religious principles of social justice and practice of the good alongside the 'end time' worldview according to Islamic eschatology). As a polyvalent, transportable and transhistorical symbol, the figure of Imam Husayn and his martyrdom religiously remodels this group's political practice.

Imam Husayn is an important character in the political and religious history of Twelver Shi'a Islam. Historical and religious consciences are culturally shaped through the frames of interpretation shared by the community. Their re-articulation as myth is a way of social awareness. A mythico-historical conscience is articulated (Hill 1988) through which historical events (the martyrdom of the Imam and conflicts among the different tendencies within Islam), the religious worldview (practical and moral principles) and contemporary events (persecutions of Shiʻa minorities, terrorism, revolutions, wars, etc.) are interpreted and reflected. Various narratives, historicities and interpretive dimensions are juxtaposed (Sahlins 1997). The martyrdom and commemoration of Imam Husayn stands as a 'structure of the conjuncture' (Sahlins 1997), demonstrating how an event acquires historical significance and is revalued through shared interpretative frames. It expresses the dialogical relationship between the (past and present) event and the (social, symbolic and historic) structure, gaining mythico-practical force.

Finally, the figure of the Imam becomes a political and religious emblem that is updated both locally in its discourses against the hegemonic powers in the framework of Latin American politics and the Arab world, and performatively every year in the commemorative ritual of 'Ashura'. Although we are not looking at grand processions or mass meetings such as are conducted in other countries, the coming-together of the local community on this date is an instance of remembrance and also a symbolic action of communication, reinterpretation and dissemination of its politico-religious memory.

References

Akmir, Abdeluahed (2011), *Los árabes en Argentina*, Rosario: Universidad Nacional de Rosario.
Anderson, Benedict (1991), *Imagined Communities: Reflections on the Origin and Spread of Nationalism*, London: Verso.
Balibar, Etienne (1990), 'The nation form: history and ideology', *Review* 8:3, 329–61.
Beckford, James A. (2001), 'Social movements as free-floating religious phenomena', in R. Fenn (ed.), *The Blackwell Companion to the Sociology of Religion*, Oxford: Blackwell, pp. 229–48.
——— (2003), *Social Theory and Religion*, Cambridge: Cambridge University Press.
Bianchi, Susana (2004), *Historia de las religiones en Argentina: las minorías religiosas*, Buenos Aires: Sudamericana.
Bokser-Liwerant, Judit (2008), 'Religión y espacio público en los tiempos de globalización', in R. Blancarte (ed.), *Los retos de la laicidad y la secularización en el mundo contemporáneo*, México DF: Colegio de México/Centros de Estudios Sociológicos, pp. 59–84.

Bourdieu, Pierre (1972), 'Les stratégies matrimonial dans le système de reproduction', *Annales Economies Sociétés Civilisations* 27:4–5, 1105–27.
Burgat, François (2016), *Comprendre l'Islam politique: Une trajectoire de recherche sur l'altérité Islamiste, 1973–2016*, Paris: La découverte.
Calvo, Nancy (2004), 'Lo sagrado y lo profano: Tolerancia religiosa y ciudadanía política en los orígenes de la república rioplatense', *Andes* 15, 151–81.
—— (2006), 'Los unos y los otros. Católicos, herejes, protestantes, extranjeros. Alcances de la tolerancia religiosa en el Río de la Plata durante las primeras décadas del siglo XIX', *Anuario IEHS* 21, 13–35.
Eessa Ibarra, Muhammed (2003), *Risalatul Mutah: El matrimonio temporal en el Islam*, Online: Biblioteca Islámica Ahlul Bait.
Eickelman, David E., and Armando Salvatore (2002), 'The public sphere and Muslim identities', *European Journal of Sociology* 43:1, 92–115.
Esquivel, Juan Cruz (2010), 'Notas sobre la laicidad en Argentina', *Debates do NER* 2:18, 149–71.
Finke, Roger (1997), 'The consequences of religious competition: supply-side explanations for religious change', in L. Young (ed.), *Rational Choice Theory and Religion*, London: Routledge.
Frigerio, Alejandro (2007), 'Repensando el monopolio del catolicismo en la Argentina', in M. J. Carozzi and C. Ceriani (eds), *Ciencias sociales y religión en América Latina: Perspectivas en debate*, Buenos Aires: Biblos, pp. 87–118.
Frigerio, Alejandro, and Hilario Wynarczyk (2008), 'Diversidad no es lo mismo que pluralismo: cambios en el campo religioso argentino (1985–2000) y lucha de los evangélicos por sus derechos religiosos', *Sociedade e Estado* 3:2, 227–60.
García Somoza, Mari-Sol (2009), 'Narrations interjectives: Identités, discours et contre-discours', MA dissertation, EHESS, Paris.
—— (2017), 'Entre Fátima et Evita: Identités, espaces de participation et de sociabilités religieuses des femmes musulmanes en Argentine', PhD dissertation, Université Paris Descartes, Paris and Universidad de Buenos Aires/CONICET, Buenos Aires.
García Somoza, Mari-Sol, and Mayra Valcarcel (2016), 'Íconos, sentidos e identidades en movimiento: estrategias, prácticas y discursos en una comunidad musulmana de la Ciudad de Buenos Aires', *Revista de Estudios Sociales* 56, 51–66.
Giménez Béliveau, Verónica (2006), 'Desafíos a la laicidad. Comunitarismos católicos y su presencia en el espacio público', in N. Da Costa (ed.), *Laicidad en América Latina: Repensando lo religioso entre lo público y lo privado en el siglo XXI*, Montevideo: CLAEH, pp. 81–92.

Giménez Béliveau, Verónica, and Juan Cruz Esquivel (1996), 'Las creencias en los barrios o un rastreo de las identidades religiosas en los sectores populares urbanos del Gran Buenos Aires', *Sociedad y Religión* 14/15, 117–28.

Goffman, Erving ([1963] 2006), *Estigma: La identidad deteriorada*, Buenos Aires: Amorrortu.

Halbwachs, Maurice ([1925] 2004), *Les cadres sociaux de la mémoire*, Paris: Albin Michel.

Hallar, Ibrahim (1962), *El Gaucho y su originalidad arábiga*, Buenos Aires: n.p.

Hervieu-Léger, Danièle, and Jean-Paul Willaime (2001), *Sociologies et religion: Approches classiques*, Paris: Presses universitaires de France.

Hill, Jonathan D. (1988), *Rethinking History and Myth: Indigenous South American Perspectives on the Past*, Chicago: University of Illinois Press.

Iannaccone, Laurence (1998), 'Introduction to the economics of religion: a survey of recent work', *Journal of Economic Literature* 36:3, 1465–96.

James, Daniel (1988), *Resistance and Integration: Peronism and the Argentine Working Class, 1946–1976*, Cambridge: Cambridge University Press.

——— (2000), *Doña Maria's Story: Life History, Memory and Political Identity*, Durham: Duke University Press.

Mahmood, Saba (2001), 'Feminist theory, embodiment and the docile agent: some reflections on the Egyptian Islamic revival', *Cultural Anthropology* 6:2, 202–36.

Mallimaci, Fortunato (2000), 'Catolicismo y liberalismo: las etapas del enfrentamiento por la definición de la modernidad religiosa en América latina', *Sociedad y Religión* 20/21, 25–54.

——— (2001), 'Prólogo', in J. Esquivel, Juan F. García, M. Hadida and V. Houdin (eds), *Creencias y religiones en el Gran Buenos Aires: El caso de Quilmes*, Buenos Aires: Universidad Nacional de Quilmes, pp. 13–31.

——— (2008), *Primera encuesta sobre creencias y actitudes religiosas en Argentina*, Buenos Aires: CEIL-CONICET.

——— (2010), 'Entre lo "que es" y lo que "queremos que sea": secularización y laicidad en la Argentina', *Sociedad y Religión* 32/33:20, 8–30.

——— (2015), *El mito de la Argentina laica: Catolicismo, política y Estado*, Buenos Aires: Capital Intelectual.

Mallimaci, Fortunato, and Verónica Giménez Béliveau (2007), 'Creencias e increencia en el Cono Sur de América: Entre la religiosidad difusa, la pluralización del campo religioso y las relaciones con lo público y lo político', *Revista Argentina de Sociología* 5:9, 44–63.

Marcilese, José (2015), 'La formación del Partido Justicialista: El peronismo, entre la proscripción y la reorganización (1958–1959)', *Quinto sol* 19:2, 1–24.
Marty, Martin E., and R. Scott Appleby (1994), *Fundamentalisms Observed*, Chicago: University of Chicago Press.
Montenegro, Silvia Maria (2002), 'Identidades muçulmanas no Brasil: entre o arabismo e islamização', *Lusotopie* 2, 59–79.
—— (2007), 'Hacia una sacralización de la Política: Reflexiones sobre las Perspectivas de Análisis del Islam Político', *Sociedad y Religión*, 28:28/29, 71–85.
Pace, Enzo (2001), 'Política y Religión en el mundo moderno: El retorno de las Guerras de Religión', *Revista de Ciencias Sociales y Religión* 3:3, 9–25.
—— (2006), 'Política de redención y redención de la política', *Ciencias Sociales y Religión* 8, 31–40.
Polleta, Francesca, and James M. Jasper (2001), 'Collective identity and social movements', *Annual Review Sociology* 27, 283–305.
Roy, Olivier (1992), *L'échec de l'Islam politique*, Paris: Seuil.
—— (2002), *L'Islam mondialisé*, Paris: Seuil.
Sahlins, Marshall ([1985] 1997), *Islas de historia: la muerte del capitán Cook, metáfora, antropología e historia*, Barcelona: Gedisa.
Sayad, Abdelmalek (1999), 'Immigration et "pensée d'État"', *Actes de la Recherche en Sciences Sociales* 129, 5–14.
Segato, Rita (2007), *La Nación y sus otros: Raza, etnicidad y diversidad religiosa en tiempos de políticas de la identidad*, Buenos Aires: Prometeo.
Shanneik, Yafa (2015), 'Remembering Karbala in the diaspora: religious rituals among Iraqi Shii women in Ireland', *Religion* 45:1, 89–102.
Stark, Rodney, and Roger Finke (2000), *Acts of Faith: Explaining the Human Side of Religion*, Berkeley: University of California Press.
Stark, Rodney, and Laurence Iannaccone (1993), 'Rational choice propositions about religious movements', in D. G. Bromley and J. K. Hadden (eds), *Handbook of Cults and Sects in America*, Greenwich: JAI Press, pp. 241–61.
Stark, Rodney, and James C. McCann (1993), 'Market forces and Catholic commitment: exploring the new paradigm', *Journal for the Scientific Study of Religion* 32:2, 111–24.
Sunier, Thijl (2009), 'Beyond the domestication of Islam: a reflection on research on Islam in Europe societies', *Journal of Muslims in Europe* 1:2, 189–208.
Todorov, Tzvetan ([1982] 1987), *La conquista de América: El problema del otro*, Mexico: Siglo XXI.

—— ([1989] 2013), *Nosotros y los otros. Reflexión sobre la diversidad humana*, Madrid: Siglo XXI.

Valcarcel, Mayra (2013), 'Mujeres Musulmanas: Identidad, Género y Religión', BA dissertation, FFyL, University of Buenos Aires.

—— (2014a), 'Sierva de Allah: Cuerpo, Género e Islam', *Revista Cultura y Religión* 8:2, 54–82.

—— (2014b), 'El Islam como objeto antropológico: Estudio en Buenos Aires', *Anuario Antropología Social y Cultural en Uruguay* 12, 155–69.

Warner, R. Stephen (1993), 'Work in Progress towards a new paradigm for the sociological study of religion in the United States', *American Journal of Sociology* 98:5, 1044–93.

Wertsch, James V. (2002), *Voices of Collective Remembering*, Cambridge: Cambridge University Press.

Yáser, Juan (1997), 'El movimiento literario americano-árabe en América Latina', in L. R. Corbinos and R. Kabchi (eds), *El mundo árabe y América Latina*, Madrid: Unesco-Libertarias/Prodhufi, pp. 331–70.

Zanatta, Loris, and Roberto Di Stéfano (2000), *Historia de la Iglesia católica en Argentina: desde la conquista hasta fines del siglo XX*, Buenos Aires: Mondadori.

4

BEKTASHISM AS A MODEL AND METAPHOR FOR 'BALKAN ISLAM'

Piro Rexhepi

Introduction

Shi'ism is theorised as the politics and poetics of Islam, the Islam of protest, as Hamid Dabashi calls it, a theology that thrives in opposition always ready to face reoccurring Karbalas, revitalising faith and commitment to set things right. It is also the colour green honouring Fatima al-Zahra, the daughter of the Prophet Muhammad, or the shining inspiration of the Twelver *tariqas* who in remembering and revering her righteous deeds and those of the Twelve Imams recount and relate the 'providential assurances that all will one day be well' (Dabashi 2011: xi). Much of the Bektashi *tariqa* is informed by the Shi'a experience – from the continued memory of Karbala, the ceaseless mourning and devotion of Imam 'Ali, to the oath to follow and emulate the ways of the *ahl al-bayt* and all those 'who sleep'. Those 'who sleep' for the Bektashis are all those *dervishes*, *babas* and the few *dede-babas* whose *turbehs* become the sites of veneration and vindication of Bektashi faith, fears and desires. To invoke them unjustly or to swear by their sacrifice is to defy the continuation of the cosmic order on whose shoulders the righteous path is maintained and passes on from one time to another since the occultation of the Imam.

From Dagestan to Dar-al-Salam and Detroit, Shi'ites opt for a more modest and discrete manifestation of their rituals than the public *ta'ziya* enactments and 'Ashura' mourning processions in Qom or Karbala. Among the Bektashis in particular, to draw attention to oneself in tremors gained by the insights of mourning is considered to disfavour one from the founder's gaze – Pir-i Haxhi-Bektash Veli (1209–71), venerated for his virtue in reticence. The more practical explanation for this understatement or *taqiyya*, Albanian and Turkish Bektashi *babas* suggest, is due to their continued persecution in the last century of the Ottoman Empire, which required modesty and mysticism to both nurture the faith and escape attention. A tension that has become part of the Bektashi way, where the public display and the private/communal becoming have taken on ceremonial features. That which one *is* in public and that which one *becomes* in the community is observed closely through the *prag*, the doorstep that divides the inside from the outside, the times outside from those within, crossing it is one of the most respected rituals of entering any Bektashi *tekke*. In most of them, kissing the *prag* upon entering and leaving is required as a commitment to contain all that is experienced inside and in one's heart and confer to the outside only that which the outside can grasp and absorb. It is why proselytising is neither practised nor preferred. An *ashik* must find their own path to the doorstep, 'take the hand' as a *nesip* and enter the voyage of the *muhib*, the seeker whose search for light is aided by the entire community and her or his spiritual guide, but prescribed by none. In the *meydan*, the *muhib* becomes united with the community through their collective *ikrar ayini*, the confession of their faith. Thus, one is never born a Bektashi, but have to strive to become one. Bektashi dervishes and *babas* love riddles and jokes, which is why those with aptitude for interpretation and humour always find it easier to enter the path – a common Albanian expression in Kosovo is: '*ne kofsh bektesh hec e mere vesh!* (if you are a Bektashi, go and figure it out!)'.

Located predominantly in Albania, North Macedonia and Kosovo, but also parts of Bosnia, Bulgaria and Greece, Bektashism is perceived as nominal Islam, resonating with the New Age vocabulary of Sufism – an example of the now academically revered peaceful 'Balkan Islam'. It is within this larger academic, policy and media differentiation of Islam that the particular regard for Bektashis, as well as Alevis in Turkey, has frequently been undertaken with the political aim of promoting a 'liberal Islam'. Muedini (2015) calls this phenomenon 'sponsoring Sufism', whereby various neoliberal projects in the larger shift from government to non-governmentality have subcontracted religious communities in 'countering radicalisation' work while simultaneously promoting religion as a means of conflict resolution for questions that are not necessarily religious (see also Hurd 2015). In this regard, Bektashis are admired as eager to 'bridge doctrinal gaps between Christianity and Islam by adopting local beliefs into reformulated theology' (Blumi 2005: 5). Endless academic categorisations have sought to define Bektashis in opposition to mainstream Sunni and Shi'a Islam. The Bektashis, writes Vickers (2008: 5), 'although generally Shia, are an unorthodox, pantheistic sect of Islam that finds God within nature and animals as well as mankind'. In observing its practices in Albanian-speaking communities, Clayer (2010: 53–69) notes that Bektashism has become the 'means of promoting "another Islam"', a 'religion' interpreted as a 'bridge between Islam and Christianity', or even as an 'Albanian religion'. This conceptualisation of Bektashis as Christian-Muslims is not recent. Coon (1955: 394) writes in the *American Anthropologist* in 1955 that 'the Bektashi, in certain respects is almost Christian'. Rooted in early twentieth century European and American scholarship undertaken in the Balkans during the decline of the Ottoman Empire (see for instance, Brailsford 1906; Birge 1937; Durham 1920, 1985; Hasluck 1925, 1929; Swire 1937), the Bektashis were also perceived as moderate Muslims by scholars who, although they had not studied Islam in other contexts, imagined a more fiery Islam further east of the Balkans. In what has become one of the most quoted texts on the tolerant and non-fanatical nature of Bektashis, 'The nonconformist Moslems of Albania', Hasluck (1925: 394) argues that the 'Bektashi gospel, so different from the conventional "fiery sword of Islam", . . . its emphasis on ethics differentiates it sharply from the other religions of the Near East which are only too often merely barren ritual, and therefore it is alive as they are stagnant'. Bektashism, concludes Hasluck (1925: 398), 'offers an Islam without rigidity or vexatious exactions'. Similarly, the focus by Western scholars on the Alevi-Bektashi in Turkey from the nineteenth century onwards has had an immense influence on how the Alevi-Bektashis have come to see and experience themselves and the ways in which they have attempted to co-opt Christian missionary conversion strategies or more recent Turkish nationalist projects of secularism (Dressler 2013; Kaya 1998). Much of this scholarship has been knowledge tied to or as a result of imperial adventures, Orientalist fantasies and, more recently, the European search for a model 'autochtonous Islam' that can service the multicultural needs of recognition and representation of a neoliberal European Union. As a Bektashi, I venture to do something else here.

In this contribution, I examine the Bektashi *tariqa* through a decolonial Islam as articulated by Sirin Adlbi Sibai's (2017) critical engagement with Islam, beyond the preservationist concerns with the past and 'not a set of dogmas and doctrines' but 'above all as an experience' to be approached through the 'decolonial option' for epistemic decolonisation (Mignolo and Escobar 2013). The decolonial approach would, as Salman Sayyid (2014: 125) points out, question

> the assertion that Muslim identity is less sturdy, less authentic and far more fictional than ethnicity or class and is therefore incapable of constituting and sustaining a collective identity is little more than a reflection of the idea that the political is impossible for the non-West.

Moreover, engaging with decolonial Islam, argues Sayyid (2016), is a process of both challenging 'Eurocentric historiography and learning the history of Muslim agency' while also 'changing the frame of reference bequeathed to us by the colonial order and internalized by the Westoxicated, and presented as the truth'. Sayyid's invocation of Jalal Al-e Ahmad's (1984) unfinished project of *gharbzadegi*, or 'Westoxification', is in part rooted in decolonial Shi'ism that questioned Cold War decolonisation binary 'alternatives' of either Soviet socialism or Euro-American capitalism, depicting both as the two sides of the same 'Occidentoxic' colonial paradigm.

Given Bektashi's imminence to Shi'ism, I am also approaching the Bektashi experience through the lens of decolonial Shi'ism as articulated by Ali Shari'ati whose reclaiming of Shi'ism 'against the nobility, against dictatorship, against capitalism, against poverty and against racism' (quoted in Dabashi 2011: 53) is more relevant today than ever. The importance of subjecting Bektashi epistemology to decolonial Islam and Shi'ism is a project of what Salman Sayyid (2016) calls 'clearing' as a way of Muslims speaking from a decolonial and autonomous position, as 'Muslim autonomy requires not only Muslims to know their *deen* but also to know their history' without which, he insists, 'any understanding of our *deen* will be stilted, and simply reproduce and reinforce Orientalism'. In the Bektashi and Balkan Muslim context this would require revisiting post-Ottoman nationalist narratives by engaging in a critical reading of nineteenth- and twentieth-century texts on Islam and Muslims in the Balkans while also examining the history of anti-colonial struggles and solidarities among Muslims in the Balkans and the larger Muslim world.

I approach Bektashism not as a religion, sect or through a sectarian and comparative lens but as Dabashi's (2011: xii) conceptualisation of Shi'ism, as a 'poem, an elegy, a eulogy, an epic, a panegyric pausing for a moment for history to recollect itself and start anew'. Last but not least, since my focus are primarily Albanian-speaking Bektashis in the Balkans, my work has been inspired by a wide range of Albanian scholars who in the last three decades have attempted to question the erasure of Muslim history and memory in the Balkans, chief among them Ervin Hatibi's work dedicated to examining the Albanian 'intellectual's dream for a final solution to the Muslim problem among Albanians' (Hatibi 2009: 145). Hatibi's work has been major in questioning the standard Albanian historical narrative saturated in anti-Muslim rhetoric that has silenced and declared 'clandestine' the works of Albanian intellectuals whose histories have given visibility to a more complex history of Islam among Albanians, beyond the standard narrative of forceful conversion under the violence of the Ottoman Empire. Habiti's work is not only important in raising public awareness of how theses of 'aggressive Islamisation' have contributed to contemporary trends of Islamophobia but also in giving visibility to muted authors such as Sherif Delvina (1998), Ferid Duka (2012) and Nexhat Ibrahimi (2004), among others, whose work provides new approaches in thinking Islam among Albanians and in the Balkans in general.

With that in mind, the contribution's first section examines the way in which the Bektashis are projected as the exemplary model for moderate Islam in the Balkans – the presentable relatives, as Hatibi (2009) notes, rather than 'rustic relations' like the mainstream Sunnis. I examine the production and proliferation of knowledge about Bektashis and Islam in the Balkans in the context of EU enlargement processes and the ways in which the region's

Muslims have been mobilised to build a European Islam and to serve as role models for other Muslims in the EU – thus coming to define the EU's borders. In the second part, I propose a decolonial approach to the study of Islam in the Balkans by bringing the question of who is given a voice and who is silenced in the study of Balkan Islam to the forefront and opening up the debate to local discussions of Islam published in Albanian, Bulgarian, Macedonian and Bosnian-Serbo-Croatian throughout Muslim communities in the Balkans, restoring Muslim subjectivity and memory to an area which has been appropriated for problematic projects of defining European borders along the lines of racial and religious segregation.

Bektashis: Model Moderate Balkan Muslims

> Interviewer: In view of what has happened in Yugoslavia, I would like to ask you about religious intolerance. Half the Albanians are Muslims, including your family. Did you receive a religious education? Is there a danger of Islamic fundamentalism in Albania now that religious practice has become free?
>
> Kadaré: I don't think so. My family was Muslim in name, but they did not practise. No one around me was religious. Besides, the Bektashi sect of Islam that is practised in Albania is very moderate, even more so than in Bosnia. So I don't think we need to worry on that score.
>
> (Kadaré and Shusha 1998)

In this excerpt from an interview given for the *Paris Review* in 1998, the Albanian writer Kadaré summons the Bektashis as a response to what had become a common ordinance among Albanian and Bosnian intellectuals in the 1990s. In responding to questions that present the genocide and expulsion of Muslims of Yugoslavia as a result of 'Islamic fundamentalism' just three years after the Bosnian Genocide and a year before the Racak Mascacre, Kadaré gave what had become a standard explanation of minimising the role of Islam in their lives and their communities as a way of easing historical European anxieties of continued Muslim presence in the Balkans, especially at the height of the post-Cold War clash of civilisations thesis that had designated the Balkans as one of the sites of such clashes. What is interesting, however, is Kadaré's claim that the 'Bektashi Islam practised in Albania is very moderate.' There are two issues with this claim. One suggests that Islam as practised in Albania is predominantly Bektashi although Bektashis constitute only between 3 and 5 per cent of the entire population. The more interesting claim is that Bektashis are moderate Muslims who should not be feared – unlike all those *other* Muslims.

In the 1990s, Bektashi became the metaphor and model for moderate Muslims in the Balkans. Hatibi points out how Western travellers have

> felt a great predilection towards the Bektashis, a predilection shared by various contemporary scholars, which was and is due to their syncretistic attitude, to the western foundation of their guidelines and lifestyle and to the consequent separation from the tradition and 'uneasy' aspects of Islam. Seen with a Western eye, we could say that the Bektashis are the 'presentable relatives', while the Sunni Muslim seem to be the 'rustic relation', those that you would prefer not to invite to your wedding. (Hatibi 2009)

The outward presentable characteristics of the Bektashis has made them favourites in both past and present curation of Albania's 'hardly Muslim' image while also appealing to the new-found interest among New Age spiritual communities in Europe and the US on Sufi teachings and practices. Among Albanians in particular, Bektashism constituted a cornerstone for self-determination claims of nationhood seen with doubt because of its Muslim majority population in the Europe of the late nineteenth and early twentieth century. This tradition continues. Speaking at a symposium on Bektashism in Tirana, the Albanian President called the Bektashis 'the main ideologists of our national Renaissance in their platform for a free and European-like Albania' and 'a main pillar for the establishment of the new state, religious harmony among faiths and religious orders' (Nishani 2014).

Seeking to promote this European-like Albania, the Bektashi establishment has seized the opportunity to engage in various 'interfaith' dialogues. In a visit to the Vatican in 2016, the head of the Albanian Bektashi Order, Haxhi Dede-Baba Edmond Brahimaj, called on everyone present at the meeting to strengthen the unity among faiths and religions in inter-religious dialogue. Meanwhile, Vatican Radio reported that the Dede-Baba represented the mystical order of Bektashis, who 'abstain from many ordinary practices of Sunni Islam'. The report also points out that unlike Sunnis, the

Bektashis 'pray only twice a day; they are not obliged to turn to Mecca; their wives are not veiled; and if they do not eat pork, the consumption of alcohol is not totally banned'. In the event that the message might have been missed between the lines, the report also adds that 'in the early years of the twentieth century, they fought alongside Christians in favor of Albania's independence, unlike the Sunnis loyal to the Sultan' and that they are seen as heretics 'among majority Sunnis' (Radio Vatican 2016). Whereas *La Stampa*, noting the importance of the meeting and the message of inter-faith coexistence both spiritual leaders sent, argues that the message the Bektashi Dede-Baba brought to Rome is of 'unique importance' since the Balkans constitute 'a real European frontier in the fight against the Caliphate' (Bernardelli 2016), the term 'caliphate' in the text not being specified. After his visit at the Holy See, the Dede-Baba travelled to Paris where, attending an event titled *La Journée de la Culture Bektashi à Paris*,[1] he declared that 'Bektashis are the representatives of the kind of tolerant and moderate Islam practised by all Muslims in the Balkans' and that they should not be confused with Muslims gone astray in the Middle East.

This representation of Bektashi Islam as Balkan Islam, acceptable to Europe, and as something that must be protected for the sake of Europe, works through an economy of fear grounded in multiple premises. The iteration of a Bektashi, as well as Balkan, Islam that must be placed in the service of, and acceptable to, Europe is not only problematic in that it nurtures divisions within Muslim communities by designating what Mamdani (2002) calls 'good' and 'bad' Muslims but it also sustains racialised spatial and temporal hierarchies that form Euro-American geopolitical positioning of their borderlands. In this constellation, the hierarchy of trusted Muslims is informed by their distance from orthodox Islam, located in the past and spatially somewhere deep in the 'Middle East', and the trusted Muslims whose proximity to Europe, spatial, spiritual and temporal, produces them as possible subjects. Within this logic, Bektashi Muslims are the favourites within the Balkans whereas the Balkans are the favourites within the Near/Middle East, and so on. The more pernicious outcome of these hierarchies of 'good' and 'bad' Muslims is their maintenance through divisions within the communities by foreign journalists and academics, who further the divisions by framing these questions along 'victims and villains' narratives. Note, for instance, how the case of two attacks on the Bektashi Harabati Baba Teke in Tetovo Macedonia in 2002 and 2009 have come to define the relations between Sunnis and Bektashis throughout North Macedonia, suggesting that 'the Bektashis are under violent pressure from the official Sunni, fundamentalist, and radical Islamic Religious Community of Macedonia' (Schwartz 2012). The same author goes on to describing the takeover of the *tekke* by a small group of extremists as 'the Sunni interlopers' who 'transformed a tower in the Harabati complex into a minaret by equipping it with loudspeakers, which sound the *adhan* regularly in the harsh, rapid-fire manner of Saudi-inspired Wahhabism', adding that 'while women pray alongside men and sing Bektashi hymns in the Bektashi Sufi rituals, the Sunni intruders turned one of the buildings of the Harabati complex into a separate "women's mosque"' (Schwartz 2014). In the same article, the author notes that while 'the Albanian Bektashis are known for their historical good relations with Catholic and Orthodox Christians and with Jews' the same could not be said about the official Sunni *'ulama'* whose relations with other religious communities, according to the author, 'have been more complicated' (Schwartz 2014). Schwartz has made several attempts to 'defend' the overall Muslim communities of North Macedonia claiming that 'Arab Islamists gained greater room for maneuver in Macedonia', that the official Islamic Community of North Macedonia is 'under tight Arab control' and that the 'fundamentalists [have] attacked the well-established Balkan Muslim tradition of Sufi metaphysical beliefs and practices but were obviously richer, while the Iranians emphasized their own past contributions to the Sufi legacy' (Schwartz 2014).

Seeking to accommodate European anxieties, like the Bektashis, other Muslim communities in the Balkans engage in similar discourse that distinguishes them as upright and moderate Muslims against the more radical ones that must be cordoned off from Europe. Local Islamic scholars and community leaders have also been engaged in producing a geo-temporally specific 'European Islam' in the Balkans. For instance, in a conference organised in 2014 by the President of the Republic of Austria, Heinz Fischer, on the subject of Muslims in the Balkans, the Bosnian Islamic scholar Enes Karčić (2014) argued that 'the traditional Islam in the Balkans is an autochthonous Islam . . . an Islam of the local cultural roots' and that

> it is our task today to strive in the path of promoting these spiritual and practical interpretations of Islam, in the context of the upcoming European and Euroatlantic integrations in the Balkans . . . Naturally, we hope that the European Union, as our de facto current and future ruler, shall respect Muslim components of the Balkans and Europe.

Merdjanova notes, whereas the head of the Albanian Muslim community described Albanian Islam as being 'very acceptable to Europe and the West because it is civil', Rešid Hafizović, a member of the Faculty of Islamic Studies at the University of Sarajevo, told her that 'the authentic European Muslims are the historical representatives of Islam in Europe' (2013: 121). El-Tayeb (2011: xxxii–xxxiii) argues how 'those perceived as non-European constantly have to prove that their presence is legitimate, for there is no space within the limits of Europe that they can claim as their own, in which their status of belonging is undisputed' – the need for performances of loyalty being the very evidence that Muslims are not perceived as European in the first place. The intensification and multiplication of post-Cold War EU borders, however, in the face of continued reiteration of 'borderless' Europe, has enacted its geopolitical borders in the Balkans where the integration of majority Muslim countries is perceived and produced as a threat to European stability and security. It is in this strategic EU enlargement and bordering processes that the Muslims of the Balkans must be projected and perceived as fundamentally different from those in the Middle East at best or threatened by Muslims from the Middle East, destabilising and radicalising the otherwise peaceful nature of Balkan Islam (Rexhepi 2015, 2016a, 2016b).

This post-Cold War pressure, where Muslims in the Balkans come to apologise for their Islam by producing themselves as Islam-free, has been the dominant form of reading and writing Muslims in the Balkans where the 'reemergence of Islam', 'rediscovery of the *Ummah*', or 'new Islam in the Balkans' are grouped under the overall 'return of God in Postcommunism' (Bougarel and Clayer 2001; Buden 2009; Ghodsee 2009; Merdjanova 2013). Similarly, studies focusing on the rise of extremist Islam in the Balkans stress the role of foreign influences in what is otherwise branded as 'European Islam'. The concept of a re-emerging Islam in the Balkans is premised on the understanding that Balkan Muslims during socialism had limited contact with the rest of the Muslim world, or that previous stronger ties were weakened or discontinued after the collapse of the Ottoman Empire, and particularly during the socialist period. In this regard, the projection of Muslims in the Balkans as post-socialist situates their histories outside of post-colonial histories and geographies.

This is particularly visible in the EU enlargement processes in the Balkans, where the integration processes serve as markers of spatialisation across the margins at which the EU comes to define its supranational legitimisation. Debating the ways in which Balkan Muslims can be mobilised in building European Islam, for instance, Dittrich and Montanaro-Jankovski (2005) argue, 'both the Balkan Muslims and the defining of the future borders of the enlarged Union ... will frame the overall context for the years to come' in the region. Albahari (2006: 28) points out how 'at these edges the identitarian, administrative, and political labor through which exclusionary hegemonies of nationhood, statehood, sovereignty, and supranational community *are being* produced (and challenged) is certainly visible'. In this context, knowledge production over Balkan Islam works through the assemblage of media reporting, academic research, and EU enlargement processes and border policies, which converge towards separating Balkan Muslims from the rest of the larger Muslim world while integrating them into the EU. This is done through the process of Eurocentric spatial and temporal configuration, which solidifies claims that the contemporary 'resurgence' of Islam in the Balkans is influenced by external actors and that 'Balkan Islam'—unlike the new foreign strains of Islam—is tolerant, secular and, most importantly, European. This systematic project of separation and differentiation not only contradicts contemporary practices of diverse Islamic observances in the Balkans but also produces Islam in the Balkans as unchanging and stuck forever in an unchanging past. From this perspective, interaction of Muslims in the Balkans with those in the Middle East is frequently produced as a potential threat to EU regional stability and security and as the radicalisation of a European type of Islam. In this context, Islam and Muslims living in the Balkans are produced as nominal non-Muslim Muslims, as white, European and mostly secular, where 'the remaining Islamic consciousness is often contaminated by crypto-Christianity, syncretic elements, popular superstitions, and non-Shari'a-conform[ing] (Sufi) mysticism' (Lederer 2015: 2).

Locating Balkan Muslims in Cold War area studies of socialist/post-socialist Eastern Europe, and now EU integration, renders them observers of larger post-colonial and Muslim worlds and not a *constitutive* part of them. This is particularly visible in counter-terrorist and surveillance scholarship and policies where the interrogation of 'radical' Islam in the Balkans is frequently read as a post-socialist phenomenon — a destabilising import from the post-colonial Muslim or Arab worlds, under the veil of various Islamic humanitarian missions during the Yugoslav conflicts. Elbasani (2015: 12), for instance, examines post-socialist Islam in the Balkans and argues that 'rich Arab associations have targeted Muslim populations in the Balkans as crucial "interlocutors" to diffuse the message of Islam in Europe', and that a substantial amount of research highlights the alarming power of influence of fundamentalist networks on indigenous practices. The substantial amount of research quoted by Elbasani is Deliso's (2007) notorious *The Coming Balkan Caliphate: The Threat of Radical Islam to Europe and the West*. Along similar lines, Bougarel (2005: 18) argues that Islamic non-governmental organisations (NGOs) from the Arab world, concealed as humanitarian organisations, use aid to persuade Muslims in the Balkans to 'fulfil their religious duties' adding that 'all of them contribute to the circulation of new religious doctrines coming from the Arab world and challenge the former monopoly of Hanafi madhhab, as well as the religious legitimacy of the heterodox practices of Balkan Islam' and that 'these new doctrines are also spread through books and pamphlets translated from Arabic, videos, and websites, and the young ulema returning from Islamic universities in the Persian Gulf' (Bougarel 2005: 18). In another scenario, Ghodsee (2009: 137) examines the ways in which Arab influences arrived in the Balkans disguised as humanitarian organisations: 'After setting up refugee camps in Macedonia during the Kosovo crisis, the Islamic charities then began to work among the Albanian Muslims in the country as well', writes Ghodsee, explaining how following the initial humanitarian relief mission, these charities went on to correct traditional Balkan Islam by introducing them to 'true' Islam.

In projecting Balkan Muslims as victims of aggressive Islamicising strategies coming from the Arab world, these studies often show Muslims in the Balkans as target populations of Wahhabi and Salafi attempts to indoctrinate and radicalise post-socialist Muslims. Warning of foreign influences among Balkan Muslims such as Saudi Wahhabism, Blumi notes (2005: 12),

> Saudi Arabia is using this rigid and confrontational doctrine to legitimize its aggressive expansionist campaign of indoctrination in the former Soviet Union (Central Asia and Caucuses), Southeast Asia, Afghanistan and Europe. Armed with billions of petrol dollars, the assault on traditional Balkan Islam, which ... was based on tolerance and syncretism, is beginning to cause significant, if yet-unseen, splits in Kosovo's religious community.

In addition to the view that radical Islam is being imported into the Balkans through humanitarian organisations coming from the Middle East, another concern in these and similar accounts is the itineration of Muslims from the Balkans to the Arab world. Writing for the British Defence Academy, Vickers (2008: 1) suggests that 'historically Albanians have practised a traditional, tolerant form of Sunni and Bektashi Islam' and that now 'a third more radical interpretation of Islam is gradually being introduced by young Albanians who have studied abroad in Islamic countries', concluding, however, that 'despite a gradual increase in the number of veiled women and bearded men ... the majority of Albania's Muslims still pride themselves on their tradition of religious tolerance and moderation' (2008: 13). The broad signifiers of Islamic and Arab countries, who according to these studies come to influence a radical interpretation of Islam among otherwise secular Balkan Muslims, not only situate radical Islam outside Europe but also project Europe as a victim under threat by Islamic and Arab influences at its borders. The clash of civilisation discourse notwithstanding, what is at stake here is how this 'danger' is articulated and materialised in EU policies of securitisation, surveillance and b/ordering.

The spatial and spiritual differentiation of Muslims in the Balkans and those in the Middle East and North Africa, however, is not so much a product of the EU as much as it is a product of the European colonial geopolitical mappings in relation to its self-referential centre: the Near East, the Middle East, the Far East, and so on. Thus, the making of Balkan Islam is a product of early European colonial excursions in the Balkans claimed by multiple European powers but particularly the Austro-Hungarian Empire, during the collapse of the Ottoman Empire (Amzi-Erdoğdular 2013; Heuberger 2001; Toleva 2012). With more than half the population being Muslim at the time however, Muslim-populated areas had to be produced as European before Europe could claim them. The colonial component of Balkan Islam is infused with ethnographic accounts and invented traditions. By 'invented traditions' I mean the fabrication of various institutional frameworks to encapsulate Islam in the Balkans after the Ottoman Empire within manageable structures, much like the invention of 'Moroccon Islam' by French colonial ethnographers in the nineteenth century (Burke 2014). The connections of colonialism and contemporary politics are demanding to follow, as Stoler (2016: 1–2) argues, they 'are not always readily available for easy grasp, in part because colonial entailments do not have a life of their own' but 'they wrap around contemporary problems' by losing 'their visible and identifiable presence in the vocabulary, conceptual grammar, and idioms of current concerns'. How can we then re-think Bektashism beyond the Euro-American experiences and contemporary concerns layered with inter-faith tolerance, Europeanisation and moderate Islam? To do this, I want to propose a critical examination of the political context in which contemporary experiences of Bektashism emerge.

Towards a Decolonial Balkan Islam

In 'Who can speak? Decolonizing knowledge', Grada Kilomba (2010: 27) asks the following questions in relation to academic knowledge production:

> What knowledge is acknowledged as such? And what knowledge is not? What knowledge has been made part of academic agendas? And what knowledge has not? Whose knowledge is this? Who is acknowledged to have the knowledge? And who is not? Who can teach knowledge? And who cannot? Who inhibits academia? And who remains outside at the margins? And finally, who can speak?

Moreover, 'for a Muslim to speak', as Sayyid (2016) states, 'requires him or her to answer a series of questions which are leading, if not misleading, so one can easily become trapped and diverted in trying to demonstrate that Islam is not inherently misogynist or Muslims are not fundamentally anti-intellectual etc'. How do we engage in the decolonial study of Islam, beyond the one engendered from the dialogical exchange debated, deployed and defined in relation to Euro-American geopolitical spatial and temporal coordinates? How to produce knowledge that is not guided by geopolitical governmentalities but that reflects the lived experience, particularly at a time when the very conceptual tools and approaches employed in the study of religion today are dominated by Western concepts (Mandair 2013).

The first attempt to rethink Bektashi, as well as Balkan Islam, is to question the production and proliferation of knowledge on Islam in the Balkans, liberated from Eurocentric analysis and categories reconsidering and re-historicising Islam in the Balkans from a Muslim perspective. This would require the important task of positionality and reflexivity of all those who speak and write about Islam in the Balkans. Here Kilomba's questions on decolonising knowledge are immensely helpful particularly as knowledge that does not confirm to academic agendas is generally provincialised, silenced or unacknowledged so long as it does not comply with the contours of established cannons of 'objectively observing the natives'.

The second more pressing question – extending on Kilomba's question of *what knowledge has been made part of academic agendas?* – is to think what seems the unthinkable in contemporary studies of Islam in the Balkans, to focus not on that which differentiates, distances and isolates Muslims in the Balkans from those elsewhere in the world as a way of attaching them to Europe, but that which brings them together – the shared histories and memories that have given birth to their current (post-)genocidal and (post-)colonial conditions. That is, to bring attention to what Stoler calls (2016: 18) social dislocations 'whose etiologies are found in labels that lead away from empire and push analysis far from colonial histories, severing those connections'. This would mean engaging in counter-genealogies that go beyond methodological nationalism bringing attention to when certain post-Ottoman spaces in the Balkans have been produced as European (Balkans) and designated for Europeanisation and other post-Ottoman spaces produced as Others (Middle East/North Africa) and must remain outside. It means to ask: what informs these designations and differentiations? How did these race-informed colonial spatial and temporal configurations influence the ways in which (post-)socialist politics are also influenced by an invitation to become European citizens at the expense of the intensification of borders in the Balkans that produce migrants as foreign to the local would-be European citizens in the Balkans? The temporal junctures that would require close attention here would be the post-World War I era and the establishment of the current mental maps and geopolitical configurations in the Balkans and the Middle East. Vitalis's (2015) work on race and the emergence of the US as a world power would be particularly illuminating and influential in rethinking what is now taken for granted as common-sense geopolitical divisions. Moreover, attention to the non-aligned period between a socialist Balkans and the decolonial non-aligned world would further trouble these seemingly coherent geopolitical mappings and parallel production of imperial spaces, borders and population hierarchies.

Decolonial Islamic studies would focus on that which has ignited and inspired shared experiences among various communities within Islam as well as broader intersectional coalitions among Muslims and other marginalised groups. This call to decolonise Eurocentric scholarship on Islam in the Balkans and elsewhere is not an attempt at an equally problematic and reactionary scholarship as Bektashis in the Balkans, like Muslims around the world, live next to other faiths and these experiences are important axes of inquiry into interfaith relations, but they cannot become anchored into political projects of racialised exclusion and erasure as they are currently being employed in the Balkans. Kancler (2017) argues that

> the countries of the former Eastern Europe, which became subsidiary States, peripherialized in its servile relation to the EU politics, show on the one hand, contempt towards 'those below them' in processes of constant hierarchization, and on the other, intensified servitude towards European colonial/imperial centers . . . [where] ethno-nationalism and differentiation with labour division on a global scale are today presented as 'liberation' from what was suppressed during decades of communism/socialism.

The tendency to focus on the identity of Muslim communities in the Balkans has also made questions of class and race almost invisible. A decolonial class-conscious scholarship would be rooted in Shari'ati's (1979: 49) interpretation of Islam as

> the first school of social thought that recognizes the masses as the basis, the fundamental and conscious factor in determining history and society

not the elect as Nietzsche thought, not the aristocracy and nobility as Plato claimed, nor great personalities as Carlyle and Emerson believed, not those of pure blood as Alexis Carrel imagined, not the priests or the intellectuals, but the masses.

For Muslims in the Balkans, particularly for those in socialist Yugoslavia, the intersection of class and faith, socialism and Islam, were neither mutually exclusive concepts nor abstract notions of political aspirations but rather lived experiences. Alija Isaković's (1990) collection and analysis of the debates that accompanied the 'Muslim question' in Yugoslavia in the 1960s and 1970s on representation, redistribution and the role of Islam and Muslims in the implementation of socialist policies point towards a more complex and complicated history than the narratives that emerged immediately after the Yugoslav wars. These remain largely overlooked debates that require further interrogation and contextualisation in the wider non-aligned decolonial politics that Yugoslavia belonged to.

Last but not least, what knowledge is not recognised, who is given visibility and voice and who is silenced are perhaps the most pressing questions when engaging in decolonising knowledge. Decolonial, feminist and queer scholars of colour have already critiqued citation politics that reproduce a specific kind of knowledge. Citational structures and politics, argues Ahmed (2013), can be a 'successful reproductive technology, a way of reproducing the world around certain bodies' where 'reproduction of a discipline can be the reproduction of these techniques of selection, ways of making certain bodies and thematics core to the discipline, and others not even part'. The most referenced works on Balkan Islam are those undertaken by Euro-American scholars whose work in the Balkans is important; however, it frequently fails to engage with local academic and intellectual debates, erasing local contributions and/or intellectual histories. To do this, at minimum, those speaking or writing of Islam in the Balkans would have to be fluent in the local languages to be able to engage in the ongoing debates within Muslim communities published in Albanian, Bulgarian, Macedonian and Bosnian-Serbo-Croatian.

Decolonising knowledge is never an easy task, particularly since imperial and Eurocentric colonial knowledge production is not only dominant and pervasive but also has the tendency to pass for common sense despite it being deeply entangled in contemporary political projects. Parallel to asking who speaks for Islam in the Balkans, why and how would be tasks of a genealogical and critical reading of primary sources and the archive as a way of understanding the political and historical circumstances under which the categorisation of Bektashis and Balkan Muslims emerges as a separate category. This does not mean the search for some mythical beginning or glorious past but simply unearthing the imperial political projects that have appropriated Islam in the Balkans for various problematic projects of defining European borders along racial and religious differentiations.

Conclusion

This contribution draws attention to the intersection between Islam and the politics of EU enlargement in the Balkans in the emergence of a homogenised representational mandate for Muslims in the Balkans, or Balkan Islam. Resurgent and re-emergent Islam serve as the discursive space in which Bektashi, Balkan and European Islam are read as tolerant and acquiescent to European values, whereas only resurgent Islam looms as a new strain of Islam invading Europe from the outside. This goal requires Muslims in the Balkans to serve as the internal Other who have to continuously prove their loyalty to Europe by policing the new borders while they perform as the model Muslim minority for Muslims inside Europe. This subtle concession that Balkan Muslims are called to make in mapping the boundaries and appropriating the ideological exclusion of other Muslims not only divides them from the larger Muslim world but also creates internal conflicts in the Muslim communities in the Balkans.

This contribution is only a modest attempt to deconstruct the invention of Balkan Islam; a great deal of work still needs to be done in interrogating the colonial archives – not as a tool and a point of reference in furthering the nationalist and Europeanising projects but as a contested site of knowledge production, racialisation, Islamophobia and empire building. In this context, I have attempted to summarise a decolonial approach to the study of Islam and Muslims in the Balkans.

References

Ahmed, Sara (2013), 'Making feminist points', *Feministkilljoys*, available at: http://feministkilljoys.com/2013/09/11/making-feminist-points/, last accessed 22 March 2017.
Al-e-Ahmad, Jalal (1984), *Occidentosis: A Plague from the West*, Berkeley: Mizan Press.
Albahari, Maurizio (2006), *Death and the Modern State: Making Borders and Sovereignty at the Southern Edges of Europe*, Working Paper 137, May 2006, University of California, San Diego: Center for Comparative Immigration Studies.
Amzi-Erdoğdular, Leyla (2013), 'Afterlife of Empire: Muslim-Ottoman relations in Habsburg Bosnia Herzegovina, 1878–1914', PhD dissertation, Columbia University, New York.
Bernardelli, Gorgio (2016), 'Francis and Albanian Bektashi leader discuss path of dialogue for Balkans', *La Stampa*, 11 May 2016, available at: http://www.lastampa.it/2016/05/11/vaticaninsider/eng/world-news/francis-and-albanian-bektashi-leader-discuss-path-of-dialogue-for-balkans-73MUlDC1sY7SC03UaYrcfK/pagina.html, last accessed 22 March 2017.
Birge, J. K. (1937), *The Bektashi Order of Dervishes*, London: Luzac & Co.
Blumi, Isa (2005), *Political Islam among the Albanians: Are the Taliban Coming to the Balkans?*, Prishtina: Kosovar Institute for Policy Research and Development.
Bougarel, Xavier (2005), *The Role of Balkan Muslims in Building a European Islam*, European Policy Centre Issue Paper no. 43, Brussels: European Policy Centre and King Baudouin Foundation.
Bougarel, Xavier, and Nathalie Clayer (2001), *Le Nouvel Islam balkanique: Les musulmans comme acteurs du post-communisme (1990–2000)*, Paris: Maisonneuve & Larose.
Brailsford, H. N. (1906), *Macedonia: its Races and Their Future*, London: Methuen.
Buden, Boris (2009), *Zone des Übergangs: Vom Ende des Postkommunismus*, Frankfurt a. M.: Suhrkamp.
Burke, Edmund (2014), *The Ethnographic State: France and the Invention of Moroccan Islam*, Oalkand: University of California Press.
Clayer, Nathalie (2010), 'Adapting Islam to Europe: the Albanian example', in C. Voss and J. Telbizova-Sack (eds), *Islam und Muslime in (Südost) Europa im Kontext von Transformation und EU-Erweiterung*, Berlin: Peter Lang, pp. 53–69.

Coon, Carleton S. (1955), 'Review of *Studies in Islamic Cultural History*. GE von Grunebaum', *American Anthropologist* 57:2, 393–5.
Dabashi, Hamid (2011), *Shi'ism*, Cambridge, MA: Harvard University Press.
Deliso, Christopher (2007), *The Coming Balkan Caliphate: The Threat of Radical Islam to Europe and the West*, Westport: Praeger Security International.
Delvina, Sherif (1998), *Pa pavarësi fetare nuk ka pavarësi kombëtare*, Tiranë: Eurorilindja.
Dittrich, Mirjam, and Lucia Montanaro-Jankovski (2005), 'Introduction', in X. Bougarel, *The Role of Balkan Muslims in Building a European Islam*, European Policy Centre Issue Paper no. 43, Brussels: European Policy Centre and King Baudouin Foundation, pp. 3–5.
Dressler, Markus (2013), *Writing Religion: the Making of Turkish Alevi Islam*, Oxford: Oxford University Press.
Duka, Ferit (2012), 'The historical background of religious tolerance in Albania', in *International Symposium: Perspectives of Religious, Cultural and Social Diversity in the Balkans Seen from a Global Perspective*, Tiranë: Prizmi Publications.
Durham, M. E. ([1909] 1985), *High Albania*, London: Virago.
—— (1920), *Twenty Years of Balkan Tangle*, London: Allen & Unwin.
Elbasani, Arolda (2015), 'Islam and democracy at the fringes of Europe: the role of useful historical legacies', *Politics and Religion* 8:2, 334–57.
El-Tayeb, Fatima (2011), *European Others: Queering Ethnicity in Postnational Europe*, Minneapolis: University of Minnesota Press.
Ghodsee, Kristen (2009), *Muslim Lives in Eastern Europe: Gender, Ethnicity, and the Transformation of Islam in Postsocialist Bulgaria*, Princeton: Princeton University Press.
Hasluck, F. W. (1929), *Christianity and Islam under the Sultans*, Oxford: Clarendon Press.
Hasluck, Margaret (1925), 'The nonconformist Moslems of Albania', *The Muslim World* 15:4, 388–98.
Hatibi, Ervin (2009), 'Ju rrëfej fytyrën e re të islamit shqiptar', *Zeri Islam* 23, available at: http://www.zeriislam.com/artikulli.php?id=764, last accessed 22 March 2017.
Heuberger, Valeria (2001), '"Imagined Orient": the perception of Islam and of Muslims in Bosnia-Herzegovina in the multi-religious Habsburg Empire, 1878–1918', in V. Heuberger, G. Humbert-Knitel and E. Vyslonzil (eds), *Cultures en colour / Cultures in Colour: L'héritage des Empires Ottoman et Austro-Hongrois en Orient et Occident / The Heritage of the Ottoman Empire and Austro-*

Hungarian Monarchy in Orient and Occident, Frankfurt a. M.: Peter Lang, pp. 33–8.
Hurd, Elizabeth S. (2015), *Beyond Religious Freedom: The New Global Politics of Religion*, Princeton: Princeton University Press.
Ibrahimi, Nexhat (2004), *Islami dhe kriza e identitetit*, Skopje: Logos-A.
Isaković, Alija (ed.) (1990), *O 'nacionaliziranju' Muslimana: 101 godina afirmiranja i negiranja nacionalnog identiteta Muslimana*, Zagreb: Globus.
Journée de la Culture Bektashi à Paris (2016), available at: http://www.aktab.ma/veille/Journee-de-la-Culture-Bektashi-a-Paris-le-25-Mai-2016_a126.html, last accessed 29 April 2017.
Kadaré, Ismail, and Shusha Guppy (1998), 'Kadaré, the Art of Fiction No. 153,' *Paris Review* 147, 195–217.
Kancler, Tjaša (2017), 'Body-politics, Trans* Imaginary and Decoloniality', *Academia*, available at: https://www.academia.edu/31557368/Body-politics_Trans_Imaginary_and_Decoloniality, last accessed 22 March 2017.
Karčić, Enes (2014), 'Muslims in the Balkans', paper presented at the Muslims in the Balkans Conference, Vienna, 10 October 2014.
Kaya, Ayhan (1998), 'Multicultural clientelism and Alevi resurgence in the Turkish diaspora: Berlin Alevis', *New Perspectives on Turkey* 18, 23–49.
Kilomba, Grada (2010), 'Who can speak? Speaking at the centre, decolonizing knowledge', in G. Kilomba, *Plantation Memories: Episodes of Everyday Racism*, Münster: UNRAST-Verlag, 2nd edn, pp. 25–38.
Lederer, Gyorgy (1999), 'Contemporary Islam in East Europe', NATO Academic Forum, May, available at: http://www.nato.int/acad/fellow/97--99/lederer.pdf.
Mamdani, Mahmood (2002), 'Good Muslim, bad Muslim: a political perspective on culture and terrorism', *American Anthropologist* 104:3, 766–75.
Mandair, Arvind-pal Singh (2013), *Religion and the Specter of the West: Sikhism, India, Postcoloniality, and the Politics of Translation*, New York: Columbia University Press.
Merdjanova, Ina (2013), *Rediscovering the Umma: Muslims in the Balkans between Nationalism and Transnationalism*, Oxford: Oxford University Press.
Mignolo, Walter D., and Arturo Escobar (2013), *Globalization and the Decolonial Option*, London: Routledge.
Muedini, Fait (2015), *Sponsoring Sufism: How Governments Promote 'Mystical Islam' in Their Domestic and Foreign Policies*, London: Palgrave Macmillan.
Nishani, Bujar (2014), 'President Nishani addressing the International Symposium on the Role of Bektashism in the Realization of Inter-religious Dialogue in the

Balkans: the Bektashian faith sowed deep roots in our soul that became a spring of tolerance and a fundamental factor of culture, patriotism and optimistic philosophy', 10 March 2014, available at: http://president.al/?p=17022&lang=en, last accessed 22 March 2017.

Radio Vatican (2016), 'Des Bektashis au Vatican', *Radio Vatican*, 10 May 2016, available at: http://fr.radiovaticana.va/news/2016/05/10/des_bektashis_au_vatican/1228830, last accessed 22 March 2017.

Rexhepi, Piro (2015), 'Mainstreaming Islamophobia: the politics of European enlargement and the Balkan crime-terror nexus', *East European Quarterly* 43:2–3, 189–214.

——— (2016a), 'From Orientalism to homonationalism: queer politics, Islamophobia and Europeanization in Kosovo', *Southeastern Europe* 40:1, 32–53.

——— (2016b), 'EUrientation anxieties: Islamic sexualities and the construction of Europeanness', in Z. Krajina and N. Blanuša (eds), *EU, Europe Unfinished: Mediating Europe and the Balkans in a Time of Crisis*, London: Rowman & Littlefield International, pp. 145–61.

Sayyid, Salman (2014), *Recalling the Caliphate: Decolonisation and World Order*, Oxford: Oxford University Press.

——— (2016), 'Muslims and the challenge of historiography: an interview with Salman Sayyid', *Jadaliyya*, 1 April 2016, available at: http://www.jadaliyya.com/pages/index/24190/muslims-and-the-challenge-of-historiography_an-int, last accessed 30 April 2017.

Schwartz, Stephen S. (2012), 'Arabs, Iranians, and Turks vs. Balkan Muslims', *The Weekly Standard*, 11 May 2012, available at: http://www.weeklystandard.com/arabs-iranians-and-turks-vs.-balkan-muslims/article/644375, last accessed 22 March 2017.

——— (2014), 'The Bektashi-Alevi spectrum from the Balkans to Iran', *Center for Islamic Pluralism*, 1 February 2014.

Shari'ati, Ali (1979), *On the Sociology of Islam*, trans. Hamid Algar, Berkeley: Mizan.

Sibai, Sirin Adlbi (2017), 'El Pensament Islámic Descolonial: Une Eina contra la Islamofóbia de Génere', *Academia*, available at: https://www.academia.edu/30070600/Hacia_un_pensamiento_Isl%C3%A1mico_decolonial_towards_a_decolonial_islamic_thought, last accessed 22 March 2017.

Stoler, Ann Laura (2016), *Duress: Imperial Durabilities in Our Times*, Durham: Duke University Press.

Swire, J. (1937), *King Zog's Albania*, London: Robert Hale.

Toleva, Theodora (2012), 'Habsburg influences in the Albanian nation-building process, 1896–1908, *Etudes balkaniques* 1, 80–103.

Vickers, Miranda (2008), *Islam in Albania*, Swindon: Defence Academy of United Kingdom.

Vitalis, Robert (2015), *White World Order, Black Power Politics: The Birth of American International Relations*, Ithaca: Cornell University Press.

5

LIVING NAJAF IN LONDON: DIASPORA, IDENTITY AND THE SECTARIANISATION OF THE IRAQI-SHI'A SUBJECT

Emanuelle Degli Esposti

Diaspora, rather than a community of individuals dispersed from a homeland, may be understood more productively as a globally mobile category of identification . . . a *process* productive of disparate temporalities (anteriorities, presents, futurities), displacements, and subjects.

Axel (2004: 27)

[Al-Khoei Foundation, Ahlulbayt Foundation, Salaam Foundation, Imam Ali Foundation and Al-Hakim Foundation]; this is one big happy family. This is Najaf in Brent.

Abu H. (Author interview, 6 August 2014)

Introduction

In the basement of Ealing Town Hall in West London, several dozen young men and women, dressed mostly in black and green, mill around a number of charity and marketing stalls. Amongst the stalls giving out food, water and tea, and those selling books about Shi'a Islam and CDs of religious eulogies (known as *latmiyyat*), are several promoting British and international charities, including the Al-Ayn Foundation, the Iraqi Children's Aid and Repair

Endeavour (ICARE), the Imam Hussain Blood Donation Campaign (an offshoot of the Islamic Unity Society and affiliated to the NHS), and the 'Who Is Hussain?' campaign. The various charities' representatives give out leaflets and flyers to the attendees, raising awareness about the work they do on the ground in Iraq and the UK and soliciting donations and offers of volunteering from the crowd.

This is a snapshot from London's second annual Imam Hussain Conference, an English-language event organised and run by a group of young British-born Iraqi Shi'ites and held on 9 November 2014. Along with a full programme of events, including speeches and talks on topics such as 'Exploring Imam Hussain's proof for the existence of God' and 'Hussain: The reality of an eternal martyr', the conference also represented an opportunity for young British Shi'ites to connect with the wider Shi'a world and be exposed to humanitarian and political trends on the ground in Iraq. The presence of charitable organisations at the conference thus constituted a way for second-generation Iraqis in the diaspora to feel connected to and participate in the shaping of Iraqi civil society. However, the fact that these charities – all of which are in some way affiliated to Shi'a religious networks[1] – represented the only meaningful link to Iraq at the event suggests that, for young British-born Shi'ites at least, orientations towards Iraq are increasingly being channelled through networks of charity and patronage that are explicitly tied to sectarian religious notions of identity and belonging. Drawing on more than eighteen months of fieldwork conducted amongst Iraqi Shi'a communities in London, this chapter takes such explicit manifestations of Shi'a sectarian identity as a starting point to theorise the ways in which political and social orientations towards Iraq within the diaspora are increasingly embedded in transnational religious networks of authority and capital, especially for the second-generation of British-born Shi'ites. In particular, I will show how the intersection of such transnational religious networks with global discourses of minority rights has shaped the creation of a sectarianised 'Iraqi-Shi'a' diasporic subject that is both directly and indirectly invested in the conflict in Iraq and that has contributed, both materially and discursively, to the fracturing of Iraqi society along sectarian lines.[2]

The argument of this chapter is two-pronged. On the one hand, I seek to draw on critical theorisations in diaspora studies and the work of postmodern theorists such as Michel Foucault and Judith Butler in order to put forward a notion of a hybridised and sectarianised Iraqi-Shi'a diasporic subject. On the other hand, I wish to elucidate how this Iraqi-Shi'a subject is simultaneously constituted by and constitutive of contemporary Iraqi identity politics via the intersection of transnational religious authority and global discourses of minority rights; and how it is able to capitalise on such discourses in the British diasporic context in order to lend legitimacy to its sectarianised vision of global politics. I will begin with a theoretical exploration of the notions of diaspora, subjectivity and identification, before moving on to a discussion of the Iraqi Shi'a diaspora in Britain and its political, social and humanitarian mobilisations towards Iraq. Crucially, in arguing for the ongoing construction of a hybridised Iraqi-Shi'a diasporic subject I should not be interpreted as claiming a unitary and homogenous diasporic experience for all Iraqi Shi'ites, or even that Iraqi Shi'ites can meaningfully be categorised as a single unit for analysis. Rather, my argumentation should be seen within the context of postmodern and psychosocial discussions of subjectivity in which the Iraqi-Shi'a diasporic subject is seen as the crystallisation of one particular socio-politico-religious discourse within the diasporic context and at a particular temporal juncture. This distinction between Iraqi Shi'ites as individuals with diverse and heterogeneous life experiences and the Iraqi-Shi'a diasporic subject will be elucidated further in the following section.

Diaspora and the Subject

In presenting a study of the Iraqi Shi'a diaspora, it is first necessary to delineate the object of analysis. Drawing on the work of critical scholars of diaspora studies (Axel 2001, 2002, 2004; Brah 1996; Brubaker 2005; Butler 2001; Hall 1990; Kinnivall Nesbitt-Larking 2009; Ong 2003; Raman 2003; Venn 2009; Werbner 2009; among others), I seek to problematise the notion of 'diaspora' as an ontological thing-in-the-world capable of being bracketed off and studied. Equally, I am sceptical of the implicit assumption that a 'diaspora' is both a pre-formed social entity and an agglomeration of individuals who have been scattered across the world and yet nevertheless all nurture an indelible link to the imagined diasporic homeland or place of origin. Rather, I take classifications of diaspora as 'a globally mobile category of identification' (Axel 2004: 27) or as 'a series of projected imaginaries of identity' (Werbner 2009:

758) as a starting point from which to theorise the formation of an Iraqi-Shi'a diasporic subject as a historically specific and temporally contingent discursive alignment. Here, my focus on the Iraqi Shi'a diaspora should be understood as a theoretical and empirical preoccupation with the various nationalistic and sectarian discourses circulated and (re)iterated within the diasporic space – and which are alternatively enacted and performed by individuals who in so doing constitute themselves as diasporic subjects – rather than a focus on the individuals *within* that diaspora. In this sense, my use of the term 'Iraqi Shi'a diaspora' refers not to Iraqi Shi'ites themselves, but to the discursively constructed 'diasporic imaginary' (Axel 2002) of Iraqi Shi'ism maintained and performed in the diasporic space; in other words, to the 'process[es] of identification [that are] generative of diasporic subjects' (Axel 2002: 412).

Central to my theoretical argument here is the concept of the *subject*, which draws on elements of Lacanian psychoanalysis to refer to the product of individual practices of identification oriented towards particular discursive subject-positions. For Lacan, social actors effect their capacity for agency through language (hence the conception of the 'speaking subject') but, in turn, 'actor behaviour is regulated by pre-existing discourses that structure the field of possible actions' (Epstein 2010: 17). It is these pre-existing discourses that shape and determine the possible subject-positions that individuals can come to occupy, and that delineate the boundaries of social and political agency. While strict Lacanian theory thus views subject-positions as mere linguistic categories or 'place-holders' (Epstein 2010), scholars such as Judith Butler (1997), Ernesto Laclau (1994) and Chantal Mouffe (2005) have engaged Lacanian discourse theory with Foucauldian conceptions of productive power (Foucault 1991, 2003) to suggest a theory of the subject that sees it as a product of discursive power relations that reach beyond the realm of language and infuse all manner of social and political relations. In this sense, subject-positions can be understood as the temporary and contingent crystallisation of certain practices and performances of identification resulting from the alignment of particular discursive structures. In such theorisations, the effect of power is not limited to the production of subject-positions, it is also constitutive of the individual's interior life, of its very understanding of self, and of its 'self-identity' (Butler 1997: 3). It is this interior psychic life that is meant by the term *subjectivity*, which should be conceptually distinguished from the anterior notion of subject-positions as positions in discursive power relations. By articulating, performing and identifying with such subject-positions (i.e. by engaging their subjectivity), individuals *are made subject* to discursive power relations. The *subject* referred to here is therefore not the individual themselves, but the way in which the individual enacts their subjectivity via identification with pre-existing subject-positions. Delineating clearly between 'the subject' as the product of identifications with discursively constructed subject-positions and 'subjectivity' as the interior psychic life of individuals thus allows us to engage directly with political subjects in and of themselves without having to take into account the problematic notion of 'self' or 'identity'. While the over-determined and unfinished process of identification and subjectivity should be noted here (Hall 2000; Howarth 2013; Stavrakakis 1999), my focus in this chapter is rather on the reification of the *Iraqi-Shi'a diasporic subject* as the product of individual identifications towards subject-positions defined by discourses of what it means to be 'Iraqi' and 'Shi'a' in the diasporic imaginary, and on the political and social effects such a subject engenders when it is mobilised towards the homeland. It is to the processes underlying the formation of this hybridised ethno-religious subject that I now turn.

'Najaf in Brent'

According to the 2011 Census of Britain, there are an estimated 73,000 Iraqi-born individuals living in the UK, with the vast majority concentrated in London (Office for National Statistics 2013). Since this figure is neither up to date nor takes into account second- or third-generation Iraqis born in Britain, it is safe to assume that the total number of diasporic Iraqis in the UK is much higher; for example, Al-Ali estimates there are at least 100,000 individuals (2007: 21), while the Iraqi Embassy estimates between 350,000 and 400,000 and the International Organisation for Migration (IOM) gives figures of 240,000, including 125,000 in London alone (IOM 2007: 8). As with any migrant population, Iraqi Shi'ites in London represent a diverse amalgam of individuals from a variety of socio-economic, class, regional, ideational and generational backgrounds, and who may have come to the UK at different times and under very different circumstances. However, although no official figures exist regarding the ethnic and religious orientations of Iraqis in the

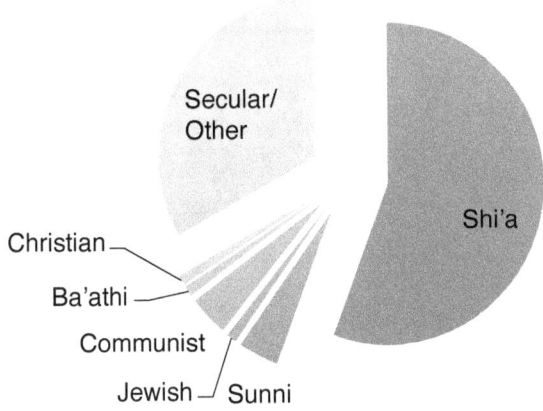

Figure 5.1 Iraqi institutions in London by political/religious affiliation. (Source: author's fieldwork.)

UK, anecdotal evidence suggests that the vast majority of these individuals come from (either secular or practising) Arab Shi'a backgrounds, and originally arrived in Britain during the 1980s and early 1990s (Communities and Local Government 2009: 7). There is also evidence to suggest that practising Iraqi Shi'ites are the most active and engaged members of the Iraqi Arab diaspora in London. Of the ninety-seven London-based Iraqi organisations I identified during my fieldwork (not including any Kurdish organisations), a total of fifty-four (or 55 per cent) either have Shi'a religious leanings or have social and/or political ties to the Shi'a religious establishment or to Shi'a political parties in Iraq (see Figure 5.1).

As well as being well-represented in civil society institutions, Iraqi Shi'ites in London also attend a number of Shi'a religious centres (known as *hussayniyyat*, sing. *husayniyya*) in the city, most of which are located in the northwest borough of Brent in and around the neighbourhoods of Wembley, Cricklewood, Kilburn, Queen's Park and Brondesbury (see Figure 5.2). This concentration of Shi'a activity in the area has led to it being dubbed London's 'Shi'a triangle' (a tongue-in-cheek reference to the oft-touted media phrase of the 'Shi'a crescent' in relation to Iran, Iraq, Syria and Lebanon) or alternatively as 'Najaf in Brent' (Bowen 2014), a reference to the Shi'a religious seminaries of the southern Iraqi city of Najaf, the home of Shi'ism's highest-ranking religious source of emulation Grand Ayatollah 'Ali Al-Sistani.

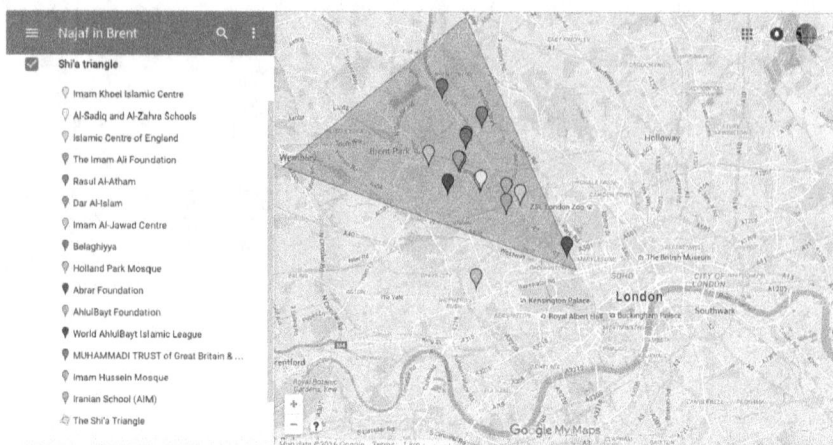

Figure 5.2 Map showing the main religious institutions in the 'Shi'a triangle' of northwest London. (Source: author's fieldwork.)

Most, but not all, of these *hussayniyyat* are run by Iraqis[3] (such as the influential Al-Khoei Foundation in Queen's Park, which is often upheld by the British government as the representative of the Shi'a Muslim voice in the UK – a status that is not always corroborated by individuals in the community), with a notable exception being the Iranian-run Islamic Centre of England in Maida Vale, which has links to the government of the Islamic Republic. The concentration of Iraqi Shi'a religious centres and institutions in one corner of northwest London has shaped the lived experience of practising Iraqi Shi'ites in the diaspora such that individuals often speak about feeling part of an 'Iraqi-Shi'a community' that is defined through its relation to the material and social fabric of the city of London (Degli Esposti 2019). For example, many of the young British-born Iraqis I interviewed[4] described how, as children growing up in London in the 1990s, their parents would regularly take them to the *hussayniyya* as a way to meet up with other Iraqis exiled in the UK and to exchange gossip and news. One interviewee, a secular Iraqi who fled the country as a young man in 1980 out of fear of being targeted by Saddam Hussein's regime (Iraq instigated a long and bloody war with Iran in August 1980 and the Baath regime took pains to eradicate anyone it considered a potential fifth column in the months leading up to the war), spoke about how he would often visit *husayniyyat* in London as a way to keep up to date with developments in Iraq:

I don't consider myself a religious man but I started to go to the mosque, or to the *husayniyya* in '91 just to get the fresh news from Baghdad. Because there by faxes the news was coming by minutes [sic]. (Interview 4)

In this sense, we can see how the *husayniyyat* and other Shi'a institutions acted as social and community 'glue' that kept exiled Iraqi Shi'ites together and allowed them to stay in touch both with each other and with developments 'back home' in Iraq. In the London context, the *husayniyyat* engendered a sense of community by acting as a physical meeting place for diasporic Iraqi Shi'ites; one that was simultaneously inscribed with religious meaning through the observance of religious rites and practices such as the annual 'Ashura' commemorations and that was oriented towards religious and political engagement with domestic developments in Iraq (Flynn 2013). Many of these institutions also maintain direct links to the political and religious establishment in Iraq[5] and act as channels for diasporic Iraqis to send and receive money, resources and information across international borders.

Significantly, then, as well as being in the demographic majority comparative to other diasporic Iraqis, Iraqi Shi'ites in London have well-established and active religious and civil society institutions through which individuals are able to mobilise, both in terms of civic participation in the home state and in terms of diasporic mobilisation towards the homeland. It is this network of Shi'a politico-religious institutions, many of which are explicitly geared towards social and political engagement in Iraq that, I argue, contributes to the formation of a diasporic Iraqi-Shi'a subject, especially for second-generation Iraqi Shi'ites born in the UK and who have little contact with Iraq itself beyond such organisational networks. Arguably, the institutionalisation of Shi'ism in London, and the material and discursive links between Shi'a spaces in the diaspora and the 'homeland' of Iraq, have contributed to the formation of a diasporic imaginary in which Shi'a religious observance has become intertwined with Iraqi nationalist sentiment, and to a diasporic Iraqi-Shi'a subject that generates certain modes of identification and belonging in individuals.

My use of the hyphenated formulation 'Iraqi-Shi'a' is significant here, as it points to the hybridised and dialectical ways in which discourses of Iraqi nationalism and Shi'a religiosity intersect in the diasporic imaginary to produce sectarianised diasporic subjects. Such forms of politico-religious sectarianism, I wish to stress, do not emanate from some form of anterior ethno-sectarian 'essence', but rather represent 'a modern constitutive Foucauldian socioeconomic and political power that produces and reproduces sectarian subjects and modes of political subjectification and mobilisation through a dispersed ensemble of institutional, clientelist, and discursive practices' (Salloukh *et al.* 2015: 3). In the case of the Iraqi Shi'a diaspora in London, the reification of Shi'a 'groupness' (Brubaker 2002) through the proliferation of Shi'a religious and civil society organisations and the alienation from the homeland engendered via the diasporic imaginary has led to the blurring of nationalist and sectarian sentiment in which manifestations of Shi'a religiosity are seen as synonymous with articulations of Iraqi nationality.[6] While in Iraq itself articulations of Shi'a religious identity were often tempered with or superceded by other forms of collective belonging, including socio-economic status, political affiliation and regional origin (Batatu 2004; Nakash 2002, 2003; Tripp 2007), in the diaspora the emphasis on ethno-national origin coupled with the freedom of religious practice offered by the *husayniyyat* allowed for the emergence of a hybridised Iraqi-Shi'a identity that had not previously existed. As one of my interviewees remarked: 'many Shi'ites prior to leaving Iraq saw themselves as primarily Najafis or Karbala'is, Communists or Da'wa Party members, secularists or nationalists – now, they're just Shi'a' (Interview 5). In other words, the circulation, articulation and institutionalisation of ethno-sectarian discourses regarding the political status of Shi'ites in Iraq has led to processes of subjectification that, in the diasporic imaginary, have produced a hybridised Iraqi-Shi'a subject where notions of 'Iraqiness' are intrinsically tied to manifestations of 'Shi'aness'. This is especially the case for second-generation British-born Iraqi Shi'ites, who, in the words of one of my interviewees, a young British-born man from a religious background, tend to 'see their Iraqiness *as* Shi'aness; they show how Iraqi they are by being more and more Shi'a' (Interview 24).

Despite the diversity of individuals comprising the Iraqi Shi'a diaspora in the UK, therefore, the experience of exile coupled with the Shi'a institutional fabric of the London context provided the necessary conditions under which a hybridised Iraqi-Shi'a diasporic subject could emerge that was qualitatively different from forms of Shi'a identification in pre-exile Iraq. Again, I am not claiming that this is the only form of subjectivity present in the Iraqi Shi'a diaspora, or even that it is necessarily the most common one, but rather that the hybridised Iraqi-Shi'a subject is a product of particular and historically contingent alignments of discursive, institutional and social practices in contemporary London that is simultaneously oriented towards the lost Iraqi homeland through material and discursive networks of transnational religious authority and capital. Having briefly outlined some of the contingent factors leading to the crystallisation of a diasporic Iraqi-Shi'a subject (other significant factors include the sectarianisation of Iraqi domestic political discourse and current ethnic and sectarian conflict in the Middle East; the British government's policies of multiculturalism and ethnonormativity; and the role of the Shi'a religious establishment, most notably through the state actor of the Islamic Republic of Iran, in shaping political discourses regarding the meaning of Shi'ism),[7] I turn to the symbolic and material mobilisations of the Iraqi-Shi'a diasporic subject with regards the way it comes to shape the behaviour and practices of individual diasporans in relation to Iraqi domestic politics.

Charity, Pilgrimage and Symbolic Capital

Having already drawn attention to the significance of Shi'a-affiliated charities in diasporic mobilisations towards Iraq, it is important to recognise how such organisations are themselves embedded in wider networks of capital and charity that are materially and symbolically invested in orientations towards the diasporic homeland. As Corboz argues, 'the materiality of social services embedded in the reality of the "here" in exile can be combined with the creation of emotional attachment to the "there" back home' (2015: 82). In other words, by investing in such charitable and patronage networks individual Iraqi Shi'ites are contributing to the discursive construction of the Iraqi-Shi'a subject as one that views the Iraqi homeland through the lens of sectarian ethno-political belonging. As one of the five pillars of Islam, charity holds an important symbolic status in the maintenance of Muslim identity, and especially for Shi'a Muslims who in addition to the annual *zakat* obligatory for all Muslims (a charitable donation amounting to 2.5 per cent of one's disposable income) are expected to give *khums*, or one-fifth of their disposable income, to the Shi'a religious establishment every year.[8] In the UK, there are a number of organisations affiliated to the Shi'a religious establishment that are authorised to collect both *zakat* and *khums* on behalf of the *marja'iyya* (including the Imam Al-Khoei Foundation), while smaller charities rely on voluntary donations such as *sadaqa* or *wikat*.

For this reason, the channelling of funds and resources to Iraq via British-based Shi'a charities and organisations has significant symbolic, as well as material, consequences in the institutionalisation of sectarian patterns of belonging and association. The very real financial links between diasporic Iraqi Shi'ites in London and Shi'a religious institutions and clerical authorities in Iraq (and to a lesser extent Iran) thus contribute to an inflow of economic capital to Iraq's Shi'a clerical elite that has significant consequences for the political situation on the ground. In particular, the blurred boundaries between political and humanitarian organisations within Iraq itself, where a weak state has led to a mushrooming of informal patronage and charity networks upheld by non-state actors (often linked to sectarian militias), means that such inflows of religious remittances are likely to reinforce existing divisions in which community and religious leaders each look out for 'their own' at the expense of wider Iraqi society (Rosen and Younes 2008). While it is difficult to verify the extent to which religious remittances from the diaspora contribute to such sectarianisation of civil and religious society in Iraq, the influx of charitable donations through religious channels may plausibly contribute to maintaining, if not creating, the current sectarian order in Iraq. In this way, 'the practice of charity [in the diaspora] reinforces the religious, social, and political leadership roles assumed by clerical benefactors' in Iraq and contributes to the fragmentation of Iraqi civil society along sectarian and confessional lines (Corboz 2015: 93).

Another channel through which diasporic remittances of capital and resources take on sectarian dimensions is in the proliferation of religious pilgrimage routes from Britain to sites in Iraq (and to a lesser extent Iran). The symbolic significance of the holy shrines of the Iraqi cities of Najaf, Karbala, Kadhimiyya, Hilla and Samarra, as well as those of Qom and Mashhad in Iran, have led to the establishment of well-trodden pilgrimage routes to these cities. As a result, there are a number of companies dealing exclusively with the organisation and running of pilgrimage networks to Shi'a shrines in Iraq and Iran (including one established by a young British-born Pakistani Shi'ite facilitating the movement of Pakistani Shi'a pilgrims to these countries), including a number catering specifically for youth-led trips such as Al-Asr Foundation and the youth division of the Islamic Unity Society. For the younger generation of British-born Iraqi Shi'ites, such trips often serve as their only real experience of Iraq, as well as providing an opportunity to meet and make friends with British-born Shi'ites outside their immediate social network.

Despite the current security situation in Iraq, such pilgrimages continue to be common (indeed, many of those I spoke to say that since they believe their death has been pre-ordained they do not see themselves as taking any inordinate risk in travelling to Iraq, and that to die on pilgrimage would ensure their soul was pure on entry to heaven), especially during the Islamic month of Muharram (during which time many organisations offer discounts and packages) and the ensuing annual pilgrimage of Arba'in. Taking place forty days after the commemoration of the death of Imam Husayn in the Battle of Karbala, the Arba'in pilgrimage is one of the largest annual gatherings of people in the world, with an estimated 17 million people taking part in 2014[9] (compare this to the 2 million that participate in the annual hajj pilgrimage to Mecca). As part of the event, pilgrims walk from the seat of Shi'a religious learning in Najaf to the shrine of Imam Husayn in Karbala (a distance of around 80 km), catered for by charitable donations and volunteers along the route.

This annual influx of religious tourists to Iraq's major Shi'a shrine cities not only reinforces the symbolic value of Najaf and Karbala in the Iraqi-Shi'a diasporic imaginary, it also provides an influx of wealth to the country, channelled through clerical and religious networks of charity and patronage, that helps maintain the authority of the Shi'a religious establishment and the increasing reification of Shi'a identity through material and discursive means. As embodied and material practices, pilgrimage and the rituals associated with it represent a mechanism for the performative and discursive articulation of Shi'a religious identity (Pinto 2007). To engage in Shi'a pilgrimage is, in effect, to make a claim regarding the representation and content of Shi'a religious identity at the same time as it reifies certain pre-existing notions of what that identity constitutes. In this sense, individuals participating in pilgrimages are simultaneously engaging with the types of Shi'a identity that are constructed and performatively enacted through the practice of pilgrimage itself; whether that be the wearing of black, crying and prostrating at shrines, the consumption of religious goods and services, fasting, prayer, or other forms of performative identity construction. In other words, to conduct a Shi'a pilgrimage is at once to make a claim regarding one's 'Shi'a identity' at the same time as such performative practices constitute the meaning of that 'Shi'a identity' in the first place through the discursive construction of the (Iraqi-)Shi'a subject.

From the above, it is possible to discern how individual practices involving the distribution of charitable and pilgrimage remittances according to religious sect, as well as the performative enactment of 'Shi'a identity' represented through pilgrimage and ritual practices, contribute to the discursive formation of a hybridised Iraqi-Shi'a subject that has come to be implicated in the ongoing sectarianisation of Iraqi domestic politics. Although it is difficult to establish the extent to which the diaspora has been materially invested in the sectarianisation of Iraqi politics,[10] it is plausible to argue that the reinforcement of the politics of sectarianism in the diasporic imaginary has taken on potent symbolic forms through the discursive construction of a hybridised and sectarianised Iraqi-Shi'a subject. For example, one of the images on the Facebook page of ICARE, a New Zealand-based charity that works with children and young people in Iraq and that has a significant London presence (such as at the Imam Hussain Conference 2014), shows a young man in army fatigues kissing the hands and feet of an elderly lady in a black *abaya*. The caption to the image reads (in both English and Arabic): 'An Iraqi soldier in Popular Mobilisation Forces kisses his mothers [sic] feet and forehead before heading into the battlefield to fight ISIS' (see Figure 5.3).

The significance of a charitable organisation specialising in providing dental care and health services to Iraqi orphans and young people posting material indicative of its support for the Popular Mobilisation Forces (PMF), an umbrella group of Shi'a militias affiliated to the Iraqi army and set up following Grand Ayatollah Al-Sistani's fatwa compelling people to fight against ISIS in June 2014, is symbolically significant. By demonstrating its support of the PMF, ICARE are discursively contributing to the construction of an Iraqi-Shi'a subject that defines itself in opposition to the radical and fringe Sunni ideology of militant groups such as ISIS. In this sense, and whilst not

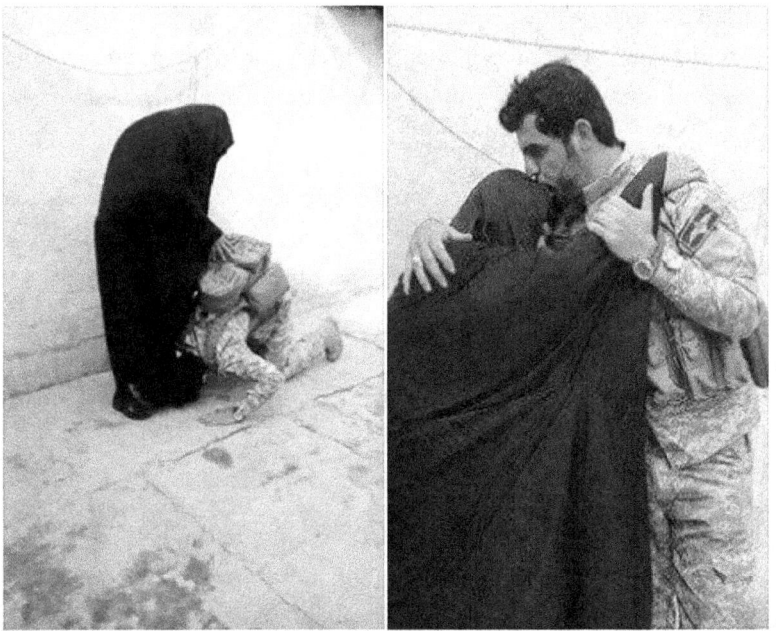

Figure 5.3 ICARE Facebook post depicting Iraqi soldier from the PMF militia. (Source: Facebook.)

wishing to flatten the nuances of the political and social reality in Iraq at the time of writing, it is possible to see how the contours of the Iraqi-Shi'a subject articulated in the diaspora have become symbolically and discursively invested in the very real sectarian dynamics of contemporary Iraqi politics. Similarly, many second-generation Iraqi Shi'ites to whom I spoke, although wishing to distance themselves from Shi'a militias such as the Mehdi Army and the Badr Brigades (one young British-born man even compared Muqtada Al-Sadr, the leader of the Mehdi Army, to Jabba the Hutt from Star Wars: 'he's the big fat ugly slug, he's the intergalactic gangster'; Interview 7), have expressed some form of symbolic support for the Popular Mobilisation Forces (one young woman even had a picture of a soldier holding the PMF flag as the home screen image on her iPhone).

Such public displays of support for the PMF are understandable given the contemporary political context in Iraq, and especially following the fatwa issued by Grand Ayatollah Al-Sistani urging Shi'ites to join the PMF in order to fight ISIS. Indeed, since the fall of Mosul in June 2014 to ISIS forces, in the Shi'a diasporic imaginary, the self-declared 'caliphate' has come to represent the same forces of 'evil' that fought and killed Imam Husayn on the battlefields of Karbala. As one young British-born man put it, speaking about the rise of ISIS in Iraq:

> These are the same people whose forefathers killed Imam Husayn . . . It is the same people who fought the Prophet. It's the same people who tried to do all these bad things in the world, you see them today. History repeats itself. It's an ideology, and the problem is that now it's become apparent to the whole world that's it uh . . . you know, it's a flawed ideology. That they don't know what to do anymore. Even the Sunnis, between me and you, they've realised that their ideology and what they believe in is a pathway to ISIS. Because it's flawed. (Interview 7)

In other words, the representation of ISIS as the spectral embodiment of 'evil' simultaneously invokes a politico-religious narrative of Shi'a victimisation and emancipation, as well as implicating localised practices of Shi'ism in wider sectarian politics that pits the essentialised categories of 'Sunnis' and 'Shi'ites' in an eternal conflict of 'us and them'. This suggests that the increasingly sectarian nature of the conflict in Iraq (most notably since the 2003 US-led invasion, and manifested by the recent rise to prominence of ISIS and the formation of the PMF) has symbolically altered the orientation of the diasporic Iraqi-Shi'a subject such that expressions of Iraqi national solidarity take on increasingly sectarianised forms, and that the problematic nature of such a conflation of Iraqi and Shi'a socio-political identities are uncritically glossed over.[11]

Shi'a Rights and the Transnational Imaginary

Such symbolic (re)iterations of a sectarianised Iraqi-Shi'a diasporic subject are inscribed in wider discourses of Shi'a victimisation that make claims regarding the political and social place of Shi'ism internationally and domestically and that are, I argue, embedded in wider global discourses of minority rights and social justice. The rise of the 'Shi'a rights' movement,[12] in which the narrative of victimisation and marginalisaition stemming from Shi'a religious doctrine (often embodied in the symbol of Imam Husayn and the Battle of Karbala) has been transferred into the diasporic imaginary via its inscription in global discourses of equality, emancipation and minority rights. Many of my research participants used the phrase 'minority within minority' to highlight the status of Shi'a Muslims in Britain (a minority of Muslims, who are themselves a minority within the wider white British population) and to make claims regarding the role of Shi'ism as a political and social discourse of emancipation. But the claiming of 'Shi'a rights' is not just limited to the British diasporic sphere; many of the same narratives and claims are being visibly and forcibly made in both the national and international imaginary by Iraqi Shi'ites in London and elsewhere (Degli Esposti 2017). Drawing on specifically Shi'a forms of aesthetics, ritual practices and politico-religious discourses, such attempts to visibly foreground the Iraqi-Shi'a subject and Shi'a minority rights can be understood as 'a form of agency' that 'brings the domain of culture and the personal under public attention' (Göle 2011: 390).

> There is an intrinsic relation between getting public, visibility and agency ... To appear always means to seem to others. It is perceived by a plurality of spectators, therefore a public is by definition pluralistic. And therefore citizenship is not prior to public appearance but *one becomes a citizen as one makes oneself visible to others* ... The questions of citizenship are always political because politics deals with difference and conflict; as one makes oneself visibly public, one also marks the transgression of boundaries and the disruption of the established frame. (Göle 2011: 390, emphasis added)

In this sense, being visibly and publically Shi'a is intricately related to claiming one's place as a citizen of the modern state, a form of citizenship that is directly invested in global models of minority rights and social equality and implicated in the politics of difference and commensurability. Perhaps the most evident manifestation of such specifically *Shi'a* politics of visibility is in the annual 'Ashura' and Arba'in marches that take place in central London on the tenth and fortieth day of Muharram respectively. Beginning at Marble Arch and progressing through Hyde Park (although for the last three years the 'Ashura' march has moved to go up Edgware Road), the marches draw thousands of devout Shi'ites from various backgrounds onto the streets and avenues of central London to profess their faith and to mourn the killing of Imam Husayn. A watered-down version of similar processions in Iraq, Iran, and other countries with significant Shi'a populations, the marches manifest aesthetically as a mass of black-swathed bodies and large, Arabic-inscribed banners, punctuated with the melodic cadences of *latmiyyat* in various languages and the rhythmical beating of bodies and drums. Alongside the religious banners, the flags of Iraq, Iran, Lebanon, Afghanistan, Iraqi Kurdistan, Bahrain, and a host of other nations can be seen (as well as the flags of Shi'a religious and political parties such as Hezbollah), along with various smaller placards and banners bearing religious and political slogans in English such as: 'Genocide committed to those who stood against tyranny'; and 'Every land is Karbala and every day is 'Ashura' (a slogan made popular during Iran's Islamic Revolution).

Since 2014, alongside such slogans of Shi'a doctrinal ideology, a sea of black signs inscribed with red and white letters have proclaimed 'Down with ISIS', or alternatively 'ISIS are the Yazid of today', and even 'Shi'a Muslims are the biggest victims of terrorism'. Such public and visible articulations of Shi'a religious and sectarian identity in explicit opposition to the politics and practises of ISIS draw on contemporary social and media tropes of Islamism and terrorism to articulate an unequivocally Shi'a political and religious message inscribed in the contemporary politics of Iraq. The public contrasting of 'Shi'a-as-victim' with 'Sunni[/ISIS]-as-oppressor' thus constructs an explicitly sectarian narrative as a way to make specific claims regarding the political place of Shi'ism in the contemporary politics of Iraq and in the world as a whole. In this way, the marches are seen as a way of publically and visibly claiming a politically invested manifestation of Iraqi-Shi'a religious identity, couched in the language of international justice and minority rights. As one young British-born Iraqi Shi'a woman active within the community put it: 'It's good to show that we're not just a minority oppressed group, that we have a presence . . . that we have a voice' (Interview 30). Another older woman I walked alongside during the 2014 'Ashura' march told me: 'We want people to stop and ask us what it's about. That's the whole point.'

During the 'Ashura' march of 2014, I was handed a leaflet entitled 'Why are we here?' that declared: 'Moses. Buddah. Jesus Christ. Cyrus the Great. William Wilberforce. Confucius. Che Guevara. Ibn Sina. Alexander Fleming. Ali Ibn Abu Talib. Gandhi. Hussain. Plato . . . We are here to continue the legacy of Hussain and his companions.' Similar examples include the setting up of stalls on university campuses by Ahlulbayt Societies (Shi'a student societies commonly known as ABSocs), the holding of English-language events (such as the Imam Hussain Conference 2014 and the Imam Hussain Slam Poetry Competition 2015), and the dissemination of information pertaining to the minority status of Shi'ites across mainstream and social media platforms (hashtags such as #YaHussain and #WhoIsHussain are used to draw attention to questions of social justice and inequality). Here, the explicit juxtaposition of the religious figure of Imam Husayn with globally recognisable figures of social justice and political emancipation inscribes the Iraqi-Shi'a subject in wider discourses on minority rights that, crucially, make claims towards the status of Shi'ism as a politico-religious identity within the global sphere. This sectarianisation of global Shi'a activism, in which articulations of Shi'a religious identity are increasingly expressed with relation to issues of Shi'a persecution, victimisation and discrimination, has political effects when transferred to the local sphere of Iraqi politics through the prism of the diasporic imaginary as it contributes to the ongoing polarisation of Iraqi political discourse in which questions of the material allocation of resources, money and public infrastructure have come to be couched in terms of sectarian 'quotas' and networks of ethno-religious patronage and clientelism.

In this sense, the global orientations of the contemporary Iraqi-Shi'a diasporic subject have real political effects with regards to the 'homeland' of Iraq, especially in the way discourses of Shi'a rights and minority justice have come to hold sway with regards to both domestic and international analyses of the Iraqi political scene – a prime example being the way in which former

Iraqi Prime Minister Nouri Al-Maliki (himself a diasporic exile for several decades before returning to Iraq post-2003) repeatedly justified his own government's sectarian and clientelist distribution of resources by appealing to the history of Shi'a marginalisation and persecution in Iraq under Saddam Hussein (Dodge 2012). While it is difficult to establish any kind of causal link between diasporic iterations of Iraqi-Shi'a identity and political consequences within Iraq itself, it is possible to trace a link between the kinds of articulations and performances circulating within the diasporic imaginary (such as the trope of 'Shi'a-as-victim', bolstered by discourses of social justice and minority rights) and the kinds of discourses gaining political salience within Iraq itself. In this sense, while the sectarianisation of the Iraqi-Shi'a subject in the diasporic context may have arisen as a result of specific historical, social and political contingencies, its symbolic and discursive resonances echo beyond the specificities of the diasporic experience to inform (though of course not entirely dictate) articulations of what it means to be both 'Iraqi' and 'Shi'a' within the Iraqi domestic context.

Najaf in Brent, London in Karbala

Throughout this chapter, I have drawn attention to the ways in which the crystallisation of a sectarianised Iraqi-Shi'a diasporic subject forged in the intersecting imaginary of global discourses of social justice and regional sectarian conflict has dialectically shaped and been shaped by Iraqi domestic politics and ongoing ethno-religious conflict. In particular, I have demonstrated how this hybridised Iraqi-Shi'a diasporic subject has both material and discursive effects on the political and social terrain of the 'home' state of Iraq. The channelling of resources, religious remittances, and symbolic capital through networks of clerical authority and patronage thus serve to reinforce the existing hegemony of the Shi'a religious establishment and embed it in clientelist relations that construct and maintain docile sectarian subjects. In this sense, the diasporic imaginary of the Iraqi-Shi'a subject is at once both a discursive construction open to symbolic articulations of identification and a precipitator of social and political action that transcends individual agency and invests the locus of political analysis in the subject of discursive power relations.

The theoretical significance of the argument here, then, is to highlight the ways in which political subjects can be productively conceptualised as distinct from acting agents as a way to interrogate the ways in which political subjects are rendered 'natural' through the inner workings of discursive power. Although my exploration of such theoretical insights in this chapter has been necessarily brief, I hope that it can open up new avenues for engaging with political agents, and in particular of thinking through the existence of diasporic subjects and their potential orientations and mobilisations towards an imagined 'homeland'.

Author Interviews

1. K. Makiya (12 February 2013)
2. Prof. J. Sassoon (18 February 2013)
3. Abu Zainab (3 March 2013)
4. D. Kashi (6 March 2013)
5. Abu R. (13 March 2013)
6. R. Momeini (24 May 2014)
7. Abu Hussain (6 August 2014)
8. Sayyid F. Bahrululoom (12 August 2014)
9. M. Al-Khoei (28 September 2014)
10. M. Field OBE (3 October 2014)
11. K. Makiya (6 October 2014)
12. H. Al-Khoei (13 October 2014)
13. D. Kashi (second interview) (17 October 2014)
14. M. Al Kadhimi (21 October 2014)
15. G. Jawad (28 October 2014)
16. H. Allawi (31 October 2014)
17. Dr A. Al-Ta'i (Abu Abeer Saleh) (6 November 2014)
18. H. Al-Hakim (11 November 2014)
19. E. Cohen (12 November 2014)
20. E. Al-Abadi (18 November 2014)
21. G. Fadil (18 November 2014)
22. M. Jawad (25 November 2014)
23. J. Hassan (26 November 2014)
24. H. Tahan (6 December 2014)
25. H. H. Al-Qarawee (9 January 2015)
26. N. Yasin (28 January 2015)

27. Um Nadia (30 January 2015)
28. M. Hariri (20 February 2015)
29. Sayyid Karbasi (20 February 2015)
30. M. Allawi (30 October 2015)

References

Al-Ali, Nadie Sadig (2007), *Iraqi Women: Untold Stories from 1948 to the Present*, London: Zed Books.
Alkhairo, Marwa Wael (2008), 'Iraqi diasporic identity across generations, struggle, and war', PhD dissertation, Georgetown University, Washington, DC.
Al-Arabiya (2014), 'Iraq's Karbala registers record number of pilgrims', 12 December, available at: http://english.alarabiya.net/en/News/middle-east/2014/12/12/Iraq-s-Karbala-registers-record-number-of-pilgrims-.html, last accessed 14 November 2015.
Axel, Brian Keith (2001), *The Nation's Tortured Body: Violence, Representation, and the Formation of a Sikh 'Diaspora'*, Durham: Duke University Press.
—— (2002), 'The diasporic imaginary', *Public Culture* 14:2, 411–28.
—— (2004), 'The context of diaspora', *Cultural Anthropology* 19:1, 26–60.
Batatu, Hanna ([1978] 2004), *The Old Social Classes and the Revolutionary Movements of Iraq: A Study of Iraq's Old Landed and Commercial Classes and of its Communists, Ba'thists and Free Officers*, London: Saqi Books.
BBC News (2014), 'Shia pilgrims flock to Karbala for Arbaeen climax', 14 December, available at: http://www.bbc.co.uk/news/world-middle-east-30462820, last accessed 14 November 2015.
Bowen, Innes (2014), *Medina in Birmingham, Najaf in Brent: Inside British Islam*, London: Hurst.
Brah, Avtar (1996), *Cartographies of Diaspora: Contesting Identities*, London: Routledge.
Brubaker, Rogers (2002), 'Ethnicity without groups', *European Journal of Sociology* 43:2, 163–89.
—— (2005), 'The "diaspora" diaspora', *Ethnic and Racial Studies* 28:1, 1–19.
Butler, Judith (1997), *The Psychic Life of Power: Theories in Subjection*, Stanford: Stanford University Press.
Butler, Kim D. (2001), 'Defining diaspora, refining a discourse', *Diaspora* 10:2, 189–19.
Communities and Local Government (2009), *The Iraqi Muslim Community:*

Understanding Muslim Ethnic Communities, London: The Change Institute, Communities and Local Government.

Corboz, Elvire (2015), *Guardians of Shi'ism: Sacred Authority and Transnational Family Networks*, Edinburgh: Edinburgh University Press.

Degli Esposti, Emanuelle (2017), 'The aesthetics of ritual – contested identities and conflicted performances in the Iraqi Shi'a diaspora: ritual, performance, and identity change', *Politics* 38:1, 68–83.

——— (2019), 'Fragmented realities: the "sectarianisation" of space among Iraqi Shias in London', *Contemporary Islam*, 13:3, 259–85.

Dodge, Toby (2012), 'Iraq's road back to dictatorship', *Survival* 54:3, 147–68.

Epstein, Charlotte (2010), 'Who speaks? Discourse, the subject and the study of identity in international politics', *European Journal of International Relations* 20:10, 1–24.

Flynn, Kieran (2013), *Islam in the West: Iraqi Shi'i Communities in Transition and Dialogue*, Oxford: Peter Lang.

Foucault, Michel (1991), *Discipline and Punish: The Birth of the Prison*, London: Penguin Books.

——— ([1982] 2003), 'The subject and power', in P. Rabinow and N. Rose (eds), *The Essential Foucault: Selections from The Essential Works of Foucault 1954–1984*, New York: The New Press, pp. 126–44.

Göle, Nilüfer (2011), 'The public visibility of Islam and European politics of resentment: the minarets-mosques debate', *Philosophy and Social Criticism* 37:4, 383–92.

Haddad, Fanar (2011), *Sectarianism in Iraq: Antagonistic Visions of Unity*, London: Hurst.

Hall, Stuart (1990), 'Cultural identity and diaspora', in J. Rutherford (ed.), *Identity: Community, Culture, Difference*, London: Lawrence and Wishart, pp. 222–37.

——— (2000), 'Who needs "identity?"', in P. du Gay, J. Evans and P. Redman (eds), *Identity: A Reader*, London: Sage, pp. 15–30.

Howarth, David R. (2013), *Poststructuralism and After: Structure, Subjectivity and Power*, London: Palgrave Macmillan.

International Crisis Group (2006), 'The next Iraqi war? Sectarianism and civil conflict', *Middle East Report* 52, 27 February.

International Organisation for Migration (IOM) (2007), 'Iraq mapping exercise: London', available at: http://unitedkingdom.iom.int/sites/default/files/doc/mapping/IOM_IRAQ.pdf, last accessed 14 November 2015.

Kadhum, Oula (2017), 'Diasporic interventions: state-building in Iraq following the 2003 Iraq War', PhD dissertation, Warwick University, Warwick.

Kinnivall, Catarina, and Paul Nesbitt-Larking (2009), 'Security, subjectivity, and space in postcolonial Europe: Muslims in the diaspora', *European Security* 18:3, 305–25.

Laclau, Ernesto (1994), 'Introduction', in E. Laclau (ed.), *The Making of Political Identities*, London: Verso, pp. 1–8.

Mouffe, Chantal (2005), *On the Political*, Oxford: Routledge.

Nakash, Yitzhak (2002), 'The nature of Shi'ism in Iraq', in Faleh A. Jabr (ed.), *Ayatollahs, Sufis and Ideologues: State, Religion and Social Movements in Iraq*, London: Saqi, pp. 23–35.

―― (2003), *The Shi'is of Iraq*, Princeton: Princeton University Press.

Nasr, Vali (2006), *The Shia Revival: How Conflicts within Islam will Shape the Future*, New York: W.W. Norton and Company.

Office for National Statistics (2013), 'Detailed country of birth and nationality analysis from the 2011 Census of England and Wales', 16 May, available at: http://www.ons.gov.uk/ons/dcp171776_310441.pdf, last accessed 22 March 2014.

Ong, Aihwa (2003), 'Cyberpublics and diaspora politics among transnational Chinese', *Interventions* 5:1, 82–100.

Pinto, Paulo G. (2007), 'Pilgrimage, commodities, and religious objectification: the making of transnational Shiism between Iran and Syria', *Comparative Studies of South Asia, Africa and the Middle East* 27:1, 109–25.

Raman, Parvathi (2003), 'A resting place for the imagination? In search of the "authentic" diasporic subject', *Himal South Asia* 16:9, 22–30.

Rosen, Nir (2006), *In the Belly of the Green Bird: The Triumph of the Martyrs in Iraq*, New York: Free Press.

Rosen, Nir, and Kristelle Younes (2008), 'Uprooted and unstable: meeting urgent humanitarian needs in Iraq.' *Refugees International*, April, Washington, DC.

Saleh, Zainab (2011), 'Diminished returns: an anthropological study of Iraqis in the UK', PhD dissertation, Colombia University, New York.

Salloukh, Bassel F., Rabie Barakat, Jinan S. Al-Habbal, Lara W. Khattab and Shoghig Mikaelian (2015), *The Politics of Sectarianism in Postwar Lebanon*, London: Pluto Press.

Stavrakakis, Yannis (1999), *Lacan and the Political*, London: Routledge.

Tripp, Charles (2007), *A History of Iraq*, Cambridge: Cambridge University Press.

Venn, Couze (2009), 'Identities, diasporas and subjective change: the role of affect, the relation to the other and the aesthetic', *Subjectivity* 26:1, 3–28.

Visser, Reidar (2007), 'The Western imposition of sectarianism on Iraqi politics', *The Arab Studies Journal* 15/16:2/1, 83–99.
Walker, Martin (2006), 'The revenge of the Shia', *The Wilson Quarterly* 16–20.
Werbner, Pnina (2009), 'The translocation of culture: "community cohesion" and the force of multiculturalism in history', *The Sociological Review* 53:4, 745–68.
Witteborn, Saskia (2008), 'Identity mobilisation practices of refugees: the case of Iraqis in the United States and the war in Iraq', *Journal of International Communication* 1:3, 202–20.
Yousif, Basem (2010), 'The political economy of sectarianism in Iraq', *International Journal of Contemporary Iraqi Studies* 4:3, 357–67.

PART II
TRANSNATIONAL SHI'A TRAJECTORIES

6

GLOBAL NETWORKS, LOCAL CONCERNS: INVESTIGATING THE IMPACT OF EMERGING TECHNOLOGIES ON SHI'A RELIGIOUS LEADERS AND CONSTITUENCIES

Robert J. Riggs

Introduction

Religion is not just transmitted via particular media. The forms of mediation should actually be regarded as an integral part of the definition of religion. Religions are to a large extent shaped by their dominant means of communication. Whether they are mainly oral, codified in writing, or further distributed in print has significance. Printing technology was an 'agent of change' in the Protestant Reformation in Europe (Eisenstein 1979), and likewise digital technologies are probably crucial to transformations of contemporary religious systems.

Throughout history, religious traditions have had to be translated (or 'transmediated') for new generations in changing contexts of communication. Religion 'cannot be analysed outside the forms and practices of mediation that define it' (Meyer and Moors 2006: 7). It then becomes paramount to explore how the transition from one mode of mediated communication to another contributes to reconfiguring a particular religious practice. The focus should be on the cultural practices of mediation rather than on the media themselves, as already suggested by the communication scholar Jesús

Martín-Barbero (Martín-Barbero and Fox 1993), based on his Latin American experiences. 'It is in the emergence of the interstices', Homi Bhabha writes, '– the overlap and displacement of domains of difference – that the inter-subjective and collective experiences of nationness, community interest, or cultural values are negotiated' (Bhabha 1994: 2). One could say the same for Shi'a religious communities, in the context of the new digital world, when ideas and institutions are contested and created through a process of mediation and, as will be discussed below, mediatisation.

However, the extent to which new media technologies are driving forces in transformations of the Shi'a branch of the Islamic religion and in the creation of third spaces of religious hybridity is a key issue that will distinguish the theoretical approach to be discussed in this chapter. By 'new media', this contribution points to the contemporary digitisation of communication. Small-scale digital media present a ritual view of the communication of new energy, as these tools are woven into daily social interaction within a variety of communities. They invite 'user-generated content' as symbolic sharing, although the transmission of view still applies when religious actors use these new media to reach out via new forms of mediation (Lundby 2013: 226).

In September 2008, assumed Sunni Salafis hacked and defaced the websites of Ayatollah 'Ali Al-Sistani and other prominent Shi'a religious authorities. In the case of Sistani, a YouTube excerpt from a Bill Maher interview ridiculing Sistani was placed over his homepage along with an anti-Shi'a polemical text. In addition, hundreds of other Shi'a websites were attacked. While the intra-Muslim virtual conflict provided material for the next day's news cycle, the real story was the increasing diversity of authorities in the Shi'a Internet world. This study examines the paradoxical results of the use of Internet technology by Shi'a *mujtahids*. Internet websites allow self-styled *mujtahids* to proliferate and diverse centres of authority to form. At the same time, these websites have adhered to common Shi'a religious conventions in content and presentation. To date, scholars have discussed the effects of Internet technology on the authority structures of Shi'a religious leaders in furthering competition for knowledge and authority (Rahimi and Gheytanchi 2008; Scholz *et al.* 2008). However, these studies neglect to highlight the increasing uniformity in thought that the Internet has encouraged. This chapter will address these two seemingly contradictory outcomes of increased uniformity and diversity in Shi'a religious leadership through the application of Arjun Appadurai's theory of the 'disjunctive order' of a 'new global cultural economy' (Appadurai 1990) and the application of theories of mediatisation as an effect of new media on Shi'a religious institutions.

Globalisation's Varying '-Scapes'

With the rise of increasing globalisation in the late twentieth century, Appadurai identifies five dimensions of global cultural flow, which he termed: (a) ethnoscapes; (b) mediascapes; (c) technoscapes; (d) finanscapes; and (e) ideoscapes (Appadurai 1990). The interaction of these five dimensions represents certain fundamental disjunctures between economy, culture and politics. He uses the suffix '-scape' to indicate that these are not objectively given relations which look the same from every angle of vision, but rather that they are deeply perspectival constructs, inflected very much by the historical, linguistic and political situatedness of different sorts of actors.

For example, an ethnoscape could be a Bahraini refugee community in Atlanta, interacting with the technoscape of shiachat.com and sistani.org to communicate with both politicised relatives in Manama and the spiritual authorities in Najaf. This same Bahraini ethnoscape uses the finanscape of Western Union wire transfers to fund both religious travellers to Najaf for education and pilgrimage and the establishment of political opposition movements in Bahrain. Simultaneously, this ethnoscape develops a mediascape in the form of independent films about the plight of Shi'a communities in Bahrain, using imagery from the holy cities of Iraq and religious iconography of the martyrdom of Husayn. The content of these mediascapes comprise ideoscapes that capture the hybridisation of certain ideas, images and terms. This hypothetical example shows the radical disjunctures that could occur between these various '-scapes' as they interact with one another, facilitated by different forms of global cultural flows.

Mediascapes and Mediatisation

Focusing on the concept of mediascapes, the media's specific impact on religion may be manifold and at times contradictory, but as a whole the media as channel, language and environment are responsible for the mediatisation of religion. Mediatisation designates the process through which core elements of a social or cultural activity (e.g. politics, teaching, religion, etc.) assume media form. As a consequence, the activity is to a greater or lesser degree performed through interaction with a medium, and the symbolic content and the structure of the social and cultural activity are influenced by media environments, upon which they gradually become more dependent (Hjarvard 2008; Schulz 2004).

Mediatisation is not to be mistaken for the common phenomenon of *mediation*. Mediation refers to the communication through one or more media through which the message and the relation between sender and receiver are influenced by the affordances and constraints of the specific media and genres involved. Thus, the specific choice of communication channel for a political speech or a religious narrative influences the form, content and subsequent reception of the speech or narrative. However, mediation in itself may not have any profound impact on the social institutions of politics or religion, as long as the institutions are in control of the communication. Mediation concerns the specific circumstances of communication and interaction through a medium in a particular setting. In contrast, mediatisation addresses the long-term process of changing social institutions and modes of interactions in culture and society due to the growing importance of media in all strands of society.

Mediatisation describes the process of social change that to some extent subsumes other social or cultural fields to the logic of the media. In the case of religion, as a channel, language and environment, the media facilitate changes in the amount, content and direction of religious messages in society, at the same time as they transform religious representations and challenge and replace the authority of the institutionalised religions. Through these processes, religion as a social and cultural activity has become mediatised. In this chapter, the focus will be on selected changes observed in Shi'a religious institutions. It will be argued that mediatisation played a significant role in enacting those changes. Through the process of mediatisation, one could argue, Shi'a religious institutions are increasingly being subsumed to the logic of the media, both in terms of institutional regulation, symbolic content and individual practices. A theory of the interface between media and Shi'a Islam must consider the media and Shi'a Islam in the proper cultural and historical context. However, the mediatisation of religion is not postulated to be a universal phenomenon, rather it is historically, culturally and geographically informed. By this process, religious imaginations and practices become increasingly dependent upon the media. As a channel of communication, the media have become the primary source (not only mediators) of religious ideas, and as a language the media has melded religious imagination in accordance with the genres of popular culture. The media as a cultural environment have taken over many of the social functions of the institutionalised religions, providing both moral and spiritual guidance and a sense of community.

How mediatisation creates new forms within religious spaces is best understood as analogous to Homi Bhabha's understanding of 'third spaces' of cultural hybridity, in this case religious cultural hybridity (Bhabha 1994). He believes that cultural articulation can take place through a continuous process of hybridity, and that such hybridity can generate relevant statements and meanings that are autonomous from existing authority. Thus, significant interpretive communities can form and these concepts and statements can result in meaningful action. Within the context of the Shi'a religious authority systems, mediatisation is creating this hybridity, leading to new meanings and social constructs.

Traditional Shi'a Religious Authority Construction

Historically, some studies of the Shi'ites have focused on centre–periphery models, whereby the complexities of the relationship between the *mujtahid* and his followers have been studied and these client-patronage relationships were thought to govern the development and control of knowledge and authority within specific urban environments (Corboz 2015; Walbridge 2001). These client-patronages developed into systems of religious tithe collection and redistribution that helped to establish centres of learning and religious pilgrimage. Echoing Raymond Williams's 'city-country' dichotomy (Williams 1973), some scholars have represented Shi'a religious authorities as based within the city – a site for religious knowledge and enlightenment – versus the country, where access to religious authorities and knowledge is limited (Marcinkowski 2004; Mottahedeh 2014). Historically, the Shi'ites in most cases have had to travel to the religious authorities in the shrine cities, as opposed to the authorities coming to the people by taking up residence in non-urban areas (Momen 1985). At the same time, the authorities continued to maintain offices and representatives in many outlying areas where the Shi'ites lived. They developed and maintained local constituencies through the strategic placement of loyal representatives who collected the *khums* tithe, mediated local disputes and transmitted messages on their behalf.

Despite the local character of Shi'a authority, since at least the second half of the nineteenth century, Shi'a *mujtahids* have represented themselves as transnational religious leaders whose authority reaches followers all over the world. The vast majority of the Shi'a religious leaders now view their position as one governing broadly over an amorphous and transnational community, unrestricted by narrowly local political concerns, but focused on the overall wellbeing of the Shi'ites (Corboz 2015; Louër 2008). The governance of this religious community sometimes demands that a *mujtahid* intervenes in political affairs, without binding him to a specific political ideology or state authority. However, despite these international aspirations and authority claims, these religious authorities primarily exerted localised authority until the late twentieth century (Walbridge 2001).

In the beginning of his book *Imagined Communities*, Benedict Anderson describes the medieval imagined religious community, prior to the rise of nationalism, where, 'Literati were adepts, a strategic strata in a cosmological hierarchy of which the apex was divine' (Anderson 2006: 15). He then explains that these literati were experts in a 'script-language', such as Latin or Arabic, which gave them privileged access to truth and that pilgrimage sites were central to the development of these imagined religious communities. Because of the rise of what Appadurai terms 'technoscapes' such as the Internet, the authority exercised by ayatollahs and the religious symbolism that surrounds the shrine cities and pilgrimage sites of Shi'a Islam has led to the development of both a modern Shi'a imagined transnational religious community, but also local Shi'a communities that adapt themselves pragmatically within the various nationalisms in which they exist. This broad network of religio-political authority is exercised in an amorphous and non-delineated fashion through the use of newly existent communication technologies.

This Shi'a transnational community is overseen and perpetuated through a variety of means, such as internationally based social service organisations, but one of the most potent is the use of the Internet to transverse traditional boundaries. In the second half of the twentieth century, these ayatollahs have taken advantage of technological advances to expand their client-patronage networks to reach a larger audience. The classical example is the use of audiotapes to disseminate Ayatollah Khomeini's messages to his followers in Iran before the revolution from his residence in France (Sreberny and Mohammadi 1994). This phenomenon represents what Peter Mandaville refers to as 'modes of translocality' (Mandaville 2001: 83).

Shi'a Islam has known a form of autonomous and institutionalised religious authority, the *marja'iyya*, since the early or mid-nineteenth century. Since that time, this institution has had either a single leader, called the *marja' al-taqlid* (a source to follow or imitate), or a number of different leaders (Walbridge 2001). Until 1970, the *marja'iyya* was most often based in Najaf and occasionally in nearby Karbala, Iraq, or Qom, Iran. From the 1970s onwards, there have been multiple centres in Najaf, Qom, Tehran, Mashhad and Beirut, although Qom in particular has risen to pre-eminence since the 1960s. These different centres compete not only for religious prominence, students and followers but also for religious taxes (*khums*) and religious tourism to holy Shi'a pilgrimage sites, another type of 'finanscape'. In the politico-religious realm, this competition among leaders has adopted a nationalist rhetoric, with the antagonism between Iran and Iraq at its focus. This power struggle was particularly apparent while Saddam Hussein was in power in Iraq. Linda Walbridge commented on this conflict, stating, 'The governments of Iran and Iraq [are] constantly trying to manipulate the *marja'iyya* and often pit various ulama against one another' (Walbridge 2001: 233).

In terms of leadership succession, the use of the term succession itself is problematic, since it connotes a rigid hierarchical structure in Shi'a Islam, instead of illustrating that this network of authority is actually gradually developed over many decades through the cultivation of institutions and constituents. In other words, there is not one moment when a *marja'* is elected to become the primary leader. Rather, his leadership is a reflection of a gradual consensus that is implicit when others defer to his leadership and socio-religious rulings. At no point in history has one leader ruled all of the Shi'ites. Additionally, leadership has not been hereditarily passed down from one *marja'* to his son. Despite these limitations, this study will use the term succession to mean the organic development of leadership within Shi'a Islam as a network of authority. This study defines network using the actor-network theory (ANT) of Bruno Latour (Latour 2005) who views a network as a descriptive entity that maps relations simultaneously material and semiotic. For example, the interactions in a school involve children, teachers, ideas (both the students' and the teachers') and technologies, the latter he broadly defines as tables, chairs, computers, stationery, and so on. Likewise, within this definition, the interactions between a *marja'*, his ideas, students, educational methodology, locale and technologies (among other things) form a single network. Latour terms each element within this network an 'actant', denoting human and non-human actors, and states that all actants in a network take the shape that they do by virtue of their relations with one another. This theory assumes that nothing lies outside the network of relations. Latour also views the network itself as an actant within larger networks. To apply this to Shi'a Islam, within the broader network of the global Shi'a community exists the Ayatollah Sistani network, the Ayatollah Khamenei network, and so on. ANT explains how material–semiotic networks come together to act as a whole (for example, a school is both a network and an actor that hangs together, and for certain purposes acts as a single entity) while continually changing as actants are added or removed.

Late Twentieth-century Changes in Media: The Internet

The rise and development of a reconstituted Shi'a transnational imagined religious community in the late twentieth century has led to a series of innovations. These innovations are due to the easing of traditional boundaries and hindrances to communication among the various Shi'a communities and the interwoven processes of economic and cultural globalisation. Nevertheless, this Andersonian concept of the transnational imagined religious community is complicated by the fact that the Shi'ites have remained largely provincial in their political engagement, focusing on substantial political gain in various nation states where they live (Fuller and Franke 1999). This paradoxical interplay of the global and local forms what Appadurai calls 'imagined worlds', that is, the interplay of multiple 'imagined communities' that are constituted by the historically situated imaginations of persons and groups spread around the globe (Appadurai 1990). These imagined worlds draw in part upon the figure of the ayatollahs, which represent continuity and innovation as an authoritative religious institutional reference point for the Shi'ites, providing both a source of cohesiveness and the potential for fragmentation. The factors that combine to hinder or enhance the authority of an ayatollah include his connection to overt political power, tribal and clan affiliations, religious educational pedigree, economic independence, administrative acumen and perceived personal piety. The ayatollahs self-legitimise their authority by using the Internet to magnify these factors.

With the rise of a global information network, powered by the Internet, these *mujtahids* have established website 'technoscapes' that play a vital role in the maintenance of local constituencies (ethnoscapes). Since a *mujtahid* bases his authority in part on his role as the guardian and producer of knowledge, the use of websites and Internet technology provides greater opportunities for constituency-building. Now anyone can access an ayatollah without going through one of his representatives or visiting him in person. At the same time this free access to knowledge represents a significant challenge to the historical control that *mujtahids* have exerted over the production and propagation of knowledge and authority within Shi'a communities. While there are still excluded groups (the very poor, rural regions without Internet access) the use of new media technologies for self-representation and message diffusion has allowed the emergence of competing religious authorities (both personalities and institutions) that seek to establish spheres of influence within the newly literate Shi'a communities. The Internet gives an individual freedom to create a following by depersonalising the experience and allows anyone to purport their authority due to the anonymity of the medium, but also due to the fact that anyone has access to the Internet, without regard for authority/legitimacy/pedigree/experience/education. The city-country dichotomy, if not abolished, is at least increasingly blurred. Additionally, the ability to raise and distribute funds over the Internet undermines the financial system that traditionally furthered this dichotomy.

Simultaneously, all religious authority figures in Shi'a communities express their authority using certain symbolic references to historical forms of authority construction such as devotion to the holy shrines, educational pedigree and social activism. The first *mujtahid* to successfully utilise the Internet for online propagation of his message was Muhammad Husayn Fadlallah (1935–2010) in Beirut in 1997. Since that time, all of the other historically prestigious religious figures in Shi'a Islam have established Internet websites with various levels of sophistication. Additionally, other Shi'a websites compete with or complement these authorities. One can see the homogeneity and heterogeneity that these technological developments hold through an examination of the four prominent *mujtahids* living in Najaf.

Case Study I: Contested Authority of the 'Four *Mujtahids*'

Beginning in the 1990s but accelerating since the 2003 US invasion of Iraq, four Najaf-based ayatollahs have come to be collectively known as the *marja'iyya diniyya* of Najaf – 'Ali Al-Sistani, Bashir Al-Najafi, Muhammad Sa'id Al-Hakim and Muhammad Ishaq Al-Fayad. During the 1990s in Iraq, Saddam Hussein increased pressure on the Shi'a religious establishment by imprisoning the leaders and their students and representatives or placing them under *de facto* house arrest. As a result of this disruption of the normal activities of the *hawza* (Shi'a religious educational centres overseen by *mujtahids*), and the simultaneous creation and rise of the Internet, these authorities turned to virtual methods of propagating their messages. At the same time, the embattled leading teacher-scholars of the *hawza* joined together in an informal alliance whereby they met regularly to consult on issues of importance to the local Shi'a community of Iraq and issued joint statements on contemporary political and social issues.

On Sistani's website, he has been depicted facing the shrine of Imam 'Ali in Najaf, a connection being drawn between his position as guide for the Shi'ites and inheritor of the charismatic leadership of the Imam. Moving to Bashir Al-Najafi, a similar juxtaposition is made. Again, on the homepage of Al-Fayyad the shrine of Imam 'Ali has been prominently displayed. Finally, the website of Al-Hakim has exhibited the same iconography. This usage of the image of the Imam 'Ali shrine in Najaf shows how the Shi'a transnational imagined religious community bases itself on the primary pilgrimage site of Shi'a Islam and the location of the premier centres for Shi'a religious education, the *hawzat*. It is also the site of a sprawling cemetery adjacent to the mosque called Wadi Al-Salam, or Valley of Peace. This cemetery is where many Shi'ites around the world have their corpses buried to be near the burial shrine for Imam 'Ali. Providing both powerful religious symbolism and an educational structure that legitimises religious elites,

Najaf remains the centre of the Shi'a imagined religious community, implementing a re-sacralisation of Shi'a Islamic historical symbols and texts. The combination of religious symbolism and web-based technology presents a combination of Appadurai's 'technoscapes', 'ideoscapes' and 'mediascapes' into one iterative process.

The similarity between the websites of these four authorities is not limited to image iconography. On each of these websites one can find a detailed intellectual biography of the individual. These biographical sections invariably detail the educational pedigree of each individual ayatollah, thus establishing their legitimacy as authoritative sources of emulation. Each website biography states that they were educated by famous twentieth-century scholar-teachers of the *hawza* such as Ayatollah Al-Khu'i (1899–1992) or Burujirdi (1875–1961), thus reinforcing their legitimacy (Al-Sistani 2019). In many cases, these biographies are accompanied by scanned copies of the *ijaza* certificates (permission to teach particular religious topics) that they received from various famous teachers in the *hawza*, further validating their claims to authority and authoritative educational pedigree.

All of their websites include a list of free downloadable writings authored by the individual *mujtahid*, easily accessible as PDF documents and zip files. These works focus on the study of Islamic jurisprudence, theology, hajj rituals and other subjects of Shi'a scholarship. By increasing access to these works, the *mujtahids* are attempting to internationalise their appeal, although, simultaneously, they are weakening their control over access to these sources of knowledge. No longer does a student need to travel to Najaf in order to gain this access. Instead the Internet 'technoscape' breaks down many of the traditional barriers: country/city; social classes; gender barriers.

The *mujtahids* historically fulfilled important roles as issuers of fatwas in response to specific questions from their constituents. On their websites, each ayatollah can receive virtual queries from their followers to which they respond within days or weeks (Sisler 2011). This serves to both spread their influence and simultaneously create a virtual version of their authority, again increasing their accessibility. Additionally, these *mujtahids* periodically intervene in local concerns of their communities through the issuance of online statements (*bayyanat*), which address specific events that affect their constituents. An example of this intervention occurred during the US invasion of Iraq, when Sistani's office called for his followers to participate in newly established electoral politics (Feldman 2005; Rahim 2005).

Yet, parallel to the emergence of methods mediation for spreading their messages and authority, the aforementioned *mujtahids* face unprecedented challenges from younger aspirants to religious authority. None in Iraq is more prominent than Muqtada Al-Sadr, scion of a respected scholarly family and leader of a youthful constituency. Al-Sadr rose to fame during the immediate aftermath of the US invasion of Iraq, when he immediately called for the withdrawal of foreign forces from Iraqi territory and commanded an armed militia that fought the US forces in Najaf in 2004. At the same time, Al-Sadr consciously represented himself within the framework of *hawza*-based authority, founded a publishing house, created Internet websites and an active social media presence, collected monetary and material donations, and oversaw the formation of a political bloc to run in successive Iraqi parliamentary elections (Bayless 2012; Cockburn 2008). Al-Sadr activated the pre-existent network of representatives (*wukala'*) who had been loyal to his father, Muhammad Sadiq Al-Sadr (1943–99). Thus, he had the ability to both raise and distribute funds over the Internet, undermining the financial system that privileged the power of the *wakils* who had sole authority to collect and redistribute the *khums* on behalf of the *marja'*, but also exploiting that historically established system to his benefit (Cole 2003; Plebani 2014). Like his senior *mujtahid* competitors, Al-Sadr utilises sacred iconography, such as images of the holy shrines in Karbala and Najaf, on his websites. Notably, he also incorporates imagery of his martyred father as well as his more-famous uncle Muhammad Baqir Al-Sadr (1935–80), making an explicit connection between their authority and his (Al-Sadr 2019).

Al-Sadr's challenge to the established authorities in Najaf represents Homi Bhaba's aforementioned hybridity effect, whereby the respect and scholarly acumen attributed to high ranking clerical figures is transferred to a much younger cleric, while restructuring the religious authority itself. This transference of authority indicates a structural and symbolic change in the landscape of Shi'a religious authority and is an outcome of mediatisation. References to younger clerics as *marja'* or ayatollah, something unthought of in past generations, becomes commonplace on social media websites. Mediatisation occurs as new religious institutions and centres have emerged to challenge pre-existing centres of authority, and Muqtada Al-Sadr is leading the way.

Case Study II: Sistani's *Khums* Collection and Redistribution as Actor-Network Development in Iran

This case study will show how Ayatollah Sistani has leveraged his use of the religious tithe called the *khums* to exert 'soft power' in his native country of Iran, largely through the conduit of his Internet network of sites. Historically, ayatollahs throughout the Shi'a diasporic communities have maintained financial autonomy from the ruling elites through the collection of a *khums* religious tithe equalling one-fifth of their annual profit after the deduction of expenses, directly from their Shi'a followers. Which ayatollah receives this *khums* is the choice of the individual believer, ostensibly based upon the perceived trustworthy character and intellectual acumen of the ayatollah. A follower can give his *khums* to the ayatollah directly in person, through donation boxes, temporary offices set up in Mecca during the hajj, or to one of his trusted representatives or representative organisations. It is the ayatollah's responsibility to then distribute this money back into the Shi'a community in the most effective way possible. This distribution can occur through religious educational institutions as well as other social service organisations such as clinics or subsidised housing. With an ever-expanding network of social services, educational facilities and information propagation, Ayatollah Sistani is cementing his status as a preeminent authority within Iran, where he has not resided since 1961 or visited since 2003.

Iran-based *marja'* have encountered increasing pressure from state authorities since the establishment of the Islamic Republic in 1979. The hybridised combination of political and religious authority in Iran has blurred the boundaries of religion and the state to the point that the *khums* is now partially subsumed under regulatory measures set in place by the Supreme Leader, 'Ali Khamenei. An example of this state intrusion is the Management Centre of the Seminary in Qom (formerly the Management Council of the Seminary), which keeps tabs on the financial assets of each individual ayatollah's office in Qom and the writings of individual teachers and students (Khalaji 2006: 26). If a student in the seminary does not adhere to Khomeini's interpretation of *wilayat al-faqih* or issues other statements that conflict with the office of the Supreme Leader, he may find that his monthly stipend is cut off by the Management Centre. The Iranian government under Khamenei has effectively brought the *khums*, a voluntary religious donation in the private sector, under state control. This process parallels Beatrice Hibou's description of the National Solidarity Fund (*Fonds de Solidarite Nationale*) in Tunisia in her book *The Force of Obedience* (2011). Hibou's analysis shows that what began as a voluntary private donation campaign in Tunisia has become obligatory and state-driven, allowing the state to exert control and patronage without taxation reform (Hibou 2011: 194–6). In the case of Tunisia, loyalty to the state replaces loyalty to a *marja'*. In Iran, since the *khums* is of fundamental importance to the establishment and perpetuation of an ayatollah's actor-network, state interference in *khums* collection and redistribution can interfere with the organic process of institution building that strengthens a *marja'*'s leadership. The state directs funds towards leaders who follow its vision for society and pressure them to appoint or support state-chosen successors in Iran. However, Sistani, who does not operate an official school in Iran and lives in Iraq, has avoided this oversight. Because he is outside of this state system, Sistani's activities in Iran have increased dramatically since the mid-1990s. His son-in-law and senior *wakil*, Jawad Shahrestani, was integral to his successful establishment of an actor-network in Iran. Shahrestani first moved to Iran in 1977 and established publishing and propagation centres under the title of the Al Al-Bayt Foundation in the early 1980s. Currently Sistani's monthly living stipends for students are the highest in Iranian centres of learning, even higher than those given by Supreme Leader Khamenei (Khalaji 2006). This indicates that Sistani receives more *khums* donations to redistribute into stipends, implying that he also has more followers than other clerics living in Iran.

He also funds many social service and educational institutions and information services in Iran including hospitals and clinics, refugee centres and research centres. One such institution is the Al Al-Bayt Global Information Centre. This centre consists of a complex set of linked Internet websites that are localised centres of information distribution and charitable contribution. These websites have individual website addresses. Sistani supported the establishment of the first part of this network in Qom in 1998, and thereafter has supported the creation of locally run websites in Najaf, Karbala, Kazimayn and Basra in Iraq, Shiraz, Tehran, Mashhad, Elam and Isfahan in Iran, Lahore and Karachi in Pakistan and websites in Turkey and Georgia, among others. They maintain online searchable Qur'an, *hadith* collections, *risalas* of leading *mujtahids*, commentaries, books about Shi'a-specific topics such as temporary marriage and *ta'ziya* rituals, online library catalogues, contact information for various *mujtahids* including their photographs when possible, interactive online forums for dialogue with the offices of various *mujtahids* and a variety of computer services (Al-Sistani 2019).

Sistani supports these and many other institutions in Iran through his collection and redistribution of *khums* income, leading to his increased local authority among his constituents in religio-social matters. Bakhshayeshi's biography of Sistani indicates that many thousands of Iranian tomans each month are spent in Iran on behalf of Sistani's organisation (Bakhshayeshi 2003). At the same time, Sistani is not dependent upon one single local constituency, because Sistani's reputation among the Shi'ites around the globe allows him to collect *khums* from a wider set of followers, increasing each year through Internet donations. Furthermore, by continually expanding the scope of his social and humanitarian services, he reinforces his self-representation as a pious individual, worthy of emulation and *khums*-contribution. This carefully cultivated self-representation has led to a self-perpetuating cycle of increased revenue from loyal followers and increased funding for various projects within Iran, despite Sistani's subtle opposition to the current structure of political authority there, as detailed in his interpretation of *wilayat al-faqih* (Al-Sistani 2019). In fact, a reputation for piety and asceticism in religious leadership is one very important component of Sistani's growing authority. Additionally, Sistani's representative, Shahrestani, has developed close ties with the various religious leaders in Iran and navigated the political authority structures with great skill.

Thus, the *khums*-collection/redistribution tool creates a client-patronage system that forms the underpinning of the ayatollah's authority and development of an actor-network within local and transnational Shi'a communities. In Iran, the office of the Supreme Leader Ayatollah Khamenei subsumed many of the prerogatives of this collection and redistribution process, but in various constituencies outside of Iran, the individual leaders continue to develop processes for collecting and redistributing the *khums*, as in the case of Sistani in Iraq or the late Sayyid Fadlallah in Lebanon. It is unknown how many devout Shi'ites follow Sistani as their *marja' al-taqlid* in Iran. Nevertheless, Sistani has funded and encouraged the development of a widespread network of social services and educational facilities that subtly challenges the perception of a monolithic clerical ruling class in Iran, and shows the religious institutional restructuring that can be enacted through mediatisation. Additionally, each aspect of the Sistani network fulfils the definition of 'actants' previously described in the aforementioned discussion on Latour's ANT theory.

Conclusion

The paradoxical results of the rise and use of the Internet 'technoscape' and 'mediascape' by Shi'a *mujtahids* both enhances their authority and simultaneously allows self-styled *mujtahids* to proliferate and diverse actor-networks to form. These leaders' websites have adhered to common conventions in content and presentation tied to historical forms of knowledge and iconography, what one would call a new mediation of sacred knowledge. Due to the nature of the new disjunctive global economy of culture, it is difficult to predict what forms these new actor-networks will take within Shi'a Islamic communities. Perhaps new social media technoscapes will create opportunities for younger and younger self-styled ayatollahs to challenge the hegemonic religious authority of Najaf. A thorough understanding of the impact of new media on Shi'a Islam must therefore be sensitive to the differences between new media and the various ways in which new media represent Shi'a Islam, transform or modify its religious content and symbolic forms, and move religious activities from one institution to another.

In this study, a framework has been developed to conceptualise the different ways new media could and already are changing Shi'a religious institutions. The developments are complex and do not necessarily have a uniform impact on Shi'a Islam. In some instances, new media may further a re-sacralisation of Shi'a Islam, as was seen in the employment of historical symbols and texts on the various *mujtahid* websites. Nevertheless, in other respects, new media undermines the authority of institutionalised Shi'a Islam. In a third instance, the economics of Shi'a Islam were employed to enact subtle social changes to create actor-networks in potentially hostile socio-political environments. At a general level, these processes share a common feature: they are all evidence of the mediatisation of Shi'a Islam. This dynamic process will undoubtedly continue to accelerate in the future, creating new actor-networks that may or may not remain tied to the centre–periphery dynamics of religious authority in Twelver Shi'a communities as it had developed in the nineteenth century. As Homi Bhabha (1990) notes in relation to the value of hybridity and cultural translation as an alternative positioning:

> for me the importance of hybridity is not to be able to trace two original moments from which the third emerges, rather hybridity to me is the 'third space' which enables other positions to emerge. This third space displaces the histories that constitute it, and sets up new structures of authority, new political initiatives, which are inadequately understood through received wisdom . . . The process of cultural hybridity gives rise to something different, something new and unrecognisable, a new area of negotiation of meaning and representation. (1990: 211)

Likewise, in the realm of new media and its impacts on religious institutions in Shi'a Islam, one can see the emergence of hybridity and a new 'third space' where tradition and innovation intersect through mediatisation and the formation of new actor-networks. It remains unclear if the impact of new media will solidify existing authority structures or challenge them in ways that reform the foundations of Twelver Shi'a Islam in the twenty-first century.

References

Anderson, Benedict (2006), *Imagined Communities: Reflections on the Origin and Spread of Nationalism*, London: Verso Books.
Appadurai, Arjun (1990), 'Disjuncture and difference in the global cultural economy', *Theory, Culture & Society* 7:2, 295–310.
Bakhshayeshi, Abdul al-Rahim Aghiqi (2003), *Faqih-e Varasteh*, Qom: Novid Islam.
Bayless, Leslie (2012), 'Who is Muqtada al-Sadr?', *Studies in Conflict & Terrorism* 35:2, 135–55.
Bhabha, Homi K. (1990), 'The Third Space: interview with Homi Bhabha', in J. Rutherford (ed.), *Identity: Community, Culture, Difference*, London: Lawrence and Wishart, pp. 207–21.
——— (1994), *The Location of Culture*, London: Routledge.

Cockburn, Patrick (2008), *Muqtada Al-Sadr and the Battle for the Future of Iraq*, New York: Simon and Schuster.

Cole, Juan (2003), 'The United States and Shi'ite religious factions in post-Ba'thist Iraq', *The Middle East Journal* October, 543–66.

Corboz, Elvire (2015), *Guardians of Shi'ism: Sacred Authority and Transnational Family Networks*, Edinburgh: Edinburgh University Press.

Eisenstein, Elizabeth (1979), *The Printing Press as an Agent of Change: Communications and Cultural Transformations in Early Modern Europe*, 2 vols, Cambridge: Cambridge University Press.

Feldman, Noah (2005), 'The democratic fatwa: Islam and democracy in the realm of constitutional politics', *Oklahoma Law Review* 58:1, 1–10.

Graham, Fuller E., and Rend Rahim Francke (1999), *The Arab Shia: The Forgotten Muslims*, New York: St Martin's Press.

Hibou, Beatrice (2011), *The Force of Obedience: The Political Economy of Repression in Tunisia*, Cambridge: Polity Press.

Hjarvard, Stig (2008), 'The mediatisation of religion: a theory of the media as agents of religious change', *Northern Lights: Film & Media Studies Yearbook* 6:1, 9–26.

Khalaji, Mehdi (2006), 'The Last Marja: Sistani and the end of traditional religious authority in Shiism', *The Washington Institute for Near East Policy*, Policy Report 59, Washington, DC: The Washington Institute for Near East Policy.

Latour, Bruno (2005), *Reassembling the Social: An Introduction to Actor-Network-Theory*, Oxford: Oxford University Press.

Louër, Laurence (2008), *Transnational Shia Politics: Religious and Political Networks in the Gulf*, New York: Columbia University Press.

Lundby, Knut (2013), 'Theoretical frameworks for approaching religion and new media', in H. Campbell (ed.), *Digital Religion: Understanding Religious Practice in New Media Worlds*, London: Routledge.

Mandaville, Peter G. (2001), *Transnational Muslim Politics: Reimagining the Umma*, London: Routledge.

Marcinkowski, Muhammad Ismail (2004), *Religion and Politics in Iraq: Muslim Shia Clerics Between Quietism and Resistance*, Singapore: Pustaka Nasional Pte.

Martín-Barbero, Jesús, and Elizabeth Fox (1993), *Communication, Culture and Hegemony: From the Media to Mediations*, London: Sage Publications.

Meyer, Birgit, and Annelies Moors (eds) (2006), *Religion, Media, and the Public Sphere*, Bloomington: Indiana University Press.

Momen, Moojan (1985), *An Introduction to Shi'i Islam: the History and Doctrines of Twelver Shi'ism*, New Haven: Yale University Press.

Mottahedeh, Roy (2014), *The Mantle of the Prophet*, London: Oneworld Publications.

Plebani, Andrea (2014), 'Muqtada Al-Sadr and his February 2014 declarations. Political disengagement or simple repositioning?', *Italian Institute for International Political Studies* 244, 1–11.

Rahim, Ahmad H. (2005), 'The Sistani factor', *Journal of Democracy* 16:3, 50–3.

Rahimi, Babak, and Elham Gheytanchi (2008), 'Iran's reformists and activists: internet exploiters', *Middle East Policy* 15:1, 46–59.

Al-Sadr, Sayyid Muqtada (2019), *The Official Website of the Private Office of His Eminence Sayyid Muqtada Al-Sadr*, available at: http://jawabna.com, last accessed 1 February 2019.

Scholz, Jan, Tobias Selge, Max Stille and Johannes Zimmermann (2008), 'Listening communities: some remarks on the construction of religious authority in Islamic podcasts', *Die Welt des Islam* 48:3/4, 457–509.

Schulz, Winfried (2004), 'Reconstructing mediatisation as an analytical concept', *European Journal of Communication* 19:1, 87–101.

Sisler, Vit (2011), 'Cyber counsellors: online fatwas, arbitration tribunals and the construction of Muslim identity in the UK', *Information, Communication & Society* 14:8, 1136–59.

Al-Sistani, Al-Sayyid 'Ali Al-Husseini (2019), *The Official Website of the Office of His Eminence Al-Sayyid Ali Al-Husseini Al-Sistani*, available at; www.sistani.org, last accessed 1 February 2019.

Sreberny, Annabelle, and Ali Mohammadi (1994), *Small Media, Big Revolution: Communication, Culture, and the Iranian Revolution*, Minneapolis: University of Minnesota Press.

Walbridge, Linda (2001), 'The counterreformation: becoming a marja' in the modern world', in Linda Walbridge (ed.), *The Most Learned of the Shi'a: The Institution of the Marja' Taqlid*, Oxford: Oxford University Press, pp. 230–46.

Williams, Raymond (1973), *The Country and the City*, London: Hogarth.

7

'STILL WE LONG FOR ZAYNAB': SOUTH ASIAN SHI'ITES AND TRANSNATIONAL HOMELANDS UNDER ATTACK

Noor Zehra Zaidi

Introduction

In April 2003, as stunning images of crowds congregating in Firdos Square in Baghdad to pull down Saddam Hussein's iconic statue beamed across the world, an unanticipated phenomenon was taking shape just further south. The American-led invasion was launched only a week after the tenth day of the Islamic month of Muharram – the day of commemoration for the martyrdom of Husayn ibn 'Ali, Shi'ism's third Imam, and his companions on the plains of Karbala in 680 CE (al-Modarresi 2014; Paton 2017). Almost immediately, the fall of Saddam Hussein led to an explosion in pilgrimage – or *ziyarat* – to the Shi'a holy shrine cities in Iraq, opening the doors for Shi'ites to visit sacred sites that had been closed to them for decades. *Ziyarat* to these Shi'a shrines was seen as a life-threatening activity for Iraqis under the Baath regime, and strict restrictions meant that few from outside Iraq were able to undertake the pilgrimage.[1] Yet in the weeks and months after the fall of Saddam Hussein, reports were published on the sea of pilgrims arriving in Iraq, undeterred by a still-lingering threat of instability, fostering the sense that Shi'a Muslims, so long deprived of the important centres of their narrative historiographies, could return 'home'. 'The pilgrims' path was walked in secret for over three decades. Hiding in alleyways and skirting fields, once a year Shi'ites would try to make their way to the holy city of Karbala under threat of arrest and persecution. But no more,' one report celebrated (Santora 2003: 11).

Indeed, the numbers back this sense of renewed vigour for *ziyarat* to Iraq, with many millions multiplying each year that passed. In April 2003, American news reported that up to 2 million people were converging on Karbala, though some senior clerics did not publicly perform rituals due to security concerns (Holgun 2003). By 2017, reports placed the numbers at up to 20 million pilgrims for the commemoration of Arba'in, which marks forty days after the death of Husayn ibn 'Ali.

As the volume of pilgrims arriving in Iraq grew, so too did the focus around the world on what pilgrimage and sacred sites mean to Shi'a Muslims. In particular, American newspapers – many of which were consumed by local American Shi'ites – revealed a mix of awe and confusion at the new spectacle emerging, one that had never been experienced or witnessed at such a scale. *Ziyarat* was labelled 'an extraordinary display of the raw power of Iraq's Shiites, the country's long repressed yet dominant sect' (Smith 2003: A1). From the front lines, journalists reported,

> The fall of Saddam Hussein has undammed a flood of Shiite Muslims . . . driven not by desire to fight Americans but by a religious devotion that United States soldiers here are finding hard to contain or even comprehend . . . 'We were expecting something like foreign fighters to get up from the spot and take potshots at us,' said Robert Robinson, 28, a sergeant from Columbus Miss. 'We didn't expect pilgrims to come for a better life or just to pray.' (Fisher 2003: A1)

For American Shi'ites, including both first- and second-generation South Asians, a new opportunity had been born – a chance to visit the shrines that the constructs of the modern nation state and the subsequent limits on mobility had denied. Now, possessing American passports that had previously made visits to Iraq near impossible, many young South Asian Shi'ites would capitalise on the massive growth in *ziyarat* tour operations and make a trip to 'rediscover' their 'roots'. Encouraged by English-speaking orators and by their experiences in Iraq, young South Asian Shi'ites would come to speak of these shrines as their displaced homelands, to articulate a sense of belonging to these distant *lieux de mémoire*, or sites of memory, as termed by Pierre Nora.²

The exhortation to undertake visitation to the shrines of Shi'a Imams would take on a renewed vigour in Muharram celebrations in Shi'a communities around the world, with orators outside Iraq and religious clerics within presenting *ziyarat* as an imperative, an act rooted in tradition that must be experienced to have a true understanding of the faith. The anthropologist Talal Asad has argued, Islam itself is a discursive tradition, a religion defined by discourses 'that seek to instruct practitioners regarding the correct form and purpose of a given practice, precisely because it is established, has a history' (2009: 14).³ *Ziyarat* was an act intrinsic to the story of Karbala itself, as the survivors of the event returned to the plains of Karbala forty days after Husayn ibn 'Ali's martyrdom, on Arba'in – and thus the ritual performance of this act has an authentic purpose and an established history, one rooted in the very early years of Islam. *Ziyarat* manuals enumerating centuries-old *ziyarat* narratives would be printed in mass quantities and then made widespread online, many outlining the benefits of *ziyarat* to Husayn ibn 'Ali that outweighed the blessings of hajj.⁴

The encouragement to perform *ziyarat* has a long theological and social history, as early Shi'a leaders sought to cement a distinct consciousness amongst their followers. According to historian Yitzhak Nakash, for Shi'a Muslims, the tragedy of Karbala and the commemoration of the events would become 'vital for reinforcing their distinct Shi'i identity and collective memory . . . to evoke every year the sorrow and memory of Karbala, and to transmit it to generations to come' (1993: 5).⁵ Since 2003, the large proliferation of pilgrimage groups has become central to this goal. For the *ziyarat* groups from the United States that have abounded in recent years, pilgrimage to Iraq has helped construct a collective memory in a diasporic community and inculcate a new generation in transnational ways of being Shi'a. Critically, it presented new ways for the *performance* of identity. The growth in *ziyarat*, paired with the background of geopolitical turmoil, has also presented a clear way of 'being sectarian', or practising sectarianism, as termed by Max Weiss (2010).⁶ For American Shi'ites, Iraq would once again become the heartland and imagined 'centre out there' of Shi'a Islam – a position Iran had long fashioned itself as.⁷ From Iraq would come images of throngs at the shrines of Husayn and his brother Abu Fadl 'Abbas ibn 'Ali, from where new orators would emerge to engage diasporic communities, moulded by the events unfolding in their homeland, and where the construction of Shi'a identity was being continuously reformed by groups travelling to and from the sacred shrines.⁸

This contribution explores the longing for Shi'a shrine cities amongst South Asian Twelver Shi'a communities in the United States, with a particular focus on Shi'a youth in New York and New Jersey.⁹ It analyses how, with the increased *ziyarat* opportunities and the expansion of tour groups to Iraq, Shi'a shrine cities have replaced the 'homeland' in the discourse of second-generation immigrants, young American Muslims who express deeper affinity to these shrines and their affairs than to the state of Shi'ites in their parents' native countries. These young Shi'ites strongly affirm that their 'home' is the United States, affirming what Avtar Brah (1996) termed 'the lived experience of a locality'. Yet in conversation they display a kind of 'homing desire' oriented towards these Shi'a shrine cities, positioning them as the 'mythic place of desire' and belonging (1996: 192). Like Seán McLoughlin, who explores how 'universal religions might create a homeland consciousness analogous to that of a diaspora', this chapter argues that the 'homing desire' for places beyond the nation state retains salience in this contemporary Muslim community (2010: 227). This sense of a homing desire directed at pilgrimage shrines – sites of collective memory – destabilises the notion of the nation state as the most self-evident unit of homeland consciousness.

This sense of longing and belonging for the Shi'a shrine cities is inextricably linked to movement – the ability to visit the imaginary 'centre out there', as coined by Victor Turner. The proliferation of pilgrimage groups allows these young South Asian American Muslims to position these shrines as symbolic and mythic sites of unity – even amongst those who have yet to visit these sites themselves. As explored by Eickelman and Piscatori, travel has been a central feature of Muslim identity and self-conception, and *ziyarat* and this current ease of mobility inspires changes 'in how Muslims conceive of and experience "Islam"' (1990: 3). Consequently, while they speak of oppression of Shi'ites as a universal concern, these young American Shi'ites are particularly concerned with affairs driven by the context of Middle Eastern current events in countries they have visited on *ziyarat* trips, spurred by a boom in popularity for Iraqi orators, many of whom accompany the most well-known pilgrimage groups.

The narrative of American South Asian Shi'ites' involvement with *ziyarat* is not a simple story of progressive ease, and the euphoria of the post-Saddam order would not last. From 2004, Iraq spiralled into sectarian violence, with militias cleansing neighbourhoods of opposing sects and waves of reprisals destabilising the country. In February 2006, Al-Qaeda in Iraq bombed the Al-'Askari shrine in Samarra, one of the holiest sites in Shi'a Islam, with fighting escalating in the aftermath. Beginning in 2011, increasing unrest in Syria would curtail visitation to the shrines of Zaynab bint 'Ali and Ruqayyah bint Husayn in Damascus. The shrine of Sayyeda Zaynab, built to honour the grave of Husayn's sister in the outskirts of Damascus, had in many ways been the most viable outlet for a transnational Shi'a consciousness in the decades that Iraq was under Baath party rule. The shrine's growth was spurred by a range of geopolitical fluctuations, allowing pilgrims from all over the world to access a site linked to the narrative of Karbala martyrology.[10] As the Syrian civil war devolved, however, the shrine would become a flashpoint of conflict between the ideologies of pro-government militias and Iranian Revolutionary Guards and Salafi-influenced opposition groups, caught within a transnational discourse increasingly focused on sectarianism. By June 2014, the group that self-declared as the Islamic State of Iraq and Syria (ISIS) was sweeping across vast swathes of Iraq and into Syria. ISIS explicitly threatened to destroy the shrines in the holy cities of Najaf and Karbala. On 31 January 2016, a series of suicide bombs killed over seventy people outside the Sayyeda Zaynab shrine in Damascus, Syria, and more attempts and bombs would follow.

These threats on *ziyarat* – both real and perceived – had a profound effect on how the Shi'a Muslims in this study thought about pilgrimage and themselves. The loss of the Sayyeda Zaynab shrine as a viable pilgrimage destination for Shi'a Muslims in the US is essential to understanding the complex ways that young Shi'ites long for the shrines of their 'history'. These simultaneous and contradictory narratives – of opening and reinvigoration and shuttering and destruction – has led to new and complex kinds of articulation of sectarianism in Shiʻa communities in the United States, one that has increasingly put them at odds with young Shiʻites in Iran and Iraq.

Tales of (Be)Longing

'There is no love more important than the love of Husayn', Zaki Haider proclaimed. A thirty-three-year-old financial analyst in New York City, Zaki describes himself as a 'secular, religious, but modern Shiʻa' – labels that seem to give him no pause or sense of contradiction. Indeed, as he spoke to me with his fiancée Shahida Kazmi, a twenty-seven-year-old lawyer who had recently passed the New York Bar Exam, the melding of 'new' and 'old' remains fluid. They explained their decision to travel to Iraq for *ziyarat* for their honeymoon as an unquestionably natural one, one that many young couples had undertaken in the first years of their marriage, despite how uncommon this practice would have been just a decade earlier. They joined an increasingly prominent tour group called Spiritual Journeys for their trip in Muharram 2014. Shahida explained,

> We know we'll take other trips together, *Insha'allah*. We'll do Europe, we'll go to a beach. But when you think the *bulava* [spiritual invitation for *ziyarat* believed to come from the Imams themselves] comes for you, we knew it was the first thing we had to do. We both have friends who did the same, [like] my cousin and his wife, and they all said to us 'you definitely have to go'.

The concept of *bulava* is not new amongst South Asian Shiʻa communities. The idea that a believer undertakes *ziyarat* at the preordained time determined for them by the Imams or God is a common concept, one that Zaki and Sakina's parents – from Multan and Karachi respectively – used in describing their decision to travel for hajj in 2001. Yet the practice of young couples performing *ziyarat* together in lieu of 'expected' vacation destinations is a recent trend, a function of new opportunities, social encouragement and financial ability. This development is reflected in the prevalence of hundreds of young South Asian Shiʻites comprising new *ziyarat* tour groups, all travelling for a variety of reasons yet finding a sense of commonality and community. The two found in the experience lifelong friends, they expressed, 'different people who were just like us, from London, Tanzania, Toronto . . .', Zaki stated.

'People might think it's strange to spend your honeymoon with hundreds of other strangers, but really we were with family.'[11]

That these two American-born young professionals could travel to a distant shrine to form bonds of solidarity that they *believed* negated all differences in region, heritage or experience involves, of course, a complex work of self-fashioning and collective memory. They expressed quite clearly that the pilgrimage enforced a sense of belonging to a place and with people far removed from their everyday lives, linking them to a kind of master narrative, as termed by Paul Connerton, into which individuals and communities can find meaning through their particular rituals and sub-narratives (see also Shanneik 2015). One can certainly question the universalising principle represented in the group, as the cost associated with undertaking a *ziyarat* at a younger age necessarily means it tailors to a class of upper-middle-class American and European Shi'ites. Spiritual Journeys, for example, is a relatively higher-end group, with costs that can range upwards of $3,000 per pilgrim. Yet that perceived sense of belonging in a transnational space amidst a diverse group of people cannot be discounted.

For Zahra Ahmed, her return trip to Karbala in 2015 was the fulfilment of a wish granted to her on her first *ziyarat* trip. She had visited Iraq and Iran in 2008 with her parents and younger sister with a group run by a long-established and more affordable tour operator based in Canada. The experience of being in Karbala left a powerful impact on her. She had spent nights at Husayn's shrine praying for intercession in a deeply personal manner, one she would not share but claims had finally been resolved to some peace. Nevertheless, the accommodations were a challenge for Zahra on her first trip, then twenty-four years old and recently graduated from the MBA programme at Rutgers Business School in New Brunswick. 'When I decided I wanted to go back, I knew I wanted to go with a better tour. I knew I wouldn't be worried about being alone once I was there,' she explained, indicating the advancement of her own personal status. 'You want to be comfortable, so I just looked for the best package. Knowing people doesn't really matter when you go to Karbala. Everyone feels like they belong together, and you meet and become close to people in your own group.' When questioned on the difference between the two visits, she claims, 'It's the same feeling as the first time. Maybe more. I really felt like our Imam was welcoming me back after all the years.' She paused, with tears forming in her eyes. 'I don't know if there's anywhere else in the world I can just go alone, but I never *felt* alone. I felt completely at home.'[12]

Thirty-two-year-old Jaffer Syed, who travelled to Iraq with his younger brother during Arba'in in 2016, gave an explanation that similarly illustrates the co-influential bonds that exist between young Shi'ites in the region. He explained that they signed up for the trip because 'so many of our friends have gone and told us that it was an amazing experience'. This most common of behavioral factors – the suggestion of close friends – led them to sign up with this group, led by Ammar Nakshawani, a dynamic young British-Iraqi orator who has gained a significant popularity in young Shi'a communities worldwide. None of their close friends had signed up for the trip, nor did anyone else from their family travel with them. It mattered little to them. 'We felt as if we were home,' Jaffer stated. Mohammad, his brother, added, 'You don't miss anyone when you're in Najaf or Karbala. It's just you and all the family you need is there.' They both admitted that they did not regularly pray *salat* (the obligatory prayers Muslims are told to perform five times a day) in their daily lives but prayed extensively at the shrines at the appointed hours; immersed in the daily rituals of pilgrimage, listening to English lectures, spending nights doing *matam* (ritual beating of chests set to lamentation poetry) and praying, they felt they had returned home. 'Sometimes I forgot it was only my first trip there,' Jaffer noted wistfully.

> I don't usually cry, but on our last trip to do *salam* to Hazrat Abbas (brother of Husayn ibn 'Ali), I couldn't stop crying. Everyone else was too. You feel like you're leaving your home and your heart there and you don't know when you'll come back.'[13]

The frequent use of 'home', the themes of longing and belonging is reflected in the older generation of South Asian Shi'ites, but as they speak of the homelands they left in India and Pakistan. Though they built their homes in the United States through struggle and sacrifice, many recalled with some nostalgia the language and culture of their homelands. Their attempts to inculcate the same loyalties in their children, however, have been met with mixed success. Many of the young Shi'ites who were interviewed have made multiple family trips to South Asia, and many understand or can speak

Urdu to varying degrees of fluency. They acknowledged, however, that when they long for a place, it is not the places of their parents' birth, places many had visited with more frequency than Iraq.[14] Instead, time and again they expressed that the places for which they long, where they feel a deep and oft-unexpected connection to, which they consider their 'homelands' are the shrine cities of Iraq. Many noted this explicitly. Like her parents and extended family, Mahjabeen Ali, twenty-two, is an active member of her local religious centre, Astaana-e-Zehra, participating in community picnics and fundraisers, youth programmes, Ramadan sessions and more. Fluent in Urdu and wearing the hijab, Mahjabeen shared that she had wanted to travel for *ziyarat* for years, sensing that her experience commemorating Karbala is not complete without the awareness of one who has walked those same streets. 'I think I feel the way about Karbala that my mom feels about Hyderabad,' she admitted. 'And I've never been there!' In this comparison Mahjabeen made explicit the replacement of the first generation's 'home' with the longing for the 'home' of Iraq. 'Every year on *chehlum* [Arba'in] when we do our *alvida'i matam* [final lamentation], I just cry and pray that next Muharram will be the year I'll go, *insha'allah*.' It is a longing to be complete that propels this desire, because 'just imaging Karbala is painful, but being there, in the heart of it, is what makes you really understand. I know how I feel now isn't the complete feeling.'[15] It is a sentiment that is echoed in numerous conversations with young Shi'ites who have yet to take the trip: the sense that *ziyarat* is an imminent desire, one that needs not be constrained by the bonds of current relationships because the transnational sense of belonging creates a sense of homecoming, of truly understanding what it means to be Shi'a. If there is a place 'out there' that these young Shi'ites feel tethered to, it is not the forgotten homelands of their parents' childhoods, but the distant shrines of Iraq – sites that are just as foreign but seem intimate, shrines many have just imagined thus far.

What is most critical in these exchanges is an emerging picture of what this focus on *ziyarat* says about issues of race, language and authenticity in young South Asian Shi'a consciousness. The replacement of the 'centre' in the young diasporic consciousness from cities in Pakistan and India to gold-domed shrines in Iraq has ties to both practical and geopolitical circumstances. The most obvious factor remains the displacement of diaspora languages, with all their various regional linguistic variations, and the adoption of English (or local vernaculars) as the central medium of communication in the assimilation process. As young Shiʻites have consciously moved into public spaces, such as the *jaloos* processions in New York City on the tenth of Muharram, an outward-oriented communicative focus, embodied by campaigns such as 'Who is Hussain?', has transformed Urdu or Hindi into a perceived 'traditional' or limited mode of communication.[16]

While geopolitical shifts have played a role in this new way of 'being sectarian' as termed by Weiss, the move of religious practice over the last two decades from private domestic spaces (where it still exists in fervour) to institutionalised spaces has also contributed significantly. Older *imambargahs* (congregational spaces for Shiʻa rituals) that were established in converted churches or old buildings are being replaced by centres built solely to accommodate their Shiʻa communities, marked as aesthetically Islamic centres. This move is not unique to the United States, with art historian Kishwar Rizvi (2015) arguing the vast expansion in transnational mosque building is rooted in new ideological agendas of Islam, sponsored by Saudi Arabia, Iran, Turkey and the United Arab Emirates. From *madrasas* in Indonesia to green-domed corner mosques in Pakistan, the prolific growth in religiously designated spaces continues. In New Jersey and New York, the largest construction project was completed with the opening of the Masjid-e-Ali centre, a large and technologically advanced complex to accommodate multiple lectures in different languages beamed across different rooms, boasting a full array of services, from daily prayer congregations and Sunday religious school to wedding receptions and burial preparation facilities.[17] Most notable was the board's decision to label the site a *masjid* – a term they argue has become co-opted by Sunni Muslims in their critique of Shiʻism. '[Sunnis] claim that Shiʻas only talk about ʻAli, but do not pray *namaz* or read Qurʼan. We didn't want to call it an *imambargah*. We wanted it to be known as a *masjid* and for it to function like a *masjid*.'[18] The space eschews many of the ornamental adornments of a distinctly Shiʻa space – markers that have come to be conflated with an Iranian Safavid era aesthetic, visual cues that Rizvi argues 'unifies the diverse communities of Shiʻi Islam' but 'also singles those monuments out for desecration and destruction' (2015: 129). At Masjid-e-Ali, along with other older Shiʻa centres, young Shiʻites are using these community spaces to advance a collective consciousness, from concerns about Islamophobia to interfaith efforts, holding question-and-answer sessions with young orators and scholars, and more. The co-option of religious institutions for a range of social and political purposes is part of a new way that young Shi'a Muslims in the region articulate and embody being sectarian. Yet these interactions are also happening beyond just traditional *imambargahs* and in the broader public sphere, or what Pnina Werbner terms 'a series of interconnected spaces in which the pleasures and predicaments of diaspora are debated and celebrated' (2002: 15). For example, the popular lecturer Ammar Nakshawani presented a talk at Rutgers University in 2014 entitled 'Karbala: past, present, future', an event sponsored by the Rutgers Ahl al-Bayt Student Association and attended by an overflowing auditorium of young Shi'a Muslims (and many of their parents) from across the region. The invocation of the Karbala paradigm, as termed by Michael Fischer, and discussions on how it remains uniquely salient in the current context in a public university setting speaks to broadened avenues in which young Shi'ites have understood what 'being Shi'a' and behaving in a sectarian manner means.[19]

This sense of Karbala as the 'authentic' homeland for a generation of South Asians who primarily only have experiences of living within the United States is equally tied to the explosion of popularity of young Arab or Iraqi orators such as Ammar Nakshawani, figures that are making an impact in English on a global scale. While the focus internationally and politically has long been on Iranian influence in transnational Shi'ism, amongst Shi'a communities in New York and New Jersey, one can see the limits of the Iranian influence and appeal and the concurrent reassertion of Iraqi clerical authority and training.[20] The names of Ammar Nakshawani, Sheikh Mohammad Al-Hilli, Hussain Al-Nashed, Mahdi Al-Modarresi, and others have gained vast following – all young scholars and lecturers who have received varying degree of formal *hawza* training but have made a mark internationally with their English lectures. Their Iraqi backgrounds endow them a cultural and spiritual capital and sense of authenticity, yet they have largely been socialised in Western contexts, living and lecturing in the UK, the US or Australia. Thus, they move easily between a Western Shi'a diaspora and their Iraqi homeland, a lived history of movement and multiple belongings that allows young Shi'a Muslims to relate to their experiences.

The popularity and demand for these young Iraqis has made them the large draws internationally during Ramadan and Muharram commemorations, with crowds estimated at over 1,500 when Ammar Nakshawani speaks at Masjid-e-Ali, the newest and largest Shiʻa centre in New Jersey. Syed Mahdi Al-Modarresi, a nephew of Grand Ayatollah Mohammad Taqi Al-Modarresi, is a founder of Ahlul-Bayt TV, the first international English-based television channel for Shiʻa programming. While these orators bring an engaging command of English, gain salience through their historical knowledge, share the same socio-cultural socialisation in the West as many of these respondents, and target issues that face young Shiʻa Muslims, they are also quite distinctly products of unfolding geopolitical circumstances that have redefined sectarianism and what 'being Shiʻa' means in the current world. They emphasise an approach to practice that is equally concerned with how the faith is perceived externally – a reaction to Wahhabi and Salafi critiques of Shiʻism as overly superstitious or even embracing *bidʻah* (innovation or heresy) and contemporary Western portrayals of Islam as reactionary. They engage with socio-cultural issues and debates, encourage engagement with other religious and political communities, and in particular call for young Shiʻites to view themselves as ambassadors of a kind of tolerant and outward-facing religion. Unlike the rote or 'traditional' Islam that respondents identify in Urdu, Hyderabadi, or other vernacular-speaking mosques, the use of English by these orators opens up a more cosmopolitan consciousness, presenting religion as a modern and assimilating force.[21]

For young South Asian Shiʻites, these figures are critical in the growth in *ziyarat* to Iraqi shrines, seen as a visible display of Shiʻa identity and solidarity in the face of ISIS and Salafi threats across the region. The influence that these speeches have had in decisions to undertake *ziyarat* is a recurrent theme in conversations with young Shiʻites. 'Listening to Syed Ammar is what made me decide to go to Karbala,' explains Abbas Jafri of his decision to join Nakshawani's Spiritual Journeys group, echoing a sentiment expressed across multiple religious centres.[22] '[It's] part of what makes you a Shiʻa.' For many of these young Iraqi scholars and orators who live their own deterritorialising diasporic experience, the construction of Iraqi shrine cities as the broader Shiʻa homeland is a natural step for what is, in fact, their homeland. Through the words of these speakers, the desires of these young Shiʻites, the collective experience of travelling to and from these shrines, and the rituals and narratives oriented towards these shrines that position them as repositories of collective Shi'a memory, these shrine cities become critical *lieux de mémoire* for this community.

This encouragement is not limited to those lecturers that travel to these communities. According to Grand Ayatollah Mohammad Sa'id Al-Hakim, one of the most senior religious authorities in Shi'a Islam, Iraq has been the true centre of Shi'ism since the time of 'Ali ibn Abu Talib's caliphate in Kufa. Al-Hakim is one of the four leading grand *marja'* (source of emulation amongst religious clerics) based in Najaf and the only Iraqi amongst the group. In conversation, he explained that Shi'ism has spread far from its roots, like the branches of a great tree. Yet the further from this centre Shi'ism spreads, the more necessary it was for its adherents to return to its roots and retain a connection to Iraq, he claimed.[23] The clerical establishment in Najaf, the oldest and most revered centre of Shi'a learning, remains extraordinarily responsive to establishing connections with foreign pilgrims. Despite his advanced age and often failing health, the most senior Grand Ayatollah, Sayyid 'Ali Al-Sistani, will spend hours daily throughout the months of Muharram and Safar and through the rest of the year meeting hundreds of pilgrimage groups, allowing many thousands of Shi'ites the opportunity to feel a personal connection to him. His message to groups from the United States in particular has remained consistent: integrate into society, be productive and law-abiding citizens, emphasise both religious and secular education, but to always maintain the link and importance of *ziyarat*.[24] The calls from the 'centre', therefore, reinforce the 'homing desire' for these young Muslims, re-affirming that they are, in fact, linked to these shrines across time and space.

Yet these scholars are quick to argue that they do not emphasise *ziyarat* to the detriment of other essential requirements of Islam, a critique they feel is often levelled against Shi'ites. As one popular Iraqi orator argues,

> If you ask me 'should I go to Hajj or go to visit the grave of Imam Husayn (AS), it is not an answer I can give. There is place for each . . . But for many years the lovers of the *ahl al-Bayt* could not visit these holy shrines, and it is my duty to remind our *mu'minin* (believers) that it is incumbent on us that

we do not leave them empty, because this is what the enemies of our Imams desire. Daesh wants to destroy them, but we do not fear them.[25]

Noticeably, the answer is not unequivocally that hajj is the mandatory pilgrimage for all Muslims. Instead, the answer retains an implicit warning that pilgrims should not allow themselves to be dissuaded from *ziyarat*. He equates the current threats on the shrine by ISIS and its allies – a distinctly modern phenomena – with the enemies of the Imams across a broad temporal range. The desire to defend the shrines, to keep visiting them in the face of opposition, and to think of them as a kind of collective homeland is reflected in the urgency with which young people speak of *ziyarat*, something not found when asked about hajj. Indeed, some interviewees expressed that they had a lifetime to complete hajj and saw it as a task for their later years. The perceived threat to the shrines of Iraq remained a real consideration. 'We don't know how long it will even be possible to go to Karbala. Something could happen to them tomorrow, God forbid,' one female Pakistani lawyer in New York City argued.[26]

This quasi-'return' to the Arab 'root' of Shi'ism, with its increased emphasis on Iraqi shrines and internal politics, raises broader questions of how and in what ways sectarianism has infiltrated into the American consciousness. Young Shi'ites are influenced by and express a growing sense that they are a community under siege transnationally, even if not locally. For example, multiple Shi'a youth within the communities that I spoke to referenced Ammar Nakshawani's lecture on ISIS, delivered in Muharram 2014, as central to their understanding of the current conflict. In it, Nakshawani ties the current iteration of anti-Shi'a violence to a long historical trajectory of Shi'a martyrology, tracing the ideological roots of ISIS to opponents of 'Ali ibn Abi Talib and the early Shi'a. He creates a genealogy of ISIS, tying together Surah Buruj of the Qur'an (ch. 85), the Prophet Muhammad's warnings to 'Ali about those amongst the early Muslims who fast, pray and recite the Qur'an but never embrace its spirit, those that Nakshawani terms 'early ISIS' amidst 'Ali's opponents at the Battle of Nahrawan. He also includes the anti-Shi'a zeal of influential pre-modern Sunni scholars such as Ibn Taymiyya (1263–1328) and Ibn Al-Qayyim Al-Jawziyya (1292–1350) and links them to the Saudi family's deal with Muhammad ibn 'Abd Al-Wahhab and the disinclination of the Shi'a to believe in a caliphate and unjust rulers. In essence, he ties the current geopolitical climate inextricably to the time of the Imams (Nakshawani 2014). Hence, the struggle becomes one as old as Shi'ism itself, invoking Nakshawani to argue that those that opposed 'Ali were the direct ancestors of the current ISIS ranks.

Underscoring all of this is a very present political concern: the influence of Saudi Arabia and its Salafi theology on anti-Shi'a forces and the attempts to turn Iraq and Syria into battlegrounds over authentic Islam. Mehek Ali travelled to Iraq in December 2015 with her parents, at a time when joint Iraqi forces were launching attacks to retake cities from ISIS control. On Friday, the bodies of Iraqi soldiers would arrive for burial at the Imam 'Ali shrine in Najaf, a scene that pilgrims could not avoid. She described, 'there were just so many bodies, just white bodies on the ground on all these lines, and all their mothers crying and screaming. I will never, ever forget that sight and hearing those mothers.'[27]

This is an image that many religious scholars in Najaf hope Shi'ites from around the world will carry with them. The images of Iraqi soldiers and volunteers, 'martyrs' in the fight against ISIS, line the entire walk from Najaf to Karbala, a path that millions walk on the days of Arba'in. Billboards with portraits of dead soldiers are ubiquitous through Karbala and Najaf, a constant reminder of the huge cost of war. A senior cleric in Najaf admitted, 'We do want people to see these pictures. They should remember how many of our people died so that *zuwwar* (pilgrims) can visit in peace.'[28] For those pilgrims from the United States that live removed from those daily threats and who travel in relative security for *ziyarat*, it is a purposeful reminder that their safety and comfort was hard won. Those images of lost soldiers left a deep impact on the Shi'ites that were interviewed, as they were meant to.

Thus, for young Shi'a Muslims in these communities in the United States, sectarian identity has come to the forefront and been redefined. The combination of the emphasis on English and outward communicative strategies, the rise and popularity of diasporic scholars and orators over the 'older guard' of Iranians, the appeal of their approach that emphasises history and discourse over mysticism, and the social influence in the sense of urgency to complete *ziyarat* has transformed how many of them see themselves. There is a distinct sense that these young people identify assertively as Shi'ites, seek new associational bonds based on this identity, yet have rejected the Iranian- or South Asian-dominated configurations of what this has meant in the past.²⁹ The idea of Iran as a theocracy or the concept of *velayet-e faqih* is removed from how these young Shi'ites orient themselves politically, and for many, South Asia was more distant, more 'foreign'. Few have visited their parent's homelands with any regularity, but even amongst those who had made the trip, the feeling of being an outsider in a place they were meant to 'belong' was acute. As a result, young South Asian Shi'ites routinely admitted that they were more tuned in to bomb attacks on shrines in the Middle East and ISIS threats against Shi'ites than they were to the routine attacks and target killings of Shi'ites in Pakistan.³⁰ For many, *ziyarat* has approximated the sixth pillar of Islam, a central tenet of the faith, and the Iraqi shrines have replaced the homelands of their parents as the sites they feel an inherent sense of belonging to. As *lieux de mémoire*, these shrines have taken on special symbolic and functional valence as sites that hold the collective memory of believers and places towards which these Shi'ites can orient.

Ironically, this sense of sectarian identification puts many of these respondents at odds with their co-religionists within Iraq. Iraqi political culture has increasingly come to downplay sectarianism as the central component of national identity. Religious clerics, politicians and ordinary Iraqis alike in the post-ISIS era have increasingly begun to speak of the need to construct a broader vision of Iraqi nationalism; Iraqis even in the shrine cities express that sectarian ties alone do not define their identity nor their relationship with the state (Zaidi 2018). Sectarian loyalty has also diminished as a driving factor in electoral behaviour (Haddad 2019). Thus, even as these young South Asian Shi'ites feel more intensely the 'homing desire' for Iraq and the Shi'a shrine cities that capture their sense of collective memory, Iraqis in that context have expressed reservations with the notion that being Shi'a is enough to capture loyalty.

Umm al-Masa'ib

Simultaneous to advocating for *ziyarat* to Iraq as essential to 'being Shi'a' in the face of growing threats, however, is a continuous effort to remind communities of the 'home' that is lost to them – the Sayyeda Zaynab shrine in Damascus, caught in the crossfires of the Syrian civil war. In many ways, the longing for Zaynab and a shrine under attack functions as a trope for a community who believe that their ancient enemies have returned again. The Karbala paradigm provides Shi'ites a framework for understanding the current geopolitical contours and internalising the notion of a faith besieged – a threat that now extends to their beloved shrines.

In a question-and-answer session held for youth in a South Asian Shi'ite centre in 2015, a popular Iraqi orator outlined what has become a common theme amongst Shi'a Muslims – that ISIS and extremist Sunni groups' attacks on the Sayyeda Zaynab shrine was a direct parallel to the events of *al-sham* in the Karbala tragedy and thus an issue that should animate all Shi'ites.[31] As Zaynab was unveiled and yet triumphant, so too have Yazid's descendants – ISIS – sought to destroy her again, this time by targeting her holy grave. Yet again the forces of Yazid would not be successful, with the Shi'a of the world ready to defend Zaynab shrine and her honour, he proclaimed. 'Again we see *umm al-masa'ib* alone in *sham*!' he lamented in the prayer at the end of the session.

> But this time, oh Sayeda, you are not alone! We call to you, oh Sayyeda, let us be among the ones who defend your holy shrine, as we could not be there to sacrifice ourselves for your Husayn, nor in the court of Yazid the drunkard when your veil was ripped from you![32]

There are obvious gendered tropes at work here with the description of Zaynab as *umm al-masa'ib*, the mother of hardships, and the link drawn between Zaynab's forced unveiling and ISIS attacks on her shrine. Narratives of Zaynab's life and character had undergone a shift through the 1970s, as she would be positioned rhetorically as the twin face of Husayn's revolution. 'One must choose: either blood or the message,' Ali Shari'ati (1981), the famed ideologue of the Iranian Revolution, had argued in a series of lectures on martyrdom given in 1972. To die would be to be as Husayn; to live like the women of Karbala and spread the message of true Islam would be to carry on Zaynab's work. In this way, *ziyarat* to the shrine of Sayyeda Zaynab was inextricably linked to *ziyarat* to Karbala – a feeling reflected in conversations with these young Shi'ites. Syed Naqvi, a member of a popular group of *noha-khaans* (reciters of rhythmic lamentation poetry) said, 'We all know *ziyarat* isn't really complete if we can't go to Sham (Damascus) . . . Our Bibi (Zaynab) is the other half of Karbala. But we've all done *niyat* (taken a vow) that *insha'allah* when [it] opens again we'll be the first ones there.'[33] From Maryam Ali, a thirty-one-year-old business intelligence analyst, came a striking statement of the charged valences these shrines have taken on: 'Bibi Zaynab's shrine is just as home to us as Imam Husayn's. No one has forgotten that. If anything, it makes the need to go to Karbala stronger.'[34] Despite the spiritual intentions, the limits of geopolitics remained a painful consideration. These South Asian Shi'ites expressed both worry for security in Damascus and fear of profiling in the United States if they travelled to Syria under the Trump administration's travel restrictions.

The construction of the shrine of Sayyeda Zaynab as a 'lost' homeland reveals the same complex processes at work in discussions of Iraqi shrine cities. The Sayyeda Zaynab shrine itself is a distinctly modern one, constructed, expanded and promoted in the age of the nation state and governed by the Syrian Murtadha family, caretakers who claim to be descendants of the Imams and who have controlled the shrine's *waqf* since the thirteenth century. In the mid-twentieth century, the site received moral and theological backing from the great Shi'a *marja'* Muhsin Al-Amin (1867–1952), a widely respected jurist who sought to coalesce and 'reform' the Shi'a community under French Mandate. The Sayyeda Zaynab shrine provided an opportunity to promote a Shi'a site that was uniquely compatible with Arab and Syrian sentiments. Yet waves of refugees, transnational Shi'a networks such as the Shiraziyyin, and Iran's increasing influence transformed the demographics and aesthetics of the shrine, now a sprawling complex marked as an unmistakably Shi'a site in the style of Persian Safavid architecture (see Zaidi 2015). There is a real tension over the question of 'heritage' and authenticity at the shrine, yet for many Shi'ites it became a centre of displaced Shi'ites longing to commemorate Karbala when Iraqi shrines were closed. That South Asian Shi'ites would consider it a 'home' equal to that of Husayn's shrine in Karbala is further complicated by the civil war in Syria. The strange alliances at play on the ground has placed Shi'ites in the position of supporting those that defend the shrine along with Iran's Revolutionary Guards – namely Bashar Al-Assad and his Russian allies. For these young Shi'a Muslims, being sectarian also means navigating these unsavory alliances, wanting to fully condemn ISIS for their attacks on Shi'a shrines but avoiding a full-throated support of the regime – or its Russian allies. All those that were interviewed avoided a defence of Assad, though many pointed out the United States' hypocritical stand in the leaders that they support in the Middle East. Many acknowledge that he remains a better option for Shi'a Muslims than ISIS, even while condemning his human rights' violations; most claim they shy away from grappling with the political connotations of the current conflict, remaining focused on their concern for the shrines in Syria. As Pnina Werbner argues, 'none of the social unities we evoke – identity, diaspora, community, nation, tradition – are consensus-based wholes; all are the products of ongoing debates and political struggles' (2002: 18). For these South Asian Shi'ites, claiming a stake in the conflict in Syria means negotiating with the broader geopolitical implications of the conflict, debating with each other about how to balance different identities.

Nevertheless, the concern for the Sayyeda Zaynab shrine as part of young South Asian Shi'ites' focus on sectarianism and the ramifications of events in the Middle East remains. 'It was the most fulfilling experience of my life to travel to Karbala,' says Ahsan Naqvi, one of the leaders of the *Anjumane Nawjawanane Ali Akber* (a collective group of *noha* reciters). 'But still we long for Zaynab.' For young Shi'a Muslims, the process of imagining themselves in relation to the 'heart' of Shi'ism remains an ongoing process.

References

Alidina, Shaikh Murtaza (2019), 'The philosophy of Ziyarat & its details', available at: http://www.duas.org/downloads/Philosophy_Ziarat_Alidina.pdf, last accessed 15 May 2019.

Asad, Talal (2009), 'The idea of an anthropology of Islam', *Qui Parle* 17:2 (Spring/Summer), 1–30.

Brah, Avtar (1996), *Cartographies of Diaspora: Contesting Identities*, London: Routledge.

Deeb, Lara (2006), *An Enchanted Modern: Gender and Public Piety in Shi'i Lebanon*, Princeton: Princeton University Press.

Eickelman, Dale F., and James Piscatori (1990) (eds), *Muslim Travellers: Pilgrimage, Migration and the Religious Imagination*, Berkeley: University of California Press, 1990.

Fischer, Michael (1980), *Iran: From Religious Dispute to Revolution*, Cambridge, MA: Harvard University Press.

Fisher, Ian (2003), 'Resolute Iranian pilgrims meet awed G.I.'s', *The New York Times*, 7 October 2003, A1.

Haddad, Fanar (2019), 'The waning relevance of the Sunni-Shia divide', *The Century Foundation Report*, 10 April 2019, available at: https://tcf.org/content/report/waning-relevance-sunni-shia-divide/, last accessed 15 May 2019.

Holgun, Jaime (2003), 'Shiites' holy march to Karbala', *CBS News*, 22 April 2003, available at: http://www.cbsnews.com/news/shiites-holy-march-to-karbala/, last accessed 15 April 2016.

McLoughlin, Seán (2010), 'Muslim travellers: home, the ummah and British-Pakistanis', in K. Knott and S. McLoughlin (eds), *Diasporas: Concepts, Intersections, Identities*, New York: Zed Books, pp. 223–9.

Masjid-e-Ali (2015), 'A glimpse into Masjid-e-Ali, NJ', 31 December 2015, available at: https://www.youtube.com/watch?v=aeD3OY_upNY, last accessed 15 May 2019.

Mervin, Sabrina (1996), 'Sayyida Zaynab: Bainlieu de Damas ou nouvelle ville sainte chiite?', *Cahiers d'etudes sur la Mediterranée orientale et le mode turco-iranien* 22, 149–62.

Al-Modarresi, Sayed Mahdi (2014), 'World's biggest pilgrimage now under way, and why you've never heard of it', *Huffington Post*, 24 November 2014, available at: http://www.huffingtonpost.co.uk/sayed-mahdi-almodarresi/arbaeen-pilgrimage_b_6203756.html, last accessed 12 December 2017.

Modood, Tariq (2005), *Multicultural Politics: Racism, Ethnicity and Muslims in Britain*, Edinburgh: Edinburgh University Press.

Nakash, Yitzhak (1993), 'An attempt to trace the origin of the rituals of 'Ashura'', *Die Welt des Islams* 33:2, 161–81.

––––––– (2003), *The Shi'is of Iraq*, Princeton: Princeton University Press.

Nakshawani, Syed Ammar (2014), 'Ammar Naqshawani on Takfiri Deobandi Wahhabi Salafi ISIS Daesh', 1 November 2014, available at: https://www.youtube.com/watch?v=FrKdhTMC1v0, last accessed 15 May 2019.

Nasr, Vali (2006), 'When Shiites rise', *Foreign Affairs*, available at: https://www.foreignaffairs.com/articles/iran/2006-07-01/when-shiites-rise, last accessed 15 May 2019.

Nora, Pierre (1999), *Rethinking France: Les Lieux de Mémoire, Volume 1: The State*, Chicago: University of Chicago Press.

Paton, Callum (2017), 'After ISIS defeat, millions of Shiite Muslims make world's largest pilgrimage in Iraq', *Newsweek*, 25 November 2017, available at http://www.newsweek.com/iraq-after-isis-defeat-millions-shiite-muslims-make-worlds-largest-pilgrimage-721470, last accessed 12 December 2017.

Al-Qummi, Ibn Qulawayh (2004), *Kamil al-Ziyarat*, New York: Al Khoei Foundation.

Rizvi, Kishwar (2015), *The Transnational Mosque: Architecture and Historical Memory in the Contemporary Middle East*, Chapel Hill: University of North Carolina Press.

Santora, Marc (2003), 'Once risky pilgrimage is forbidden no more', *The Times of India*, 21 April 2003.

Shaery-Eisenlohr, Roschanack (2007), 'Imagining Shi'ite Iran: transnationalism and religious authenticity in the Muslim world', *Iranian Studies* 40:1, 17–35.

—— (2008), *Shi'ite Lebanon: Transnational Religion and the Making of National Identities*, New York: Columbia University Press.

Shanneik, Yafa (2015), 'Remembering Karbala in the diaspora: religious rituals among Iraqi Shii women in Ireland', *Religion*, 45:1, 89–102.

—— (2017), 'Shia marriage practices: Karbala as *lieux de mémoire* in London', *Social Sciences* 6:3, 100.

Shari'ati, Ali (1981), *Martyrdom: Arise and Bear Witness*, Tehran: Ministry of Islamic Guidance.

Smith, Crai (2003), 'Elated Shiites, on pilgrimage, want U.S. out: huge numbers attend long-banned rites', *The New York Times*, 22 April 2003, A1.

Szanto, Edith (2012), 'Following Sayyeda Zaynab: Twelver Shi'ism in contemporary Syria', PhD diss., University of Toronto, Toronto.

Turner, Victor (1973), 'The center out there: pilgrim's goal', *History of Religions* 12:3, 191–230.

Weiss, Max (2010), *In the Shadow of Sectarianism: Law, Shi'ism, and the Making of Modern Lebanon*, Cambridge, MA: Harvard University Press.

Werbner, Pnina (2002), *Imagined Diasporas Among Manchester Muslims: The Public Performance of Transnational Pakistani Identity Politics*, Oxford: James Currey.

Who is Hussain (2019), available at: www.whoishussain.org, last accessed 15 May 2019.

Zaidi, Noor Zehra (2015), 'The Prophet's Other Messengers: Sayyida Zaynab, Bibi Pak Daman and the Construction on Shiite Sacred Geography', PhD diss. Philadelphia: University of Pennsylvania.

—— (2018), 'From Shi'as to Iraqis, and Pakistanis to Shi'as: nationalism, transnationalism and sectarianism in modern Iraq', *Conference on Rethinking Nationalism, Sectarianism and Ethno-Religious Mobilisation in the Middle East*, University of Oxford, 27 January 2018.

8

FROM A MARGINALISED RELIGIOUS COMMUNITY IN IRAN TO A GOVERNMENT-SANCTIONED PUBLIC INTEREST FOUNDATION IN PARIS: REMARKS ON THE 'OSTAD ELAHI FOUNDATION'

Roswitha Badry

Introduction

Over the past decades, the reformist (*maktabi*) branch of Iranian Ahl-e Haqq (Yaresan) has undergone a stupendous metamorphosis that, although showing similarities with other former *ghulat* groups, nevertheless seems to be unique. The transformation process started three generations ago in Iran with the writing down of the community's religious tenets, which had previously been transmitted orally. It was Nur Ali Elahi (d. 1974), called 'Ostad Elahi' by his admirers, who was mainly responsible for reconciling the doctrines of the Ahl-e Haqq with Twelver Shi'a Islam by placing them in the context of the esoteric Shi'a. Subsequently, his son Bahram Elahi (b. 1931) gave his father's teachings a universal dimension by publishing books in French for the growing Western community and by establishing the Ostad Elahi Foundation in Paris (2000) that is said to teach 'ethics and human solidarity' according to Nur Ali Elahi's concepts. The Foundation was even granted NGO special consultative status with the United Nations Economic and Social Council (ECOSOC). This contribution will focus on the web presentation, the activities and networks of the Foundation. It will be argued that the community has tried to benefit from a booming Western interest in esotericism and a global ethos.

The Challenges of Modernity

Since the nineteenth century the MENA region (Middle East and North Africa) has witnessed a series of reform and social movements that have tried to come to terms with the challenges posed by Western colonial interventions (including missionary efforts), state efforts at modernisation, and the influx of new secular ideologies. In time, other hitherto marginalised religious groups were also certain to react to these challenges in order to adapt their tenets of belief to the altered socio-political and cultural conditions, and to reposition themselves in the emerging modernised society and state.

The so-called *ghulat*, or extreme Shi'a communities[1] (Turkish Alevis, Syrian Alawites/Nusayris, Ahl-e Haqq, henceforth AH), offer a particularly interesting example. Over centuries they were accused of heresy or even worse of polytheism, excluded and/or oppressed by the mainstream religion. They lived for the most part in remote areas, in secluded communities, and preserved their orally transmitted esoteric, gnostic teachings and secret rituals, which by tradition were only available to the initiated. With the advent of modernity, it became clear to some segments of the communities that they had to modify their belief system at least partially, if it was to be meaningful and relevant in the new contexts.

The transformation and self-identification process was mainly promoted by educated members of the communities and went through various stages that started in earnest in the twentieth century. As a result, some groups managed to gain new visibility. However, this transformation and re-positioning must be considered as still unfinished since re-interpretation of religious heritage and cultural identity is an ongoing process that correlates with changing historical and social contexts. Adaptations, modifications and re-adjustments to new conditions have not been unanimously accepted, and it has to be kept in mind that the respective communities are heterogeneous and far from being one unit. The initial transformation came as a result of greater access to (secular) education, of migration to urban cities, of writing down religious tenets which had earlier been transmitted orally, and subsequently reformulated, and in response to the rising demand among the intellectual elite for individualisation. A further development occurred in the contexts of diaspora, where the communities were and are in competition with a plurality of other religious positions.

This contribution is about the reformist (*maktabi*) branch of Iranian AH[2] which, despite similarities with other *ghulat*, has undergone a metamorphosis over the past decades that is unique. The transformation has to be seen against the background of serious challenges in Iran since the mid-nineteenth century, among them the emergence of new religions (Babis, Baha'is), of popular social movements (Tobacco Protest, Constitutional Revolution), the rise and fall of the Pahlavi dynasty with its ambitious modernisation programme, and finally the Islamic Revolution with the establishment of the Islamic Republic. At the same time, Iran has been exposed to divergent external interferences, first by European colonial powers (Britain, Russia), then by the USA.

Much research has been done on the Iranian AH,[3] and the development of the reformist branch has also been dealt with in several articles by Ziba Mir-Hosseini (1994b, 1997). Therefore, I will focus on the most recent phase since the establishment of the 'Ostad Elahi Foundation' in Paris.

Remarks on the Historical Background of the Ahl-e Haqq: Origins and Development until the Twentieth Century

Ahl-e Haqq, literally 'people of truth', are primarily found in western Iran (in Luristan, Kurdistan and Azerbaijan) and in some regions of northeastern Iraq. Their preferred self-designation in Iran is Yaresan,[4] while in Iraq they are usually referred to as Kaka'is.[5] Origin, development and categorisation of the AH are subjects of controversy, not only among scholars but also among adherents and sympathisers or supporters of the group. The traditional narrative of the religious community, which up to the twentieth century was preserved in the form of orally transmitted religious poems (*kalam*, mainly in Gurani Kurdish language), offers a mythical and legendary description of its history, without attaching great value to chronology or to a coherent and systematic account. To outsiders, the belief system of the AH resembles a mixture of pre-Islamic (*inter alia* Zoroastrian)[6] and Islamic (above all Shi'ite and Sufi) elements. Cardinal doctrines and rituals are inconsistent with mainstream Islam (Geranpayeh 2007: 4, 7), among them the belief in a series of consecutive divine incarnations in human form, each of them accompanied by four or five helper angels (During 2005), also in the transmigration of souls (Freitag 1985: 259–60)[7] with the aim of purification and lastly perfection of the soul, and the non-observance of the main pillars of Islam. Despite divergent opinions on the origin, all observers agree on the eminent importance of Sultan Sehak (variant readings Sohak, Sahak, Ishaq) to all AH subgroups (Mokri 1997; Moosa 1988: 214–23). This historical figure (who flourished most probably in the late fourteenth or early fifteenth century, that means at a time when many popular Sufi groups appeared) is revered as the fourth great theophany and regarded as the founder of the specific Sufi path (*maslak*) of the AH. Compared to Sultan Sehak, 'Ali ibn Abi Talib, the first Shi'a Imam, plays only a minor role, though he is seen as the second manifestation of God (Moosa 1988: 245–54).

Traditionally, a hierarchy of ritual specialists called *seyyeds* (a hereditary and endogamous class of eleven lineages[8] known as *khandan*, literally 'family', 'dynasty') and subordinate religious experts (including commoners) are responsible for the initiation ceremony and other rituals[9] and for preserving and transmitting the *kalams*. The relationship between *seyyed* and initiated commoner is similar to the *pir-murid* (master-disciple) relationship in Sufi brotherhoods, and the *seyyeds* receive annual religious dues from their adherents; also, intermarriage is taboo (Leezenberg 1997: 166–7; Mir-Hosseini 1994a: 271). Followers of the various families constitute sub-communities of the AH with minor differences in belief and religious ceremonies (van Bruinessen 2013). Up to the twentieth century, the faith was restricted to those born into the community.

As a result of both the obscure history and the organisational structure of the AH, the community may be (self-)identified as a separate religion (*din, madhhab*) (BBC Persian 2015), a particular branch of Shi'a religion, a specific Islamic spiritual path or a distinct ritual of Sufi (Dervish) brotherhoods.[10]

The Crystallisation of the Reformist (*Maktabi*) Branch

The transformation process in the twentieth century initiated by the Elahi family can be summarised as passing through three stages, which went hand in hand with an increasing opening up to the outside world. The growing visibility was accompanied by a change in the use of media, of strategy, methodology, the clientele or audience addressed, and a progressive evolution of the teachings. The latter included the negation and/or modification of original traditions.¹¹

Hajj Ne'matollah Jayhunabadi (1871–1920), the father of Nur Ali Elahi (1895–1974), born a commoner, started his reform with a challenge to the traditional authorities. After a severe illness and a kind of spiritual rebirth, he felt obliged, 'by God's command' and as the 'messenger of the Lord of the Hour',¹² to unify the diverse subgroups of the AH. A contemporaneous Christian missionary reports that Ne'matollah twice proclaimed the speedy advent of the Lord (Stead 1932: 188–9; see also Mir-Hosseini 1997: 182; Moosa 1988: 208). After this failed to be realised, he retreated and gave up his claims to leadership. However, he dedicated the remaining years of his life to writing down the secrets of the AH in Persian in a more systematic way, though his methodology, literary style and argumentation is considered rather traditional. These manuscripts (*Shahnama-ye haqiqat*, *Forqan al-akhbar*) were not published within his lifetime, but he seems to have taught their content to a growing number of followers.¹³

The second stage began in the early 1960s when his son, later referred to as 'Ostad (Master) Elahi' by his admirers, attempted to reconcile the AH teachings with the mainstream dogma of Twelver Shi'a Islam and to present the AH as a Shi'a mystical order whose adherents follow the *shari'a*. His methodology is related to the standard type of justification used by Shi'a scholarship (Qur'an, *hadith*, *ijtihad*), and he re-interpreted (or ignored) allegedly heretical elements of the AH belief. His Persian publications, *Borhan al-haqq* (1963)¹⁴ and *Ma'refat al-ruh* (1969),¹⁵ are characterised by a tendency to objectification and adjustment to the socially conditioned verbal practices of the contemporary religious discourse. A major focus of both works is on the refutation of 'misunderstandings', 'distortions' and 'false accusations' with respect to two principles that have always been regarded as core doctrines of the AH: the belief in the seven incarnations of the Deity and metempsychosis. The first is held to be the place of Manifestations of God – the state attained when one ('the saint') reaches the level of *haqiqat* (truth of reality), the last stage on the mystical path following *shari'at*, *tariqat*, and *ma'rifat* (knowledge of God). Accordingly, the author claims that the AH's belief in the soul donning a series of 'garments' should not be confused with the doctrine of transmigration of souls. Moreover, Sultan Sehak is not only the founder of the AH Sufi order but also identified as a descendent of the eighth Shi'a Imam. In contrast to his father, Nur Ali Elahi[16] had given up his secluded life as an ascetic in 1920 to pursue his studies in Kermanshah, Qom and Tehran. After completing his legal studies in 1933, he started a career as a judge and prosecutor in different parts of the country. His retirement in 1957 enabled him to devote his energies to writing and guiding his growing number of disciples and supporters, among them new converts – middle-class Tehranis with a non-AH background. He composed commentaries, notes and glosses on his father's works and authored the aforementioned 'Proof of the Truth' and 'Knowledge of the Soul'. According to experts of his works, a complete picture of his understanding of AH doctrine requires the inclusion of his unpublished writings in Gurani, intended to be read only by AH initiates. However, even his posthumously published statements (*Asrar al-haqq* 1991, 2 vols) 'are not consistently marked by a concern for a conformity with Shi'ite Islam' (Algar 1998).

The innovations in the third phase are credited to Bahram Elahi (born 1931) who after medical studies in France returned to Iran in 1964 in order to teach *inter alia* at the University of Tehran and (subsequent to a 'spiritual transformation') to fulfil his mission to guide others in the tradition of his 'Master', that is, his father. He not only compiled the above-mentioned pronouncements of his father but also authored two books in French for supporters in the West: *La voie de la perfection* (1976) and *Le chemin de la lumière* (1985).[17] Both books were later translated into English (1987, 1993; 1993), though with substantial alterations. The English versions as well as further translations into other European languages helped to spread Ostad Elahi's thought to wider circles. Bahram Elahi gave the teachings of his father, who is now presented as the last manifestation of the divine essence, a universal dimension, and his texts show 'the influence of both traditional Sufi literature and contemporary Western self-awareness manuals' (Mir-Hosseini 1997: 190). Thus, he deems the esoteric dimension of every 'true religion' to be 'unique and the same for all', however different in terms of their exoteric dimensions. Finally, he established the Ostad Elahi Foundation in Paris (2000) that is said to teach 'ethics and human solidarity' according to Nur Ali Elahi's concepts. The short biography on the Foundation's website informs us that the President has spent the past years either in Europe or in the USA, being engaged in translating his father's work and in lecturing at French and American universities. Meanwhile, he has published further books[18] that try to represent spirituality as a precise and experimental science.

The Establishment of the Foundation (2000)

On the occasion of its tenth anniversary, the *Fondation Ostad Elahi – éthique et solidarité humaine* produced a video documentary on the formation process of the organisation, its aims, activities and collaborations (Fondation Ostad Elahi 2016b). In fact, the short film merely summarises the content of the website, but it is nevertheless instructive because of the persons interviewed. Several prominent persons who were involved in some way or another in the process of establishing the Foundation and its later acceptance as a non-governmental organisation with special consultative status to ECOSOC express their admiration for Ostad Elahi and the Foundation inspired by his philosophy. They attest to the originality of the thoughts of this 'great spiritual figure' and 'sage'. According to the statements of the members and supporters, the idea of establishing a foundation surfaced in 1995 when devotees of the Ostad arranged ceremonies of commemoration in Paris (and also in London, New York and Los Angeles) on the centenary of his birth. Apart from an exhibition,[19] followers in Paris organised a symposium at the Sorbonne entitled *Le Spirituel: Pluralité et Unité* to which, for instance, James W. Morris, a renowned specialist in the field of classical Islamic mysticism and translator of *Ma'rifat al-ruh* into English (2007, 2009), contributed with a paper on the different aspects of Ostad Elahi's spiritual teaching (Morris 1996).[20] Finally, following the application for recognition as a public interest foundation (*fondation reconnue d'utilité publique*) and a long process of review, the 'Ostad Elahi Foundation – Ethics and Human Solidarity' received the required official approval and came into being by decree of the Prime Minister and Minister of the Interior of France on 27 January 2000.

Self-presentation of the Foundation on its Website

The official website (Fondation Ostad Elahi 2016a) provides information on the general profile of the Foundation, its status, aims ('mission'), activities, collaborations and publications. The website is bilingual, English and French, though details – for example on the conferences, workshops, publications –

and a list of (national and international) partners are only given in French. As the full title of the institution already indicates, its main objective is the advancement of individual, practical ethics in different contexts (family, education, work, business, and so on), in order to promote better understanding and 'true solidarity' among human beings. Although the Foundation states that it is inspired by the ethical concept of its eponym, and indeed propagates his ideas (in the reading of his son Bahram) in a number of publications, it insists that the intention is not to impose norms or rules, but rather to share practical experiences in an interdisciplinary and intercultural approach. Therefore, it organises conferences, seminars, research projects, and/or cooperates with educational institutions in the preparation of teaching units (didactic modules).

Decision on the activities is taken by the Board of Directors. After their ratification, the managing or executive director is responsible for their implementation. The Board of Directors consists of ten members (the only members of the organisation): the 'Charter Members' include the President Bahram Elahi, his wife Minou[21] and his younger brother Chakhrokh (born 1950), an ophthalmic surgeon, practising in France. The Advisory Body comprises three representatives: one non-permanent of the Ministry of the Interior, and two long-standing members, representing the Council of Europe[22] and Sorbonne University[23] respectively. The other members of the board (two women and two men) are leading experts in various fields (business, finances, social affairs, media, and so on) with connections to national and international authorities and institutions. The vice president of the Foundation, Maria Camilla Pallavinci, who belongs to a prominent family of Italian nobility and manages several companies, deserves particular mention.

Since 2000 and 2002, the Foundation has organised conferences whose aim is to reflect on and deepen knowledge on ethical, spiritual and cultural values that may promote tolerance and reconciliation. The topics of the annual conferences are mentioned (in English and French) and hyperlinks lead to additional information (only in French) on the programme and publication of the conference proceedings. Although the website is regularly updated, it is conspicuous that since 2012 no more 'Study Days', which were, as explicitly said, open to the public, seem to have been held. By contrast, the 'Days of Human Solidarity', an initiative that came up in response to the terrorist attacks of 11 September 2001 in the USA, had been organised annually since 2002, but the last entry on the English-language website is for 2013 whereas the French was updated until 2015. In addition, videos of the 'Study Days' since 2008 are available on the 'Web TV of the Foundation'. Another important field of activities relates to 'Research and Education in (applied) Ethics'. In collaboration with several other institutions, among them French, Swiss and Canadian higher institutes of learning, teaching modules on ethics are developed and implemented, books are published (for example, the 'Daily Ethics Series, based on public lectures that are delivered on seminars organised by the foundation'), and biennial prizes for teaching and research in ethics are awarded (fourth edition in 2014). With regard to its involvement with ECOSOC, the website points to 'round tables' that the Foundation has organised since 2006 (until 2013) in order to contribute to the Council's work. As a result, the Foundation was granted the special consultative status with ECOSOC in July 2008. Similar to the number of French public interest foundations,[24] the number of NGOs which have attained consultative status has been steadily increasing since the beginning of the 1990s. Whereas in 1946, only forty-one NGOs were granted consultative status by the Council, the number jumped to more than 700 in 1992 (UN-ECOSOC 2011) and (in 2014) to more than 4,000 organisations, most of them (2,926) in special consultative status (far fewer in 'general consultative status' and about a fourth on the 'roster status'; UN-ECOSOC 2014). The application process and main requirements to be fulfilled by potential candidates are outlined in a brochure entitled 'Working with ECOSOC: an NGOs Guide to Consultative Status' (UN-ECOSOC 2011). Apart from 'a transparent and democratic decision-making mechanism and a democratically adopted constitution, . . . a representative structure, appropriate mechanisms for accountability', and so on (UN-ECOSOC 2011), an NGO to be eligible for a special consultative status is required to have 'a special competence in, and are concerned specifically with, only a few of the fields of activity covered by ECOSOC' (UN-ECOSOC 2011). It comes as no surprise that the Ostad Elahi Foundation in its profile on the 'Integrated Civil Society Organizations System' has expanded its 'areas of expertise and fields of activity' in a way that complies better with the objectives of ECOSOC. In addition, it lists a number of the UN 'Millennium Development Goals' it supports (UN-ECOSOC 2016a). Up to the end of April 2016, the Ostad Elahi Foundation has submitted several statements to ECOSOC (2011: 19–20, 22–3). However, the required quadrennial report (UN-ECOSOC 2011: 37–9), which the Foundation should have submitted in June 2012 (a new report would be necessary in mid-2016), is neither available on its website nor on the 'CSO Net'.[25]

At the end of this short description of the website, one may ask: and what about the AH? No (explicit)[26] reference is made to the AH anywhere on the website, even under the section headed 'Who was Ostad Elahi' who is depicted as 'a philosopher, theologian, and musician' who was born 'to a family of notables'. Only if a visitor desires more information on the person, will he or she be lead to the official website of Ostad Elahi (2016)[27] and will find, for instance, the information, that AH literally means 'Devotees of the Truth' and that 'among the great figures of this mystical and religious order was Hadj Nematollah, Ostad Elahi's father'. In the same place, under the entry 'Philosophy' of Ostad Elahi, which is said to be 'comprehensive' and to have been influenced by 'Greco-Persian Philosophy and Persian Mysticism', AH culture is defined as 'a specific mystical Kurdish culture'. In this context, we also find a reference to 'Greco-Islamic philosophy', whereas otherwise connections to Islam are ignored.

Critical Evaluation of the Foundation's Website and Links

The Foundation makes obvious efforts to represent itself as an enlightened, progressive,[28] humanist (During 1998: 123–4), secular and open-minded organisation, a vanguard of a modern, rational and ethical approach to religion or spirituality. However, an analysis of its website (including the hyperlinks) raises several questions.

Foundations are often accused of lack of transparency, paucity of information, insufficiency, particularism, paternalism, amateurism,[29] and so on (Jensen 2013: 107–9). The same seems to be true in the case of the Ostad Elahi Foundation. Due to the limited space available to me, I will name just a few examples: the first concerns the funding structure. French law requires a public interest foundation to have an endowment sufficient to enable the organisation to fulfil its intended purpose. The law does not stipulate a minimum endowment or amount. However, it is often cited that in practice a minimum of one million Euro 'is necessary to guarantee a stable and steady stream of income to a public utility foundation' (France, Council on Foundations 2015). ECOSOC, for its part, emphasises that it 'does not provide funding or financial support of any kind to any organization which it partners. However, social networking at ECOSOC events allows organizations to expand their contacts . . . to explore possible partnerships and joint ventures with various stakeholders' (UN-ECOSOC 2011: 7). In its profile on the 'Integrated Civil Society Organization System' the Ostad Elahi Foundation makes the following specification on their funding structure: 'Foreign and international grants, donations and grants from domestic sources', as well as (unspecified) 'royalties' (UN-ECOSOC 2016b). Compared to the profiles of other civil society organisations working with ECOSOC, the last-mentioned resource is unusual. Does the term include the religious dues paid by the 'initiated commoner' to his *sayyid-pir* responsible for his initiation?

The second point concerns missing details or confusing statements on the aims of the Foundation, and the overstatements about the eponym and other spiritual figures of the Elahi family. Much of the information available on the website and hyperlinks is vague and full of redundancies. No definition for ethics is given, there is no differentiation between norms, principles or values, and the relation between spirituality, religion, philosophy and mysticism remains obscure. To the outsider, the explanations often turn out to be either utterly banal or unintelligible. Under the heading 'Presentation of the Foundation' (with the same content as under 'Home'), for instance, we find a note on 'the awareness that human life continues after our physical death – an assumption that is now the subject of serious scientific investigation . . .' (Fondation Ostad Elahi 2016a). This and other remarks on 'natural' (also referred to as 'authentic') spirituality are only comprehensible when we take Elahi's conception of the stages of the 'perfection of the soul' and the (original) AH tenets on reincarnation and transmigration of souls into account, which Nur Ali Elahi had re-interpreted in his books in Persian in order to prove the compatibility of AH belief with Twelver Shi'a Islam. With respect to a major field of the Foundation's activities, that is teaching ethics, one would expect to hear something about the effects and/or difficulties experienced in practice when trying to convey ethical principles. Moreover, the question arises of whether an ambitious project of cultivating 'a universally shared body of knowledge on ethics' (Fondation Ostad Elahi 2016a) does not need an outreach to the grassroots level, that is, the wider public. Limiting the 'mission' and discussions to expert panels and tiny elite circles does not seem to be very helpful, and making an appeal for an 'ethics devoid of all self-interest' is rather unlikely to succeed in our times.

Thirdly, there are several omissions and inconsistencies in the self-presentation. On the one hand, these are due to the character of the writings of Ostad Elahi, including the contradictions between the books in Persian and those in Kurdish language, which had been posthumously edited and published. On the other hand, the omissions and inconsistencies are the result of the ambitious goal of the Foundation to take his works as the basis of a shared esoteric essence of all religions. This project necessarily and unavoidably leads to a shortened presentation of Ostad Elahi's views, mostly consisting of easily understandable ethical principles and maxims that fit the main objective. In this respect, it is interesting to have a look at the description and selected excerpts of the works of the eponym. Moreover, it is conspicuous that among the partners and affiliations with other organisations there is no mention whatsoever of the Nour Foundation in New York, a public charitable and non-governmental organisation founded in 1985. This foundation, which attained special consultative status with ECOSOC in 2009, has similar objectives to those of the Ostad Elahi Foundation and also claims that its conception 'was inspired by the inclusive philosophy of the late Ostad Elahi' (Nour Foundation 2016). The only indication of the existence of the predecessor and affiliate of the Ostad Elahi Foundation is made on the official site of Ostad Elahi – though at the very end of links to resources on his works (Foundation Ostad Elahi 2016a). Hence, the relation between both foundations is far from being clear. Does the discreet mention of the Nour Foundation point to a rivalry and different orientation between the two foundations, or is it intended to disguise more complex interconnections and further networks?

In general, both foundations highlight the fact that the dissemination of ethical (or spiritual) values, a strategy they support, is needed to address major problems of contemporary societies, but by failing to address how this new ethical awareness will generate 'true solidarity', the focus is kept on the strategy and by extension on the foundation itself as provider of this strategy. Though they emphasise that they only want to offer a forum for discussions and research on ethics and/or spirituality, the ideas of Ostad Elahi (and his relatives)[30] – in the reading of Bahram and other members of the Foundation – are so omnipresent that this claim is somewhat hard to believe. What is more, in the postmodern perspective there is no absolute version of reality, no absolute truth, because religious truth is highly subjective and resides within the individual.

Contextualisation and Concluding Remarks

It can be argued that the Ostad Elahi Foundation has tried to benefit from a booming Western interest in esotericism (Hammer 2009: 2–5) as well as from initiatives to formulate a global ethos. With regard to the first mentioned phenomenon, several scholars speak of a 'spiritual revolution' (Jankowski 2002: 70; see also Heelas and Woodhead 2005; Tacey 2004). The recent public interest in the spirit is explained as a reaction to the crisis and erosion of traditional religious institutions, the rise of fundamentalisms, especially in the three monotheisms, and the surge in materialism, inhumanity and economic rationalism. This increased fascination with the spiritual is set within a (postmodern) cultural context characterised by a subjective turning away from life as obligation to something like established authorities and towards an emphasis on inner, personal sources of meaning, significance and authority (Heelas and Woodhead 2005: 2–7; Jankowski 2002: 71; Tacey 2004: 2–5). The market offers a multitude of competing products – spirituality without religion and without God as well as various forms of neo-spirituality, among them neo-Sufism and neo-Kabbalah, which are all severed from their respective traditional framework (Laude 2013: 5). On the other hand, the past decades have seen various efforts to promote the universal values shared by all religions. In the early 1990s, the Swiss Catholic priest, theologian and prolific author Hans Küng (b. 1928) initiated a project called 'World Ethos' ('Global Ethics'),[31] which attempts to describe what the world's religions already have in common (binding values and standards such as the 'Golden Rule';[32] Morris 1996: 140). In his opinion, an awareness of this common basis is a precondition to contribute to the peace of humankind. Küng's ideas were integrated in the document 'Towards a Global Ethics: An

Initial Declaration' which was signed at the 1993 Parliament of the World's Religions by religious and spiritual leaders of the world. Later his project would culminate in the UN sponsored 'Dialogue Among Civilizations'. At the end of August 2000, 2,000 representatives of the world's faiths gathered at the UN in New York for a 'Millennium World Peace Summit' which led to the formation of the World Council of Religious Leaders, whose aim is to offer 'the collective wisdom and resources of the faith traditions towards the resolution of critical global problems', and thereby to support the work of the UN and its agencies 'in our common quest for peace' (World Council of Religious Leaders 2016). Further initiatives of the same organisation were launched in the following years.

Emphasising ethos and virtues in reflections on social issues has always appealed to very diverse thinkers. However, to believe that promoting universal ethics might solve the complex causes of our world's conflicts is going to remain a pipe dream. As long as the foundations and organisations mentioned are beneficiaries of the present global (hegemonic) system, they cannot generate more progressive, structural change. They are in fact impeding thorough social change. Even their often-standardised rhetoric – when describing their work and themselves in decidedly self-admiring, vainglorious terms – cannot obscure this fact.

Nevertheless, on the *zahir* level, their 'outer history', the transformation of the *maktabi* branch of the AH from a small splinter group in Iran to something like a missionary society with the ambition to disseminate their messages to the Western hemisphere, can be read as a success story, at least in the short run. However, outreach to the broader public included the breaking down of complex tenets of belief to uniform messages, hard to distinguish from other groups or associations with a similar agenda (at least for the outsider), and the adaptation to the national and/or international rules, agendas and strategies of performance. In the long run, this development may put the survival of the Foundation(s) at risk. The 'inner truth' of the Ostad Elahi Foundation, however, remains obscure, and is up to now only accessible to the insiders, the 'initiates', who may still adhere to some aspects of the original ideas of the AH.

References

Algar, Hamid, James W. Morris and Jean During (1998, last updated 2011), 'Elāhī, Ḥājj Nūr 'Alī: i. *Biography* and ii. *Teachings* and iii. *Music*', in *Encyclopaedia Iranica*, available at: www.iranicaonline.org, last accessed 11 January 2019.

BBC Persian (2015), 'Dar-khāst-e payravān-e 'Ahl-e Ḥaqq' az rahbar-e Irān barāy-e bāz-negari dar qānun-e asāsi', 20 March 2015, available at: http://www.bbc.com/persian/iran/2015/03/150320_|45_yaresan_khamenei_letter, last accessed 3 December 2015.

Bruinessen, Martin van (2013), 'Ahl-i Ḥaqq', in *Encyclopaedia of Islam Three*, available at: http://referenceworks.brillonline.com/entries/encyclopaedia-of-islam-3/ahl-i-haqq-COM_22840, last accessed 11 January 2019.

Delshad, Farshid (ed., trans.) (2013), *Nūr 'Alī Elāhī: Ma'refat al-Rūḥ – Zur Erkenntnis der Seele. Eine persische Schrift zur Mystik aus dem 20. Jahrhundert. Übersetzung und Kommentar*, Berlin: Schwarz.

During, Jean (1997), 'Le système des offrandes dans la tradition Ahl-e Haqq', in K. Kehl-Bodrogi, B. Kellner-Heinkele and A. Otter-Beaujean (eds), *Syncretistic Religious Communities in the Near East*, Leiden: Brill, pp. 49–64.

—— (1998), 'A critical survey on Ahl-e Haqq Studies in Europe and Iran', in T. Olsson, E. Özdalga and C. Raudvere (eds), *Alevi Identity: Cultural, Religious and Social Perspectives*, Richmond: Curzon, pp. 105–26.

—— (2005), 'Notes sur l'angéologie Ahl-e Haqq', in G. Veinstein (ed.), *Syncrétismes et hérésies dans l'Orient seldjoukide et ottoman (XIVe–XVIIIe siècle)*, Paris: Peeters, pp. 129–52.

Floor, Willem (2009, last updated 2012), 'Judicial and legal systems: v. judicial system in the 20th century', in *Encyclopaedia Iranica*, available at: www.iranicaonline.org, last accessed 28 April 2016.

Fondation Ostad Elahi (2016a), *Fondation Ostad Elahi – Ethique et solidarité humaine (Paris)*, website, available at: http://www.fondationostadelahi.com/, last accessed 28 April 2016.

—— (2016b), *10ème anniversaire de la Fondation Ostad Elahi*, film réalisé à l'occasion du 10ème anniversaire de la Fondation Ostad Elahi – éthique et solidarité humaine, available at: https://www.youtube.com/watch?v=oFG-9Ra6upU, last accessed 29 March 2016.

France, Council on Foundations (2015), 'France – current as of July 2015', available at: http://www.cof.org/content/france, last accessed 11 March 2016.

Freitag, Rainer (1985), *Seelenwanderungslehren in der islamischen Häresie*, Berlin: Schwarz.

Geranpayeh, Behrouz (2007), 'Yaristan – Die Freunde der Wahrheit. Religion und Texte einer vorderasiatischen Glaubensgemeinschaft', PhD diss., University of Göttingen, Göttingen (submitted 2006, published 2007), available at: http://hdl.handle.net/11858/00-1735-0000-000D-F224-9, last accessed 15 April 2016.

Halm, Heinz (1982), *Die islamische Gnosis: Die extreme Schia und die ʿAlawiten*, Zurich: Artemis.

—— (1984, last updated 2011), 'Ahl-e Ḥaqq', in *Encyclopaedia Iranica*, available at: www.iranicaonline.org, last accessed 15 April 2016.

—— (2001, last updated 2012), 'Ḡolāt', in *Encyclopaedia Iranica*, available at: www.iranicaonline.org, last accessed 15 April 2016.

Hammer, Olav (2009), 'Esotericism in new religious movements', in J. R. Lewis (ed.), *The Oxford Handbook of New Religious Movements*, Oxford: Oxford University Press, pp. 1–24, available at http://www.oxfordhandbooks.com, last accessed 15 April 2016.

Hamzeh'ee, M. Reza (1990), *The Yaresan: A Sociological, Historical and Religio-Historical Study of a Kurdish Community*, Berlin: Schwarz.

—— (1997), 'Methodological notes on interdisciplinary research on Near Eastern religious minorities', in K. Kehl-Bodrogi, B. Kellner-Heinkele and A. Otter-Beaujean (eds), *Syncretistic Religious Communities in the Near East*, Leiden: Brill, pp. 101–17.

—— (2009a, last updated 2011), 'Ahl-e Ḥaqq: ii. Initiation Ritual', in *Encyclopaedia Iranica*, available at: www.iranicaonline.org, last accessed 15 April 2016.

—— (2009b), 'Kurdische Religionen und die Authentizität ihrer oralen Traditionen', in C. Allison, A. Joisten-Pruschke and A. Wendtland (eds), *From Daēnā to Dîn: Religion, Kultur und Sprache in der iranischen Welt. Festschrift für Philip Kreyenbroek zum 60. Geburtstag*, Wiesbaden: Harrassowitz, pp. 321–31.

Heelas, Paul, and Linda Woodhead (2005), *The Spiritual Revolution: Why Religion is Giving Way to Spirituality*, Malden, MA: Blackwell.

Hodgson, M. G. S. (1965, first published online 2012), 'Ghulāt', in *The Encyclopaedia of Islam, second edition*, Brill Online.

Jankowski, Peter J. (2002), 'Postmodern spirituality: implications for promoting change', *Counseling and Values* 47:1, 69–79.

Jensen, Courtney (2013), 'Foundations and the discourse of philanthropy', *Administrative Theory & Praxis* 35:1, 106–27.

Karl Schlecht Foundation (2015), website, available at: http://www.karl-schlecht. de/en/foundations/projects-of-ksg/global-ethic-foundation/, last accessed 10 December 2015.

Küng, Hans (1990), *Projekt Weltethos*, Munich: Piper.

—— (2002), *Dokumentation zum Weltethos 2002*, Munich: Piper.

—— (2012), *Handbuch des Weltethos: eine Vision und ihre Umsetzung*, Munich: Piper.

Laude, Patrick (2013), 'Spirituality in a postmodern age: challenges and questions', *Studies in Spirituality* 23, 43–60.

Leezenberg, Michiel (1997), 'Between assimilation and deportation: history of the Shabak and the Kakais in Northern Iraq', in K. Kehl-Bodrogi, B. Kellner-Heinkele and A. Otter-Beaujean (eds), *Syncretistic Religious Communities in the Near East*, Leiden: Brill, pp. 155–74.

Minorsky, Vladimir (1921), 'Notes sur la secte des Ahle-Haqq (deuxième partie)', *Revue du monde musulman* 44–5, 205–302.

—— (1960, first published online 2012), 'Ahl-i Ḥaḳḳ', in *The Encyclopaedia of Islam, second edition*, Brill Online.

Mir-Hosseini, Ziba (1994a), 'Inner truth and outer history: the two worlds of the Ahl-i Haqq of Kurdistan', *International Journal of Middle East Studies* 26:2, 267–85.

—— (1994b), 'Redefining the truth: Ahl-i Haqq and the Islamic Republic of Iran', *British Journal of Middle Eastern Studies* 21:2, 211–28.

—— (1997), 'Breaking the seal: the new face of the Ahl-e Haqq', in K. Kehl-Bodrogi, B. Kellner-Heinkele and A. Otter-Beaujean (eds), *Syncretistic Religious Communities in the Near East*, Leiden: Brill, pp. 175–94.

Mokri, Mohammad (1997, first published online 2012), 'Sulṭān Sehāk', in *The Encyclopaedia of Islam, second edition*, Brill Online.

Moosa, Matti (1988), *Extremist Shiites: The Ghulat Sects*, Syracuse: Syracuse University Press.

Morris, James W. (1996), 'La pensée d'Ostad Elahi', in M. Meslin (ed.), *Le Spirituel: Pluralité et Unité* (Symposium 1995, Sorbonne), Cahiers d'Anthropologie Religieuse, vol. 5, Paris: Presse de l'Université, pp. 137–47. [English version 'The different aspects of Ostad Elahi's spiritual teachings', in ibid. pp. 1–16.] Available at http://hdl.handle.net/2345/4027, last accessed 15 April 2016.

—— (2007), *Knowing the Spirit*, New York: State University of New York Press.

—— (2009), *Ostad Elahi on Spirituality in Every Day Life*, Kuala Lumpur: Centre for Civilisational Dialogue.

Nour Foundation (New York) (2016), website, available at: http://www.nour.foundation.com/, last accessed 15 April 2016.

Olsson, Tord (1998), 'Epilogue: The scripturalization of Ali-oriented religions', in T. Olsson, E. Özdalga and C. Raudvere (eds), *Alevi Identity: Cultural, Religious and Social Perspectives*, Richmond: Curzon, pp. 199–208.

Ostad Elahi (2016), Official Site of Ostad Elahi, 1995–2016, available at: http://ostadelahi.com/, last accessed 29 March 2016.

Al-Qāḍī, Wadad (2003), 'The development of the term ghulāt in Muslim literature with special reference to the Kaysāniyya', (reprint) in Etan Kohlberg (ed.), *Shīʿism*, Aldershot: Ashgate, pp. 169–94.

Raei, Sharokh (2009), 'Der Zusammenhang zwischen den religiösen Traditionen der Khaksar und denen der Ahl-e Haqq: eine Perspektive zum historischen Verständnis der Khaksar-Derwische', in C. Allison, A. Joisten-Pruschke and A. Wendtland (eds), *From Daēnā to Dîn: Religion, Kultur und Sprache in der iranischen Welt. Festschrift für Philip Kreyenbroek zum 60. Geburtstag*, Wiesbaden: Harrassowitz, pp. 349–55.

Stead, F. M. (1932), 'The Ali Ilahi sect in Persia', *The Moslem World* 22:2, 184–9.

Tacey, David (2004), *The Spiritual Revolution: The Emergence of Contemporary Spirituality*, Hove: Brunner-Routledge.

UN-ECOSOC (2011), *Working with ECOSOC – an NGOs Guide to Consultative Status*, New York: United Nations, available at: https://csonet.org/content/documents/Brochure.pdf, last accessed 29 March 2016.

—— (2014), *List of non-governmental organizations in consultative status with the Economic and Social Council as of 1 September 2014; Note by the Secretary General*, New York: United Nations, available at: http://csonet.org/content/documents/E-2014-INF-5%20Issued.pdf and http://csonet.org/index.php?menu=99#1, last accessed 29 March 2016.

—— (2016a), NGO Branch, website, available at: http://esango.un.org/civilsociety/showProfileDetail.do?method=printProfile&tab=1&profileCode=7155, last accessed 22 April 2016.

—— (2016b), 'Integrated CSO System' (Information on organisations by region and in Consultative Status with ECOSOC, etc.), available at: http://esango.un.org/civilsociety/login.do, last accessed 22 April 2016.

—— (2016c), 'Statements submitted by the Ostad Elahi Foundation', available at: http://esango.un.org/irene/?page=viewProfile&type=ngo&nr=7155&section=9, last accessed 29 March 2016.

Weightman, Simon C. R. (1964), 'The significance of Kitāb Burhān ul-Ḥaqq', *Iran* 2:1, 83–103.
World Council of Religious Leaders (2016), website, available at: http://www.millenniumpeacesummit.org/wc_about.html, last accessed 29 April 2016.

PART III

'ALID PIETY AND THE FLUIDITY OF SECTARIAN BOUNDARIES

9

IDEAS IN MOTION: THE TRANSMISSION OF SHI'A KNOWLEDGE IN SRI LANKA

Arun Rasiah

Origins

Twelver Shi'ism emerged in Sri Lanka following the Islamic Revolution in Iran in 1979. The political upheaval that inaugurated the fifteenth Hijri century also heralded an important shift in the transmission of religious knowledge. Disseminated widely, Iranian publications found a Sunni Muslim audience curious about different expressions of Islam. Interest in Shi'ism eventually solidified into the establishment of a small Shi'a community. In subsequent years, students and scholars attended the centre of traditional learning, *hawza 'ilmiyya*, in Qom and returned to Sri Lanka to found educational institutions, embodying an alternative intellectual order to that of majority Sunnism. This chapter surveys the scholarly networks that undergird the Shi'a community and enable the transmission of knowledge in Sri Lanka.[1] Bound by conceptions of religious authority, the Shi'ites gather for religious observance and instruction in centres led by local *'ulama'* and intellectuals. In the face of numerous challenges, they have adapted global discourses to address concerns in the aftermath of the civil war (1983–2009) and an atmosphere of rising anti-Muslim hostility. Their double minority status in relation to the

Sunni community and the national polity has led many of them to observe dissimulation (*taqiyya*) as a security measure (Medoff 2015). Into this multilayered context persecuted minorities from Pakistan and Afghanistan have sought sanctuary, and the Shi'ites have played a crucial role in their resettlement. As asylum seekers and refugees on the margins of larger society, they share a sense of exile that resonates with narratives of oppression concerning the Prophet's family, the *ahl al-bayt*, and their followers. A distinctive Shi'a identity has formed in this environment, one that connects to the indigenous heritage of Sri Lankan Islam, enculturated through practices of learning, and echoing trans-local, trans-regional and global perspectives. The community that has developed represents all socioeconomic backgrounds spread throughout three geographic areas: Colombo and the Western Province, the Kandyan Highlands, and the Eastern Province.[2] Almost exclusively from Sunni backgrounds, and thus integrated into Muslim society, the new Shi'ites number several hundred families, but no more than a thousand individuals, to attempt an estimate.

The transmission of knowledge has been essential to the contemporary formation of the community of Shi'a Muslims, which in turn is composed of smaller, disparate sub-sections. It outlines a scholarly network embedded within a transnational political economy of knowledge production. At its core, individual teachers and students engage in practices of learning, from study and teaching to translation and authorship. The interrelation of teachers, students and texts to the larger discursive, institutional and international context broadens the conventional scope of Islamic education, often focused exclusively on the *madrasa*. Based on the movement of individuals and textual materials, the scholarly network has become formally organised through affiliated institutions of learning and channels of patronage (Noor 2008: 17–18). Travel to and from centres of traditional religious learning in the Middle East connects regions and brings socio-religious prestige to locals able to make the journey abroad. Short trips for pilgrimage or extended formal study have strengthened the network and allowed ideas to circulate.

South Asia's long tradition of Islamic learning is especially rich on the Indian subcontinent. At one time the 'connective systems' that linked the Safavid and Mughal cultural spheres influenced the *madrasa* curriculum in North India and transmitted texts of Shi'a philosophy, including the works of Mulla Sadra (circa 1571–1635), which currently experience a resurgence of interest (Robinson 1997: 151–84). Among the Shi'ites of India, Lucknow has been the most important centre in the north, while Hyderabad influenced the Carnatic region. These areas, however, are steeped in a Persianate literary culture that embraces Urdu, as distinct from the Dravidian languages of the south. The coastal areas of South India, Sri Lanka and the Maldives, united by the Shafi'ite school of Sunni jurisprudence, can be also thought of as a maritime arena with links purportedly reaching back as far as Hadramawt, Yemen. This trans-local sphere, made up of distinct zones with similar features, is closely connected to the Middle East for study and the Gulf states, in particular, for employment. The practice of Sunni Islam here differs markedly from, and predates, the post-Mughal environment although it also adopted the Nizami curriculum.[3] However, the presence of Shi'ism is comparatively limited with significant pockets in Madras in Tamil Nadu and around Bangalore in Karnataka. Kerala has had a similar trajectory in the development of Shi'ism as that of Sri Lanka.[4]

Like many other Muslims around the world, Sri Lanka's Sunni community initially expressed vigorous support for the Islamic Revolution in Iran of 1979. The charismatic figure of Ayatollah Khomeini and the energy of the movement heightened receptivity to political writings of key figures, particularly the *'ulama'*, but also partisan intellectuals such as Ali Shari'ati and Jalal-e Ahmad. The literature, arriving by post as well as from visitors and diplomats, included the committed journalism of Iranian newspapers and magazines like *Echo of Islam* and *Mahjuba*, but featured other genres as well, particularly ideological tracts and scholarly treatises. Iranian cultural organisations, such as the Islamic Propagation Organisation (IPO) and the World Organisation for Islamic Services (WOFIS), distributed complimentary books and periodicals. Thinkers who combined traditional *hawza* and university education, such as Mortaza Motahhari (1920–79) and Muhammad Husayn Beheshti (1928–81), were counted as highly influential sources of the current running through Iran. Translations of these materials found a sympathetic audience in the urbane, English-educated generation of Jamath-e Islami (JI) activists based in Colombo, who became the first to absorb the ideas of political Islam as represented by contemporary Iranian Shi'ism. An elite of activist intellectuals, steeped in Sunni reformist thought, thus crystalised into the vanguard Organisation to Support the Islamic Revolution in Iran (OSIRI). They presented the unfolding events to the broader community in English and Tamil, the vernacular and literary language of Sri Lankan Muslims, a practise that continues today through social media. Emerging from the Sri Lanka Muslim Students Federation (SLMSF) and Jamath-e Islami, OSIRI staged public demonstrations of solidarity with the Revolution on the basis of unity across schools of thought in Islam. Over time, the imperative of political unity matured from tolerance into appreciation of theological difference. The act of sustained political support eventually led to a number of key figures refocusing their religious orientation to Twelver Shi'a theology and Ja'fari jurisprudence, representing an epistemological shift within Sri Lankan Islam. From the initial group of supporters, Muslim activists accepted invitations to visit Iran to tour religious sites. Thereafter, several Sri Lankan students embarked for long-term study in Qom, where they joined growing numbers of international *hawza* students. After attending Madrasa Imam Khomeini, the first cohort returned to Sri Lanka in 2004. An ongoing relationship developed with Sri Lankan students attending *madrasas* in Qom, known widely as the *hawza 'ilmiyya* or institutionally as Mustafa International University (MIU) at present.[5] On return, they faced numerous challenges in an uncertain environment of ethnic tension and religious competition, but have remained committed to the teachings of contemporary Twelver Shi'ism.

The infusion of Islamic thought from post-revolutionary Iran contributed to intellectual change in suggesting an alternative to Shafi'ite traditionalism and reformist Sunni thought. The transmission of Shi'a ideas by institutions of learning in Iran and disseminated by publishers based in Qom and Tehran provided the intellectual basis for the establishment of an indigenous Shi'a community. Since then it has grown quietly, advancing by way of political and intellectual discourse. In the interim, however, the Sunni organisations that once supported the Revolution had turned away from Iran during the war with Iraq in the early 1980s. The Iraqi embassy published books, organised seminars for *'ulama'* and intellectuals, and arranged trips to Iraq to sway Muslim opinion. Later, the influence of literature from Saudi Arabia fomented discontent with the Islamic Republic. A continuous flow of Salafi counterpropaganda contributed to the hardening of anti-Shi'a attitudes. While several pro-Revolution Sunni thinkers and activists continued to serve as a bridge or buffer between communities, Shi'ites remained numerically small, yet disproportionately influential due to their integration into Sunni life.

The intelligentsia has been at the forefront of the transmission of Shi'a ideas into Sri Lanka. This group comprises scholars and students of the Islamic disciplines (*'ulum al-din*) as well as activists and professionals without formal religious training. Familiar with Islamic political discourse across schools of thought, these intellectuals are the driving force of local Shi'ism. Visiting Iran was a decisive moment in forging trans-regional ties, one that offered a direct encounter with Shi'ism in practice, moving beyond political slogans and into cultural and social experience. Through dialogue and literature, the original adherents shared knowledge with family and friends, peers and neighbours. In this way, what appeared as a foreign import has gradually moved into a stage of indigenisation. An aspect of the process of localising Shi'ism related the Prophet's family, the *ahl al-bayt*, to established cultural practices in Sri Lanka. Purported evidence of this connection included reference to lyrics of extant Arabic-Tamil litanies, oral poetry that extolled 'Ali and Fatima, Hasan and Husayn, and the popularity of the names of the *ahl al-bayt*. While processes of indigenisation differ by region all tap into the specificities of local heritage. Outside the major urban centres of Colombo and Kandy, the community has relied on a younger generation to transmit knowledge in the Muslim areas of the Eastern Province.

Ideas

Critical concepts animate the history of ideas even in minority settings with fragile institutions of higher learning and uneven conditions for intellectual activity. The reception of Shi'a ideas in a multireligious environment such as Sri Lanka has elapsed over several stages, first emphasising the explicitly political before turning to theological debates. While Shi'ism has been widely regarded as critique for its oppositional political character, beneath this dimension lies a substantive critical engagement that returns to the primary sources of Islam. The investigation, though initiated by political events, has resulted in a reconstruction of religious thought. Thus critique, while indubitably political, is ultimately scriptural, theological and historiographical in rebuilding the edifice of Islam. In this way the intellectual project of establishing Shiʻism can be considered a form of renewal (*tajdid*) seeking to revitalise received wisdom. Perhaps the foremost example of such a critical concept is *wilaya*, the notion of 'authority' or 'guardianship'. With the advent of Shiʻa ideas, *wilaya* has entered the religious lexicon with new inflections. This term encapsulates a key principle of Shiʻism that has implications for cosmology (*wilaya takwiniyya*) and the structure of religio-political authority (*wilaya i'tibariyya*). It expands on the sense of religio-political authority insofar as representing the relationship of God to creation, with political reverberations from the station of Imamate, in contrast to secular views of governance. In terms of textual transmission, this idea has reached Sri Lanka by way of multiple disciplines, from philosophy and mysticism to political and social thought. Its premier manifestation is the contemporary notion of *wilayat al-faqih*, a subject of ongoing controversy, but supported almost unanimously among the new Shiʻa communities. Ironically, extended study in Qom has produced some ambivalence towards the concept and its application. Debate on such matters tends to be limited, however, to the comparatively advanced scholars whose numbers are few but who wield authority subtly without imposing the concept.

With regard to transmission of knowledge in the new Shiʻa community of Sri Lanka, four groups can be discerned in a typology of 'seekers of knowledge': religious scholars, students, intellectuals, and visiting scholars, all from disparate social backgrounds and localities. They are predominantly male but not exclusively; women also attended the *hawza* in Iran. While these four groups may be delineated, alternatively the point is not to create artificial separations, but to identify distinctive qualities of overlapping groups. Some individuals are formally designated as scholars, though many are still in training, while others informally study on their own as independent thinkers with other vocations, yet all make significant contributions to knowledge production. This latter group will be called 'intellectuals' for convenience.

Scholars

Scholars and students are integrated into circuits of learning, an appropriate metonym considering recent shifts in technology. The materiality of texts and sites figure into the system as tangibles, in which sacred books and holy places also have a symbolic quality. In this scholarly network ideas circulate as fluid epistemes that have taken shape trans-locally in diverse ways and forms, for example in the translation from Arabic to Tamil of *Al-Sahifa al-Sajjadiyya*, and its travels from South India to Sri Lanka. The translation of this canonical text, commissioned by an Iranian organisation, took place under the auspices of a Khoja community near Bangalore, which afforded the Sri Lankan translator a suitable environment to carry out his work while protecting his anonymity. Printed in Bangalore by Ameed Publishers in 2005, the book was then distributed in Sri Lanka. Similarly, cooperation among Twelver Shi'a Muslims in Madras and Sri Lankan Shi'ites have been aided by senior figures who express support for translations in Tamil.

For religious scholars undertaking traditional study, the preliminaries (*muqaddimat*) cover language proficiency in Persian and Arabic. As for subject matter beyond linguistics, jurisprudence and its principles comprise the official discipline. In its Aristotelian form, logic is the mainstay of the scholastic curriculum and especially required for philosophy, a late addition to the *hawza* curriculum though an extracurricular but respectable pursuit. As comparative theology rather than dialectics, *kalam*, integral to the project of vernacularising Shi'ism and establishing intercultural relations in Sri Lanka, is often seen as inadequate to the task in its current framework. *Hadith* studies also have value in disputation. There are only a handful of religious scholars in various stages of training. It is still too early to judge to what extent a scholar will advance in the established course of study.

Another dimension to the scholarly network has arisen from the diffusion of new technologies into Sri Lanka. This virtual network brings the digital transmission of religious knowledge to a new audience, disrupting notions of centre and periphery based on traditional distribution networks. Wide availability of smart phones and tablets in Sri Lanka offers access to a multitude of applications that include the Qur'an with translation and commentaries, digital libraries of textual materials in the Islamic disciplines, devotional materials (such as supplications and *a'mal* handbooks), news sites, and so forth. Direct private access to these texts also results in decentralisation and individualisation of learning, potentially refiguring the structure of intellectual authority. The digital transmission of knowledge delivers a variety of textual materials directly into the hands of community members, typically through the ubiquitous smartphone and associated platforms of tablets, laptops and desktop computers. The virtual network digitally interconnects the Shi'a heartland of Iran, Iraq and Lebanon to 'peripheral' locations like Sri Lanka that share a geographic and cultural distance from long established Shi'ism. The social media application Whatsapp provides a way to share and comment on textual messages and a constant stream of *hadith*, sermons, news and opinion reaches the individuals and communities scattered throughout the island and to members who reside abroad. News from similar minority Shi'a Muslims occasionally interlinks disparate communities in Africa and Asia into something of a post-1979 'International' (Mallat 1993: 7). However, based on the information disseminated by community members, their orientation remains focused towards Middle Eastern centres of religious learning in Qom and Najaf, which still exert authority over knowledge.

Students

The *hawza* students (*talib*, pl. *tullab*) who matriculated from a *madrasa* in the hinterland to a comparatively more cosmopolitan institution in Colombo, Qom or Tehran carried with them the weight of family and community expectations. Historically, students and scholars alike endeavoured to undertake the journey in search of knowledge, *rihlat talab al-'ilm*, a central motif of Islamic education (Eickelman and Piscatori 1990; Touati 2010). Today an aura of reverence for this endeavour lingers and the greater distance one moves the more prestige associated with one's studies. For many students who would later identify as Shi'a the initial step in their scholarly travels took place not overseas but within the country, when as youth they left their homes to reside in 'the Arabic colleges' of the Eastern Province (Asad 1993: 36–8). At this stage of learning youngsters exchanged conventional family life for immersive study in the Sunni *madrasa*. They embraced Shi'ism later, but as boarding school students formed bonds that would last through their years in Qom. Even as youth, broad respect for Islamic studies earned them the honorific, *maulavi* used affectionately up to the present. The appellation carries a trace of irreverence, perhaps because locals have known them since they were mischievous boys. Remaining within a cultural sphere similar to their own hometowns, they came into contact with other Muslims from outlying areas. At this point they followed the Shafi'ite *madhhab* and studied the subjects of Arabic, Qur'an and Islamic law. Training in Arabic grammar and rhetoric provided the linguistic foundation for continuing studies in the Islamic disciplines and would later serve them well in Qom. Predictably, students occupied the bottom rung in the hierarchy of knowledge, but the further they proceeded both academically and geographically the more respect they accrued. Other factors raised their rank: religiosity, scholarly potential, family background (including marriage ties) and individual resourcefulness.

In the early period of their academic careers, students had no guarantee they would enter professions related to Islamic scholarship. Whatever their occupational status, however, they remain indispensable to the overall system of knowledge transmission. Obviously, without students, education, in the sense of handing down sanctified knowledge to a new generation, cannot proceed. It is imperative that schools fill seats and advance students to the next level, institutions of higher education. At first, the Arabic college was the key area of student recruitment for scholarships to Iran. Today, with an established community, members send forth their own children for study abroad in Iran. Few of the students are sons and daughters of *'ulama'*, but usually hail from families working in the fishing, farming and retail sectors of the Eastern Province. This region differs strikingly from the Sinhalese majority areas of the central hill country and Western Province. The towns and villages from Batticaloa south along the coast to Amparai in the Eastern Province, where this research was conducted, have some of Sri Lanka's highest concentrations of Muslims. Residents had lived through the insecurity of the ethnic conflict, especially volatile on the eastern front, with daily incidents ranging from disappearances and extrajudicial killings to massacres (McGilvray 2008). During this time of paramilitary and state terror the intellectual formation of the first batch of *madrasa* students took place. It was with no small measure of relief then that the classmates left for Iran.

The opportunity to study in Qom marked a significant development in the cultural and religious relations between Sri Lanka and Iran, but in particular for the former. While at first only a handful of students completed this journey, it cemented ties between the fledgling community in Sri Lanka and the *hawza 'ilmiyya*. The first Sri Lankan student arrived in the 1980s during the period of the Iran-Iraq War but he is considered something of an anomaly. It was in the mid-90s that more students arrived, with the single longest stay lasting from 1994 to 2004. Travel to Qom caused an upheaval in their lives and while they managed to escape one of the ethnic conflict's main theatres it also removed them from the familiar surroundings of their upbringing. Their tenacity had helped to navigate checkpoints and curfews, and exercise *taqiyya* in unfamiliar mosques. In comparison, they appreciated the relative ease of *hawza* life, in spite of annoyances such as having to explain themselves constantly. As perpetual minorities, their numbers paled in comparison to Indians and Pakistanis, whose expectation that they speak Urdu aroused considerable indignation. Notwithstanding unfamiliarity with Sri Lanka, they fondly recalled dormitory life in the international school, Madrasa Imam Khomeini, where they formed close friendships with diverse international students. At first, they were placed in an accelerated six-month programme aimed at Persian proficiency. Arabic foundations from *madrasa* days facilitated the Sri Lankans' acquisition of Persian, which they found easy enough to learn. Like many Qom alumni, upon returning home they have continued to speak Persian with each other, which operates as a marker of their shared experience and identity. Having travelled to Iran for Islamic studies, the students were warmly welcomed by extended family members, the Shi'a community and Sunni Muslim society. Depending on the town they lived in, these alumni of Qom used *taqiyya* as circumstances demanded, usually in response to the strength of local Salafism.

Of this group that found employment in the field of education back in Sri Lanka, the most common were the vocations of madrasa teacher, itinerant Qur'an teacher serving both Sunnis and Shi'ites, while one continued tertiary studies in Iran, as a doctoral student at the University of Tehran. Advancing the transmission of knowledge and development of the community, *hawza* students participated in founding a new madrasa north of Batticaloa, Manbaul Hudha Arabic College in Valaichchenai, the first such institution in the region that served Sunni and Shi'a students. There, a new generation, trained by *hawza* graduates, prepared to study in Qom.

Intellectuals

The admittedly vague category of intellectual may not be useful if conceived too broadly. The objective of classifying intellectuals separately from other groups is primarily to distinguish them from the conventional trajectories of religious scholars and students and to draw attention to their public role.

While Sri Lankan *'ulama'* share a similar disposition, their religious training gives them knowledge in the Islamic disciplines in Arabic and Persian that other kinds of intellectuals are not privy to. An intellectual may combine forms of educational training or have none at all. Here it includes independent thinkers without formal training, university-trained academics, professionals, authors and artists, and religious figures on contingent assignments, such as preachers visiting during the month of Ramadan. Among the pillars of the community are a number of professionals, primarily lawyers, teachers, engineers and accountants, who speak English fluently and debate well, lending the community stature and bearing a subtle influence on society at large. The elite occupational status of the intellectuals gives them broad credence and facilitates a public role representing the community and its ideas, while internally playing an important administrative and financial role in the community. This group shares the attribute of being conversant in global discourses of Sunni and Shi'a Islam, while being attuned to social, cultural and political conditions in Sri Lanka. They express anti-imperialist sentiments, rooted in post-war Third World politics and the turn to political Islam.

Aside from those whose primary vocation is seeking knowledge, the community at large also shares in the experience of religious pilgrimage and educational travel by way of *ziyara* and short-term study in Qom. Such activities offer opportunity for rank and file community members who are not formally affiliated to Islamic educational institutions to experience study and travel, which connects the regions through interpersonal contact and is enhanced by social media networks. Overall the community has reinforced an intellectual orientation in that numerous members have undergone a significant transformation in accepting Shi'a Islam. In part, this is because they must be able to articulate arguments in favour of their (double) minority position. The ability to build a convincing argument is not solely the preserve of professionals but incumbent on all because of their proximity to Sunni family, friends and neighbours. Informal dialogue around the similarities and differences of Islamic schools of thought pervades community gatherings. In broader discussions with associates outside the community, if one had a degree of comfort to disclose Shi'a leanings, they articulated their position and refuted counterarguments. One technique was to provide a scriptural proof illustrated by evidence from *hadith* and published in Tamil pamphlets distributed to sympathetic Sunnis. Another strategy was to engage co-religionists in a vociferous critique of Salafism. Although cautious to disclose Shi'a beliefs, intellectuals felt comfortable in publicly discrediting 'Wahhabism'. Their tactics included historicising Wahhabism by recounting the movement's origins in Najd and drawing attention to relations with Western imperial powers. By delimiting the theological framework, they prepared the ground for a comparative understanding of Islam from within.

The older generation deliberately linked the new form of knowledge to the cultural heritage of Sri Lankan Muslims. This didactic technique defended Shi'ism in polemical style as another form of orthodoxy rather than a non-normative practice outside the fold of Islam. At the same time, a reminder of long-standing veneration of the *ahl al-bayt* blurred the sharp distinction between Sunnis and Shi'ites. The community, by inviting Sufi *tariqa* leaders to accompany them on visits to Iran, have been able to influence the broader Sunni discourse on Islam. This was evident in the content of sermons in mosques, in which the *khatib* praised 'Ali b. Abi Talib over the loudspeakers using *'alayhi al-salam* (peace be upon him) rather than the standard *radi allahu 'anhu* (may God be pleased with him). In this way new perspectives on the *ahl al-bayt* circulated among Sunni parishioners as well.

Itinerants

Visiting scholars included foreign authors and activists on tour, university professors from overseas, Iranian *akhunds* on assignment, *hawza* students on leave, and endangered scholars seeking refuge. As itinerant intellectuals they joined community activities on a temporary basis before returning home or being dispatched to a new post. During Ramadan 2015 a professional Qur'an reciter (*qari*) visited the community's main centre from Iran. At his send-off on the eve of Eid Al-Fitr leaders formally received him with a display of gratitude and public recognition of his 'sacrifice' in leaving family to spend time in Sri Lanka. In his remarks, a senior community leader, a retired civil servant, also gently expressed the wish that the reciter would encourage authorities in Iran to be more consistent in sending people in future 'to enrich the experience of the people of Sri Lanka during the month of Ramadan'.

Another visitor served as the centre's resident *'alim*, a Shi'a scholar from Pakistan who led the prayer and delivered sermons. He had evaded likely assassination in Lahore when authorities discovered his name on an extremist hit list. After studying in Qom, he had obtained a doctorate in philosophy at the University of Tehran, where Ayatollah Khomeini's daughter-in-law chaired his dissertation committee. Unable to find full employment as a university lecturer, he sought an income on the religious lecture circuit, where he gained popularity by introducing *hawzawi* philosophical knowledge to mourning assemblies (*majalis*) during Muharram in Pakistan. As a student of Ayatullah Taqi Misbah Yazdi in Qom, he had been exposed to the stream of Islamic philosophy in the Sadrian tradition. He asserted that this novel content based on his *hawza* and university studies offered a unique style of homiletic discourse that attracted growing audiences. His rising celebrity also alerted paramilitary *takfiri* groups. Lashkar-e Jhangvi, Ahle-Sunnat Wal Jama'at, Tehrik-e Taliban and their precursors have systematically assassinated notable Shi'a figures, including religious leaders and professionals. Unable to protect him, the police insisted he leave the country immediately. From that point, his odyssey as an asylum seeker began. In Sri Lanka, anti-Shi'a rhetoric remained largely at the level of symbolic violence, in the sense of hate speech involving threats and even vandalism, unlike the mass murder and targeted killings of high profile individuals in Pakistan since 1987. Continuing strife there has increased Shi'a migration and altered the composition of the community. The influx of asylum seekers from Pakistan, including Ahmadis and Christians, rose dramatically from 2012 and reached a peak of 1,338 in 2013. There was a marked difference in attendance at community programmes in Colombo during field visits in 2012 and 2015, by which time Pakistanis and Afghans had a discernible presence. Since 2015, their numbers have increased and unverified accounts suggest that at present they constitute the majority of attendees.

Sites

The Shi'ites have established sites designated for religious gatherings and education such as community centres, *madrasas*, *husayniyyas*, and rented venues for regular programmes or annual conferences. The Islamic Centre, a nondescript two-storey building with a retail storefront surrounded by a high metal fence, was until recently located on the same narrow road as a popular *jamia* mosque in a residential suburb of Colombo. Serving as the national headquarters of the island-wide Shi'a community, the centre housed administrative offices, held religious programmes and hosted visitors. Programmes included daily prayers and a full range of commemorations in the Twelver Shi'a tradition, such as group supplications, Ramadan *iftars*, Muharram *majalis* and Eid celebrations. In Colombo there are three Shi'a organisations, the Cultural Centre affiliated to the Iranian diplomatic mission, the offices of Mustafa International University, and the local community's Islamic Centre. What distinguished this last site from the Iranian organisations is its indigenous and autonomous character, in which the original group of Sri Lankan Shi'ites form the leadership and organise activities independently of Iranian influence. The ground floor had a central prayer room (*musalla*), kitchen and two guest rooms. Four small rooms on the second floor were used as offices. A conference table upstairs was used for meetings while impromptu gatherings were held in the *musalla* surrounding the prayer times. Visitors from other parts of the country or abroad slept on the *musalla* carpet, and during Ramadan a college student from the Eastern Province occupied a guest room to prepare for exams. The storefront on the ground floor was used informally for business ventures.

Combining functions of *masjid* and office, the multipurpose Islamic centre recalled the idea of the legendary Dar al-'Ilm, the medieval institution of learning with a library in Baghdad that featured more debate and discussion than formal instruction. In providing a place to stay for the traveller, it also evoked the hidden places of vulnerable Shi'a communities, a sanctuary for refugees and locals alike. This meaning also coheres with the idea of Qom as a 'sanctuary of knowledge', a place in which *'ilm* was safeguarded historically and where the *ahl al-bayt* themselves, as well as their descendants and followers, took refuge. Significantly, the building functioned as a temporary safe house for extra-national refugees from the region. This group included migrants from neighbouring countries seeking to certify refugee status before settling abroad permanently. In particular religious and ethnic minorities from Pakistan and Afghanistan entered Sri Lanka after the United Nations designated it a sub-regional sanctuary country, an irony not lost on the island's alienated Tamils, especially those living under military occupation in the Northern Province, and Muslim Internally Displaced People (IDPs). As resident *'alim*, the Pakistani asylum seeker lived in one of the guest rooms. Other Pakistani asylum seekers and Afghan Hazara refugees visited the centre for religious occasions as well as for meetings with the community's senior scholar. In addition to his translation of Islamic texts he served as a UNCHR (the United Nations Refugee Agency) translator, and the hosts used English and Persian to communicate. The resident *'alim* noted that while European states have superior infrastructure and resources to accommodate refugees, they are not guaranteed entry and could be returned forcibly to their countries of origin, which contributed to the appeal of Sri Lanka as an intermediary destination. Caught in the political limbo of statelessness they shared anxieties of an uncertain future. The centre provided a critical space to interact among themselves, exchange information and relieve pressure by engaging in religious and social activities.

Texts

Texts in circulation, both classical and modern, include Arabic and Persian curricula such as *Jami'a al-Muqaddimat* and *Amuzesh-e Falsafeh (Philosophical Instructions)* studied by junior and intermediary *hawza* students and advanced scholars. Political works published after the revolution, mostly in English, but also in Arabic and Persian, have been widely distributed and comprise the writings of Khomeini, Motahhari, Beheshti and Shari'ati. Original materials in Tamil, Sinhala and English, usually pamphlets and short articles, target an indigenous audience. Finally, there are seminal works translated into Tamil. Thus far the most significant Shi'a text translated from classical Arabic into modern Tamil for a regional audience is the collection of supplications *Al-Sahifa Al-Sajjadiyya* (Zayn Al-'Abidin 2005), attributed to the fourth Imam, 'Ali ibn Al-Husayn or Zayn Al-'Abidin. The Tamil translation included an introduction which presented a biography of Zayn Al-'Abidin, a history of its transmission, and an account of its significance for imparting the teachings of the *ahl al-bayt*.

Translation of this text involved a battery of tasks. At the most technical level it required expertise in both the original's classical Arabic and modern literary Tamil. The translator, writing under the *nom de plume* 'Farazdaq' (after the Arab poet who was imprisoned for composing a verse in praise of

Zayn Al-'Abidin), had studied extensively in Qom and attained mastery of Arabic and Persian, in addition to his fluent Sinhala, Tamil and English. Formerly a prominent activist in the Sunni community, he had hosted a popular *da'wa* programme. His erudition and humility have earned him unanimous respect and a position as the community's foremost scholar and senior leader. He undertook the project of translating *Sahifa* in South India to protect the nascent community from political repercussions. As a guest of the Khoja community, he spent six months at work on the translation in Alipur, a town on the outskirts of Bangalore, Karnataka. The book was then printed in India, owing in part to cheaper production costs, but also so that it could be exported to Sri Lanka on the grounds that it posed less of a threat as a foreign product. Without 'raising the alarm' concerning the Shi'a presence in Sri Lanka, Farazdaq thus performed a service to the community while taking appropriate measures to ensure its security. To accomplish this, he interpreted political conditions and the sociocultural context of the book's reception. The 'offshoring' of textual production also demarcates a wider scholarly network in which the act of translation becomes a trans-regional affair that interconnects communities by crossing national borders and ethnic boundaries, while establishing ties of patronage and fraternity. This episode also illustrates the practice of *taqiyya* as an instance of dissemblance to safeguard the believers and the emergent faith. Several thousand copies of the book were disseminated across Sri Lanka.

Though a canonical source for daily practice, *Sahifa* does not have a public function, unlike the collective recitation of *du'a kumayl*. Thus, it falls upon the worshipper to take advantage of the text, for example in reading the prayer for each day of the week. At the close of Ramadan, the resident *'alim* in Colombo, the Pakistani exile, exhorted the audience to read the *du'a* for the last day of the month in *Sahifa*. He encouraged his co-religionists to recognise the importance of supplications from the Imams, 'particularly the prayers from *Al-Sahifa Al-Sajjadiyya*', and to take advantage of them by way of reading and recitation. He went on to remind listeners 'to recite prayer 45 in *Sahifa Kamila* and a special prayer from Imam Sajjad for the day of Eid Al-Fitr'. While recitation in the original is meritorious purely for the blessings (*baraka*), the speaker brought attention to understanding the meaning of the supplication. In emphasising comprehension, he echoed a common refrain, the community's focus on individual meaning-making rather than rote memorisation or recitation. Whereas the collectivity of the *jamat* is highly valued in Sunni circles, individuality has pride of place in the Shiʿa community. Supererogatory devotions in private homes are an as important religious practice of the Sri Lankan Shiʿites as congregational prayer, which is stressed more among Sunnis. Indeed, when a senior religious scholar or leader is not present it is common for Shiʿites to perform the daily prayers solitarily. However, the community meets frequently in their autonomous spaces for communal worship.

Religious texts in practice have didactic and devotional purposes, and bind together the community in private reading and communal recital. Certainly, the translation of *Al-Sahifa Al-Sajjadiyya* edified the translator as much as the projected audience in Sri Lanka, whose reading habits have shifted away from tangible volumes to digital applications. Traditional study and scholarly activity may still rely on hard textual materials, but for the majority of the community the relevance of the book as we know it is under question. Just as traces of the older Arabic-Tamil script have vanished due to disuse, so too conventional Islamic libraries have also begun to look obsolete, at least based on the appearance of their abandonment.

Patrons

Patronage both enables and constrains knowledge production in Sri Lanka. Historically, political and commercial elites could underwrite religious education through direct support of individual scholars or by establishing pious endowments (*awqaf*) to finance *madrasa* study and teaching as well as upkeep of properties. Scholarship without patronage is also common, perhaps even the norm, but requires sufficient income from employment or independent wealth. Failing that, a student, especially with a family, learns to live very simply. Sometimes financial considerations forced Shiʿites to flee home and shelter in the Islamic Centre hidden in the crowded capital. Difficult economic conditions in the Eastern Province have led to a cycle of borrowing for basic needs and the concomitant inability to service debts. Others have undertaken dubious business ventures in tight times, often leaning on family members by pooling resources to make initial investments. When deals failed to pay off and relatives or friends came around to recoup their loans, the borrowers absconded. On the run from debt collectors, Sunni and Shi'a men, including seminary students, can be found far from home living on the streets. Such difficult circumstances incentivise the search for work abroad as well as contribute to the maintenance of local ties of patronage.

Two major streams of patronage from the Middle East have had a decisive influence on the transmission of new kinds of Islamic knowledge in Sri Lanka. Saudi Arabia has been at the forefront of support for Salafi learning, castigated by its opponents under the catch-all 'Wahhabism'. Meanwhile, Iran has financed Shi'a educational, religious and cultural activities including subsidising travel, founding institutions and funding projects that strengthened ties between *hawza* and community.

For the majority Sunnis in Sri Lanka, the various government agencies and private organisations of Saudi Arabia have exercised financial power and brought religious prestige to reshape Islamic thought into a reformist Salafi mould. Foreign influence has operated through support for institutions, scholarships, contests, publishing and pilgrimage. While only limited numbers claim formal membership in Salafi organisations such as the All Ceylon Salaf Council (ACSC), those who espouse reformist ideas, receive funding and adopt the Gulf style of dress (white *thobes*, black *niqabs*, long beards, etc.) are much larger, giving the impression of a widespread shift in Sunni practice. This has been described as a trend of 'Arabisation' and has been the subject of Buddhist nationalist condemnation as well as Sufi resistance that has resulted in vandalism and violence, including fatalities.

Anti-Shi'a opinion in the public sphere has intensified in the last ten years. Due to the apparent lack of a sizeable Shi'a community, sectarian conflict had until recently been seen as irrelevant to Sri Lanka. However, the escalation of international sectarianism has also impinged on local discourse down to the village level. Meanwhile the Shi'a community had been hiding in plain sight. In 2014 rumours began to circulate on social media about their whereabouts and even specified the name of the road and their location in an unmarked building near a popular *jami masjid* in Colombo. While no incidents were reported in the capital, smaller Shi'a centres have been vandalised in small towns. Not far from Batticaloa accusations multiplied regarding a certain madrasa spreading *rafidi* (rejectionist) ideas.[6] The image of a young schoolteacher with an Iranian scholar appeared on posters distributed during Ramadan 2015 and heightened anxieties in the area. Generally, the policy of *taqiyya* has insulated Shi'ites from physical threat but there are gradations of the practice and it is an open secret, particularly if it is known that the accused studied in Qom, as in this case. The *ustad* (teacher) directly confronted the perpetrators who mocked and threatened him physically, albeit mildly. The tenor of such threats has been raised since then. In Friday sermons at Sunni mosques, preachers vilified Shi'a teachings so consistently some wondered whether it was a concerted policy during the month of fasting. The situation declined thereafter when the official body of *'ulama'* issued a ruling that condemned Shi'a Muslims as outside the boundaries of the Muslim community. That the *takfiri* position has been legitimated in scholarly circles gives credence for the Muslim public at large to police 'non-believers'. Saudi patronage, through refurbishment of physical sites, endowments and scholarships, has thus effected significant discursive and material change in the broader Muslim community. In this climate, Sunnis must consider whether to keep silent or speak out and be branded as Shi'a sympathisers, potentially falling victim to similar propaganda. As a minority group itself, Sri Lanka's Sunni Muslim community is not empowered to use the state apparatus against the Shi'ites. However, even Sunni expressions of solidarity with global organisations such as the Muslim Brotherhood or Tabligh Jamaat earn the label *hizbi* (supporters of Islamic groups and political parties) or 'false Salafis'. More troubling, the imperative of enforcing conformity by Saudi-supported groups has resulted in the destruction of shrines (*ziyarams*), cemeteries, hospices (*khanaqas*), and other sites which Sufi, *madhhab*-based Shafi'ite and Shi'a Muslims are known to visit. Some observers have argued that on occasion the agenda of Sunni reformism has even converged in practice with that of Sinhala Buddhist nationalists such as Bodu Bala Sena (BBS) in attempting to expunge traces of Islam – or *bid'a* in Salafi parlance – from the island.[7]

Pressures related to patronage are not limited to the Saudi agenda. Iranian support also presents challenges. The *hawza* provided enough assistance for students integrated into Iranian educational networks to subsist on the monthly stipend (*shahriyya*) for food, housing and family expenses. However, there is debate regarding the efficacy of implementing an imported pattern of community building. That blueprint privileges Iranian culture in prioritising acquisition of Persian over Arabic, though the latter has deep linguistic roots on the island. Moreover, it involves support for political stances taken by the Islamic Republic, such as adopting modes of political performance, that is, staging public demonstrations. The small and increasingly vulnerable community disagrees on the wisdom of making their presence felt. This divergence in strategy reflects less about differences regarding quietism versus activism, an enduring debate regarding the role of the clerical establishment in politics, than it does about the importance of a pragmatic gradualism.[8] Despite consensus on political issues, their cautious stance has been interpreted not as strategic practicality, but opposition to Iran, which has engendered criticism of the community's founders. Without a support system beyond the immediate family, Shi'a students face enormous pressure, compounded by social and political dictates. A former *hawza* student who has remained financially independent dared to criticise the conditionalities that accompany foreign patronage and mocked other students and scholars within the orbit of Saudi or Iran as 'dancing for money'.

One frame through which to understand relations of patronage is that of the political economy of knowledge production.[9] Its merit resides in focusing attention on the trans-regional economics of education and scholarship. The outline of political economy provides a structure to interrelate key elements of knowledge 'production' such as education, scholarship and publishing, with aspects of economic exchange. Here economic exchange may include commercial and financial activity, patronage and distribution of resources, charitable giving, employment, volunteering, tuition and pilgrimage. In spatial terms, situating the network geographically interconnects regions that traverse the boundaries of nation states, in this case South Asia and the Middle East, but also trans-locally in the example of Sri Lanka, South India and the Maldives. However, it is problematic if the framework skews our understanding of religious education towards purely instrumentalist ends. While it is important to ascertain material concerns, these cannot be elevated while confining pious motivations strictly to worldly goals. Such a skeletal framework, absent of tools for exploring asceticism in religious life, threatens to diminish the value of ideas on their own terms and selflessness independent of financial considerations. Although the commodification of religious knowledge is normative in all materialistic societies, the pursuit of knowledge cannot be entirely constrained by objectives of seeking position and remuneration. As often as not, seekers of knowledge expect impoverishment and marginalisation, particularly when belonging to a minority facing exclusion from the mainstream. In the Kandyan highlands even well-educated Muslims from reputable families who had been identified as Shi'ites reflected that it was increasingly difficult for their children to marry. However, such social barriers did not deter them from their religious commitments. A similar resolve to overcome ostracism and financial hardship can be found among students and scholars.

Directions

The peregrinations of scholars and students aid in revitalising Islamic knowledge in Sri Lanka. Alongside them, the movement of travellers and refugees brings new populations and perspectives to bear on the cultural and intellectual life of Muslims. The remittances and investments of workers and entrepreneurs further alter the character, and perception, of Sunni Muslim society, which remains highly visible in spite of its minority position. All in all, migration of people and ideas infuses a cosmopolitan energy into Shi'a communities. A trans-regional network of scholars and students links the Middle East to South Asia, primarily Iran to Sri Lanka, but extends in other directions as well, notably to the Gulf states, South India and the Maldives, and further afield to Australia, Europe and North America. The small number of individuals associated with this incipient network does not indicate its lack of importance. Since 1979, Twelver Shi'a thought has taken root for the first time in the multireligious landscape of Sri Lanka and the dynamic configuration of scholars and students connected to the broader Muslim community enables the observer to chart the movement of ideas. It is possible to discern a network of learning that involves knowledge transmission on a variety of fronts from informal study to the formation of educational institutions.

Anchored in political support for the Islamic Revolution, a critical re-examination of foundational sources gradually effected a change in religious outlook. One cannot stress enough the profundity of this transformation, reflecting a lasting process of study, discussion and debate. Yet to consider a Sunni Muslim's movement towards Shi'ism as an instance of 'conversion' misses the mark. This misnomer suggests the turn to another religion altogether. Without doubt accepting Shi'ism entailed a dramatic shift in conceptual framework and worldview, as well as in models of authority and ethical practice. Sources of emulation shifted in a re-evaluation of the Prophet's companions and the elevation of his family. Nevertheless, common to major schools (*madhahib*) of Islam are axiomatic beliefs such as the 'two testimonies' (*shahadatayn*) and the three foundational principles of religion (*usul al-din*), monotheism, prophethood and resurrection. Indeed, investigation into Shi'a perspectives involves a re-examination of the foundational sources of Islam, the Qur'an and *hadith*, employing canonical texts in the Sunni tradition such as Bukhari and Muslim. By positioning the Qur'an as primary criterion and exploring ostensible contradictions within Sunni literature, students precluded accusations of relying on controversial (Shi'a) sources. To aid in debate they also discussed modern polemical texts that present comparisons of *hadith*-based narratives. As an example of this critical practice, a *madrasa* student could present proofs for the Imamate of 'Ali b. Abi Talib, using the Qur'an, *hadith* and logic. As students gained skill in debating, they relied on memory to cite verses of the Qur'an and recount *hadith* to solidify their case with proofs, but also as a rhetorical flourish. It was thus possible to launch a critique from within that did not resort to external (non-Sunni) sources to establish the point. In this way, an internal dialogue took place, which also provided flexibility in concealing their sympathies. Intriguingly, community members rehearsed arguments in favour of Shi'a accounts among themselves long after having accepted the premises. In that the Sunni-Shi'a debate is not likely to be resolved, the discussion never concluded but constituted an enduring exercise, a key element of intellectual life illustrated in divergent ways across the community.

Finally, it should be noted that a Sunni Muslim's departure from a *tariqa* for a Salafi organisation (or vice versa) is never regarded as an act of conversion, although the change in thought and practice is arguably as profound as that of embracing Shi'ism. Rather than 'conversion', a more suitable term is 'reorientation' within Islam. In fact, the reorientation of Muslims, whether from one *madhhab* to another, or from mysticism to Islamism, and in many kinds of creative fusion, is a constant recurrence. 'Conversion' troubles matters when positing an either/or dichotomy, and sets the expectation that one side unequivocally repudiates the other, which is no doubt commonplace.

More disconcertingly, the term conversion potentially legitimates the Salafi view that Shi'ism lies beyond the limits of Islam, and establishes a justification for rectifying action. On the other hand, members of the Shi'a community who support the unity of Muslim schools of thought display a subtler approach in their comradery with '*tarīqa* men' (affiliates of Sufi orders) that suggests a spectrum of beliefs on a single continuum.

As elsewhere, Middle Eastern patronage to local groups constitutes a wider politics of distribution, in which Saudi Arabian and Iranian organisations among others compete for influence. As religious rivalry threatens to deteriorate into physical confrontation, stakeholders inscribe battlelines between majority and minority religions. Among Muslims, supporters of Sunni reformism condemn practices as being contaminated with polytheism. This attitude motivates attempts to eviscerate the living sites and architectural remnants of Sufism, and substitute them with a standardised Islam limited to mosque and *madrasa*. Oiled with financial incentives, the reformist campaign has gained adherents seeking a 'purified Islam'. It has also galvanised opposition, an informal alliance of *madhhabi* Sunni, Sufi and Shi'a Muslims that form an uneven resistance to varieties of Salafism and Wahhabism. Composing a multilayered field of contestations, majority Sinhala nationalists vie with minority Muslims, while Salafis dispute with Sufis, and Sunnis of all stripes condemn the all but invisible Shi'a Muslims. For their part the Shi'ites of Sri Lanka have tried to disrupt such facile divisions by engaging with shared foundational sources in sophisticated practices of discursive reasoning, towards fashioning another approach to questions of Islamic thought and life.

References

Algar, Hamid (1969), *Religion and State in Iran 1785–1906: The Role of the Ulama in the Qajar Period*, Berkeley: University of California Press.

Asad, M. Kamil (1993), 'Muslim education in Sri Lanka: the British Colonial Period', *Journal of Muslim Minority Affairs* 14:1–2, 35–45.

Eickelman, Dale, and James Piscatori (eds) (1990), *Muslim Travellers: Pilgrimage, Migration, and the Religious Imagination*, Berkeley: University of California Press.

Fasenfest, David (2010), 'A political economy of knowledge production', *Critical Sociology* 36:4, 483–7.

Haniffa, Farzana (2016), 'Stories in the aftermath of Aluthgama', in J. C. Holt (ed.), *Buddhist Extremists and Muslim Minorities: Religious Conflict in Contemporary Sri Lanka*, Oxford: Oxford University Press, pp. 164–93.

Mallat, Chibli (1993), *The Renewal of Islamic Law Muhammad Baqer as-Sadr, Najaf and the Shi'i International*, Cambridge: Cambridge University Press.

McGilvray, Dennis (2008), *Crucible of Conflict: Tamil and Muslim Society on the East Coast of Sri Lanka*, Durham: Duke University Press.

Medoff, Louis (2015), 'Taqiya i. In Shi'ism', in *Encyclopaedia Iranica*, available at: http://www.iranicaonline.org/articles/taqiya-i-shiism, last accessed 11 January 2019.

Noor, Farish (2008), *The Madrasa in Asia: Political Activism and Transnational Linkages*, Amsterdam: Amsterdam University Press.

Robinson, Francis (1997), 'Ottomans–Safavids–Mughals: shared knowledge and connective systems', *Journal of Islamic Studies* 8:2, 151–84.

Sakurai, Keiko (2015), 'Making Qom a centre of Shi'i scholarship: Al-Mustafa International University', in M. Bano and K. Sakurai (eds), *Shaping Global Islamic Discourses: The Role of al-Azhar, al-Medina and al-Mustafa*, Edinburgh: Edinburgh University Press, pp. 41–72.

Touati, Houari (2010), *Islam and Travel in the Middle Ages*, Chicago: University of Chicago Press.

Zayn al-'Abidin, Ali b. Husayn (2005), *Saḥīfa Sajjādīya*, trans. Farazdaq, Bangalore: Ameed Publishers.

10

LIMITS OF SECTARIANISM: SHI'ISM AND *AHL AL-BAYT* ISLAM AMONG TURKISH MIGRANT COMMUNITIES IN GERMANY

Benjamin Weineck

Introduction

'Although, or maybe even because the duality of Shi'ism and Sunnism dominates both academic and political discourse on Islam, inner-Islamic movements may counter such polarized narratives' (Heine and Spielhaus 2008: 25). This finding refers to the results of a survey conducted in 2008 by the German Bertelsmann Foundation called *Religionsmonitor*.[1] In the survey 19 per cent of the Muslim respondents refused to identify with one of the questionnaire's three possible items of inner Islamic belonging, that is, Sunnism, Shi'ism and Alevism.

This indifferent share hints at three interrelated aspects that are to be recognised in coming to terms with contemporary Shi'a identity formations in Germany and beyond. First and foremost, there is the issue of seemingly divergent self-descriptions of actors, called 'inner-Islamic movements' here, on the one hand, and academic or political conceptions and categories, on the other. Secondly, there is the reasoning for such an 'incongruence' or incommensurability, posing the question of the relation of academic and political speaking/writing and its reception among those who are the subject of such discourses. And thirdly, these two aspects urge the interrogation of the contexts in which such sectarian fault lines are used in making and representing their collective religious identity. Granted that sectarian borders do yield the potential for political mobilisation and are frequently referred to in contexts of conflict (for example, in cases such as Iraq or Yemen) they are apparently less visible or highlighted in contexts where such political mobilisation is not required or otherwise hindered. As such, Heine and Spielhaus also emphasise that the identification as either Sunni, Shi'ite or Alevi is more important in national contexts where these identities are politically charged and thus amenable for mobilisation (2008: 25). In this context, with regard to the German-language Shi'a magazine *Al-Fadschr* published by the Iranian-funded Islamic Centre in Hamburg, Liselotte Abid has observed that this magazine 'avoids a characteristic Shii appearance' (2013: 17) and instead seeks to reach out to all German-speaking Muslims. During my fieldwork among Shi'a communities in Germany between 2015 and 2017,[2] the question emerged to what degree these communities and individuals articulate their religiosity and practices as specifically 'Shi'ite'. Many of my interlocutors in the field renounced the label 'Shi'ite' as being political and favoured a self-identification as 'Muslim' instead – which yet again urges us to investigate modes and means of articulating collective belonging among these 'other Shiites' (Monsutti *et al.* 2007: 7)[3] beyond sectarian matrices. Furthermore, I came across cases in which Shi'ites as well as Alevis refer to semiotics, practices and discourses that they share with each other and represented themselves as 'friends of the *ahl al-bayt*' (*ehlibeyt dostları*) rather than as either Shi'a or Alevi.

Therefore, the present contribution investigates cases from the Shi'a field in Germany and asks for the relation of specific Shi'a, 'Islamic' or other categories that serve as markers of collective identity among these groups. Based on the observation in my fieldwork among Turkish-speaking Shi'a and Alevi groups in Germany, the notion of belonging to the family of the Prophet, the *ahl al-bayt* (*ehlibeyt* in the Turkish rendering), is far more widespread than specific sectarian modes of articulating religious identities. I will argue that too strict sectarian notions of inner-Islamic plurality and difference do not suffice to grasp such forms of 'Alid piety'[4] or 'ahl al-baytism' (McChesney 1991: 33) which continuously exceed and subvert sectarian boundaries among Sunnis, Alevis, Twelver Shi'ites or Nusayri-Alawis, for example.

While academic and political language, as illustrated in the quote at the beginning of this chapter, may remain heavily invested with confessional notions of inner-Islamic plurality and difference, the examples I shall speak about here bear witness of the fact that alternative concepts for such a plurality are already (and have for a long time been) on the table – in need of further testing for their applicability in different Islamicate social contexts. Therefore, this chapter illustrates, through the lens of Turkish-speaking Shi'a communities, on the one hand, the diversity of *ahl al-bayt* and Shi'a-oriented articulations of Islam in Germany. On the other, it also seeks to draw attention to these nuances in the field in between seemingly stable confessional or sectarian identities and the dynamics evolving around them and their border-crossing. Yet, the examples I would like to discuss also illustrate that denominational boundaries such as Shi'a, Alevi or Nusayri-Alawi do not lose their importance for drawing on specific historical narratives, practices or dogma. Instead, the focus on a shared repertoire of symbols and the shared veneration of the *ahl al-bayt* by Alevis, Shi'ites and, to a lesser extent, Nusayri-Alawis may blend out these denominational boundaries and describe a discursive space in which the importance of genealogy and charisma narrow down sectarian differences between these groups and enable them, for example, to conduct common ritual practices and join in festivities, such as *ghadir khumm*.[5] The examples given in this chapter furthermore illustrate a web linking various different Twelver Shi'a, Alevi and Nusayri-Alawi communities in a network of '*ahl al-bayt* communities' in which different charismatic persons from Turkey interact in festivities such as *ghadir khumm* and thereby articulate a mutual belonging to the followers of the *ahl al-bayt*.

As such, it seems necessary to investigate the relation of specifically Shi'a Islamic conduct, on the one hand, and other forms of articulation, practice and discourse that integrate other inner-Islamic denominations in an imagination of *ahl al-bayt* Islam, on the other. In doing so, it is also argued for the necessity to contextualise the emergence, operation or un-doing of sectarian boundaries instead of ossifying them through academic and political discourses on the seemingly timeless Sunni-Shi'a conflict.

"Alid Piety' and 'Ahl al-Baytism' as Analytical Concepts

As early as Marshall Hodgson's classic 'How did the early Shi'a become Sectarian?' (1955), it was noted that the veneration of the Prophet's family is by no means exclusive to Shi'a Islam. Hodgson argues:

> So many-sided is the sentiment – in *ḥadîth*, in the Ṣûfî orders, in guilds, in popular tales – that not only in its support of the original 'Alid claims but in its whole piety Sunnî Islâm can be called at least half Shî'ite. Yet, there were Shî'ites who still refused the half loaf, and formed themselves into sects. (Hodgson 1955: 4)

Such observations on 'Alid loyalty and veneration of the Prophet's family, the *ahl al-bayt*, was further described by researchers for very different contexts in time and place. To name but a few examples, Robert McChesney coined the term '*Ahl al-Bayt*ism' in order to describe practices and beliefs in his research at the 'Alid shrine in Mazar-e Sharif (1991: 33, 268). In his work, he looks at the rediscovery of 'Ali's tomb there at the end of the fifteenth century and traces the history of the shrine and its social environment from the sixteenth to the twentieth century. McChesney urgently stresses that it is problematic to speak of anything that happens in and around the shrine as specifically 'Shi'a practices' or as manifestations of 'folk Islam'. He argues:

> At the same time, however, there was and is the phenomenon of popular or folk religious practice and belief, which does not necessarily reject the legal tradition but goes in other directions in search of meaning. In present-day writing this aspect of Islam is often subsumed under the heading 'Sufi Islam' or 'dervish Islam' after one of its more visible manifestations. But again popular religious belief and practice both encompassed and transcended the somewhat limited phenomenon of the dervish brotherhoods. If one wishes to apply a label to the kind of religious manifestation represented by the tomb rediscovery that is more informative than 'Shi'i' or 'dervish' and more specifically Islamic than 'folk' or 'populist', perhaps the most suitable would be *ahl al-bayt*ism, the special reverence for the immediate family of the Prophet Muhammad. (McChesney 1991: 33–4)

After McChesney, Vefa Erginbaş has used the concept *ahl al-bayt*ism in order to characterise narrations of early Islamic history by early modern Ottoman historians like Enveri (d. 1460), Mustafa Ali (d. 1600) or Katip Çelebi (1657) who, according to Erginbaş, broadly and openly displayed 'Alid loyalty, venerated the *ehlibeyt* and partly even cursed the first three *rashidun* (Erginbaş 2013: 53). Referring to Hodgson's observation, Feener and Formichi also draw on the idea of 'Alid piety in describing the dynamics of sectarianism and shared cultural repertoire among Sunnis and Shi'ites in Southeast Asia (Feener and Formichi 2015: 4).[6]

These examples have in common that they focus on practices of veneration of the Prophet's close family by Sunnis – a veneration that exceeds the esteem that is generally held, also by Sunnis, for the Prophet's offspring. They suggest that *ahl al-bayt* veneration is no hallmark exclusive to Shi'ism and in fact antedates the development of the historical Shi'a. Although it came to be associated with one of Shi'ism's central characteristics, there is and ever was considerable disagreement as to whom the term *ahl al-bayt* actually applies and whom it integrates. The Qur'anic verse is not clear in this matter, because of grammatical inconsistencies with the preceding verses, as Brunner (2014: 5) has pointed out: in Qur'an 33.33 it says 'God desires only to remove defilement from you, o people of the house, and to purify you completely' (*yuridu allah li-yudhhiba 'ankumu 'r-rijsa ahl-al-bayti wa-yutahhirakum tathiran*, Brunner's translation). Here, the male plural suffix *-kum* is used, while the immediately preceding verses use the female suffix *-kunna*, as they address Muhammad's wives only. According to Brunner, such an unspecific formula gave rise to tentative interpretations, and was also applied to, for example, Abu Bakr and 'Umar, who both were father-in-law of the Prophet and thus rendered such a tie based on marriage on a par with blood-relationship (Brunner 2014: 7). Such an open and contestable understanding of the *ahl al-bayt* also enables Islamicate currents with a Shi'a tinge in Germany to refer to themselves as 'friends of the *ehlibeyt*'. As such, they oftentimes stress a mutual belonging to the *ehlibeyt* more than they draw on a more specific (sectarian) register in terms of Shi'a, Alevi or Nusayri-Alawi.

In the following, I would like to investigate two examples of such *ahl al-bayt*-oriented articulations of Islam in Germany. The first example depicts Alevis in Berlin, represented by the organisation called *Oniki İmam Yolu*

(The Way of the Twelve Imams) that is also listed among others under the umbrella organisation of Shiʻa groups in Germany, the Islamic Community of Shiʻite Congregations in Germany (*Islamische Gemeinschaft der schiitischen Gemeinden in Deutschland*, IGS). The other example investigates Turkish-speaking Shiʻites from Iğdır in eastern Turkey, *caferis* as they call themselves in Turkish. I would like to discuss these examples as articulations of *ahl al-bayt* Islam, as neither of the denominational, religio-political terms 'Shiʻa' or 'Alevi' may grasp practices and discourses within these articulations of Islam. Furthermore, I also favour the term *ahl al-bayt* Islam over syncretism here, as the latter suggests too much a mixture of two or more segregated elements with clear-cut boundaries. An idea of *ahl al-bayt* Islam, on the other hand, also does justice to many different forms of conduct in Islamicate contexts, be they in Germany, Turkey or elsewhere, which are not sufficiently described by sectarian labels such as Shiʻa or Alevi.

Shiʻism, ʻAlid Piety and *Ahl al-bayt* Islam in Germany

Though small in number, Germany's Shiʻa population is highly diverse in its ethnic, linguistic and socio-religious composition. While earlier works on Muslims in Germany, such as Spuler-Stegemann's (1998: 42), speak of approximately 125,000 Shiʻites, recent and more sophisticated inquiries assume around 200,000 (Mirbach 2008: 76). Hamideh Mohagheghi differentiates between 120,000 Shiʻites of Iranian and about 80,000 of Afghan background (Mohagheghi 2007: 123), while Heine and Spielhaus, according to the results of the previously mentioned inquiry by the Bertelsmannstiftung, name a share of 9 per cent of Shiʻites among the Muslim population in Germany (approximately 360,000) (Heine and Spielhaus 2008: 24).[7] Although there are no official data, my fieldwork further suggests that there are Shiʻa Muslims among Iraqis, Lebanese and Pakistanis living in Germany as well. The ethno-religious composition of the Shiʻa communities in Germany is also characterised by the ramifications of several migration waves since the 1960s: Iranians, Turkish labour migrants, Lebanese, Iraqi, Afghan and Pakistani refugees uphold their ethnic identity by means of religion and ritual activity. Furthermore, there are some German converts, but also Turkish Sunnis, who mainly converted in the 1980s being attracted by the success of the Islamic Revolution in Iran,[8] and several Turkish Alevis, who see their activity within Shi'a communities or as Shi'ites not as a conversion but as an articulation of their 'true' 'Ali-centred form of Islam.

There are almost 200 Shi'a organisations and associations in Germany, which display in most cases rather national or ethnic identities and are thus usually organised around language as their common marker of belonging (Langer and Weineck 2017: 224). Examples of such organisations are predominantly to be found among Iraqi as well as Turkish- and Azeri-speaking Shi'a communities. Others instead articulate a broader, 'Islamic' outlook, such as the Islamic Centre Hannover,[9] and others. This corresponds to Thielmann's findings from the wider Muslim field in Germany. He also stresses that there are broadly speaking two different kinds of organisational structures: ethnically oriented institutions, on the one hand, and supranational and more *umma*-oriented ones on the other (Thielmann 2012: 154). Both types of organisations have in common, however, that they do not articulate a specific Shi'a character in their names but rather promote either national/ethnic or more generally 'Islamic' ideas of collective reference and mutual belonging. Yet, there is also a considerable number of organisations that use references to the Prophet's family, the *ahl al-bayt*, as their common denominator. Among the 198 Shi'a organisations in Germany that I identified during my fieldwork, there are thirty-five that use this very term, either in its Turkish or Arabic rendering, in their names. Mohagheghi also points to the early attempts at organising the various different scattered Shi'a organisations under one umbrella, which was to coordinate the activities of the different '*Ahl al-Bayt* communities' (Mohagheghi 2007: 125). By 2006, there were forty-five such '*Ahl al-Bayt* communities' listed within the Islamic Council of the '*Ahl al-Bayt* Communities' in Germany[10] – a body that was installed in conjunction with activities by the Islamic Centre in Hamburg, one of the oldest and most famous Shi'a institutions in Germany providing both religious and educational activities. These communities, however, do not necessarily refer to the term *ahl al-bayt* in their names (Nassab 2017). This *Ahl al-Bayt* Council was soon to be replaced by yet another umbrella organisation in order to connect the work of the various different Shi'a communities in Germany. In 2009, the above-mentioned Islamic Community of Shi'a Congregations in Germany (IGS) was founded in Berlin, and there are by now around 150 organisations listed under its umbrella. Interestingly enough for our argument here, there are also Alevi organisations being represented by the Shi'a umbrella organisation, among them the *Oniki İmam Yolu* (The Way of the Twelve Imams) in Berlin (IGS 2017).

Ahl al-Baytism among Alevis: 'The Way of the Twelve Imams e.V.', Berlin

The organisation *Oniki İmam Yolu* was founded in the 1980s. Most of its members are Alevis from the traditional Alevi settlements in Anatolia, Bingöl, Muş Erzincan, Erzurum, Antep and Maraş Çorum; but there are also Twelver Shi'ites from Iğdır and Nusayri-Alawis from Hatay among the members of this organisation.

There are round 500,000 Alevis in Germany. Many of them perceive Alevism as part of Islam, while there are also voices that conceptualise Alevism as a distinct tradition outside of Islam; there is, for example a specific chair for Alevi theology at the Academy of World Religions at Hamburg University. The example of the *Oniki İmam Yolu*, on the other hand, represents an articulation of Alevism that strongly emphasises narratives and concepts shared with Shi'a Islam. Therefore, these examples – although numerically a minority within the Islamic and also the specifically Shi'a field in Germany – may serve to also discuss methodological problems aligned with too narrow an understanding of inner-Islamic denominations and their perceived boundaries which implicitly copies a Christian model of confessionalism.

The name *Oniki İmam Yolu* already hints at a rather Shi'a-oriented character of this form of Alevi-Islam. An informant, let us call him Onur,[11] is a *sayyid* from the Alevi *ocak* of Kureyşan. The Alevi *ocak*s are patrilineal lineages of descent which developed around Anatolian holy figures with an Alevi pedigree – a pedigree that endows the *sayyids* with legitimacy as religious specialists and that furthermore plays an important role in the social stratification of Alevi communities. As such a religious specialist, called *dede* among Alevis, Onur also conducts a *cem* ceremony every two weeks, as he says, 'in order to let their Anatolian roots not to fall into oblivion'.

He further stresses that, from inception, the organisation was more Shi'a-oriented than other Alevi organisations in Berlin, such as the *Berlin Alevi Toplumu* (Berlin Alevi Community). As such, many of the members display specifically Twelver Shi'a practices in that they follow, for example, the *taqlid* of Grand Ayatollah Sistani or Khamenei – a characteristic usually not to be found among other Alevi organisations and individuals. While some of the Alevis in *Oniki İmam Yolu* omit the five obligatory prayers – as many Alevis do – Onur himself emphasises their importance, referring to the Hymns of Shah Ismail Safavi (known among Alevis under his pen-name Hata'i) in which the obligation to pray was mentioned. Shah Ismail (1487–1524) was the founder of the Safavid dynasty in Iran who also declared Twelver Shi'ism as official religion of the state in the early sixteenth century. His poems belong to the most important sources for bestowing practice and conduct in Alevism with legitimacy. In the context of the daily prayer, Onur also emphasises that at the shrine of Hacı Bektaş in Anatolia, another important figure in Alevi Islam, members of the congregation usually pray using clay tablets during prostration called *turbah* or *mohr*, as is common or obligatory in Shi'ism as well.

The organisation's website likewise brings together Alevi and Shi'a semiotics (see Figure 10.1). There are, on the one hand, blessings and pieces of wisdom by Pir Sultan Abdal, another Anatolian Alevi dervish who lived at the turn of the sixteenth century. On the other hand, there are also slots dedicated to the 'fourteen infallibles' (*ondört masum*) and the *ehlibeyt*. Here we find *ahadith* concerning the *ehlibeyt*, blessings by 'Ali or dates deemed important for the *ehlibeyt mektebi*, as it is called here. Using the term *mekteb* (school) for the *ehlibeyt* followers suggests a certain degree of institutionalisation and coherence and further contributes to the notion of the *ehlibeyt* as an important marker of a specific inner-Islamic current. The website also displays an interesting appropriation: a saying placed at the bottom of the website says '*İlimden gidilmeyen Yolun Sonu Karanlıktır*' – 'The end of the path that leads astray from knowledge is darkness', which is usually connected by Alevis with Hacı Bektaş, the mentioned Alevi saint. These words are attributed to 'Ali here and thus connect this wisdom, widely known and referred to by Alevis, with the closer family of the Prophet, immediate successor of Muhammad and first Imam in Twelver Shi'ism.

As such, Onur and his organisation represent a specific articulation of Islam that does not fit the common denominational categories of either Shi'a or Alevi alone; rather, these two collective categories and their specific narratives, symbols and semiotics are combined and produce an articulation of Islam beyond these two denominations – an articulation that heavily draws

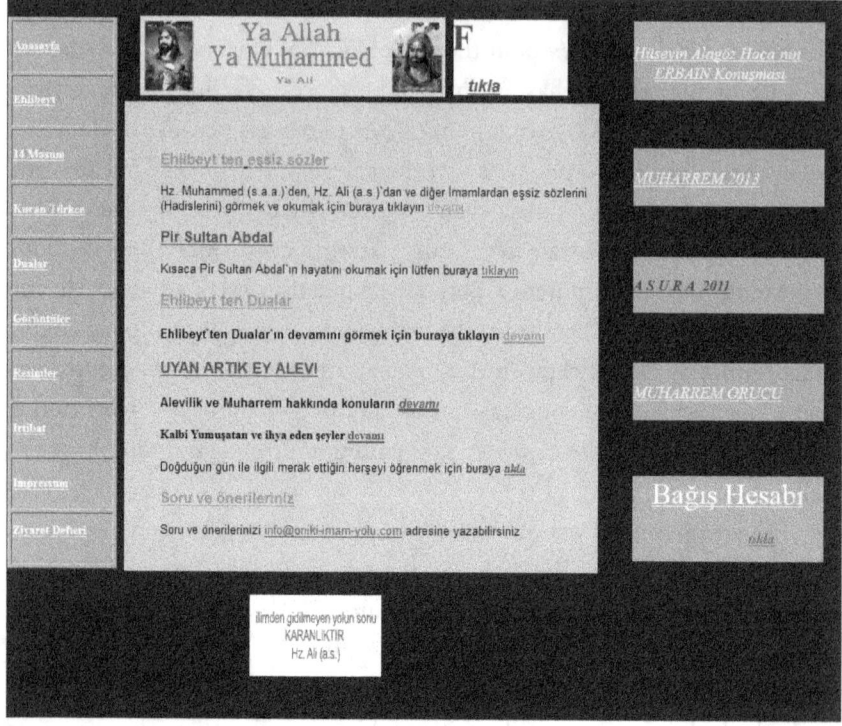

Figure 10.1 Website of *Oniki İmam Yolu*.

on the *ehlibeyt* as a source of cohesion. Although, as I mentioned before, such an articulation of Alevi-Shi'a Islam is not very widespread, it is not limited to this single example either. A prominent organisation in Turkey, the *Dünya Ehlibeyt Vakfı* (World Ahl Al-Bayt Foundation) likewise promotes an idea of Alevi Islam that heavily promotes Shi'a ritual practices and narratives; for example, Ali Kirazli, who was a representative of the organisation in Europe, holds that all Alevis should follow Shi'a forms of prayer (Gorzewski 2010: 204).

Apart from the fact that the *Oniki İmam Yolu* is organised within the Shi'a umbrella organisation IGS, some of their activities also hint at yet other aspects of this organisation being part of a transnational network of followers of the *ahl al-bayt*. For example, in December 2014 Ali Yeral, the director of the Hatay-based *Ehl-i Beyt Kültür ve Dayanışma Vakfı* (EHDAV, Ehlibeyt Culture and Solidarity Foundation), visited the *Oniki İmam Yolu* and gave a talk, which is obtainable on Youtube. In this presentation he further elaborated the importance of *ahl al-bayt* networks and articulated a vision of unity and community beyond sectarian boundaries:

> In order to follow the path of the *ehlibeyt*, to be an Alevi by heart, to be *hüseyini* by heart or *caferi*, we have to know about what is right and what is wrong according to [the teachings of] the *ehlibeyt*. (Yeral 2014)[12]

For the sake of our argument here, it is less important what Ali Yeral has in mind when he discerns right and wrong in terms of *ehlibeyt* teachings. More important are the categories that he refers to and that belong, in his perspective, to the *ehlibeyt*: Alevi, *hüseyini* and *caferi*. Yeral does not differentiate in his enumeration between Nusayri-Alawis from Syria and southern Turkey, a religious minority that he himself belongs to, and Anatolian Alevis, but it may be assumed that he summons both currents – major differences in terms of religious history and practice notwithstanding – under the one term Alevi. While the Nusayri-Alawis are an Arabic-speaking group that originates in ninth century Iraqi and *ghulat*-Shi'a contexts and that live along the Syrian and southern Turkish coastline, the Anatolian Alevis mostly stem from Turkmen and Kurdish tribal millieus of Ottoman Anatolia and came into contact with Shi'ism through military and Sufi bonds with the Iranian Safavids (Arinberg-Laarantza 1998: 152).

As such, the term Alevi increases its inclusivity and may include anyone who is a follower of 'Ali in the broadest sense, as this accommodates the original meaning of the term.[13] The concept of the *ehlibeyt* furthermore connects these Alevi groups with other forms of venerating the Prophet's offspring and which Yeral addresses by the term *hüseyini* – those who orient themselves to one of 'Ali's sons. Also referring to the *caferis*,[14] as the Twelver Shi'ites in Turkey are called, enables Yeral to reach out to these forms of 'Alid piety and include them as well in his imagination of those following the path of the *ehlibeyt*.

Ahl al-Baytism and Ghadiriyye: The Ehlibeyt Art and Cultural Organisation in Nuremberg

The other example I would like to discuss is represented by another organisation, the *Ehlibeyt Kultur- und Kunst Verein* (Ehlibeyt Cultural and Art

Organisation) in Nuremberg and their *ghadir khumm* celebrations. While the example above represented a case where Alevi and Shi'a practices and discourses are shared, the example of the Ehlibeyt Cultural and Art Organisation is slightly different: most of the members here are Turkish-speaking Caferi Shi'ite from Iğdır in eastern Anatolia and as such are rather homogeneous according to their common migratory background. The Caferis are Twelver Shi'ites from Turkey who used to live close to the Iranian and Armenian border. Although there had been Caferis residing in Istanbul since the eighteenth century (Zarcone 1993: 98), many Caferis from eastern Anatolia migrated to Istanbul in the 1950s and 1960s and began to publicly articulate their religion and culture from the 1980s onwards, also through the public display of rituals (Baylak 2011: 15). Like many other Shi'a organisations in Germany, their organisation bears the term *ehlibeyt* in its name. There are only a few examples where an organisation uses the label 'Shi'a': for example, the Iraqi Shi'a Cultural Organisation (Irakisch-schiitischer Kulturverein e.V.) in Munich. Most of the communities instead employ other aspects from a Shi'a register, such as Hüseyin, Al-Mahdi or, as here, *ehlibeyt*.

I visited their *ghadir khumm* festivities in October 2015,[15] which were conducted – *nota bene* – in an Alevi *cemevi* that the members of the Ehlibeyt Cultural and Art Organisation rent from time to time, whenever their own location is too small for their activities. The *ghadiriyye* celebrations especially lend themselves to reach out to and connect with all different forms of 'Alid communities, as this is the one occasion where 'Ali's legitimacy as Muhammad's successor is both commemorated and reproduced.[16]

For the *ghadir khumm* celebrations in 2015 the *ehlibeyt* organisation had also invited Ali Yeral and Cevat Gök, a Shi'a cleric from Istanbul. During his talk, Ali Yeral, who also gave talks to the above-mentioned Alevi association, mainly focused again on the unity of the Islamic *umma* in general and the *ehlibeyt* in particular. As representative of an Nusayri-Alawi organisation from Hatay, his being invited to a Twelver Shi'a *ghadiriyye* in Nuremberg personifies the degree not only of transnational networking among these communities, but also bears witness to the fact that these denominational boundaries may easily be overcome, especially on occasions such as *ghadir khumm*.

According to Yeral, *ghadir khumm* represents unity as it was on that occasion, when Islam was rescued from division and decline, as he said (*'ayrımcılıktan ve yok olmaktan kutarıldı'*). Interestingly, arguing like this, he excludes all those voices that do not perceive of *ghadir khumm* in this manner: one could also argue that the incident of *ghadir khumm* was indeed the point where the division of Sunni and Shi'a Islam was incepted into the early Muslim community. In doing so, Yeral articulates implicitly a Shi'a or *ehlibeyt*-oriented version of unity, that not only excludes Sunni perceptions of *ghadir khumm*, but also integrates different Islamicate currents, such as Nusayri-Alawis, Twelver Shi'ites or Anatolian Alevis into his idea of Islamic unity. On the occasion of the *ghadiriyye* in Nuremberg, he also brought in the aspect of national unity in concert with a mutual commemoration of Ali's designation: celebrating *ghadir khumm* and the national marker of being Turkish as common points of reference furthermore strengthen the ties of the *ehlibeyt* communities, to which he, as a Nusayri-Alawi belongs, as well as the Twelver Shi'a Caferis from Iğdır.

Likewise, on the occasion of *ghadir khumm*, Cevat Gök spoke of a path on which 'Alevis and Shi'ites are those following the way of the *ehlibeyt*, not the Yezid one' (*'Yezid yolunun değil, ehlibeyt yolunu takip eden Aleviler ve Şiiler'*). Positioning Yazid bin Mu'awiya vis-à-vis Alevis and Shi'ites, he rhetorically unites the latter two as being opposed to Yazid who is held responsible for Imam Husayn's martyrdom in Karbala by both Shi'ites and Alevis. Drawing on the *ehlibeyt* as a common denominator of Shi'ites and Alevis enables Gök and Yeral to articulate an imagination of unity that integrates such different denominations as Twelver Shi'ites, Anatolian Alevis and Nusayri-Alawis despite specific and considerable differences in their history, religious conduct, ritual practice, and so on. The mutual engagement in commemorating 'Ali's designation as Muhammad's legitimate successor appears here as the most important aspect in forging the community of the *ehlibeyt* and transcending sectarian boundaries that may be drawn according to other aspects of religious history, ritual practice or dogma.

Networking *Ahl al-bayt* Communities

Both Gök and Yeral represent an understanding of the *ahl al-bayt* that is widespread among Shi'a discourses and embraces Muhammad's closer family and the Twelve Imams. Likewise, both are able to reach out to the different currents within this form of *ahl al-bayt* Islam, be it Nusayri-Alawis, Anatolian Alevis or Twelver Shi'ites: both were invited to Germany on the occasion of the *ghadiriyye* in 2015, where both of them joined the festivities – despite their different sectarian backgrounds. Yeral, himself a Nusayri-Alawi and director of an *ehlibeyt* organisation, was invited to an Alevi organisation in Berlin and a Twelver Shi'a organisation in Nuremberg: the share of common ground and their mutual belonging to the *ehlibeyt* enabled them to link up in a transnational network of followers of the *ehlibeyt*. It is furthermore important to emphasise that their mutual engagement in this network is not perceived of as 'border-crossing', or as active undoing of sectarian boundaries; rather, the aspect of identification as friends or followers of the *ehlibeyt* is emphasised. Their mutual engagement in the network of *ehlibeyt* communities defines these communities more than any narrow sectarian label such as Shi'a, Alevi or Nusayri-Alawi.

In this regard, Spies has argued for contexts of researching religious plurality and/or hybridity where the researcher must also take into account that the subjects in question may not intentionally do or undo sectarian boundaries, but are rather indifferent towards them: 'they [the subjects of research] do not necessarily measure traditions against each other, look for equivalents or try to resolve differences' (Spies 2013: 123). The quote from the beginning of this chapter hints at a 19 per cent share of indifferent positioning by respondent Muslims in between Sunnism, Shi'ism and Alevism in Germany. The statistical problem of unspecific items may be one side of this coin. The other side, however, may be incommensurability as mentioned by Spies.

Interestingly enough, during the *ghadiriyye* celebrations – but also on other occasions, like Yeral's talk in the *Oniki İmam Yolu* – the focus on the unity of the *ehlibeyt* seems to be far more important than, for example, establishing clear boundaries to Sunni Islam. During my fieldwork I also frequently came across the opinion that 'Shi'a' was a political label while the subjects in question would call themselves nothing else but 'Muslim'. This again may underline the finding that Heine and Spielhaus mentioned: labels such as Sunni or Shi'a gain importance in national contexts in which these markers are politically charged. If this is not the case, or if these markers do not lend themselves to political mobilisation, then the degree of identification with them is less distinctive. This, in turn, may yield articulations of Islam that do not rely on a political or academic register of inner-Islamic plurality and difference, but draw on other forms of collective belonging, such as being friends of the Prophet's family, which may include very different currents – both from an ʿAlid and Shiʿa spectrum, but from Sunnism as well.

As illustrated, it is problematic to speak of specifically Shiʿa communities in these mentioned cases: although Shiʿa semiotics or ritual practices are displayed, the actors themselves are reluctant to label their activities as specifically Shiʿa and instead tend to draw different boundaries of Islamic belonging. Thus, more nuanced analytical categories are in order if we are to come to terms with such articulations of Islam. The examples given here also highlight another important character. On the one hand, they are both rather small communities that keep a low profile and thus do not aim at representing the majority of Shiʿites in Germany. On the other, this rather marginal position may enable articulations of Islam that do not necessarily have to follow hegemonic (for example, Iranian-funded Twelver Shiʿism) understandings of Islam.

Conclusion

The term *ahl al-bayt* Islam was used here in order to grasp practices of articulating forms of Islam in Germany that are incommensurable with sectarian borders among different ʿAli-oriented Islamicate currents such as Alevis, Nusayri-Alawis and Twelver Shiʿites. While the majority of the existing literature on the phenomenon of 'Alid piety' and '*ahl al-bayt*ism' focuses on the veneration of the Prophet's family by Sunni Muslims, this chapter investigated contexts in which currents with an ʿAlid or Shiʿa tinge unite as *ehlibeyt* Muslims. Thereby, relying on a small but working network of *ehlibeyt*-oriented scholars, these *ehlibeyt* Muslims create a discursive space in which their respective sectarian identities are blended out in favour of a broader idea of following the *ahl al-bayt*. The term *ahl al-bayt* Islam may thus serve as a concept to grasp such articulations of Islam that emphasise common points of mutual reference among Twelver Shiʿites, Alevis or Nusayri-Alawis. Describing the mentioned practices and narratives according to a confessionalised scheme of academic language does not come to terms with such a common discursive space, in which Shiʿites as well as Alevis of different currents may participate and transcend their respective denominational boundaries. It also accommodates the widespread veneration of the Prophet's family, which is, as McChesney holds, often labelled Shi'a, but also applies to other contexts – be they Alevi, Nusayri-Alawi or Sunni.

I would further suggest that these self-identifications beyond sectarian categories must not be (mis)understood in terms of hybridity, or syncretism: this would not only contradict the emic understanding of representing a legitimate form of Islam that unites different 'Alid currents as friends of the *ehlibeyt*. It is, furthermore, theoretically and methodologically problematic, as these concepts would reproduce rather essentialised and confessionalised notions of Muslim plurality. Granted that the term *ahl al-bayt* Islam is likewise a concept born out of academic categorisations and classifications, it nevertheless moves outside denominational boxes and hints at a shared repertoire of diverse groups in articulating specific Islamicate individual and collective subjectivities. Furthermore, it does so without perceiving of such articulations in terms of syncretism, in which allegedly clear-cut boundaries are overcome.

References

Abid, Liselotte (2013), 'Expressing Shi'ite identities in a European context. The example of an Islamic magazine in German language: Al-Fadschr/Al-Faǧr from Hamburg', *Wiener Zeitschrift für die Kunde des Morgenlandes* 103, 9–24.

Aksünger, Handan (2015), 'Antrittsvorlesung: Die Suche nach dem Einvernehmen. Ein dialogisches Prinzip der alevitischen Lehre', in H. Aksünger and W. Weiße (eds), *Alevitische Theologie an der Universität Hamburg: Dokumentation einer öffentlichen Antrittsvorlesung*, Münster: Waxmann, pp. 25–40.

Aringberg-Laanatza, Marianne (1998), 'Alevis in Turkey – Alawites in Syria: similarities and differences', in T. Olsson, E. Özdalga and C. Raudverre (eds), *Alevi Identity*, London: Routledge Curzon, pp. 151–66.

Baylak, Aysen (2011), *Visibility Through Ritual: The Shiite Community in Turkey: An Ethnographic Survey on Muharram Processions*, Saarbrücken: LAP Publishers.

Bernheimer, Teresa (2013), *The Alids: The First Family of Islam, 750–1200*, Edinburgh: Edinburgh University Press.

Brunner, Rainer (2014), 'Ahl al-bayt', in A. Walker and C. Fitzpatrick (eds), *Muhammad in History, Thought, and Culture: An Encyclopaedia of the Prophet of God*, Santa Barbara: ABC-Clio, pp. 5–9.

Erginbaş, Vefa (2013), 'The appropriation of Islamic history and Ahl al-Baytism in Ottoman Historical Writing 1300–1650', PhD dissertation, Ohio State University, Columbus.

Feener, Michael, and C. Formichi (2015), 'Debating Shiism in the history of Muslim Southeast Asia, in M. Feener and C. Formichi (eds), *Shi'ism in Southeast Asia: 'Alid Piety and Sectarian Constructions*, Oxford: Oxford University Press, pp. 3–15.

Gorzewski, Andreas (2010), *Das Alevitentum in seinen divergierenden Verhältnisbestimmungen zum Islam*, Berlin: ebv-Verlag.

Heine, Peter, and Riem Spielhaus (2008), 'Sunniten und Schiiten in Deutschland: Eine Kurzbetrachtung zu den Ergebnissen der Bertelsmannstudie', in S. Huber (ed.), *Religionsmonitor 2008: Muslimische Religiosität in Deutschland, Überblick zu religiösen Einstellungen und Praktiken*, Osnabrück: Bertelsmann Stiftung, pp. 24–31.

Hodgson, Marshall G. (1955), 'How did the early Shi'a become Sectarian?', *Journal of the American Oriental Society* 75:1, 1–13.

—— (1974), *The Venture of Islam. Conscience and History in a World Civilization, Vol I: The Classical Age of Islam*, Chicago: University of Chicago Press.

Islamische Gemeinschaft der schiitischen Gemeinden Deutschlands – IGS (2017), website, available at: http://www.igs-deutschland.org/, last accessed 11 January 2017.

Langer, Robert, and Benjamin Weineck (2017), 'Shiite "communities of practice" in Germany: researching multi-local, heterogeneous actors in transnational space', *Journal of Muslims in Europe* 6:2, 216–40.

McChesney, Robert D. (1991), *Waqf in Central Asia: Four Hundred Years in the History of a Muslim Shrine, 1480–1889*, Princeton: Princeton University Press.

Mirbach, Ferdinand (2008), 'Islam in Deutschland, Islam in der Welt', in S. Huber (ed.), *Religionsmonitor 2008: Muslimische Religiosität in Deutschland, Überblick zu religiösen Einstellungen und Praktiken*, Osnabrück: Bertelsmann Stiftung, pp. 76–83.

Mohagheghi, Hamideh (2007), 'Die Schiiten', in I. Wunn (ed.), *Muslimische Gruppierungen in Deutschland: Ein Handbuch*, Stuttgart: Kohlhammer, pp. 114–28.

Monsutti, Alessandro, Silvia Naef and Farian Sabahi (2007), 'The other Shiites. From the Mediterranean to Central Asia, an introduction', in A. Monsutti, S. Naef and F. Sabahi (eds), *The Other Shiites. From the Mediterranean to Central Asia*, Frankfurt a.M.: Peter Lang, pp. 7–15.

Nassab, Hosseini (2017), Die Offizielle Website des Großajatollah Hosseini Nassab, available at: http://www.hoseini.org/proj-ger.htm, last accessed 11 January 2017.

Özyürek, Esra (2015), *Being German, Becoming Muslim: Race, Religion and Conversion in the New Europe*, Princeton: Princeton University Press.

Religionswissenschaftlicher Medien- und Informationsdienst e. V. – REMID (2016), 'Mitgliederzahlen: Islam', 28 September, available at: http://remid.de/info_zahlen/islam/, last accessed 12 January 2017.

Shanneik, Yafa (2015), 'Remembering Karbala in the diaspora: religious rituals among Iraqi Shii women in Ireland', *Religion* 45:1, pp. 89–102.

Spies, Eva (2013), 'Coping with religious diversity, incommensurability and other perspectives', in J. Boddy and M. Lambek (eds), *A Companion to the Anthropology of Religion*, Chichester: Wiley Blackwell, pp. 118–36.

Spuler-Stegemann, Ursula (1998), *Muslime in Deutschland: Nebeneinander oder Miteinander?*, Freiburg: Herder.

Thielmann, Jörn (2012), 'Die Sunna leben in Deutschland: Von der Entstehung islamischer Felder und muslimsicher Techniken des Selbst', in P. Schrode and U. Simon (eds), *Die Sunna leben: Zur Dynamik islamischer Religionspraxis in Deutschland*, Würzburg: Ergon, pp. 149–72.

Yeral, Ali (2014), 'Presentation at the Oniki İmam Yolu', available at: https://www.youtube.com/watch?v=IMin4lN_sD4, last accessed 12 January 2017.

Zarcone, Thierry (1993), 'La situation du Chi'isme à Istanbul à la fin du XIXe et au début du XXe siècle', in T. Zarcone and F. Zarinebaf-Shahr (eds), *Les Iraniens d'Istanbul*, Louvain: Peeters, pp. 97–111.

11

'FOR 'ALI IS OUR ANCESTOR': CHAM *SAYYIDS'* SHI'A TRAJECTORIES FROM CAMBODIA TO IRAN

Emiko Stock

Summer 2014: M., S. and C., early twenties, seem astray in the city of Qom, Iran.[1] They are Chams, Cambodian Muslims. None speaks or reads a word of Persian – or Arabic – just yet, but all have a year to learn. None are religious experts just yet, but all are entering a programme that will make them so in a few years (numbers unsure), years with little journeys back to Cambodia (returns uncertain). They are Muslims in a vastly Buddhist country. They are Chams among a Khmer majority.[2] And they are *sayyids* – descendants of the Prophet – born Sunnis, now 'going Shi'a', as they say themselves, as others say about them. Shi'a: yes and no, they rejoin, not yet, maybe, yet to be. For this movement towards the other side of Islam – if sides there ever were – is ongoing, trying, and all very contemporary. But Shi'a, certainly, for sure, very precisely, very soon, probably as it has always been, or at the very least as it should always be from now on. Or so whisper the ancestors, read the chronicles, inscribe the lineages. In all this, there is a clear imprecision, a constant uncertainty that we may need to write and read with. Taking in all those apparent contradictions, this chapter attempts to look at the recent Shi'a connections tied by (a few) Cambodian Cham Saeths (the transcription of *sayyid* in Cham) who so-happen to be Sunnis. It could be tempting to anchor those trajectories as conversions, and to ground them in Iran where those travels to Shi'a seminaries take place, or strictly in the contemporary since they have been carried out in recent years. Instead, I suggest a *long durée* perspective inspired by those primarily concerned and those living along side them – may they be staying in Cambodia and not going to Iran, may they be staying Sunnis and not going Shi'a. Doing so implies three things:

- First, it requires patience from both the ethnographer and the reader for what may appear to be contradictory positions, fragmented statements and partial utterances, for it is exactly what such an ethnography is made of, and has to remain loyal to. This contribution will therefore stay away from much of a context: numbers and background will be scarce, not only to follow this texture of imprecision, but also to respect the anonymity of my interlocutors who would be easy to identify if I was to spell out their regions, demographics and timelines.
- Second, by making Saeths the core of its object, this ethnography works against an erasure of the complexity of the Cham social networks under the single label of 'Chams' as a unified ethno-religious group, and instead contributes to a trans-local study of *sayyids* as one of 'Sayyido-Sharifology' as defined by Morimoto (2004).
- Third, this approach contributes to a historical anthropology that does not take Sunnism and Shi'ism as two opposite and contrasted poles, but rather situates a certain 'Alid piety in which Cham Saeths – whether they consider themselves Sunnis or Shi'ites – sit comfortably in between.

Weaving ethnographic observations and historical materials fairly familiar to scholars of Southeast Asia's Islamisation,[3] I refer to the notion of 'Alid piety as it was first elaborated by Hodgson (1955), and further developed by Feener and Formichi (2015). In this chapter, I will show how this notion of 'Alid piety takes on its full meaning among Cham Saeths who, rather than furthering a Shi'a/Sunni divide, reassert the ethereal quality of such a separation.

By not taking Sunnism and Shi'ism as a starting point, but opting to follow certain forms of 'Alid piety as they emerge through ethnography, I further Hodgson's questioning of the border between both when he said, in his study of the early history of Shi'ism, that 'the Shi'a was not yet a sect; there can as yet be no division of Islam between Shi'ite and Sunni – Shi'a and 'Uthmaniya were merely positions with regard to the imamate, not comprehensive divisions of the faithful' (Hodgson 1955: 3). Hodgson reminds us that 'in its whole piety Sunni Islam can be called at least half Shi'ite' (1955: 4). He does so because rather than looking at 'what we took for basic Shi'ite principles' (1955: 1), Hodgson re-casts those principles as inherent forms of a devotionalism to 'Ali and his family, the 'people of the cloak' (*ahl al-kisa*), and by extension the larger family of the 'people of the house', the *ahl al-bayt*,[4] which can be found across sectarian divisions later elaborated by reformist agendas. Focusing on 'Alid piety then allows

> for a reframing of our views on the widespread reverence for 'Ali, Fatima and their progeny that emphasizes how such sentiments and associated practices are seen as part of broad traditions shared by many Muslims, which might or might not have their origins in a specifically Shi'i cultural identity. (Feener and Formichi 2015: 3)

For Feener and Formichi, 'Alid piety can be defined as 'aspects of Islamic belief and practice expressing special reverence for the *ahl al-bayt*' (2015: 4). They remind us that those elements of 'Alid piety were widespread across Southeast Asia long before the Iranian Revolution (2015: 4), therefore moving away from the recurrent practice of matching references to the *ahl al-bayt* as inherent traces of Shi'ism in the scholarship on the region's Islamisation. In this chapter, it is to similar elements of 'Alid piety found among Chams in general, and Saeths in particular, that I will attend, as a way to provincialise forms of devotion to the *ahl al-bayt* away from Shi'ism and Iran altogether.

'For 'Ali is Our Ancestor': Shi'a as *Ahl al-bayt*

M., S. and C. have recently arrived in Iran. They have arrived in Qom, a city they knew nothing of, waiting in a plaza burnt out by the sun even more than a New Year heatwave back home would. M., S. and C. carry into those new Shi'a studies afar something that brings it all to a close: something of being Saeth – or *sayyid*.[5] It is in this being *sayyid*, that the contemporary move from

Sunni to Shi'a is carved. It is in the *long durée* history of Chams and Saeths, that the division between the two – Sunni and Shi'a – melts into the unity of a lineage, an aspiration to a line, the continuity of a genealogy. It is in all this, that it all goes back to 'Ali: 'for 'Ali is our ancestor'.

When the ethnographer comes to consider those connections to Shi'a – rather than conversions into Shi'a, she thinks along with her interlocutors who return the sentence 'For 'Ali is our ancestor' as reason. A sentence floating in elusiveness not only because ethnographic refusal has to be taken into account – after all, why talk when all sits in too well without saying – but also because 'going Shi'a' is in itself a process marked by uncertainty, caught in the moment, seized by potentialities rather than by the assertion of conversion or pilgrimage. This is not to mean that Chams are unsure of what they are doing, unclear of where they are going, 'ignorant' of what is happening, how and why. This may be more about how Chams are sure of other things, found in the clarity of alternative modes of knowledge, some that dwell in the sentence: 'For 'Ali is our ancestor.' It is in following this line, which names 'Ali as an ancestor, that I attempt to trace modalities of Islam and the thread that entangles Sunnism and Shi'ism.

In this chapter, I will suggest Iran as a new place on an old timeline of historiography, and Shi'ism as a devotion to and love of 'Ali, exactly where Sunnism leaves a trace. By this, I mean that I will not refer to my interlocutors and my sources as inherently Shi'a, for most could be described as Sunni if we were going for the usual categorisation. Yet, as this categorisation proves to be of little use, I will step away from it entirely unless otherwise required. What I will do, instead, is to discuss the different genealogical claims put forth by Cham Saeths in relation to the *ahl al-bayt*, through Prophet Muhammad's son-in-law 'Ali, in order to unpack the statement "Ali is our ancestor'. This will bring in a series of doubles: that of being 'Alid no matter which "Ali' is referred to, that of being Fatimid through another Fatima, that of evoking other figures connected to the *ahl al-bayt* and their progeny. A lineage that may bring in spectres of 'Alids who are not Fatimids (like Muhammad Hanafiyyah), alternative Imams blurring the Iranian connection into Southeast Asian Islamisation (like Zayn Al-'Abidin), Iranian kings calling on Persianate trends rather than Shi'itisation (like Nurshivan) and endless sojourners becoming familiar strangers as they bear lines of continuity (like Al-Aydarus from Hadramawt). Through those different lines of '*sayyid*ness', I will demonstrate the close ties that Saeths maintain with an ideal 'Ali that should enable us to understand notions of 'conversion' in a less drastic way, in modes that do not necessarily affect much of the daily, change your life, switch your soul, shake your core. In the manner of connections: something of interactions, something of affinity, something of threads of relatedness that we can see as links of genealogies. In other words, if it is a common and broadly expressed love and devotion for 'Ali that Chams – and notably Saeths – are furthering when they become 'Shi'a', there may be nothing peculiar to Shi'ism that leads them into this process. Maybe this has very little to do with Shi'ism or Sunnism. Maybe this has nothing to do with converting out or in. Maybe this is more about one's positions and compositions in full openness and fluidity.

> The van flies by the house, dusting off the road, a smoulder of red earth settling on their faces. A car follows through, and then another van and yet another car. They look like good rentals, definitely not the kind to go around, sure enough a sort of expedition to Phnom Penh – the capital – is in plans.
> Uncle A. draws a cigarette puff, eyes locked on the road where the procession passed:
> 'They are treated like kings . . . That's just too much.' His lips snap down the smoke.
> Uncle B.'s left plastic boot is attempting to scratch off the plantations' liquid rubber sticking to his right ankle:
> 'Well, we're *ahl al-bayt* after all, that's kind of like being kings.'
> He leaves the boots to rest and turns to the ethnographer as he says the last part, searching for her agreement, hoping for a justification.
> Her eyes holding on to the gone convoy, she asks: 'Who's that?'
> Uncle A.: 'Just a couple of kids heading there,' his chin pointing to a far horizon. We both know he speaks of 'Iran', which was all over a neighbourhood rumour for the past few days: this is where a couple of new students are going.
> Uncle A.: 'I mean, it's normal to have your family taking you to the airport, but now it's like the whole village is going, that's enough already.'

Uncle B., almost chanting to himself, half-jokingly, half-meditatively: 'We are the *ahl al-bayt*, we are the *ahl al-bayt* . . .'
Uncle A. turning to him, loud: 'So am I . . . Who cares?!'
Uncle B. tickles Uncle A. who jumps in surprise.
Uncle A. tickles back.
Uncle B. responds with another round.
They may be a while.

Uncles A. and B. are neighbours, cousins and friends, closing up to seventy each. Both of them are Cambodians, Chams, Saeths. Both of them are Muslims. They have always been Sunnis, just like their parents and grandparents before them, or at least just as Chams have always been described.[6] A few years ago, unlike his wife, unlike his family, unlike his neighbour, and unlike a few relatives outside of the village, Uncle B. became Shi'a. Uncle A. has, unlike his brother, unlike his morning coffee seller, unlike his cousin the-energetic-widow-next-door, or unlike his so-educated-and-knowledgeable nephew, remained Sunni. Uncle A. explains that he stays right here in Sunnism because that is what his ancestors did, why change? Uncle B. explains that he moved into Shi'ism because that is where his ancestors were from, for they are all descendants of 'Ali and 'Ali, it is said, is Shi'a. For Uncle B. it is not about change either, but about going back to normality, one that may have been put into brackets for a while, brackets now to be re-opened. It is about making continuity out of disruptions.

This is how most, if not all, stories of becoming Shi'a – or at least connecting to it – have been subtitled here since they started less than a decade ago: it is a certain going back rather than something apparently new. It may have started just now, but it all comes from centuries away.[7] Surely, it is a one-man story, as we can easily imagine: an old respectable saint preaching the truth about Islam through charisma and knowledge acquired in deep introspection and decades of careful reading and attentive life going. There is a long white beard in that image, one we cannot quite do away with just yet. And yet, it is all wrong: because it was then a young adult, shy and skinny, pink cheeks and dove eyes, not talkative but assertive maybe, a cosmopolitan 'nerd' surely, who travelled around the Middle East for his studies and his quest for more. Curious of his own *sayyid* genealogy, searching for threads into the cloak of the *ahl al-bayt*, interested in history, always a listener to elders' stories, he was eager to know the rest of it, hungry for all of it. He has read, studied and travelled places. Knowledge and charisma sometimes wear unexpected understated cloaks. Now back in the village, in hiding always, maybe for discretion, maybe also because slipping away is just what shy 'nerds' tend to do. Some call him Cousin-Hidden-Imam. He is the one who started to follow a road into seminaries in Qom, wearing a Shi'a trend some may say. Something new for all of those whom, like him and before him, studied through Sunni scholarly lineages in Malaysia, Egypt, Mecca and Thailand. Nothing new to those who had always seen 'Ali as their main anchor into Islam, nothing new to those who always claimed to be his descendants, to belong to the *ahl al-bayt* lineage. Cousin-Hidden-Imam tries out Qom for Qur'anic and *fiqh* studies, and invites a few younger relatives on the way. Each time he comes back to Cambodia, there are more discussions about Shi'a and the *ahl al-bayt* in the village. By now even words like 'Karbala' do not sound so strange anymore. And there it is: one of the main *sayyid* communities in Cambodia now has some Shi'ites and some Sunnis living side by side. For after all, the same line of genealogy to the *ahl al-bayt* has not moved.

'Ali Hanaphiah: 'Alid and Fatimid Piety Doubling Here and There

It is no coincidence that it all started with *sayyids*, that it is *sayyids* who first and foremost have been interested in, curious about, and attracted to Shi'ism. For, after all, what Cousin-Hidden-Imam and others along with him may be after when they tried out Shi'a and Iran may be just rehearsed forms of '*sayyid*ness', it may just be about threading the line back to the *ahl al-bayt*. Here, I am following not only Cousin-Hidden-Imam and his Saeth fellow Shi'ites, but also the work of Kazuo Morimoto (2004, 2012), which calls for a systematic, transnational and interdisciplinary study of *sayyids*. Centring my research around the example of Cambodian Cham *sayyids* allows us not only 'to understand [*sayyids*] respective societies better' (Morimoto 2012: 4) but also to recast the 'love and devotion' for the Prophet's family as not solely Shi'a, but rather as defining the 'contours of a transectarian tradition' (Morimoto 2012: 2, 16). I follow Morimoto's suggestion for a Sayyido-Sharifology[8] to serve as a comparative study of scattered kinsfolk of

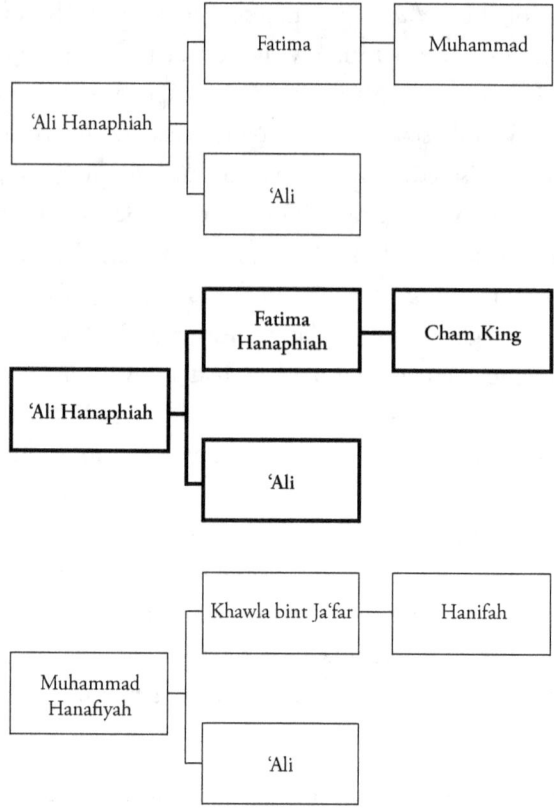

Figure 11.1 'Ali Hanaphiah (and his doubles).

the Prophet Muhammad: a systematic, transnational, and trans-disciplinary project, that would take the category of *sayyid*/sharif as a central object of enquiry. The aim, for Morimoto, is to work against the usual marginalisation of *sayyids* and sharifs to the side of the studies of Islam, which tends to take for granted the social or historical reverence supposedly attached by Muslims to the descendants of the Prophet. For Morimoto, Sayyido-Sharifology goes against the usual pattern of learning about *sayyids* as something secondary to your primary study of something more 'important' (2004: 91). Here, my starting point is a study with Saeths about their trajectories towards Shi'a Islam and Iran, rather than a study of conversions to Shi'ism and journeys to Iran that would lead me back to question *sayyids*' positionality in the making. This reflects my own ethnographic journey, which started with Chams among which Saeths prominently figured. As this research approach unfolded, I too, along with other Saeths, started to hear about newly ongoing and exciting matters we all became very curious about: Shi'a and Iran. This method may also explain why I am, for the time being, focusing this research on the '*sayyid*ness quality' of Shi'itisation and the importance of the *ahl al-bayt* reference, although I am aware that the dynamics underlying the relationship between Shi'a and *sayyid*ness are more complex and would need some later refinement that may contradict the present pages.

Turning attention to those Saeths who have become connected to something referred to as 'Shi'a', I leave this category open as in this particular village and lineage – the village of Uncle A. and B., of Cousin-Hidden-Imam and of a couple of 'kids from around the block' jumping into vans with a brand new set of denim-shirt-jacket-and-backpack – Shi'a is both very familiar and still left open to more to come, something of an imprecision. The only thing sure is that it is related to the *ahl al-bayt*[9] and that it is connected to 'Ali, the 'Ali that links all Saeths to the Prophet Muhammad's lineage.

'Ali is indeed seen by quite many Chams – including non-Shi'ites and non-Saeths – as a paternal ancestor of sorts, as well as the first Islamiser.[10] By extension, most of the first Muslim envoys from the Champa court to the Chinese court were named 'Ali, which may prove the presence of 'Alid descendants in Southeast Asia as early as the seventh century (Wade 2010: 374).[11] Saeths mainly, and other Chams too, refer to 'Ali and his son 'Ali Hanaphiah as the head of the lineage that brings being Cham together with becoming Muslim. The story goes like this:[12] 'Ali arrives among Chams where he meets a beautiful Cham princess. He falls in love with her. Her name is Hanaphiah, Fatima Hanaphiah. 'Ali already has a wife back home, Fatima. However, here he meets our Fatima, the Cham Fatima, Fatima Hanaphiah. They have a child together. A son is about to be born, a son himself to be named 'Ali, after his father; and Hanaphiah, after his mother: 'Ali Hanaphiah. Yet, there is too much trouble in the air, too much trouble in the land of the 'Arabs', over there where 'Ali has his home. 'Ali leaves to tend to this war, goes away and never comes back, for he will die there. The other 'Ali, the Cham 'Ali, 'Ali Hanaphiah, will never meet his father. Yet, other versions talk of him going to Mecca to pay a visit and help out in the war (probably Karbala). 'Ali and 'Ali do not know each other but they do meet and they do recognise each other immediately. Probably this is what happens when people are meant to be together. Sometimes 'Ali Hanaphiah is a very strong man, a hero made of power and powers. Sometimes the boy is still a boy: the storyteller is now embraced by a smile coming to his face, as he recalls: "Ali loved his son so, so dearly. He would never go about without him. He would always carry him around on his shoulders. Hasan-Hosen sometimes become(s) jealous, because he/they have to walk alone.[13] Sometimes, Fatima she gets angry, but she too calms down. Those father and son, they loved each other . . . Really, really loved each other.' Love lasts, wars come: 'Ali Hanaphiah joins the fight with his brothers Hasan and Husayn (Hasan-Hosen), and as the myth goes, all die. Other versions say *they* died and *he* survived, and came back to the Chams where he started the line. Others say he started the line, and then left: and still lives, up to now, somewhere in hiding today. 'It has to be in a mountain somewhere, I guess. Or maybe down a well. No one knows for sure . . .'[14] From this union – that of this Fatima (Hanaphiah) and this 'Ali (ibn Abi Talib) – a son is born, and with him all Chams, say some; only Saeths, insist others.

What is interesting here is the importance, the preponderance of the figure of 'Ali. Most, but not all *sayyids* in the world trace their line from an 'Alid branch, positioning 'Ali at the core of their lineage. However, all *sayyids* – 'Alids or not – refer to the Prophet for common ancestry. For Saeths too, the figure of Muhammad is central: if we are sons of 'Ali, who is from the House of the Prophet, we have to be by default, by association, by way of consequence, descendants of the Prophet too. We too are from the cloak, we too are the *ahl al-bayt*. However, 'Ali was not the son of Muhammad, he was his son-in-law. The Saeths' line is then a *sayyid* one only on the side, by association, since it is in the couple 'Ali and Fatima (daughter of Muhammad) that the family of the cloak, the people of the house, takes its roots. Are Saeths then really descendants of the *ahl al-bayt* as Uncle B. insists in his chants, in his prayers, in his tickles?[15] While 'Ali stands in Shi'ism as the ideal figure of virtue and strength, he nonetheless remains a side-line. After all, he is the last one invited to join in the cloak. How come, then, can Saeths insist on a *sayyid* line sliding away from its core: Fatima? This draws our attention to the female line of our story, to that lady Hanaphiah who is somehow, in all coincidence, also called Fatima. While she is clearly not *the Fatima*, mother of Hasan and Husayn, *the Fatima* daughter of Muhammad, she becomes a sort of double that enables a genealogy to repeat itself. Through the name *Fatima*, Hanaphiah may as well be *a sort of Fatima*. Also, could it be a coincidence that our boy is named 'Ali, just like his father, so that people would alternatively refer to one 'Ali or the other? In other words, just like the presence of the 'Alid-Fatimid family is *only* inferred, it is also *always* inferred, turning the lineage, through its doubles, into one inherently *both* 'Alid and Fatimid at the same time. In addition, something even more unique happens here: while stories similar to that of 'Ali Hanaphiah can be found elsewhere in Southeast Asia, through the figure of Muhammad Hanafiyah,[16] the hero is localised – rather than presented as a visiting stranger – only in the Cham version. In other words, what Fatima Hanaphiah engenders in her (Cham) womb may just be a (Cham) 'Ali. What Fatima Hanaphiah lacks here, in her own genealogy of not being truly *ahl al-bayt*, of having no inscription whatsoever in the genealogy of the People of the House traditionally reported by both Shi'ites and Sunnis, she makes up for in bearing across the name of another Fatima, her double, but also in being Cham. As Cham society is traditionally matrilocal even among patrilineal Saeths, Hanaphiah – the mother – being Cham, is something that matters here. 'Ali came to her. He did not stay, but that does not matter, that happens; he just came to her, that indeed matters, a lot.

The Cham *sayyid* genealogy is therefore one that opens up to an 'Ali essential yet passing by, a mother anchored locally which doubles with the potentials of a Fatimid line, and a core ancestor – 'Ali Hanaphiah – who keeps on coming and going, complicating this thing of being inherently from here and somewhere else, while grounding Saeths themselves at the core of the House of the Prophet. If 'Alid piety is indissociable from Fatimid piety, they are also both to be found elsewhere – where 'Ali's home is – and here – where 'Ali Hanaphiah is from and comes back to. Through the double of 'Ali Hanaphiah and 'Ali and through the double of Fatima Hanaphiah and Fatima, our story turns the strange into local and complicates our notions of outsider/insider just as it anchors 'Alid piety into a Fatimid one. This begs the question of how strange could anything 'Shi'a' be, if it is located in one's own genealogy and narratives of origins? What remains at the core of it all then is this: a love and devotion for an 'Ali and Fatima of one's own, rather than a particular import of Shi'a exegesis or ideology. Yet, 'Ali Hanaphiah is not the only composition of 'Alid piety played along with going Shi'a or going to Iran. Sometimes it even comes as an erasure: 'Ali Hanaphiah, some say, is 'not the real story, this is not correct, that's fiction you know. Actually, you won't even find the story among Shi'ites.'

Of Persian Kings in Southeast Asia: Shi'a Before Shi'a

This denial of 'Ali Hanaphiah as not being the 'real' ancestor of Saeths, or at least not the one enabling them to be recognised as descendants of 'Ali, may be something more recent, something found as one searches for absolute truths and proven facts in the seminaries of Qom. Nevertheless, tracing ideas as if one could catch them in their flow is quite impossible, as stories are exchanged from one to another and do travel around the country. More probably, different versions of different stories have long circulated side by side, taking a life of their own, flirting, getting a little too close if you ask those of us who want an easy reading, if you ask the ethnographer who is now unable to disentangle them.

Here, the words of a Saeth Uncle listing his own potential lineages

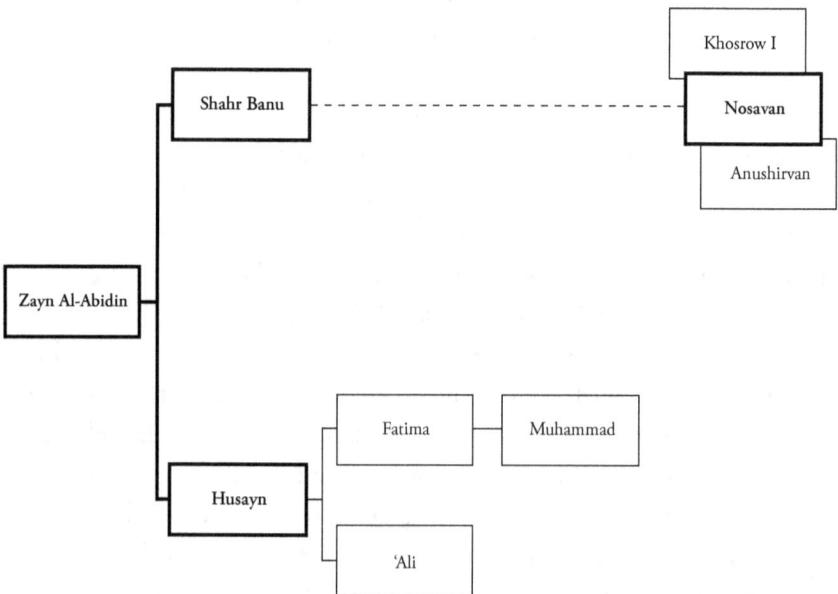

Figure 11.2 From Zayn Al-'Abidin to Nosavan.

resume it best: 'Seinol Abidin . . . 'Ali Hanaphiah . . . Al Idrus . . . I am quite unsure about all those really . . . The elders they had so many stories . . . It's hard to remember everything you know . . . I think . . . I think we all come from Hosen.' I have already discussed at length 'Ali Hanaphiah and will make sure to return to Al Idrus later on. For now, I am mostly interested in the mention of Seinol Abidin and Husayn himself as bearers of the lineage continued beyond 'Ali.

> Uncle has just finished preparing the cameras for tomorrow's wedding. I am sitting by, while Little-Cousin-Easy is struggling with the internet to upload an on-the-spot editing app for his phone. He hopes to try out some filming during the ceremony. Uncle chats away, and asks whether I'll be going to Iran soon, he wants to send some dry meats, medicine and money to Little-Cousin-Skinny who feels quite isolated there. I explain that I am still waiting for my visa but hope I will be joining a Shi'a studies seminar, that I may be able to understand a little bit more about the *sayyids*' lineages with some research there. Little-Cousin-Easy looks up and says that he thinks he knows the school where I will be studying, it's probably where he too used to study, he says. Uncle seems reflexive and then takes back the conversation: 'They must know a lot there. Because the descendants of Hosen are Chams but the descendants of Hasan are Iranians.' I ask more from Uncle: 'Hosen had a son. Seinol Abidin. He came to Malaysia and that's how the line goes. No wait . . . That's Jafar. No. No that comes after . . . Wait . . . I am not sure . . .'

Most of the time the ethnographer is left with this, with the 'unsure' for sole answer. Sometimes she is thrown a bit of luck, and she gets to layer up:

> [Several months later] I am in the Phnom Penh's apartment of Uncle's cousin. The couple also mentions that the *sayyids* come from two branches: the Hosen one is military, the Hasan one is religious. That's why 'we Saeths' are always militaries and always in trouble, they joke. They add that their ancestors came from Yemen through Malaysia/Indonesia.

We have several implications to unpack here: a certain connection to Iran and a *husayni* line that is both inherently Cham and military. A lineage finding its sources in what could be a classic of *sayyids* in Southeast Asia: the

Hadrami connection (Yemen) rooted in Malaysia or Indonesia, to which I shall return. Mainly, we have a new character coming through: Seinol Abidin.

The first Seinol Abidin – or Zayn Al-'Abidin – we can think of, along with Uncle, is also known as 'Ali ibn Husayn, son of Husayn, and one of the only survivors of the battle of Karbala. To some, I can imagine that the genealogy of Cham Saeths invoking 'Ali, Husayn and now Zayn Al-'Abidin may seem too much to handle. There is another reference that could help us connect all those lines together: 'Nosavan', who has long been at the core of the debates on early 'traces of Shi'a' among Chams, and who will help us discuss those 'Shi'a trends' before Shi'ism came to be.

Nosavan often appears in the nineteenth-century scholarship on Chams, at the head of a list of gods and kings sitting somewhere between Brahmanism and Islam (Aymonier 1890: 153; Cabaton 1906: 11, 1907: 137–8; Delaporte 1880: 417–18; Durand 1907: 321). All authors agree to identify Nosavan with *Anurshivan the Just*, a title pointing to the first Sassanid king Khosrow I (531–79). For researchers of Southeast Asian Islamisation in general, and with a particular interest in the role played by Chams in the process, Nosavan as the first king of Chams promised to finally answer the scholarship's anxiety to demonstrate 'early Shi'a traces':[17] (1) eponymous of Khosrow, Nosavan can be an identifier of an Iranian influence, and therefore confirm early Southeast Asian exchanges with Iranians; (2) while mentioned in manuscripts that have nothing to do with Islam, and even more, among Brahmanists, his association in the pantheon with 'Allah can direct to Islamisation; and finally (3) as he is always associated with 'Ali, this opens the possibility of a Shi'a figure.[18] Again, this double repeating itself: 'Ali and Shi'a. Shi'a conversions for 'Alid connections. The references to Nosavan, albeit very light and the effect of many crossed re-citations among very early sources in colonial Cham studies, will be re-re-cited in later research on Cham Islamisation as a key element to demonstrate the possibility of Shi'a and Persianate trends (Fatimi 1963: 51; Manguin 1979: 278; Schafer 1967: 11; Setudeh-Nejad 2000).

We *may* now have traces of a heroic kind of figure who *may* have been Iranian. That could enable us to place an imaginary Iran on a *long durée* Cham history. What could this have to do with our Zayn Al-'Abidin? Zayn Al-'Abidin, son of Husayn, is also son of Shahr Banu, daughter of the last emperor of the Sassanid dynasty. If we follow Zayn Al-'Abidin's line on his mother side then, all the way up, we find Khosrow I, first Sassanid king, also known as Anurshivan the Just. So: on one side Husayn and the cloak, on the other side Nosavan and 'something like Iran'.[19] This completes too nicely our circle to be merely coincidental. And yet, here comes a random quote, from a random discussion, an ethnographic snapshot among many:

> We are now talking of the Khmer Rouge massacres in the village of Pa-Saeth-Who-Became-My-Father. I'm trying to see if Uncle knows more about what happened to Grand-Pa and the girls, if anyone knows what happened after they were all forced out of the car. He doesn't respond to that, but instead he says 'That village. It is particular. They are neither Po [descendants of Cham royal lineages] nor Saeth, they are both. They are all called Van. That's because they come from Nosavan, they come from Iran.' Then he goes on describing the men in the picture around Grand-Pa at the mosque opening, probably in the late 1960s, he says. Among all of them, there was one who had indeed survived, but he is dead now, he passed away just a few months ago.

They are called Van. They come from Nosavan. They come from Iran. They have a supplementary quality, that of being both *sayyids* and descendants of the Cham kings – Po – that of being both from here and from there.[20] Given the rarity of any references to Nosavan even when the ethnographer stubbornly tries hard to find any, this sentence sticks in the air, especially given the context – the discussion is about something else entirely, I do not expect Nosavan and even less Iran to come out of this. Yet, this sentence seems again too much of a coincidence, adding to others: Nosavan was an ancestor too, just like Husayn and Zayn Al-'Abidin, and 'Iran' – or at least something Persianate behind the word – comes back in as the lasting effect left by an imprint of origins. Our Shi'a connections now seem anchored in a (glorious) past that had little to do with Shi'a and all to do with mighty lineages inscribed in what would become Iran, or at the very least a land of ancestors. Iran then, becomes a moment – that of Nosavan and his lineage somehow Saeth – rather than a place. Iran makes history in the past and in the yet to be of Qom studies for Little-Cousin-Easy and Little-Cousin-Skinny. Iran becomes a time-space where and when Shi'a connections can be made. And yet, Iran can have come through different lines of space and times itself. One of them is the Hadrami connection to Southeast Asia.

One Step in and out of Being 'Arab': The Hadrami Connection

In Southeast Asia, narratives of Islamisation often carry Hadrami lines of Southeast Asian *sayyids* (Freitag 2003; Ho 2006). A frequent trope in those stories – also common among Saeths in Cambodia – is the union between an 'Arab' – often a *sayyid* traveller – and a local princess. The Hadrami line can already be read as an imprint coming out of some of our previous field notes, where the Saeth couple from Phnom Penh say that their ancestors came from Yemen through Malaysia/Indonesia; and when confused, another Uncle recalls 'Al Idrus' as one of the many possibilities in the bundle of potential genealogies. The Al-Aydarus line is the main lineage from which Southeast Asian *sayyids* – located mainly in Indonesia and Singapore, and to some extent Malaysia – trace their affiliation. The line finds its origin in Abu Bakr Al-Aydarus, who in the early sixteenth century came to be the founder of the Sufi branch of the Ba 'Alawiyya in Aden, where he became a saint and patron (Ho 2006). In the sixteenth century, Abdullah Al-Aydarus, one of Abu Bakr Al-Aydarus' descendants, sets off for Aceh, and starts what is now known as a long line of descendants of Hadrami *sayyid* travellers and local women, most of the time daughters of ruling elites and royalties. One of those children – referred to as *muwallads* – was the son of Abdullah Al-Aydarus and the princess of Aceh. The boy was named Zayn Al-'Abidin and was the first of the Al Aydarus to migrate to Johor, where he too marries a

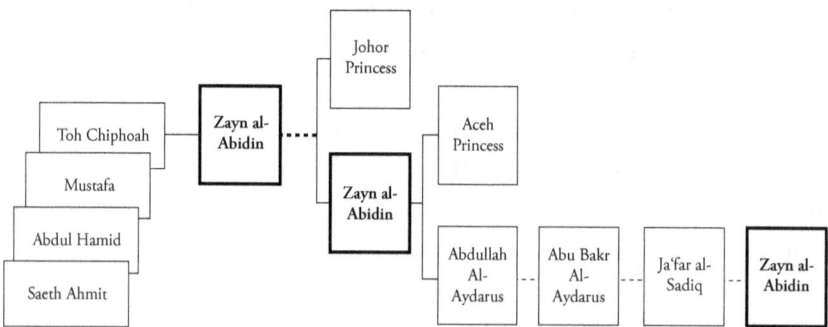

Figure 11.3 Repetitive Zayn Al-'Abidins.

local princess and takes up the Malay title of 'Tun'[21] (Winstedt 1932: 51, 58). Could this be Uncle's very own Seinol Abidin, as we saw above, or rather, just one more layer to the many Zayn al-'Abidins melting in Saeths' lineages? If the Al-Aydarus descendants have therefore spread throughout Southeast Asia and constituted new Muslim communities, we could ask why would it not be the case among Chams? A field note to line this up:

> Toh Chiphoah / Mustafa / Abdul Hamid / Saeth Ahmit was the first [ancestor] to have arrived in Cambodia. He is gone now . . . After everything [here implying everything he/we has/have been through] his tomb can't be found, it's right under that military base now . . . Nothing left . . . Even Cousin-Minister he has tried, but he can't go there, you can't see the grave . . . Anyway, so Phoah was the son of Al Idrus who was from Terengganu. He had first came to Champa, then came to Cambodia . . . I mean back then it was only one country anyway. He had four wives: a Khmer, a Chinese, and two Chams.

The reference to Terengganu here is interesting, not only because this Malaysian sultanate is said to be the first one to have received Islam (Andaya and Ishii 1993: 514; Wade 2010: 389), but also because the very Zayn Al-'Abidin Al-Aydarus just mentioned above, gave birth to a line that would later on settle in Terengganu and found its sultanate in the eighteenth century (Ali al-Haji Riau 1982: 70). Another line of Hadrami *sayyids*, another descendant of Al-Aydarus, one of the many that may be haunting Uncle when he refers to Seinol Abidin and Al Idrus, when his cousins think of Yemeni ancestors coming through Malaysia and Indonesia, when forebears of desecrated tombs found origins in Terengganu.

Here, we may think that we have lost track of our Shi'a connections into readings transporting us into Hadramawt and Indonesia and Malaysia but away from 'Alids and Iran. It does not have to be the case. We can further the Iranian thread of thought – materialised by 'Iran' – into the quote we had at the beginning: right after mentioning Zayn Al-'Abidin, Uncle hesitates, thinking the right person may be 'Jafar' instead. It is tempting here to connect Zayn Al-'Abidin to his descendant Ja'far Al-Sadiq, sixth Imam in Shi'a Islam, and founder of the Ja'fari school of jurisprudence. The name of Ja'far is now and then referred to as a sort of ancestor or religious guide by some Chams, but it is not that frequent, and he is not necessarily one of the main figures repetitively invoked to speak of lineages.[22] What interests me most though, is how we can connect those seemingly episodic 'Iranian' references doubling as 'Shi'a' references – from Nurshiwan to Zayn Al-'Abidin and Ja'far Al-Sadiq – in today's Cham oral history, with narratives in Indonesia related to the Wali Songo, the nine saints who first Islamised the archipelago.

It may seem strange to step out of our lineages of Cham Saeths in Cambodia and jump away into Indonesia to continue our quest. Yet, this will be no surprise to those familiar with the Wali Songa as many of their narratives connect them to Iranian origins, on the one hand, and to Cham royal lineages, on the other. In light of the cryptic ethnographic pieces I just laid out, what I will now try to do is to tie those loose ends together.

And Along Came the Wali Songo: Iranian and Cham Traces in the Region's Islamisation

In order to read the narratives of the Wali Songo with an eye on both Iranian and Cham lineages as indissociable, we need to begin with the legend of the *Putri Cempa*. The story, contained in Javanese literary texts, tells of a Cham princess who becomes the wife of the king of Majapahit (currently in Java, Indonesia) in the fourteenth century (Lombard 1987: 314; Manguin 1979: 261–2). While the story always brings – through many variations in its multiple versions – the Islamisation of Java as a result of this union, what should interest us the most here, is yet again a line on the side, that of the sister of the princess who had remained in Champa where she had been married to an 'Arab'. Here it is difficult not to imagine a *sayyid* of sorts, since up to now, it is frequent for Chams – and some other Southeast Asians – to collapse the two – *sayyids* and Arabs – together (Ho 2006; Jonge and Kaptein 2002). In some versions, the couple has two sons, in others only one. The son will visit the aunt-princess in Java and become Sunan Ampel, one of the nine saints of Java (Lombard 1987: 314–15; Manguin 1979: 262; Raffles 2010: 128).[23] Sunan Ampel's original name is generally Raden Rahmat or Sayid Rahmat. While '*raden*' marks a royal lineage in Javanese – which would translate the '*po*' lineage of the mother – 'sayid' clearly indicates the father's *sayyid* lineage. We know little about Sunan Ampel's father, but some texts clearly identify him

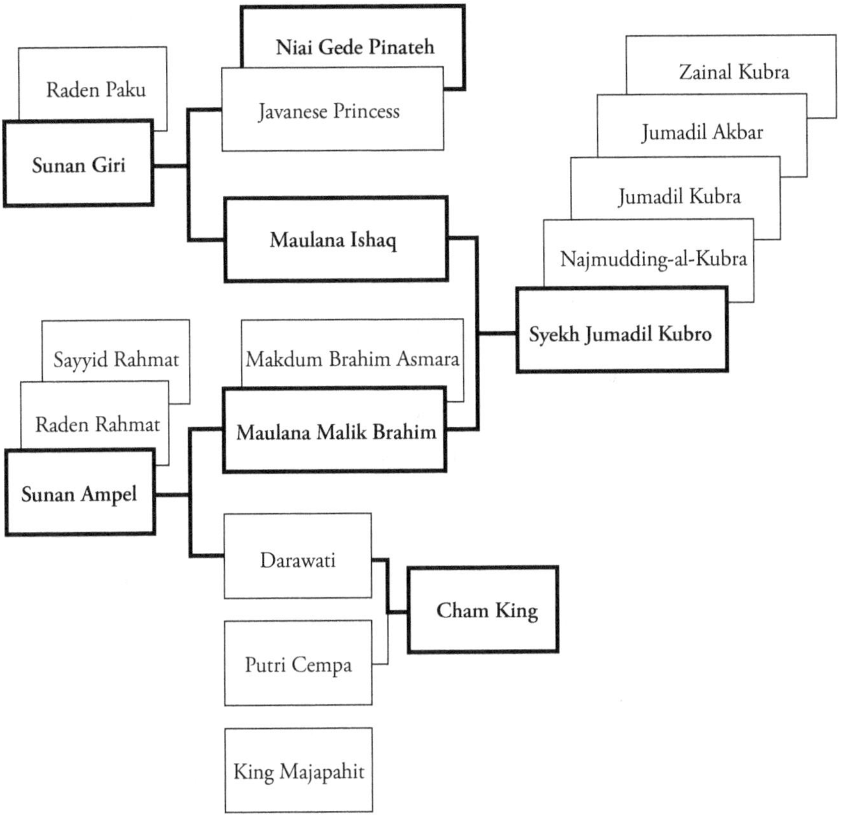

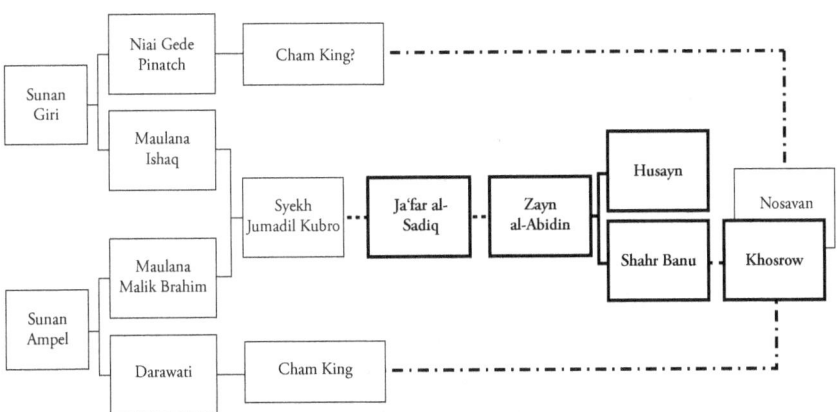

Figure 11.4 Wali Songo (Part I).

Figure 11.5 Wali Songo (Part II).

as Makdum Brahim Asmara or Maulana Malik Brahim, who was himself the first Wali Songo in the sixteenth century. Maulana Malik Brahim interests us here, because his name translated an affiliation to Samarkand and therefore to Persianate horizons. As he came to Java with both his father – Syekh Jumadil Kubro more famous in Java as Sunan Gunung Jati – and brother Maulana Ishak, we may have more to draw from by following them.

Under the name of the father – Syekh Jumadil Kubro – we could find a student of Najmuddin Al-Kubra who had lived in the Khorasan in the thirteenth century, and founded the mystical order of the Kubrawiyya (van Bruinessen 1994: 306). While van Bruinessen acknowledges the discrepancy of the dates, he also notes that 'a number of different historical and legendary persons have merged into an ideal character' (van Bruinessen 1994: 305). What interests us then, along with van Bruinessen, is not so much the absolute accuracy of the hard facts of history but rather the trace left by the name of this 'almost omnipresent character in the sacred history of Islamic Java . . . to whom all the saints of Java appear to be related somehow' (van Bruinessen 1994: 318). Najmuddin Al-Kubra quickly becomes in Javanese Jumadil Kubra, Jumadil Akbar, and even Zainal Kubra: this 'Zainal' seems to be doubling here the 'Seinol' of Uncle, and the Zayn Al-'Abidin, the son of Husayn. In other versions, Jumadil Kubra is the son of Ja'far Al-Sadiq (van Bruinessen 1994: 321), bringing us back to where we started, to a line of 'Alid piety via Husayn.

The connections of Jumadil Kubra – and something Persianate – to Chams and Champa can be now furthered. First, he is always connected – as a father, grandfather or preceptor – to our Wali Songo Raden Rahmat/Sunan Ampel and Raden Paku/Sunan Giri. Sunan Giri's father is Maulana Ishaq, sometimes brother of Maulana Ibrahim, father of Sunan Ampel. This makes Sunan Ampel and Sunan Giri cousins. And if – as some versions point to – Jumadil Kubra is the grandfather, we then have the following lineage: Sunan Giri/Sunan Ampel > Maulana Ibrahim Maulana Ishaq > Jumadil Kubra > Ja'far Al-Sadiq > Zayn Al-'Abidin > Husayn on the paternal line, and Nosavan | Nurshiwan | Khosrow on the maternal line.[24] By going back to Husayn, the paternal line implies a Shi'a narrative that can be pursued into Iranian origins through his mother line – Shahr Banu and Khosrow. By going back to Khosrow, a line emphasising the Iranian heritage leads us back into a yet-to-be Shi'a through a Husayn soon-to-come. What this tentative puzzle of genealogies brings forth then, is yet again this doubling of 'Shi'a'/'Iran' lineage on both sides.

However, the double implication of Shi'a/Iran is not the only issue that happens in the life-stories of our saints: through their own maternal line, they are partly Cham, something of importance as we have seen earlier on with Hanaphiah. While we have already explained that Sunan Ampel was the son of Maulana Ibrahim and a Cham princess, the life story of Sunan Giri, albeit more complex, may offer yet some other Cham potentials.

Raden Paku/Sunan Giri's mother is not a Cham princess but the daughter of a Hindu Javanese king who refuses to convert to Islam. His father, Mulana Ishak, failing in his conversion attempts, leaves; the kingdom is plagued; the king threatens to kill the boy yet to be born (Raffles 2010: 128–9), or is thrown into the sea in a chest which is fished out of the sea at Gresik (Ricklefs 1993: 10). The baby is taken away into protection and will be raised first by Niai Gede Pinateh – to whom we will return – and afterwards by Raden Rachmat/Sunan Ampel, who will provide him with his religious education (Raffles 2010: 129). It is only later on that Sunan Giri will meet Mulana Ishak[25] and learn that he is his father (something that echoes quite well our 'Ali Hanaphiah's late encounter with his unknown father 'Ali). The foster mother – Niai Gede Pinateh – is from Cambodia for sure, but could she have been Cham? In Raffles, she is banned from Kamboja (Cambodia) because of sorcery accusations,[26] and is taken into protection by the Javanese king who entrusts her as the political and commercial head of the port (Raffles 2010: 129). I am suggesting that she could have been Cham (from Cambodia) because, while we often equate Chams with Champa now, at a time when kingdoms fluctuated in borders and affiliations, and ethnonyms were not fixed, 'from Kamboja' could have meant being Cham from Cambodia just as 'from Champa' could have been the term attached to Chams, no matter where they came from. Po Dharma has also pointed out that Cambodia and Champa are often confused in Malay chronicles in reference to 'Kembayat Negara' (Dharma *et al.* 2000: 23), a note that could probably be applied to our Javanese texts. In any case, what we have here are two key lineages of Southeast Asian Islamisation which combine Cham and Iran into a *sayyid* lineage: Raden Rachmat/Sunan Ampel has a Cham mother and an Iranian father and Islamises parts of Indonesia; Raden Paku/

Sunan Giri has (potentially) a Cham foster mother and an Iranian father, in addition to a Cham/Iranian foster father in the figure of Raden Rachmat/Sunan Ampel. But in using those Javanese texts, one may ask why should this all matter and connect to Cham Saeths in today's Cambodia who, as far as I know, do not refer to those narratives.

To attempt an answer, it might be useful to connect the Kubra lineage more directly to our Saeth lineages within Cambodia then. We may even be able to do so by looking at the Cham royal chronicles themselves, in which a fifteenth century king is named Po Kabrah, an interesting similarity of names and time frames (Dharma 2000: 184; Dharma *et al.* 2000: 17).[27] Also, we already know that Maulana Brahim went to Champa where he found his wife the Cham princess. While – as far as I know – the Javanese sources do not speak of any travels to Champa/Cambodia on Ishak's end, the geography of tenth-century Iranian explorer Ibn Rusta does mention that an Arab merchant named Abu 'Abd Allah Muhammad bin Ishaq had spent two years at the court of the Khmer ruler at Angkor (Ferrand 1913: 69).[28] The name is too closely related to the idea of our Maulana Ishaq not to be noted.[29] The dates are too far apart for sure, but again, it is the continuity of an idea, the insertion of recurrent figures in a seamless line of ancestors that we should intend to establish here. Arabs double with Iranians, strangers with locals, 'Alids with Fatimids. This, in the end, may be all that is left of our quest for all things 'Shi'a'.

Epilogue: In Lieu of Shi'a Traces

This is what is left to the ethnographer to work with when it comes to those 'Shi'a traces' scholars from the last century were so anxious to demonstrate. This is what is left when she tries to follow lines of Saeth history and lineages of *sayyid* genealogies. And as she tries, a sentence comes back, yet another Uncle who, in his car, during a ride, throws out 'there were at least three lineages among the Saeths' and then leaves it at that, pulls the car right then, right there, as we arrive at our destination, gets out of the car opening arms of joy as our host comes to us. And that is it, never comes back to the sentence, leaves it there, even when the ethnographer attempts to pick it up. There is yet another abstract from my very early fieldnotes, in a completely different context, as I am sitting with a non-Saeth, a non-Po, a former soldier and sympathiser of the FULRO,[30] who reminisces over his childhood in the 1950s and what he now takes to be the outdated social structures of the Pos and Saeths – and notably some of their endogamic rules. The system, he says, incorporated more groups than that, more threads: some military, some royal. Probably both. They must have been all of that and more he concludes.

Probably a little bit of this and a little bit of that, something of Po and Saeth and more. Probably something of the tickles Uncle A. and B. exchange when they agree to disagree. Something about doubles repeating themselves throughout. Something about lines entangled having a burn out. Something that cannot be reduced to just a dualism, for it may always allow for more. This is, maybe, where this chapter finds its limits: too often I have spoken of narratives of 'Alids among *sayyids* as if they were only proper to the latter; too often I have talked of Shi'ites and *sayyids* as if they were equivalent. But there is more to it: probably a little bit of this and a little bit of that. I have tried to pull out many threads of a mesh of lines. Those lineages break like thin spider webs the second you try to hold on to them. Yet, just like a net, they surely hold on to us now, as they hold Saeths and *sayyids* together in 'Alid piety, a love, a devotion for 'Ali and his family that comes in many forms. What I have been trying to suggest here is not to tug so much at all those strings that weave us back into the cloak, as it is a garment of complex and intricate design. Rather, I have tried to show that it is in their dividing and doubling quality that those story lines thread traces of genealogies and absences together. It is in attending to those lines cosying up in the cloak, that we can situate Shi'itisation not as a new process of conversion but as a continuous mode of devotion, as a threading of connections. What it means to go Shi'a for Uncle A. and Uncle B., for Cousin-Hidden-Imam, Cousin-Little-Easy, Cousin-Little-Skinny and some of their neighbours, friends, relatives, is not to be found in change, for there is little of that. Yet, it is not a confirmation that Chams or Saeths were all Shi'ites from the beginning, that those 'Shi'a traces' much in expectation are finally coming together. Maybe, in the end, all this is a reassertion of a certainty in sitting comfortably in between, always. The idea of 'Alid piety developed by Hodgson (1955) and Feener and Formichi (2015) proves very productive here, to rethink the Shi'a/Sunni divide that our many Uncles A. and B., in their common hope to remain true to their *sayyid* ancestors, would probably have little patience for.

The division between Sunni and Shi'a clearly melts in those many lines towards the House of the Prophet, towards our Uncles' very own *ahl al-bayt*. It may be one – of the many – contributions that the Sayyido-Sharifology hoped by Morimoto could bring to the study of Islam beyond its too often ascribed regional borders (e.g. Middle East/Southeast Asia) in order to 'identify the contours of a trans-sectarian tradition' (Morimoto 2012: 16).[31]

In this chapter, I have often equated traces of Shi'a and lines of *ahl al-bayt* just as the tradition in Islamic Studies in general, and in Islamic Southeast Asian Studies in particular, often tend to do. I have followed, to repeat Hodgson's observations, 'what *we* took for basic Shi'ite principles' (my emphasis; Hodgson 1955: 1). I have placed an 'Alid for a Shi'a, and vice and versa. I have done so maybe because I too long for things we can hold on to, for crutches this article could walk the reader through. After all, we did take a lot of turns on our way to some of this Saeth 'Alid piety. And yet, it is to the contrary that I aim, to 'a corrective to the persistent conception . . . that the attitudes favourable to *sayyids* and *sharifs* must always be linked to Shi'ism . . . [while they] have been a phenomenon widely attested in what we may call "intercessional Islam"' (Morimoto 2012: 9). Elements of devotion to the *ahl al-bayt* should not then be reduced to Shi'a traces for two reasons:

- First, because this would merely repeat 'stricter forms of distinction between Sunni and Shi'i that have emerged in the modern period, driven by the reformist agendas' (Feener and Formichi 2015: 4). As Hodgson warned us more than half a century ago, 'Islamists, both Muslim and Western, have had a way of absorbing the point of view of orthodox Islam' (Hodgson 1955: 5), something we may want to stop repeating, if we too want to truly get caught in tickles of connections.
- Second, because reducing Shi'a to traces within a broader 'mainstream Islam' implies that Shi'a practices are at best artefacts of obsolescence and margins barely framing an orthodox centre.[32] While documenting the existence of Shi'a communities in Southeast Asia proves difficult, 'it is possible to trace diverse lines of devotionalism to the *ahl al-bayt* in terms of broader, non-sectarian traditions of 'Alid piety across the long-term Islamisation of the region' (Feener and Formichi 2015: 15), going against the reassertions of margins and centres.

Finally – if it has to be so – when it comes to the current attempts of 'going Shi'a' among Chams – who so-happen-to-be Saeths – focusing on Shi'itisation would lead us nowhere. We could look at what people think and how they feel about young gents going to 'Iran' and families being a little too 'out there' about it, as Uncle A. seems to think. We could talk about what kind of renewal in Cham Islamic ideologies may bring back Shi'ism, shall it grow outside of a particular location and lineage. We could tend to the pride of mothers longing for sons in countries unknown of, just as we could try to find what institutional powers are behind that – as if that matters to mothers. But we would miss the point that for those Chams, for those Saeths, the brackets of history are merely reopening, disruptions can now continue. The many torn up threads to 'Ali can now be seamed together, the many absences of silenced ancestors in genealogical cloaks can now take full presence.

References

Ali al-Haji Riau, Raja (1982), *The Precious Gift: Tuhfat Al-Nafis*, ed. and trans. Virginia Matheson Hooker and Barbara Watson Andaya, Kuala Lumpur: Oxford University Press.

Andaya, Leonard (1999), 'Ayutthaya and the Persian and Indian Muslim connection', in K. Breazeale and B. Adulyadej (eds), *From Japan to Arabia: Ayutthaya's Maritime Relations with Asia*, Bangkok: Toyota Thailand Foundation, pp. 119–36.

Andaya, Barbara, and Yoneo Ishii (1993), 'Religious developments in Southeast Asia c. 1500–1800', in N. Tarling (ed.), *The Cambridge History of Southeast Asia*, Cambridge: Cambridge University Press, pp. 508–71.

Aymonier, Étienne (1890), 'Légendes historiques des Chames', *Excursions et Reconnaissances* 14:32, 145–206.

Baried, Baroroh (1976), 'Shi'a elements in Malay literature', in S. Kartodirdjo, *Profiles of Malay Culture: Historiography, Religion, and Politics*, [Jakarta]: Ministry of Education and Culture, Directorate General of Culture.

Birchok, Daniel Andrew (2015), 'Locating the descendants of 'Ali in South-West Aceh: the places of 'Alid piety in late twentieth-century Seunagan', in C. Formichi and M. Feener (eds), *Shi'ism in Southeast Asia: 'Alid Piety and Sectarian Constructions*, Oxford: Oxford University Press, pp. 165–87.

Brakel, L. F, and L. F Brakel (1977), *The Story of Muhammad Hanafiyyah: A Medieval Muslim Romance*, The Hague: Martinus Nijhoff.

Brakel, L. F, Junaidah Salleh, Mokhtar Ahmad and Nor Azman Shehidan (1988), *Hikayat Muhammad Hanafiyyah*, Kuala Lumpur: Dewan Bahasa dan Pustaka, Kementerian Pendidikan Malaysia.

Bruinessen, Martin M. van (1994), 'Najmuddin Al-Kubra, Jumadil Kubra and Jamaluddin Al-Akbar: traces of Kubrawiyya influence in early Indonesian Islam, *Bijdragen Tot de Taal-, Land- En Volkenkunde* 150:2, 305–29.

Cabaton, Antoine (1906), 'Notes sur l'Islam dans l'Indochine française', *Revue Du Monde Musulman* 1, 27–47, in N. Abdoul-Carime, Nasir (ed.) (2003), 'Réimpression et commentaire de l'article d'Antoine Cabaton : "Notes sur l'Islam dans l'Indo-Chine française"', *AEFEK – Association d'Echange et de Formation pour les Etudes Khmères*, available at: http://aefek.free.fr/bibliotheque Documents00010583.html#I001b5ddd, last accessed 29 February 2015.

—— (1907), 'Les Chams musulmans de l'Indochine française', *Revue du Monde Musulman* 2, 129–80.

Collins, William ([1996] 2009), 'The Chams of Cambodia', in *Ethnic Groups in Cambodia*, Phnom Penh: Center for Advanced Study, pp. 2–110.

Cowan, H. K. J. (1940), 'A Persian inscription in North Sumatra', *Tijdschrift Voor Indische Taal-, Land- En Volkenkunde* 80, 15–21.

Daneshgar, M, F. B. A. Shah, Z. B. Mohd Yusoff, N. Senin, S. F. Ramlan and M. R. B. Mohd Nor (2013), 'A study on the notions of 'Ali Ibn Abi Talib in Malay popular culture', *Journal of Shi'a Islamic Studies* 6:4, 465–79.

Delaporte, Louis (1880), *Voyage au Cambodge*, Paris: C. Delagrave.

Dharma, Po (2000), 'L'Insulinde Malaise et Le Campā', *BEFEO* 87:1, 183–92.

Dharma, Po, Gérard Moussay, and Abdul Karim (eds) (2000), *Nai Mai Mang Makah / La princesse qui venait du Kelantan*, Kuala Lumpur: Kementerian Kebudayaan, Kesenian dan Pelancongan Malaysia, Ecole française d'Extrême-Orient.

Durand, E. M. (1907), 'Notes Sur Les Chams: VII. Le Livre d'Anouchirvan', *BEFEO* 7:1, 322–39.

Fatimi, S. Q. (1963), *Islām Comes to Malaysia*, Singapore: Malaysian Sociological Research Institute.

Feener, Michael, and Chiara Formichi (2015), 'Debating "Shi'ism" in the history of Muslim SEA', in C. Formichi and M. Feener (eds), *Shi'ism in Southeast Asia: 'Alid Piety and Sectarian Constructions*, Oxford: Oxford University Press, pp. 3–16.

Ferrand, Gabriel (1913), *Relations de voyages et textes géographiques arabes, persans et turks relatifs à l'Extrême-Orient du VIIIe au XVIIIe siècles*, Paris: E. Leroux.

Freitag, Ulrike (2003), *Indian Ocean Migrants and State Formation in Hadhramaut: Reforming the Homeland*, Leiden: Brill.
Guillot, Claude (2004), 'La Perse et Le Monde Malais: Échanges Commerciaux et Intellectuels', *Archipel: Études Interdisciplinaires Sur Le Monde Insulindien* 68, 159–92.
Ho, Engseng (2006), *The Graves of Tarim Genealogy and Mobility across the Indian Ocean*, Berkeley: University of California Press.
Hodgson, Marshall G. S (1955), 'How did the early Shi'a become sectarian?', *Journal of the American Oriental Society* 75:1, 1–13.
Jonge, Huub de, and N. J. G Kaptein (eds) (2002), *Transcending Borders: Arabs, Politics, Trade and Islam in Southeast Asia*, Leiden: KITLV Press.
Lombard, Denys (1987), 'Le Campa vu du sud', *Bulletin de l'Ecole française d'Extrême-Orient* 76:1, 311–17.
Lombard-Salmon, Claudine (2004), 'Les Persans à l'extrémité Orientale de la Route Maritime (IIe A.E. – XVIIe Siècle)', *Archipel: Études Interdisciplinaires Sur Le Monde Insulindien* 68, 23–58.
Manguin, Pierre-Yves (1979), 'L'introduction de l'Islam au Campa', *BEFEO* 56, 255–87.
Marcinkowski, Christoph (2008), 'Aspects of Shi'ism in contemporary Southeast Asia', *The Muslim World* 98:1, 36–71.
—— (2015), 'Shi'ism in Thailand: from the Ayutthaya period to the present', in C. Formichi and M. Feener (eds), *Shi'ism in Southeast Asia: 'Alid Piety and Sectarian Constructions*, Oxford: Oxford University Press, pp. 31–49.
Marrison, Geoffrey (1955), 'Persian influences in Malay life (1280–1650)', *Journal of the Malayan Branch of the Royal Asiatic Society* 28:1, 52–69.
Morimoto, Kazuo (2004), 'Toward the formation of Sayyido-Sharifology: questioning accepted fact', *The Journal of Sophia Asian Studies* 22, 87–103.
—— (2012), 'How to behave toward Sayyids and Sharifs: a trans-sectarian tradition of dream accounts', in Kazuo Morimoto (ed.), *Sayyids and Sharifs in Muslim Societies: The Living Links to the Prophet*, London: Routledge, pp. 15–36.
Ner, Marcel (1941), 'Les Musulmans de l'Indochine Française', *BEFEO* 41, 151–200.
Petrů, Tomáš (2016), '"Lands below the Winds" as part of the Persian cosmopolis: an inquiry into linguistic and cultural borrowings from the Persianate societies in the Malay world', *Moussons* 27, 147–61.
Raffles, Thomas Stamford ([1852] 2010), *A History of Java*, vol. II, Cambridge: Cambridge University Press.
Ricci, Ronit (2015), 'Soldier and son-in-law, spreader of the faith and scribe:

representations of 'Ali in Javanese literature', in C. Formichi and M. Feener (eds), *Shi'ism in Southeast Asia: 'Alid Piety and Sectarian Constructions*, Oxford: Oxford University Press, pp. 51–62.

Ricklefs, M. C. (1993), *A History of Modern Indonesia since c. 1300*, Stanford: Stanford University Press.

Schafer, Edward H. (1967), *The Vermilion Bird: T'ang Images of the South*, Berkeley: University of California Press.

Setudeh-Nejad, Shahab (2000), 'The encounter between Champa and Persia: research on the impact of West-Asiatic cosmology in Southeast Asia', *SPAFA Journal* 10:3, 5–18.

Shine, Toshihiko (2009), 'The symbolic role of literacy as a standard to distinguish the Raglai from the Cham', *Senri Ethnological Studies* 74, 129–72.

Wade, Geoffrey (2010), 'Early Muslim expansion in South East Asia, eighth to fifteenth centuries', in R. W. Hefner (ed.), *The New Cambridge History of Islam*, vol. 6, Cambridge: Cambridge University Press.

Wieringa, Edwin (1996), 'Does traditional Islamic Malay literature contain Shi'itic elements? 'Ali and Fatimah in Malay Hikayat literature', *Studia Islamika* 3, 93–111.

—— (2000) 'Taming the text: the incorporation of the Shi'itic hero Muhammad Hanafiyyah in a Sundanese version of the Prophetic Tales', in L. Chandra (ed.), *Society and Culture of Southeast Asia: Continuities and Changes*, New Delhi: International Academy of Indian Culture and Aditya Prakashan, pp. 355–64.

Winstedt, R. O. (1932), 'A history of Johore (1365–1895 A.D.)', *Journal of the Malayan Branch of the Royal Asiatic Society* 10:3, 1–167.

Wyatt, David K. (1974), 'Review article: A Persian mission to Siam in the reign of King Narai', *Journal of the Siam Society* 62, 151–7.

EPILOGUE

12

SHI'A COSMOPOLITANISMS AND CONVERSIONS

Mara A. Leichtman

This volume, the proceedings of a 2016 conference at the University of Chester, is an important collection of chapters about Shi'a minorities. Bringing together scholarship inclusive of contributions from emerging scholars, Scharbrodt and Shanneik have also facilitated a cross-regional dialogue about Shi'a minorities in the Middle East, South and Southeast Asia, Eastern and Western Europe, North America and Latin America among regional experts who would not normally be in conversation with one another. These diverse case studies provide evidence for just how widespread Shi'a Islam is globally. Furthermore, this volume enables some comparison of the similarities faced by Shi'a minorities, but also, significantly, their differences, depending on the local contexts in which they are based, and their varying positions as migrant communities or indigenous religious minorities. I have regularly faced surprised reactions – sometimes verging on doubt – that Shi'a Islam is prominent in Africa from those who encounter my scholarship or hear about my research. Recent interest by journalists and policy-makers in Africa as another geographical playground for Saudi Arabian–Iranian tensions similarly mischaracterises the local variations of Shi'a Islamic history and depicts Shi'a minorities as pawns of Iran who lack their own agency.[1] This volume is an important step towards correcting some of these misconceptions.

I was invited to reflect on these contributions through the lens of my own research on Shiʻa cosmopolitanisms in Africa. Doing so will also bring in the African context, which is lacking as an additional chapter case study in this volume. My book (Leichtman 2015) outlines a theory of Muslim cosmopolitanism for Shiʻa communities. I argue that the prominent approach of transnationalism had too many limitations (see also Leichtman 2005), with a focus – at least in the earlier literature – on first-generation immigrants primarily located in North America and Europe, without comparison to other world regions. Importantly, this scholarship also ignores the impact of colonialism. I stress that transnationalism cannot be limited only to sending and receiving countries as relationships between migrant, home country, host country and tertiary countries are key factors in the creation of a transnational community. For Shiʻa communities, as evidenced in this volume, and as I will describe below, Iran and Iraq are important tertiary focal points. These critiques are also especially relevant when examining South-South religious connections. I posit that for more established diaspora communities, movement between home and host country and economic and political embeddedness are no longer central criteria, as put forward by the earlier literature. Instead, ethnic groups maintain transnational characteristics through self-identification and definition by others, imagining the motherland, and upholding religious and sometimes political ideologies.

I chose to ground my analysis instead in the literature on cosmopolitanism.[2] Whereas this term in the social sciences has different meanings from its earlier use in moral and political philosophy, cosmopolitan studies is an emerging interdisciplinary field despite the lack of theoretical and methodological agreement (Delanty 2017). Anthropologists – among other scholars – have argued against cosmopolitanism as an elite phenomenon grounded in Western approaches to history and modernity, favouring a more popular or working-class 'rooted' and 'vernacular' cosmopolitanism that is about engaging with others and can be found in locations that are not necessarily urban (see Werbner 2008). Calhoun envisions cosmopolitanism as about cross-cutting 'webs of specific connections that position us in the world – from friendship and kinship through national states or religions to markets and global institutions' (Calhoun 2017: 198). Delanty proposes a basic definition of cosmopolitanism that avoids the pitfalls of relativism and universalism: 'alternative conceptions of what constitutes community as co-existence and as a broadening of horizons whether on national or transnational levels' (Delanty 2017: 5).

Choosing theories of cosmopolitanism over transnationalism also enabled me to bring together my two case studies of Shi'a minorities in Senegal: the Lebanese diaspora and indigenous Senegalese Muslims who identify as Shi'a. Although cosmopolitanism can also be a problematic concept, I envision it as a tool that facilitates a move beyond the political boundaries of geographic borders inherent in notions of transnationalism. The moral and ethical foundations of the cosmopolitan outlook, for me, also provide a framework for understanding both Shi'a minority communities, whereas I found that transnationalism is best applied to certain studies of migrant communities and not to indigenous populations who do not necessarily move across borders. I also conceptualise cosmopolitanism as simultaneously transcending the political as it is shaped by local and international politics. For example, in historicising this conflict between ethics and politics in the context of Shi'a Islamic movements, I analysed the role of the 1979 Iranian Revolution and 2006 Lebanon War through attempts to promote universalism and global dissemination to other Muslim contexts, and not in terms of particular and more localised Islamist agendas. I found that as Ayatollah Ruhollah Khomeini's ideologies travelled, in my example to West Africa, the revolution's violence and distinctly Iranian political message likewise transformed into Muslim pride and Islamic humanitarianism. The revolution's legacy continued to live on as Senegalese Shi'ites in the 1980s and 1990s sought knowledge about Islamic jurisprudence and combined religious proselytising with the work of economic development through Islamic NGOs. Cosmopolitanism thus allowed me to more deeply engage with processes of globalisation and localisation, which I examine in my book through various historical moments, shifts in religious identity, and constant tensions between the moral and the political.[3]

Turner (2017) has argued for a cosmopolitanism of the sacred, where religion is the driving force behind the origins of cosmopolitanism. Cosmopolitanism is, however, a fundamental ethical conflict for Islam. If cosmopolitanism, according to Appiah (2006), is 'universality plus difference', can religious minorities such as the Shi'a promote a cosmopolitanism highlighting difference before universality, or promote a universality that will apply to a particular delineated group? This collection of chapters, while not specifically grounded in theories of cosmopolitanism, provides some material for rethinking these questions. Furthermore, establishing the historical existence of cosmopolitanism in the Muslim world (Hoesterey 2012; Lawrence 2010; Zaman 2005; Zubaida 2002) demonstrates that Islam has always been cosmopolitan and that the concept is not limited to Western Enlightenment ideals, a much-debated topic in the literature. Yet, if scholars are not careful, cosmopolitanism can still introduce the dangers of liberal bias, and behind it, the same old dominant power relations.

Thus, I envision Muslim cosmopolitanism to be at once universalist in identifying (to some extent) with the global Islamic *umma* (Muslim community-at-large) and rooted in local culture and histories. The ethical model of cosmopolitanism outlined in my book could be used to theorise a global religious movement and, simultaneously, to analyse the politics of communities envisaged in marginality (Bhabha 1996). This flexible notion of cosmopolitanism could be creatively moulded, celebrated, or hidden in response to minority identity politics and the reality that difference, especially ethnic and religious difference, is not universally applauded. This volume additionally addresses these challenges for Shi'a minorities in certain ethnic, national and political contexts. In this epilogue, I will reflect on several themes that emerge from these chapters. First are the geographical and intellectual cosmopolitan linkages that bring diverse Shi'a communities together; second are local challenges of being minorities within minorities; and finally are lexicons of religious conversion, which many of these authors have creatively avoided.

Geographical and Intellectual Shi'a Cosmopolitanisms

It is significant that some chapters in this volume demonstrate how certain communities gravitate more towards Iran, while others envision Iraq as their preferred predominant centre of Shi'a learning or history. This reminds the reader that Iran is not the only Shi'a player on the global stage. Minority Muslim communities have agency in deciding which Shi'a 'centre' they lean towards – or distance themselves from.

Formichi presents a fascinating overview of physical and moral geographies of Shi'a Islam in Indonesia, which is linked in different ways with Shi'a in Iran, but also in Lebanon and Kuwait. She highlights how her interlocutors were attracted to Shi'a intellectual and philosophical thought and *not* its political embodiment, something my own research has argued in the very different context of West Africa. Interestingly, Indonesian Shi'ites did not prioritise ritual performativity. Formichi portrays the tensions between exogenous Islamic knowledge and financial networks on local educational institutions and communities. On the one hand, she argues, external connections are necessary for the survival of Indonesian Shi'ism and provide legitimacy, opportunities and visibility; but on the other hand, local community members fear that foreign intervention could obliterate local religious practices while making Shi'a communities a target of Sunni extremist groups. Importantly, Formichi maintains that Indonesian Shi'ites feel compelled to display connections to Iran, even if they do not feel this connection themselves.

Rasiah likewise examines the scholarly networks that enable the transmission of religious knowledge in Sri Lanka among its small nascent Shi'a community. Travel to and from centres of traditional religious learning in the Middle East connects geographical regions and brings prestige to those able to travel. Religious ideas similarly circulate transnationally from shorter trips for Islamic pilgrimage or extended journeys for formal study. Rasiah highlights South Asia's long history of cosmopolitan Shi'a connections from Safavid and Mughal influences. He demonstrates how geography matters; whereas northern Indian Shi'a centres have the most affinity with Persianate literary culture, southern coastal areas, such as Sri Lanka, are more connected legally to Shafi'i schools of jurisprudence and geographically to Hadramawt, Yemen. South Asians gravitate towards the Middle East for Islamic study and to the Gulf states for employment.[4] In fact, it was during the time of paramilitary and state terror in Sri Lanka when the first class of madrasa students went to Iran for their intellectual formation. Having presented a range of cosmopolitan Islamic connections, Rasiah also highlights the local frictions for Sri Lankan students who return from studying in Qom, Iran. Yet despite ethnic tensions and religious competition in their home communities, they remain committed to the teachings of contemporary Twelver Shi'ism.

My own scholarship has also addressed similar conflicts surrounding assumed local Shi'a connections to Iran. Senegalese Sunni Muslims presumed

Senegalese Shi'ites were funded by Iran, and Shi'a community leaders had to work hard to break these stereotypes. The Iranian ambassador or other Iranian officials do periodically attend Senegalese Shi'a events out of religious solidarity, but Senegalese Shi'a organisations refuse to accept funding with conditions attached, which is often the case with Iran. Funding might come instead from the production generated locally by development projects run by Shi'a organisations, and some receive assistance from the Lebanese Shi'a community in Senegal, as well as from private individual donations. These days charitable contributions come from Kuwaiti or other Arab Gulf businessmen, in addition to partnerships with Middle Eastern, African, and/or Western NGOs. Senegalese Shi'ites similarly detach religion from national politics, and adapt Shi'a Islamic practices to Senegalese culture. As such they firmly declare that they are not like Iranian or Lebanese Shi'ites; they are *African* or *Senegalese* Shi'ites.

Whereas Iran has been described as the primary geographical and intellectual focus for the communities depicted in some of the book's chapters, other minority Shi'a populations gravitate more towards the Shi'a centre that has long been Iran's intellectual and geographical competitor: Iraq. These two Shi'a poles are not dichotomous, as Rasiah reminds us by recalling how in Sri Lanka Sunni organisations once supported the Iranian Revolution, but turned away from Iran in the early 1980s during the war with Iraq. Iraqi embassies, like Iranian embassies, also disseminated books, organised religious seminars and arranged trips to Iraq to sway Muslim and even non-Muslim opinion.[5] These Iran-Iraq inter-Shi'a rivalries provide an additional competitive axis to the Saudi-Iran Sunni-Shi'a tensions. Saudi Arabia, of course, likewise disseminates religious literature with Salafi counter-propaganda, which contributes significantly to global anti-Shi'a attitudes. Yet Rasiah notes that Sunni Muslims (such as those in Sri Lanka) declare solidarity not only with Salafi groups but also with other global Sunni Muslim organisations including the Muslim Brotherhood and Tabligh Jamaat. It is extremely important to avoid examining Muslim networks in a vacuum, and this collection of chapters brings together important case studies of under-studied communities that contribute to broadening general knowledge about the growth of Shi'a Islam globally.

Degli Esposti focuses on the relationship between the Iraqi Shi'a diaspora in London and the homeland in Najaf, arguing that global discourses of minority rights have shaped the political terrain of Iraq-in-conflict. She provocatively illustrates the sectarianisation of the Iraqi Shiʿa diaspora through religious remittances, voluntary donations, pilgrimage routes, and the distribution of information and resources. This has real consequences on and political gain for the increasingly sectarian nature of ongoing conflict in Iraq. Young British-born Shiʿites of Iraqi origin remain orientated towards Iraq, with their self-conceptions of identity and belonging channelled through networks of charity and patronage. Yet, so true for many migrant communities, diasporic identities change significantly from the homeland. Degli Esposti points out that in Iraq, Shiʿites self-identified as being from Najaf or Karbala, as members of the Communist or Daʿwa Party, or as secularists or nationalists. In Britain, these Iraqi identities transformed as they were categorised religiously by others simply as Shiʿa. Furthermore, the diasporic identity of second-generation Iraqi Shiʿites born in the UK was shaped through a transnational network of Shiʿa politico-religious institutions explicitly geared towards social and political engagement in Iraq. Shiʿa religious observance thus became intertwined with Iraqi nationalist sentiments, particularly as boundaries blurred between political and humanitarian organisations. Degli Esposti powerfully demonstrates how religious remittances from the UK (and elsewhere) can reinforce existing divisions in Iraqi society, and pilgrimage routes to Iraqi Shiʿa holy cities can similarly provide an influx of wealth to the country. In this way, Iraqi diasporas can help maintain the authority of the Shiʿa religious establishment in Iraq.

Religious pilgrimage, in particular, can play a powerful role in the competition between Iran and Iraq for Shiʿa hearts and minds. Since the fall of Saddam, Shiʿites from around the world began to walk between the holy Iraqi cities of Najaf and Karbala in commemoration of the fortieth day following the death of Imam Husayn. Known as Arbaʿin, this has become the largest annual pilgrimage, surpassing even the *hajj* to Mecca. Degli Esposti describes its significance for Shiʿites of Iraqi origin in Britain. Zaidi's fascinating chapter extends the draw of Iraqi holy cities to first- and second-generation South Asian Shiʿites in the United States, who not only prefer to go on religious pilgrimages to Iraq over Iran, but also choose to visit Iraq over their own countries of origin, such as Pakistan. The Iraqi Shiʿa shrines thus began to displace actual homelands in South Asia as this diasporic community took trips to Najaf and Karbala to 'rediscover' their 'roots'. Zaidi additionally links the connection to Iraq to the community's interactions with English-speaking orators of Iraqi origin in the United States who were able to bypass linguistic obstacles of second-generation South Asians who never mastered Urdu, while tapping into their desire for religious knowledge and their cosmopolitan search for belonging.

These examples demonstrate how Iraq is once again becoming the Shi'a heartland, overtaking Iran's claims to this status, which benefitted from the inability of Shi'ites to travel to Iraq during the rule of Saddam Hussein. Zaidi also credits the growing stature of Iraq's Shi'a shrines in part due to the ongoing conflict in Syria, which eliminated the Sayyida Zaynab shrine in Damascus as a possible pilgrimage destination. These findings that young American Muslims are expressing more affinity to Iraqi shrines, including following the country's political affairs, over taking interest in the state of Shi'a in the 'forgotten homelands of their parents' childhoods', India and Pakistan, is tremendously significant. My own research confirmed that Lebanon remained the emotional homeland for Shi'ites of Lebanese origin in Senegal. Even though many of the second and third generations had never been to Lebanon, some were able to combine a visit to their villages of origin as part of a package tour organised by the Lebanese shaykh in Senegal, who annually leads the community on the pilgrimage to Mecca with a stopover in Lebanon. Some pilgrims also opted to visit the Shi'a shrines in Iran as part of this visit, integrating the holy religious sites with their ancestral Lebanese homeland. Iraq is very likely an additional destination today, which was not possible during my earlier fieldwork that largely took place in 2002–3 during the build-up to the Iraq war. Yet as Shi'a diasporic identities become more cosmopolitan, geopolitics continues to be a constraint. While Iraq has become safer, American Shi'ites increasingly worry about being profiled by the Trump administration if they travel to Syria, Iran or Iraq.

The return of symbolic value to Najaf and Karbala with the defeat of Saddam cannot be ignored. As such, it continues to surprise me how the Saudi-Iranian rivalry dominates the Western imaginary.[6] Local Shi'a politics in Iraq – as well as in Lebanon – serve as contemporary frames of references for Shi'a minorities globally. Degli Esposti highlights how the greatest enemy for Shi'ites in Iraq was ISIS, and the Sunni-Shi'a struggle became localised in Iraqi sectarian politics through a different narrative of 'Shi'a victimisation and emancipation . . . that pits the essentialised categories of "Sunnis" and "Shi'ites" in an eternal conflict of "us and them"' (Degli Esposti in this volume). Zaidi also notes how images of Iraqi soldiers and 'martyrs' in the fight against ISIS paved the roads walked by pilgrims between Najaf and Karbala. Similar to how images of Lebanese martyrs lining the streets of south Lebanon drummed up transnational political allegiance to Hizbollah, the Iraqi martyrs reminded local and foreign Shi'ites of the large cost of war and the price Iraqi Shi'ites paid to protect the shines for a peaceful pilgrimage. ISIS is thus depicted as today's 'Yazid', the villain in the epic Shi'a annual re-enactment of the fateful battle of Karbala of 680 CE where Imam Husayn, his family and his army were martyred by the Umayyad army. Degli Esposti describes how Iraqi diaspora Shi'ites contrast 'Shi'a-as-victim' with 'Sunni/ [ISIS]-as-oppressor', engaging in the politics of sectarianism in Iraq through invoking the language of international justice and minority rights. Yazid becomes personified in other contemporary local political conflicts in South Asia as well (see Rasiah), and as Israel and the United States in Lebanon (Deeb 2005).

Chapters in this volume have thus positioned minority Shi'a communities between Iranian and Iraqi geographical axes. Yet some contributions also acknowledge how the Internet and social media provide alternative online geographies for Shi'a authority, similarly reaching congregations near and far. Riggs examines the websites of Shi'a clerical leaders, in particular that of Ayatollah Sistani, showing how, on the one hand, websites have enabled a greater ability to maintain and build constituencies, but on the other hand such technology can lead to a loss of control over the production and dissemination of religious knowledge, and thereby of religious authority. This open technology platform gives diverse religious leaders an arena in which to compete for a literate population eager for accessible knowledge. Riggs suggests that the Internet thereby facilitates the formation of new centres of authority, inverting the historical dynamics of centre–periphery. Yet, while welcoming diversity, the Internet can also encourage uniformity in thought, and Riggs credits technology for certain changes in long-standing Shi'a beliefs and practices. For example, the ability to raise and distribute funds via the

Internet can undermine the financial system that privileged the power of the *wakils*, representatives of the *maraji'*, the highest Shi'a religious references. *Wakils* once had sole authority to collect and redistribute the *khums*, the Shi'a religious tax of one-fifth of wealth that, in part, supports the charitable activities of the *maraji'*.

Authors of other chapters similarly note the importance of technology. Rasiah discusses the digital transmission of knowledge that connects the 'Shi'a heartland' of Iran, Iraq and Lebanon to more 'peripheral' locations such as Sri Lanka, which are not only geographically but also culturally distant. Shi'ites now share *hadith* (sayings of the Prophet Muhammad), religious news and commentaries via Whatsapp. Badry offers a case study of the Ostad Elahi Foundation in Paris, a French government-sanctioned Iranian Public Interest Foundation also granted special consultative status as an NGO with the United Nations Economic and Social Council. In particular, Badry examines the web presentation of this organisation against the growth in Western consumption of esotericism and global ethos. Shi'a cosmopolitanisms are ever-changing, from one geographical and intellectual centre to another, while religious authority becomes decentralised through the digital transmission of knowledge. What readers should take away from this volume is that the Iranian version of Shi'a Islam does not dominate global Shi'ism.

The Shi'a as Double Minorities

Alongside the global and cosmopolitan interconnections of various Shi'a communities are their local struggles as double minorities, or minorities within minorities, which is another common theme depicted in this collection of chapters. We cannot underestimate the intersection of religion and social class, especially when examining Shi'a minorities that have historically been disadvantaged politically and economically as often persecuted communities. Social class is also one factor by which certain communities might retain ties to Iran (or Iraq) for financial reasons even if this might be a problematic association for them politically and in terms of self-identity.

Unlike Shi'a Islam in Indonesia and Sri Lanka that emerged from Sunni Muslim traditions inspired by the Iranian Revolution, Garcia-Somoza and Valcarcel paint a very different picture of Shi'a Islam in Buenos Aires, Argentina, as a minority religion in a predominantly Catholic state. The religious field opened in Argentina with the return to democracy in 1983 that brought with it a climate of tolerance towards ethnic and cultural minorities. The authors outline the history of *arabidades* ('Arabness') and *musulmanidades* ('Muslimness'), which they equate with the formation of 'political Islam'. A by-product of a growing Arab diaspora in South America (see also del Mar Logroño Narbona *et al.* 2015), Argentinian Muslims were connected to the Islamic 'revival' encouraged by the Iranian Revolution. Garcia-Somoza and Valcarcel describe the tensions between local and global Islam; some sermons were delivered in Spanish catering to converts and others not fluent in Arabic, whereas Argentines of Arab origin publicly celebrated their Arab culture and heritage during festivals through dance, food, customs and ancestry. In the Argentine context, as elsewhere, the religious is not detached from the political dimension, and Muslims demonstrate against certain national and international hegemonic powers in the name of social justice. The authors thus present Shi'ism as a political project that reads Argentine national politics against the Iranian Revolution and applies the figure of Imam Husayn to local struggles as a symbol of resistance against oppression.

Rexhepi's chapter presents another intriguing and under-studied example of Bektashi Muslims in the Balkans. Informed by the Shi'a experience, this community opts for *taqiyya*, or dissimulation, in their religious practices. Unlike the public mourning processions and proselytism of Shi'ites elsewhere and described in some of the other chapters, the Bektashi way of life requires modesty and mysticism, in part due to their continued persecution in Turkey and Albania from the time of the Ottoman Empire. A different political understanding of Islam emerges in the context of Eastern Europe. Very much connected to the politics of European Union enlargement, the Balkans favours a more tolerant Islam 'acquiescent to European values', which Rexhepi critically labels an invented Balkan Islam. He thus argues for a decolonised Shi'a Islamic lens through which to understand Albanian-speaking Bekhtashis.

In another European context, Badry places the Ostad Elahi Foundation in between two overlapping discourses. First is a discussion of *ghulat*, or extreme Shi'a communities (inclusive of Turkish Alevis, Syrian Alawites/Nusayris and the Iranian Ahl-e Haqq, the subject of this chapter). Even more marginalised than other Twelver Shi'a communities, these religious minorities have long been accused of heresy or even polytheism, and excluded and/or oppressed by mainstream religion. Within their countries of origin, practitioners of these religions often reside in remote areas in secluded communities, necessary to preserve oral esoteric and gnostic traditions. Badry highlights a 'modern' transformation of the reformist branch of the Iranian Ahl-e Haqq ('People of Truth') organisation when the founder's son, Ostad (Master) Elahi, reconciled Ahl-e Haqq teachings with mainstream Twelver Shi'a dogma. Additionally, through migration and the Foundation's establishment in Paris, the once insular and protected traditions from Iran reached a wider Western and online audience attracted more broadly to alternative forms of esotericism. Ironically, reaching a double (or even triple or quadruple) minority status enabled this branch of the Ahl-e Haqq movement to become somewhat more mainstream.

Stock's creatively poetic chapter on Cham *sayyids* from Cambodia also examines a community of minorities in multiple capacities: Muslims in a predominantly Buddhist country; Chams among a Khmer ethnic majority; and Sunni Muslims 'going Shi'a'. Cham *sayyids* are more oriented towards Iran, where they travel to study in Shi'a seminaries. Stock additionally highlights how these Cambodian Shi'ites claim descent from the Prophet Muhammad, but through his daughter Fatima and son-in-law 'Ali, presenting an alternative narrative of descent for *sayyids*, which she refers to as 'Saeths' in the local context.

In addition to new ways of thinking about minorities within minorities, these chapters raise other important points that are unfortunately underdeveloped in the volume: questions of social class, race, and language among Shi'a communities. Zaidi notes that spiritual journeys to Iraq are not cheap, and such organised trips cater to American and European Shi'ites of an upper middle class. She mentions that native languages – with their regional variations – are often displaced in the diaspora in favour of the adoption of English as the primary medium of communication. This occurs not only in the United States, she argues, but also in the global Shi'a diaspora. One example is the 'Who is Hussain?' campaign that is transforming Muharram (in Zaidi's case study in the United States, but I also recently observed this in East Africa) into an outwardly-oriented annual event for communicating the positive and peaceful values of Imam Husayn to a larger non-Shi'a audience. Yet this example of cosmopolitan Shi'ism, very much in line with the worldwide prominence of interfaith movements, can also be contrasted to the rather different account given in this volume by Degli Esposti about how transnational connections to shrines in Iraq contributed to the sectarianisation of second-generation Iraqi Shi'ites in London.

Zaidi went so far as to suggest that for affluent South Asian Shi'ites in the United States, *ziyarat* to Iraq (and sometimes to Iran) might become 'the sixth pillar of Islam', but only for those who can afford the luxuries of this kind of organised travel. Social class as well as English as the new global language of Shi'a diasporas thus provides the possibility for South Asian diaspora Shi'ites to develop their religious identities through seeking new associational bonds and rejecting past Iranian and South Asian dominated configurations. Rexhepi likewise stresses this intersection of class and faith, but in the particular context of the Balkans, also that of socialism and Islam. The political and demographic make-up of various social contexts, often a factor in the determination of class, is yet another variable. For example, Rasiah highlights that Sri Lanka's Sunni Muslim community, itself a minority group, is not empowered to use the state apparatus against Shi'ites. This is also a common discourse I heard among Shi'ites in East Africa. When Islam itself is a minority religion, particularly in a secular state that offers protection against religious discrimination, this can limit local tensions between Sunni and Shi'a groups when they are both closely monitored by the government in countries that fear violence by Islamic extremist groups.

Lexicons of the Fluidity of Shi'a Identity

Finally, I want to raise one last theme hinted at in some of the volume's chapters: lexicons of Shi'a identity. In my own research, I hesitatingly labelled the process of becoming Shi'a 'conversion' – in quotation marks – because I wanted my scholarship to speak to a larger academic literature about the search for religious identities. I did not perceive of this shift towards a Shi'a identity as a radical break (Meyer 1998) from Sunni, Sufi or Salafi Islam. Engaging with the concept of conversion enabled me to debate different notions of religious change, which is only sometimes connected to colonial power politics (Comaroff and Comaroff 1991) and critiqued as a concept emerging directly out of Christianity (Asad 1996).

In the West African context, discussions of religious conversion must be grounded historically in the spread of Islam in the eleventh century, when merchants opened up trade routes (Levtzion and Pouwels 2000; Loimeier 2013). Clerics introduced Islam to the masses through both military conquest and peaceful persuasion. Islam spread most rapidly throughout parts of West Africa through the Sufi orders during the colonial period. Marabouts (Sufi Islamic leaders) gained immense following as a result of French treatment of Senegalese and were often outspoken against the oppression of colonial rule. Islam served in part as a cultural ideology, preventing Senegalese 'assimilation' into French ways.

In my book, I define conversion as

> a change in religion over time, involving a transformation of one's religious culture resulting from multiple factors including social networks with other believers, a discovery of key religious texts, and a response to a particular location in both time and place. (Leichtman 2015: 168)

It was interesting to ponder if converting to Islam in Africa, or even 'converting' from one branch of Islam to another, entailed different processes and motivations than converting from a 'traditional religion' to a 'world religion'. In the West African context, scholars must recall the very famous classical debates about African conversion (Horton 1971, 1975a, 1975b; Fisher 1973, 1985). Senegalese Shi'ites were similarly attracted intellectually to Islamic texts and jurisprudence and found answers to questions they had long been seeking in other Islamic traditions. In the same way that literacy elsewhere and at other times has served as a time bomb of reform (Fisher 1973) and has enabled the forging of connections with congregations from afar (Ranger 1993) or even within the same nation (Anderson 1983), Shi'a texts provided alternative answers to questions about Islam. Augis (2002) even argues that Muslims who make an intrafaith conversion are reading the Qur'an for the first time as a result of participating in reformist organisations that advocate for Qur'anic literacy.

I posit that becoming Shi'a was one way certain Senegalese, especially those who were highly educated and relatively affluent, attempted to escape the colonial legacy, the weakness of the Senegalese state, and growing structural inequalities in their country through adopting a religious model that for them had been successful elsewhere in combating the West. In Senegal, there was already an accepted practice of converting from a 'traditional' African religion to Islam and Christianity, or from one interpretation of Islam to another, which was essential in the formation of Shi'a networks. Conversion to Islam, and the knowledge that came with it, was a means of achieving higher status at a younger age (Mark 1978); challenging elders' authority (Searing 2003); and gaining access to new resources for predicting, explaining and controlling events in a world penetrated by external social forces (Simmons 1979). In sum, conversion radically altered local configurations of power, kinship, wealth and inheritance. Conversion was additionally about assuming new identities in situations of historical and social change that undermined old systems of status, themes also explored by scholars of conversion to Christianity (see Hefner 1993; Keane 2007, Meyer 1999; van der Veer 1996).

Like some of the contributors to this volume, I acknowledge that many Muslims do not consider the change in affiliation from Sunni to Shi'a Islam a conversion. Senegalese Shi'ites, I found, were not opposed to the term conversion, although they did not themselves use this word. In the Wolof language, *tuub* refers to complete reversal from an attitude of denying to one of accepting, which was too radical a concept to be applied to Senegalese Shi'ites, and one not generally used for 'people of the book'. I sometimes heard the term *tajdid* in Arabic (*renouveller* in French), translated as 'religious renewal' or 'revival'. More popular was the Arabic term *tasha'a*, literally translated as 'to be affiliated with or partisan of' and meaning 'to accept or enter the Shi'a school'. The Senegalese Peul ethnic group referred to converts as *perdo mbotu*. This was translated as 'migrating from the cloth that ties the baby to its mother's back', that is, straying from one's parents' tradition. This means that in addition to being exposed to new ideas, the convert must also be ready to leave the native religion. This Peul discourse enabled a broader thinking of processes of conversion and modernity. My book describes how one could be both Shi'a and Senegalese if one embraced nationalism and cosmopolitanism, globalisation and assimilation, Sunni and Shi'a Islam. This (trans-)national conversion pushes theories of religious change to a new level as converts simultaneously searched for their place both outside and inside their traditions. Furthermore, although converts were convinced that their way was the true way, they did not compel others to accept their views, nor did they forbid Sufis from practising or even learning about their own traditions in Shi'a spaces.

In fact, some Senegalese converts kept their feet in both Sunni and Shi'a traditions, and I made the case that Shi'a Islam was made more Senegalese (and more cosmopolitan) through the ways in which various Islamic traditions converged. Indeed, converts believed that only by spreading religious tolerance and coexistence could they assist Senegal in becoming a country of peace and economic development. In my book, I give the example of one Senegalese religious scholar who served both as *wakil*, Shi'a representative, for Iranian Ayatollah Khamenei as well as *muqaddam*, an authorised Sufi representative, for a local Senegalese Tijani leader. This cleric did not renounce Tijani Islam, but built upon the notion of *njebbel*, the vow of obedience to a marabout, and his immense Islamic knowledge enabled him to go beyond the requirement within the Tijani order that disciples not follow any other doctrine. I apply an older term to this process, that of 'adhesion' (Nock 1933: 7), which referred to the possibility of participating in religious groups and rituals without assuming a new way of life, of adopting 'new worships as useful supplements and not as substitutes'. Baum (1990) similarly contends that conversion in Africa need not involve the renunciation of one's former religious system.

I therefore read with great interest the resistance of some of the authors in this volume to labelling the process of becoming Shi'a 'conversion'. Instead, they prefer other discourses emerging out of South and Southeast Asian studies: 'Alid piety, an inclusive notion of *ahl al-bayt,* and even the concept of 'Sayyido-Sharifology' (Morimoto 2004). Some chapters also suggest, going back to the earlier discussion of Iran not being as predominant a Shi'a power as readers might presume, a subtle difference in communities or families who might trace their Prophetic genealogy to either Arabian or Persianate roots.

For example, Rasiah notes that if a Sunni Muslim leaves a *tariqa* (Sufi order) for a Salafi organisation (or vice versa) this is never regarded as an act of conversion. He acknowledges that this change in thought and practice can arguably be as profound as a Sunni Muslim embracing Shi'a Islam. Instead of 'conversion', Rasiah proposes the concept of 'reorientation' within Islam. He stresses how the reorientation of Muslims is a regular occurrence, whether from one *madhhab* (Islamic legal school of thought) to another, or from mysticism to Islamism, or through many 'creative fusions' that combine a multitude of beliefs and practices. He raises some important points for not using the term 'conversion' to describe this process. In addition to the 'either/or' dichotomy, with the expectation that one religious choice unequivocally repudiates the other, he also suggests that 'conversion' could potentially legitimate the Salafi view that Shiʿism lies beyond the limits of Islam. In reality, he argues, Shiʿites in Sri Lanka display a more subtle approach to religious change that 'suggests a spectrum of beliefs on a single continuum'.

The Shiʿa communities in Germany frequented by Weineck have a different approach to contemporary Shiʿa identity formations. Weineck's interlocutors renounced the label 'Shiʿite' as too political and instead self-identified simply as 'Muslim'. The Shiʿa population in Germany is comprised of Alevis in addition to Twelver Shiʿites. Weineck suggests that both groups preferred to represent themselves as 'friends of the *ahl al-bayt*' in an effort to move beyond more specific and sectarian modes of religious identification. Weineck makes a strong case for this more inclusive belonging to the family of the Prophet (*ehlibeyt* in Turkish) and argues, drawing on McChesney (1991), that 'sectarian notions of inner-Islamic plurality and difference' that are too strict 'do not suffice to grasp such forms of 'Alid piety or "ahl al-baytism"'.

Academic as well as policy language remains heavily invested with confessional notions of religious difference. Yet Weineck, like several other contributors to this volume, calls for alternative concepts that recognise the religious plurality that has long existed locally. Turkish speakers in Germany are only one example of the diversity of *ahl al-bayt* and 'Shiʿa-oriented' communities. Confessional and sectarian identities can sometimes be very fluid, and as Rasiah has already noted, boundaries between Sunni and Shiʿa, let alone boundaries within various Shiʿa communities, including Twelver Shiʿa, Alevi or Nusayri, are not always clear-cut. My book examines similarities between Sufis and Shiʿites in Senegal, who share common symbols, a veneration of the family of the Prophet, local genealogies, the charisma of religious leaders, and the practice of visitation of shrines. Some Shiʿites even suggested that the roots of Sufism come from Shiʿa Islam, and I explore revisionist histories of the spread of Islam to Africa (Leichtman 2015: 215–20). Sectarian labels such as Sunni, Shiʿa or Alevi do not capture the diversity of religious identifications, and, as some of the authors of these chapters have noted, communities themselves are reluctant to self-identify as such.

Stock likewise protests the concept of 'conversion', positioning her scholarship as contributing to a historical anthropology that does not take Sunnism and Shi'ism as two opposite and contrasting poles. Like Formichi, she prefers the idea of 'Alid piety to describe Cham Saeths, whom she depicts as sitting comfortably between the two dominant branches of Islam. As Formichi and Feener argue, focusing on 'Alid piety allows

> for a reframing of our views on the widespread reverence for 'Ali, Fatima and their progeny that emphasizes how such sentiments and associated practices are seen as part of broad traditions shared by many Muslims, which might or might not have their origins in a specifically Shi'i cultural identity. (Formichi and Feener 2015: 3)

For Formichi and Feener (2015: 4), 'Alid piety can be defined as 'aspects of Islamic belief and practice expressing special reverence for the *ahl al-bayt*'. This notion is further developed to enable the bypassing of Shi'a politics: the authors argue that elements of 'Alid piety were widespread across Southeast Asia long before the Iranian Revolution. In this manner, Stock chooses this terminology to further provincialise *ahl al-bayt* forms of devotion, distancing them from 'Shi'ism' as dominated by Iran.

In her quest for a more useful lexicon, Stock additionally draws upon other scholarship. Morimoto (2004) called for a 'Sayyido-Sharifology' to serve as a 'comparative study of scattered kinsfolks of the Prophet Muhammad: a systematic, transnational, and trans-disciplinary project, that would take the category of Sayyid/Sharif as a central object of enquiry'. Stock proposes an 'Alid piety of doubles for the Cambodian context, where the local personality of 'Ali Hanaphiah exists alongside Imam 'Ali, the Prophet Muhammad's cousin and son-in-law and the first Shi'a Imam who succeeded the Prophet after his death. Similarly Fatima Hanaphiah parallels the Prophet Muhammad's youngest daughter Fatima, who married Imam 'Ali and gave birth to Imams Hasan and Husayn, key figures for Shi'a Muslims. Stock's 'Alid piety of doubles further complicates Shi'a identity and genealogy where the spectrums of Cham Saeths include 'that of being 'Alid no matter which "'Ali" is referred to, that of being Fatimid through another Fatima, that of evoking other figures connected to the *ahl al-bayt* and their progeny'. Stock outlines another kind of lineage, one inclusive of 'Alids who are not Fatimids, one of alternative Imams like Zayn Al-'Abidin who blur the Iranian connection to Southeast Asian Islamisation, and one of other sojourners who settle in Cambodia and bring with them lines of continuity to other geographical regions (such as the Hadramawt in Yemen). Through these different lines of '*sayyid*ness' and the close ties maintained by Saeths to what Stock refers to as an ideal 'Ali and Fatima, she proposes a less drastic understanding of processes of 'conversion'. Stock tells a fascinating, if at times confusing, story of local Cham outsiders turned insiders as 'Alid piety becomes anchored in a specific Fatimid piety.

These chapters thus highlight the importance of recognising the diversity of Shi'a minority communities in many different contexts. Genealogies are fundamental to making claims to one's Islamic, if not specifically Shi'a, lineage, and as scholars of religion we cannot undermine the importance of local genealogies (Ho 2006; Morimoto 2012). Awareness of the politics of labelling becomes even more important when examining minorities within minorities, including those communities who intentionally keep a low profile and choose not to follow hegemonic Iranian understandings of Twelver Shi'a Islam.

Final Thoughts

In sum, this book does more to question and problematise underlying assumptions about Shi'a Islam than it does to clarify them, and this is in itself an essential contribution. In presenting a wide range of unique and understudied case studies of minority communities who are often not included in more mainstream discussions of Shi'ism, this volume makes a strong case for acknowledging the diversity of Shi'a Muslims. As I endeavour to do in my own work, Scharbrodt and Shanneik also bring together examples of indigenous Shi'a minority communities alongside Shi'a diasporas in a variety of relevant contexts. This multiplicity of examples brings me back to the notion of cosmopolitanism, as there is no single manner in which to understand or position Shi'a Islam.

I would like to return to one point I raised earlier: is cosmopolitanism a fundamental ethical conflict for minority articulations of Islam that highlight difference before universality? Just as anthropologists have stopped trying to come up with a universal definition of religion, limiting our grasp of cosmopolitanism to Kantian Enlightenment ideals, or to inherently being anti-Islamic (Held 2010), is not a productive debate.[7] This collection of chapters, while not specifically grounded in theories of cosmopolitanism, provides rich material for exploring a range of Shi'a geographies and ideologies, articulations of minority status, and lexicons for avoiding the term 'conversion'. As I similarly explore in my book, Shi'a rituals and points of reference have distinct meanings for different Shi'a communities, especially those who are already 'double minorities' and marginalised in other political, social and economic contexts.

Shi'a Islam can therefore be 'deradicalised' (from its Iranian revolutionary ideologies or other national political contexts) and familiarised as it caters to local community needs in Africa, Asia, Europe, and other worldwide diasporas. Some Shi'a religious leaders even know when to emphasise Shi'a Islam as an all-inclusive (not foreign minority branch of) Islam, developing a universalist language of Islamic humanism that does not establish a division between Sunni and Shi'a Islam.[8] As I argue elsewhere (Leichtman 2015), it is precisely the unique ways in which cosmopolites mould, adapt and integrate foreign philosophies and religious practices into distinctly local understandings that enables the assertion of their rights to membership as both 'citizens of the world' and autochthons at home. In so doing they transform Shi'a Islam into a universalising while differentiating identity.

Muslim cosmopolitanism embraces religious, political, socio-economic and cultural difference. Liberal-secular visions of religious pluralism have thus never been at odds with Shi'a Islam. As my book argues, to be cosmopolitan is to command religious discourses and to create a ritual community by incorporating a variety of customs and traditions. Shi'a differences are thus refracted and reconfigured into Shi'a universalism through the coexistence – and not necessarily the convergence – of multiple Islamic traditions. As such, and as this volume demonstrates, Shi'a Muslim cosmopolitanism is also inescapably political, both in how it chooses to engage – or similarly to disengage – from certain local and global debates.

References

Ahmad, Attiya (2017), *Everyday Conversions: Islam, Domestic Work, and South Asian Migrant Women in Kuwait*, Durham: Duke University Press.

Anderson, Benedict (1983), *Imagined Communities: Reflections on the Origins and Spread of Nationalism*, London: Verso.

Appiah, Kwame Anthony (2006), *Cosmopolitanism: Ethics in a World of Strangers*, New York: W. W. Norton.

Asad, Talal (1996), 'Comments on conversion', in P. van der Veer (ed.), *Conversion to Modernities: The Globalization of Christianity*, New York: Routledge, pp. 263–73.

Augis, Erin (2002), 'Dakar's Sunnite women: the politics of person', PhD diss., Department of Sociology, University of Chicago.

Baum, Robert M. (1990), 'The emergence of a Diola Christianity', *Africa* 60:3, 370–98.

Bhabha, Homi K. (1996), 'Unsatisfied: notes on vernacular cosmopolitanism', in L. Garcia-Moreno and P. C. Pfeiffer (eds), *Text and Nation: Cross-Disciplinary Essays on Cultural and National Identities*, London: Camden House.

Calhoun, Craig (2017), 'A cosmopolitanism of connections', in B. Robbins and P. Lemos Horta (eds), *Cosmopolitanisms*, New York: New York University Press, pp. 189–200.

Comaroff, Jean, and John L. Comaroff (1991), *Of Revelation and Revolution: Christianity, Colonialism, and Consciousness in South Africa*, vol. 1, Chicago: University of Chicago Press.

Deeb, Lara (2005), 'Living Ashura in Lebanon: mourning transformed to sacrifice', *Comparative Studies of South Asia, Africa and the Middle East* 25:1, 122–37.

Delanty, Gerard (2017), 'Introduction: The emerging field of Cosmopolitanism Studies', in G. Delanty (ed.), *Routledge Handbook of Cosmopolitanism Studies*, London: Routledge, pp. 1–8.

Del Mar Logroño Narbona, María, Paulo G. Pinto and John Tofik Karam (eds) (2015), *Crescent Over Another Horizon: Islam in Latin America, the Caribbean, and Latino USA*, Austin: University of Texas Press.

Fisher, Humphrey J. (1973), 'Conversion reconsidered: some historical aspects of religious conversion in black Africa', *Africa* 43:1, 27–40.

—— (1985), 'The juggernaut's apologia: conversion to Islam in black Africa', *Africa* 55:2, 86–108.

Formichi, Chiara, and M. Feener (eds) (2015), *Shi'ism in South East Asia: 'Alid Piety and Sectarian Constructions*, Oxford: Oxford University Press.

Hefner, Robert W. (1993), 'Introduction: World building and the rationality of conversion', in R. W. Hefner (ed.), *Conversion to Christianity: Historical and Anthropological Perspectives on a Great Transformation*, Berkeley: University of California Press, pp. 3–44.

Held, David (2010), *Cosmopolitanism: Ideals and Realities*, Cambridge: Polity.

Ho, Engseng (2006), *The Graves of Tarim: Genealogy and Mobility across the Indian Ocean*, Berkeley: University of California Press.

Hoesterey, James B. (2012), 'Prophetic cosmopolitanism', *City and Society* 24:1, 38–61.

Horton, Robin (1971), 'African conversion', *Africa* 41:2, 85–108.

—— (1975a), 'On the rationality of conversion, part I', *Africa* 45:3, 219–35.

—— (1975b), 'On the rationality of conversion, part II', *Africa* 45:4, 373–99.

Keane, Webb (2007), *Christian Moderns: Freedom and Fetish in the Mission Encounter*, Berkeley: University of California Press.

Lawrence, Bruce B. (2010), 'Afterword: Competing genealogies of Muslim cosmopolitanism,' in C. W. Ernst and R. C. Martin (eds), *Rethinking Islamic Studies – From Orientalism to Cosmopolitanism*, Columbia: University of South Carolina Press, pp. 302–27.

Leichtman, Mara A. (2005), 'The legacy of transnational lives: beyond the first generation of Lebanese in Senegal', *Ethnic and Racial Studies* 28:4, 663–86.

—— (2015), *Shi'i Cosmopolitanisms in Africa: Lebanese Migration and Religious Conversion in Senegal*, Bloomington: Indiana University Press.

Leichtman, Mara A., and Abdullah Alrebh (2018), 'Shi'i Islamic preaching in the African periphery: the Dakar sermons of Lebanese Shaykh al-Zayn', *British Journal of Middle East Studies* 45:1, 58–78.

Leichtman, Mara A., and Dorothea Schulz (eds) (2012), 'Introduction to special issue: Muslim cosmopolitanism: movement, identity, and contemporary reconfigurations', Special Issue, *City and Society* 24:1, 1–6.

Levtzion, Nehemia, and Randall L. Pouwels (ed.) (2000), *The History of Islam in Africa*, Athens: Ohio University Press.

Loimeier, Roman (2013), *Muslim Societies in Africa: A Historical Anthropology*, Bloomington: Indiana University Press.

Mark, Peter (1978), 'Urban migration, cash cropping, and calamity: the spread of Islam among the Diola of Boulouf (Senegal), 1900–1940', *African Studies Review* 21:2, 1–14.

Mbembe, Achille (2017), 'Afropolitanism', in B. Robbins and P. Lemos Horta (eds), *Cosmopolitanisms*, New York: New York University Press, pp. 102–7.

McChesney, Robert D. (1991), *Waqf in Central Asia: Four Hundred Years in the History of a Muslim Shrine, 1480–1889*, Princeton: Princeton University Press.

Meyer, Birgit (1998), '"Make a complete break with the past." Memory and postcolonial modernity in Ghanaian Pentecostalist discourse', *Journal of Religion in Africa* 28:3, 316–49.

――― (1999), *Translating the Devil: Religion and Modernity among the Ewe in Ghana*, Edinburgh: Edinburgh University Press.

Morimoto, Kazuo (2004), 'Toward the formation of Sayyido-Sharifology: questioning accepted fact', *The Journal of Sophia Asian Studies* 22, 87–103.

Morimoto, Kazuo (ed.) (2012), *Sayyids and Sharifs in Muslim Societies: The Living Links to the Prophet*, London: Routledge.

Nock, A. D. (1933), *Conversion: The Old and the New in Religion from Alexander the Great to Augustine of Hippo*, Oxford: Oxford University Press.

Ranger, Terence (1993), 'The local and the global in southern African religious history', in R. W. Hefner (ed.), *Conversion to Christianity: Historical and Anthropological Perspectives on a Great Transformation*, Berkeley: University of California Press, pp. 65–98.

Searing, James F. (2003), 'Conversion to Islam: military recruitment and generational conflict in a Sereer-Safen village (Bandia), 1920–38,' *Journal of African History* 44:1, 73–95.

Simmons, William S. (1979), 'Islamic conversion and social change in a Senegalese village', *Ethnology* 18: 4, 303–23.

Turner, Bryan S. (2017), 'The cosmopolitanism of the sacred', in G. Delanty (ed.), *Routledge Handbook of Cosmopolitanism Studies*, London: Routledge, pp. 188–97.

van der Veer, Peter (ed.) (1996), *Conversion to Modernities: The Globalization of Christianity*, London: Routledge.

Werbner, Pnina (2008), 'Introduction: Towards a new cosmopolitan anthropology,' in P. Werbner (ed.), *Anthropology and the New Cosmopolitanism*, Oxford: Berg, pp. 1–29.

Zaman, Muhammad Qasim (2005), 'The scope and limits of Islamic cosmopolitanism and the discursive language of the 'ulama'', in miriam cooke and B. B. Lawrence (eds), *Muslim Networks from Hajj to Hip Hop*, Chapel Hill: University of North Carolina Press, pp. 84–104.

Zubaida, Sami (2002), 'Middle Eastern experiences of cosmopolitanism', in S. Vertovec and R. Cohen (eds), *Conceiving Cosmopolitanism: Theory, Context and Practice*, Oxford: Oxford University Press, pp. 32–41.

NOTES

Chapter 2

1. Pseudonym.
2. Unless differently indicated, the material presented is from my own fieldwork notes.
3. In Javanese it literally means '*santri*-place', referring to the educational institution where students (*santri*) study classical Islamic subjects and pursue an orthoprax communal life. For more see Denny (2017) and Federspiel (2017).
4. Al-Mustafa University is an international academic institute moulded as a *hawza* seminary, with several international affiliate schools. See Sakurai (2015).
5. Out of 200 million Muslims, unofficial estimates suggest that Shi'a Islam counts a following of around 2.5 million, equivalent to 1.2% of the Muslim population, and 1% of the total population. According to Jalaluddin Rahmat (chairman of IJABI), government statistics in 2011 reported 500,000 followers whilst the highest estimation counted them at 5 million. According to IJABI there should be about 2.5 million Shi'ites in the archipelago (TEMPO 2012). Indonesian Shi'ites could thus be more than the country's followers of Confucius (at 0.72%). They represent a larger proportion than the USA's entire Muslim

population (set at 0.8%; Pew Forum 2010). However, the issue of who is a Shi'ite is not related to the census and raw numbers only, calling into question how we define Shi'a affiliation.
6. For a more detailed discussion of 'Alid piety in Southeast Asia, see Feener and Formichi (2015).
7. Pseudonym.
8. Mission statement of the all-Indonesian Assembly of Ahlul Bait Associations (*Ikatan Jama'ah Ahlul Bayt*, IJABI), available at http://www.majulah-ijabi.org/visi-dan-misi-ijabi.html, last accessed 17 January 2013.
9. Pseudonym.
10. Indonesia was founded on the base of *pancasila*, the 'five principles', that sanctioned Indonesia as a non-confessional state (i.e. *kebangsaan*, nationalism; *per-kemanusiaan*, humanitarianism; *permusyawaratan-perwakilan*, deliberation among representatives; *kesejahteraan*, social welfare; and *ketuhanan*, belief in One God). For more on *Pancasila*, see Formichi (2012: 79–80) and Feith and Castles (1970: 40–9).
11. Personal communication with ICC Director Mohsen Hakimollahi, Jakarta, 8 June 2010.
12. For a more detailed description of Festival Tabot as took place in the 1990s, see Feener (2015).
13. Feener also explains in much detail the process of Tabot's 'secularization' during the New Order regime.

Chapter 3

1. Translated by Ian Barnett. We would also like to thank Oliver Scharbrodt and Yafa Shanneik for their contributions and bibliographical suggestions.
2. In the first survey on 'Religious Beliefs and Attitudes in Argentina' conducted by CEIL-CONICET's Society, Culture and Religion research team, based on a sample of 2,403 cases, the data collected demonstrate that, while the Argentine religious field presents a degree of internal pluralism and diversity of religious alternatives, it is nevertheless still characterised by the continuous dominance of Christian culture: 76% of the individuals surveyed professed Catholicism, 9% professed Evangelical Christianity, whereas just 11.3% professed atheism or agnosticism, or no religion at all. The percentage of those professing Islam is very low: just 0.2% of the total population (Mallimaci 2008: 6).
3. The religious field in Argentina is regulated and demarcated by a state body – the Secretary of Worship, part of the Ministry of Foreign Affairs and Worship –

through the so-called 'National Register of Religions', a monitoring mechanism whose regulatory function is assigned to members of the core of the Catholic Church organised around the CEA (Argentine Episcopal Conference). This mechanism not only regulates the borders of the religious field, determining who is in and who is out through prior approval by this body; it also demarcates the majority religious tradition of Argentine society, namely, the Christian faiths. Available at https://www.mrecic.gov.ar/es/registro-nacional-de-cultos/ (last accessed 3 March 2016).
4. By *visibility* we are referencing what Goffman conceptualised as *perceptible* and *tangible* features. The degree of visibility is distinct from the knowledge of an attribute (or stigma), the force with which it is imposed and the focus of attention: before talking about a degree of visibility, it is necessary to specify the others' decoding capability (2006: 64–6).
5. Part of this account can be found in Ibrahim Hallar's work, *El Gaucho y su originalidad arábiga* (1962) as well as a line of reasoning regarding the arrival of the Arabs and Muslims since the early days of the conquest of the American territory in his 1959 work, *El descubrimiento de América por los árabes*. In his 1962 description, Hallar draws a parallel between the Argentine gaucho and Andalusian *moriscos* (Muslim converts to Christianity): 'Nobody's children. Stellar figures of our pampas. Untameable, rebellious, fierce, generous and free, they cut a swathe through cowardice, greed and slavery. They laid the foundations for a homeland in war-time and made it endure in peace-time. / They belonged to no race but were an amalgam of all strains; or rather, they were a social class of their own, with those foregoing attributes, their great Arabian originality affirmed without fear of misunderstanding' (Hallar 1962: 3). He reinforces his argument by drawing attention to the Arabic origin of the word 'gaucho': *chauch*, a 'drover of animals'. The author thus traces back the origins of the Arabs' arrival in America in a mythico-historical story. With the process of conquest, Hallar argues that, as a result of the expulsion of the Moors from Spain and their forced conversion, many *moriscos* were forced to cross the sea to the Americas. In the River Plate region more precisely, he tells us that Andalusian *moriscos* 'were allowed unions with 20, 30 or even 40 indigenous women' (1962: 5), and this mixture 'first with the Indians, and the blacks that came after them intervened in the ethnic makeup of the Argentine people'.
6. We understand the formation of the nation as an imagined political community as suggested by Benedict Anderson (1991).

7. Taken from the Argentine Islamic Arab Association (AAAI) webpage, available at http://arabeislamica.com/historia/ (last accessed 3 March 2016).
8. Our concept of memory draws on a work by Maurice Halbwachs (2004), for whom a group's memory and collective representation are embedded in an ideology that helps unite the group's members, hence the importance of 'solidarity' and social ties. For Halbwachs, asking oneself about 'the forgetting' and the weakening of social bonds is a tool to analyse the ways a group's or society's memories are constructed. Memory, however individual and intimate it appears in reality, is a social construct: when individuals remember, they do not do so alone but through references (markers, supports) that allow them to recall, complete and reconstruct the past. Memory – 'remembering' – presupposes a reconstruction made in the present from references to the past. These social references of memory – the social frames of memory – are not rigid links of notions and images but dynamic structures, continually adjusting to new events in the present. In modernity, this memory is fragmented and pluralised, giving rise to a multiplicity of memories that respond to each of the multiple identitarian memberships (Hervieu-Léger and Willaime 2001: 204).
9. Following Goffman, we see personal identity as a conceptualisation developed by the individual within a variety of structures where ties with others are forged and stabilised. Personal identity is defined by the 'positive mark' or 'identity support' – in other words, others' knowledge of an individual – and by the unique combination of elements in the life history adhering to the individual by means of these identity supports. It is the result of a reflective activity and the concept the individual has of her- or himself (2006: 57–79).
10. *Assalam, El Diario Sirio Libanés, Natu-Islam, Sautilhak, La Gaceta Árabe, Ad-Difah, An-Nahda, Bandera Árabe, El Misionero* and others.
11. This is not the case with the Maronite Arabs or Orthodox Christians, who, due to their greater affinity with the local Catholic context, were able to found their places of worship earlier, since settling in Argentina, and were more active and visible compared to Muslims.
12. Field data from in-depth interviews and informal conversations with the members of the community (García Somoza 2009, 2017). The fieldwork began in July 2007 and was conducted by Somoza García as part of her MA dissertation and later developed in greater depth as part of her doctoral research, being continued as of 2013 by Valcarcel as part of her MA dissertation and current doctoral research. The interviews encompassed more than forty women between the ages of eighteen and sixty-five, from both Muslim and converts'

families. The interviewees were drawn from the educated urban middle-class participating in different areas of the Argentine Islamic community's social, cultural and religious life. In parallel with these interviews both researchers participated in various religious, social and political spaces during their respective periods of fieldwork. They also conducted a joint survey of community press archives and material produced by Muslim institutions based in the city of Buenos Aires.

13. The above data was collected from interviews with members of the institution and sources taken from the community's official website, available at http://arabeislamica.com/historia/ (last accessed 3 March 2016).
14. Field data obtained from interviews with members of the institution (García Somoza 2009) and data published on its webpage, available at http://arabeislamica.com/historia/ (last accessed 3 March 2016).
15. Available at http://organizacionislam.org.ar/educacion/universidad.htm (last accessed 3 March 2016).
16. Available at http://www.umma.org.ar/?page_id=403 (last accessed 3 March 2016).
17. When we talk about the 'Floresta group' or the 'Floresta community', we are adopting the native forms of denomination, which indicate institutions or communities according to the area they are based in. In the city of Buenos Aires most Shi'a institutions are located in the Floresta and Flores districts.
18. A centre belonging to Argentina's Jewish community, founded in 1894 and located in the city of Buenos Aires. On 18 July 1994 the AMIA headquarters in Pasteur Street was the target of a car-bomb attack. This was the most serious attack on the Jewish community in Argentina in its history. The judicial inquiry, which displayed significant irregularities and received wide media coverage, has to this day been unable to clarify the facts and prosecute the perpetrators.
19. The interview was conducted in April 2010 with a forty-year-old woman of Muslim-Arab origin (Valcarcel 2013: 30).
20. Established by Act No. 2559, passed by the Buenos Aires legislature on 29 November 2007 and coming into effect on 13 December 2007, the event was promoted by FEARAB but has been suspended in recent years due to administrative differences with the Buenos Aires City Government.
21. The comment was made during a dance show in the garden of the Sivori Museum on 15 May 2010. Field notes compiled by Valcarcel.
22. Field notes, 15 May 2010.

23. Interview conducted on 26 August 2013.
24. '*Revolución colorida*' (Colourful Revolution) or '*Revolución de la Alegría*' (Joyful Revolution) are ironical terms for the current government in Argentina and Mauricio Macri's political programme used by sectors opposed to the Cambiemos alliance. They refer to the aesthetics and slogans of Mauricio Macri's 2015 presidential campaign. The metaphor was inspired by the use of balloons and coloured confetti at Cambiemos rallies. It is possible to read this statement – rather ironically referring to a 'Colourful Revolution' running counter to the interests of the people – in parallel with the events of Iran's so-called 'Green Revolution' of 2009. The two social processes nevertheless differ in form and content: the 'Green Revolution' being a popular movement driven by liberal sectors calling themselves the 'Green Movement' in reference to the colour of Islam; the 'Colourful Revolution' being an ironic term used by the political and social opposition for the alliance of liberal centre-right political parties incarnated in Cambiemos. The Green Movement never came to rule in Iran, whereas the Cambiemos alliance has been in power since 10 December 2015. Neither phenomena may be extrapolated directly, but they may be analysed as standing in line with the ideology that represents the Floresta community against movements or parties whose worldview is seen as contrary to the interests of the people. For an analysis of the Green Movement five years on, see http://www.huffingtonpost.com/akbar-ganji/iran-green-movement-five-years_b_5470078.html (last accessed 20 February 2016).
25. Statement shared by a member of the community on the Facebook page of the At-Tauhid Mosque on the occasion of the thirty-seventh anniversary of the Revolution. The Spanish original reads as followed: 'El 11 de febrero se conmemora el aniversario de la Revolución Islámica liderada por Imam Ruhullah Al Jomeini (RA), fue el triunfo de un pueblo sojuzgado por una monarquía absolutista, tirana y opresora, puesta por la mano del imperio norteamericano a partir del derrocamiento por la CIA de Mohammad Mosadegh en 1953. / 37 años de luz y de prosperidad devuelta no sólo al pueblo iraní, sino a toda la Ummah Islámica, en lo que se puede graficar como el verdadero comienzo del Despertar Islámico . . . Pero a su vez, el Líder luminoso empezó otra lucha: La de educar a su pueblo, la de construir un nuevo paradigma pleno de dignidad y honor basado en el Islam, en las enseñanzas del Corán, del Profeta Muhammad y su Familia Purificada (AS). Pero también como ejemplo para un mundo islámico sumido en el letargo y a merced del colonialismo indirecto. / Recuperó el petróleo para su pueblo, hizo desaparecer prácticamente el analfabetismo,

incentivó la ciencia – Irán es líder en nanotecnología – fomentó la actividad y participación de la mujer en el seno de la sociedad – el 64% de la población universitaria en Irán es femenina – y llevó a la República Islámica a ser un país poderoso, industrializado y referente innegable en Medio Oriente ... Hoy la República Islámica de Irán se erige como un Faro Claro y Fuerte, como pilar estoico de la resistencia anti-imperialista en la región, y soporte fundamental para otros movimientos de Resistencia como el palestino y el libanés, como aliado leal de Siria en esta tragedia, también impuesta por los conocidos de siempre. El pueblo iraní ha salido a festejar sus 37 años de renovada libertad, y manifestando que la Revolución está viva y saludable, declarando con su presencia en las calles que ninguna 'revolución colorida' puede vencer a un pueblo convencido de lo que ha elegido para su forma de vida. Salud y Victoria para Tan Resplandeciente Revolución Islámica.' Available at https://www.facebook.com/mezquita.attauhid/ (last accessed 11 February 2016).

26. Signed in January 2013, during Cristina Fernandez de Kirchner's presidency, by the Argentine Republic and the Islamic Republic of Iran to continue the investigation into the attack on the AMIA. It provoked intense debates within and beyond the Argentine Jewish community. On 21 December 2015, early in Mauricio Macri's new administration, the Federal Chamber of Criminal Cassation was declared unconstitutional. Available at http://www.pagina12.com.ar/diario/elpais/1-288090-2015-12-12.html and http://www.pagina12.com.ar/diario/ultimas/20-288829-2015-12-22.html (last accessed 20 February 2016).

27. Available at http://www.radionacional.com.ar/?tag=gustavo-moussa, broadcast on 22 January 2015 (last accessed 20 February 2016).

28. Available at http://www.organizacionislam.org.ar/portada/somos.htm (last accessed 20 February 2016).

29. In a similar vein, during the presentation of the seminar on Islamic culture held by the University of Buenos Aires, Masuma Assad stated: 'The most pressing issue for me is the issue of women. We feel it is important to include this issue mainly because there are many stereotypes surrounding the image of Muslim women. And we know how these stereotypes serve certain interests, how new subjectivities are created from them and ultimately how these stereotypes stigmatise others, foreigners, people who are different, and bring about segregation and xenophobic attitudes.' Available at http://organizacionislam.org.ar/educahcion/universidad.htm (last accessed 3 March 2016).

30. Within the Floresta community, *nikah al-mut'a* or *mut'a* is a mechanism for

the lawful satisfaction of sexual desire if there is no possibility of contracting a permanent marriage. A dowry must be provided, as in a permanent marriage, and a term is set for the contract. The woman must pronounce a formula in Arabic, saying: 'I give myself to you in marriage by virtue of the dowry (x) for the period (x),' and the man must state that he accepts the marriage. The contract can be renewed but, in the event of being terminated, a period of *'idda* (two menstrual cycles) applies. Unlike a permanent marriage contract *mut'a* does not give the woman any right to inherit, but does to any children born from it. The institution of *mut'a* has to be practised in a devout and moderate way so as not to create a negative image of Islam (Eessa Ibarra 2003: 26).

31. Insurance or prevention could be closer to the meaning of the Spanish words *recaudo* or *precaución*.
32. 'Patria Grande' (Great Homeland) is a term commonly used by social movements and certain political groups as a basis to refer to Spanish American nations' common sense of belonging. The term was popularised in 1922 with the play 'La Patria Grande' (The Great Homeland) by the writer and politician Manuel Ugarte.
33. The 1948 Palestinian exodus as a result of the Arab–Israeli War and the formation of the State of Israel. The term *nakba* means catastrophe. The event is commemorated every year on 15 May.
34. Established in the City of Buenos Aires through Act No. 2559, passed on 29 November 2007. The event has not been held for several years.
35. For further information, see our article in *Diversa. Red de Estudios de la diversidad religiosa en Argentina*, available at http://www.diversidadreligiosa.com.ar/blog/allahu-akbar-dios-es-grande-pero-no-hace-la-guerra-claves-para-comprender-la-instrumentalizacion-politica-de-lo-religioso/ (last accessed 3 March 2016).
36. Apart from some prayer rooms (*musalla*), the Muslim community has just three mosques in the city of Buenos Aires; only one of these, located in the Floresta district, belongs to the Shi'a tradition. The At-Tauhid Mosque is home to the Argentine Islamic Organisation. The Shi'a community has other institutions throughout the country, affiliated around the Federation of Islamic Entities of the Argentine Republic (FEIRA). These institutions include the José Ingenieros Alawite Association, located close to the boundary between the city of Buenos Aires and Greater Buenos Aires.
37. Set up by Ayatollah Khomeini to demonstrate Muslim solidarity for Palestinians. It is held on the last Friday of the month of Ramadan.
38. The Quebracho Revolutionary Patriotic Movement, led by Fernando Esteche

and Raúl Lescano, was formed in 1996. It is a popular political organisation that includes ideological tendencies ranging from Peronism to Marxism. Its political praxis is characterised by road blocks, '*escraches*' (public protests), and the use of hoods and self-defence batons by its members.

39. The Federation of Arab American Entities was inspired by ideas discussed at the Congress of Overseas Immigrants in Damascus, Syria, in 1965, when the project to create a federation of (not necessarily Islamic) Arab entities was gaining ground. It was only at the start of the 1970s that numerous members of the Argentine Arab community sought through its entities to form a common space to unify and coordinate their community actions. This project gave rise to the First Arab Congress of 1971 in the city of San Miguel de Tucumán, Argentina, at which the foundations were laid for the Confederation of Argentine Arab Entities under the acronym FEARAB Argentina, finalised on 28 October 1982 in the city of Santa Fe, Argentina. Subsequently, on 19 October 1973 in Buenos Aires, FEARAB America was founded: a fourth-level organisation created with the aim of uniting all the FEARABs across the American continent. Available at http://www.fearab.net/arquivos/?eFh4fDY4 (last accessed 3 March 2016).

40. The Federation of Islamic Entities of the Argentine Republic is an organisation that brings together sixteen entities and six Islamic communities across the country, most of them Shi'ites and Alawites, http://www.feira.org.ar (last accessed 3 March 2016).

41. The Memorandum of Understanding between Argentina and Iran was signed in 2013 in the city of Addis Ababa, Ethiopia, between the government of the Argentine Republic under President Cristina Fernández de Kirchner and the government of the Islamic Republic of Iran. The agreement, consisting of nine points including the creation of a Truth Commission, was established to advance the legal action linked to the terrorist attack on the Argentine Israeli Mutual Association (AMIA) headquarters in Buenos Aires on 18 July 1994. For several years, Iran had refused to cooperate with Argentina in the court case against Iranian citizens, and the Argentine government consequently viewed the Memorandum as a step in the right direction. But in spite of the Argentine side's efforts, Iran's parliament did not pass it, and it was declared unconstitutional by the First House of Argentina's Federal Chamber. Although the Memorandum never came into force, it sparked a number of legal disputes and strong opposition from a sector of Argentina's Jewish community and politicians associated with the present Macri government. With the triumph of Cambiemos in the 2015 elections, there was a further attempt to make the agreement permanent,

but on 21 December 2015, the Federal Chamber of Criminal Cassation definitively declared the Memorandum unconstitutional.

42. Available at (1) http://www.lanacion.com.ar/1610173-delia-y-esteche-reivindicaron-a-la-agrupacion-terrorista-hezbollah; (2) http://www.lanacion.com.ar/1611238-elisa-carrio-denuncio-a-persico-y-delia-por-su-participacion-en-un-acto-antisemita; and (3) http://www.lanacion.com.ar/1613190-investigan-a-delia-y-persico-por-apologia-del-crimen (last accessed 3 March 2016).
43. *Montoneros* (*Movimiento Peronista Montonero* – MPM) was an Argentine urban guerrilla group, active during the 1960s and 1970s.
44. Available at http://www.sergiobergman.com/el-rabino-bergman-dijo-que-el-memorandum-con-iran-es-inconstitucional-y-no-sirve/ (last accessed 3 March 2016).
45. Available at http://www.lanacion.com.ar/1341387-cristina-kirchner-partio-a-medio-oriente-en-gira-oficial (last accessed 3 March 2016).
46. Available at http://ain.com.ar/envia.php?nota=2057 (last accessed 3 March 2016).
47. Available at http://www.clarin.com/sociedad/Concluyo-Ramadan-Ano-Nuevo-Judio_0_333566757.html (last accessed 3 March 2016).
48. 'Cambiemos' is the name of the PRO-led alliance with other political forces (the Radicals, the Civic Coalition, etc.) through which Mauricio Macri stood for president in 2015.
49. Peronist-oriented electoral alliance formed in 2003 and currently led by Cristina Fernández de Kirchner.
50. An Argentine political party that arose from the Peronist movement and was founded on 17 October 1945 (a date which was later celebrated as Peronist Loyalty Day). In October 1945, several organisations converged on the Plaza de Mayo in support of the then Labour Secretary, General Juan Domingo Perón, in opposition to the ruling conservative sectors. After 17 October 1945, Perón and other union leaders united to create the Labour Party, which emerged from the union of the Labour, Radical Civic Union Renewal Board and Independent parties. On 24 February 1946, Perón won the elections with a landslide majority. After the election, he replaced the Labour Party with the Single Party, after which he created the Peronist Party (James 2000: 164), which ruled until 1955. Subsequent to the 1955 coup d'état, the Peronist Party was banned and underwent a period of clandestine organisation (Marcilese 2015) that lasted until 1971, changing its old personalist name to the Justicialist Party, by which it is still known today. The Justicialist Party currently represents a large part of the

Peronist movement and some politico-syndical sectors aligned with Peronism. For more about Peronism, see James (1988, 2000); Marcilese (2015); Mallimaci (2016).
51. Field data obtained and recorded by Mayra Valcarcel.
52. The spiritual state of someone who believes in the omnipotence and omnipresence of God.
53. Field data recorded by Valcarcel on 24 October 2015. A commemoration attended by some 60–70 people.
54. For one of the interviewees it was vital to clarify that it is forbidden to harm oneself. Anyone who harms her- or himself on certain processions in Iran or other regions is in breach of religious precepts.
55. We take the meaning from the notion of 'strategies' given by Bourdieu (1972): 'Les strategies n'appliquent pas des principes ou des règles. Elles choisissent le répertoire de leurs opérations.'
56. Records consulted in the Archives of the Congress of the Argentine Nation, the National Library of the Argentine Republic, and the General Archive of the Nation.
57. Interviews conducted by the authors during their own ongoing research.
58. We understand the category of 'other' in the sense of otherness developed by Todorov (1982, 1989). Otherness is the product of social relations and can be defined on the basis of a triple axis (1982): a positive or negative judgment (the axiological level); the action of approaching or distancing in the relationship with the other (the praxiological level); and the ability to know or ignore the other's identity (the epistemological level). The category 'others' designates those who do not form part of the cultural and social group 'us'. In this sense Todorov understands that the 'us/others' relationship also crystallises 'the diversity of peoples and the human unit' (1989).

Chapter 4

1. The event was organised to also mark the 170th anniversary of the birthday of the Albanian Bektashi poet Naim Frashëri with references to his 'pantheism' and additional references to various European Orientalists, including Max Choublier, who found the Bektashis to have realised a true 'Franciscan life' (*Journée de la Culture Bektashi à Paris* 2016).

Chapter 5

1. The Al-Ayn Foundation, for example, has a statement on its website declaring that 'since its establishment, Al-Ayn has enjoyed the support and blessings of the Supreme Religious Authority Grand Ayatollah Al-Sayyid Ali Al-Hussaini Al-Sistani', the highest religious authority in Shi'a Islam (https://www.alayn.co.uk/basic-page/religious-authority, last accessed 20 May 2017); while the website of the Imam Hussain Blood Donation campaign includes quotes from various Shi'a scholars outlining the religious importance of giving blood (https://ius.org.uk/giveblood/islamic-opinion, last accessed 20 May 2017).
2. It should be clear that I am not suggesting that the diaspora is solely responsible for the rise of sectarian tensions within Iraq – indeed, to attempt to reduce the complex politics of ethno-religious identity within the Iraqi context is highly problematic – rather, the argument of this chapter should be taken within the context of the existing literature on the history and politics of sectarianism within Iraq (Batatu 2004; Dodge 2012; Haddad 2011; Tripp 2007; Yousif 2010; among others) in order to shed light on the ways in which identity constructs within the diaspora have contributed to the ongoing sectarianisation of Iraqi society, both materially and symbolically.
3. Since Iraqi Sunnis are a minority in Britain, practising Muslims tend to frequent mosques run by members of Britain's other Muslim communities (such as the well-established South Asian Muslim community); as such there are no Sunni mosques I am aware of that are run specifically by or for Iraqis (a fact that was often commented on by my research participants). Iraqi Shi'ites, however, although not the largest community of practising Shi'ites in London, dominate the institutional religious and community fabric of the city and in this sense represent the most visible Shi'a minority in the capital (Degli Esposti 2019).
4. I conducted a total of thirty formal interviews and fifty-two informal interviews with both male and female Iraqis of various ages, classes and political affiliations and who had come to the UK at various times or been born here.
5. For example, Dar Al-Islam in Cricklewood serves as the headquarters of the Islamic Da'wa Party in London; while the Al-Khoei Foundation in Queen's Park is the official representative of the late Grand Ayatollah Sayyid Al-Khoei and now the unofficial representative of Grand Ayatollah Sayyid 'Ali Al-Sistani; and Rasool Al-Adham serves as the representative of religious emissary Sayyid Shirazi (to name but a few).
6. There are arguably significant historical reasons behind the association of Iraqi

national identity with Shiʻa sectarian affiliation, especially as a result of the persecution many Shiʻites felt subjected to under Saddam Hussein's Sunni-dominated Ba'ath party (for discussions of the emergence of a Shiʻa politico-sectarian identity in Iraq, see International Crisis Group 2006; Nasr 2006; Rosen 2006; Visser 2007; Walker 2006; among others).

7. The processes of subjectivity and subject-formation in the Iraqi Shiʻa diaspora – and the forms of political agency they engender – are the focus of my forthcoming book, and as such will not be discussed at length here.

8. Individuals usually give their *khums* to their chosen *marjaʻ* (Shiʻa scholar), who in turn has the right to distribute the money as they see fit or, if necessary, keep it for their own needs (but never for a profit, according to Shiʻa doctrine). Unlike the *zakat*, the *khums* is specifically intended to be given to the earthly representatives of the Imam (i.e. the religious establishment) and, as a result, tends to be channelled into supporting Shiʻa families and organisations in Iraq and Iran.

9. Figures vary between 15 and 20 million, but this estimate comes from BBC News (2014). Iraq's Defence Minister Khaled Al-Obeidi gave the figure of 17.5 million for 2014, comprised of 13 million Iraqis and 4.5 million foreigners from sixty different nations (Al-Arabiya 2014).

10. Since the focus of this chapter is on the symbolic and discursive contours of the Iraqi-Shiʻa subject, questions regarding the mobilisation of the diaspora towards the homeland fall outside the scope of the current discussion. For works that do engage with such issues, see Alkhairo (2008), Kadhum (2017), Saleh (2011) and Witteborn (2008).

11. While the structurally sectarian nature of the Ba'th regime under Saddam Hussein, coupled with the decades of poverty and deprivation under the US-imposed sanctions, undoubtedly contributed to the sectarianisation of Iraqi Shiʻa subjectivity within Iraq itself, the focus of this chapter is on the shifting contours of ethno-religious identity within the diasporic context and thus a nuanced discussion of sectarian identities within Iraq is not entered into here.

12. The US-based organisation Shiʻa Rights Watch, for example, distributes a weekly online newsletter detailing discriminatory practices and sectarian persecution against Shiʻites worldwide, as well as running an iPhone and Android app.

Chapter 7

1. Fieldwork notes, interview with Sayyid Mohammad Husayn Al-Hakim, son of Grand Ayatollah Mohammad Sa'id Al-Hakim, 3 October 2017, Najaf.
2. As termed by French historian Pierre Nora (1999), a *lieu de mémoire* can refer to a place, object, symbol or concept that is imbued with significance in popular collective memory. Yafa Shanneik (2017) makes the link between *lieux de memoire* and Shi'a identity.
3. Asad (2009) notes that traditionally anthropologists have dealt with the diversity of 'Islams' by distinguishing between the text-based practice of the towns and the 'saint-worshipping, ritualistic religion of the countryside', arguing that both types formed in different ways under different conditions. These distinctions are, of course, not distinct, but in the case of American Shi'a Muslims they are merged in young Shi'a Muslims who prefer a rationalist interpretation of the faith, yet are emotionally tied to these distant shrines.
4. Online sources would extensively quote the collated volume of *Kamil al-Ziyarat*, collected by the renowned fourth-century AH Twelver Shi'a scholar Ibn Qulawayh. The book itself would be reprinted internationally, including in large quantities by the Al Khoei Foundation (Al-Qummi 2004). Online *ziyarat* guides similarly encourage the practice based on the historical rootedness of the practice, quoting classic collections such as *Kamil al Ziyarat* and *Bihar al-Anwar*, compiled by the famed Safavid Shi'a scholar Mohammad Baqir Al-Majlisi. These guides have been replicated and incorporated into online manuals and Internet appeals on some of the most popular Internet platforms (see Alidina 2019).
5. Similarly, Yafa Shanneik (2015: 89–102) argues that Iraqi Shi'a women in Ireland engage in 'collective remembering' to legitimise their particular sectarian identity and existence within Islam.
6. According to Max Weiss, sectarianism 'is a way of being in the world that depends upon a set of cultural markers and social practices, a framework capable of holding familial, local, regional, and even international loyalties together' (2010: 13).
7. The concept of 'the centre out there' was coined by Victor Turner (1973) to describe the affiliation that pilgrims feel for their sacred sites, as well as the notion that pilgrimage to these centres creates a condition of *communitas*, a unity that exists only within the pilgrimage structure.
8. Vali Nasr (2006) illustrates the new centrality of Iraq: 'Since 2003, hundreds of thousands of pilgrims, coming from countries ranging from Lebanon to

Pakistan, have visited Najaf and other holy Shiite cities in Iraq, creating transnational networks of seminaries, mosques, and clerics that tie Iraq to every other Shiite community, including, most important, that of Iran . . . The Middle East that will emerge from the crucible of the Iraq war may not be more democratic, but it will definitely be more Shiite.'

9. For this contribution in particular, I spoke to about 200 Shi'a Muslims across Ramadan, Muharram and Safar in 2014–15 in the New York/New Jersey area, primarily from Mehfil Shah-e-Khorasan in Englewood, New Jersey, Masjid-e-Ali in New Brunswick, New Jersey, Al-Khoei Center in Jamaica, New York, Astaana-e-Zehra in Manalapan, New Jersey, Bait-ul-Qaim in Delran, New Jersey, and Islamic Institute of New York in Woodside, New York. Real names have been changed where requested for publication.

10. Sabrina Mervin (1996) has detailed the changing demographics around the Sayyeda Zaynab shrine in the latter part of the twentieth century, with an influx of Iraqi migrants fleeing Saddam Hussein's persecution, Iranian religious seminary (*hawza*) students flocking to newly opened institutions in the 1970s, and groups of predominantly Sunni Palestinian refugees setting up camps around the shrine. Edith Szanto (2012) has also done ethnographic work on the layout and current demographics of the shrine.

11. Real name changed by author. Fieldwork notes, interview with the author, 19 December 2014, Mehfil-e-Shah-e-Khorasan.

12. Real name changed by author. Fieldwork notes, interview with the author, 12 November 2015, Bait-ul Qayem.

13. Fieldwork notes, interview with the author, 6 December 2014, Masjid-e-Ali.

14. Interestingly, this longing amongst young pilgrims is not concurrent with a lack of belonging in their everyday lives, as most do not exhibit the same sense of alienation that studies on European Muslim communities depict. The majority of those interviewed express the belief that they are well-integrated into their larger communities – work, diverse friend groups, or educational settings – yet feel compelled to take this step to both influence their own lives and shape their local religious communities. Though they express concern about the rising tide of Islamophobia they witness on the news and through word-of-mouth, interestingly, none of those interviewed believed that they had experienced it directly or in any serious manner. In particular, while they mentioned it was a concern for all Muslims, many had not faced it personally. 'We don't grow those long beards and we don't have those intense imams,' one college-aged man explained to me. Still, they argue that it remains a factor for the younger children, those in early

years in school who have to associate with children they argue are 'uneducated' or 'uniformed' about Islam.
15. Fieldwork, interview with the author, 13 November 2015, Astaana-e-Zehra.
16. The 'Who is Hussain' campaign is a decentralised organisation that allows Shi'a communities around the world to mobilise around particular local campaigns – helping the homeless, blood drives, food banks, and more – to spread a message of Karbala linked to social justice. 'We are made up of individuals of many cultures, languages, religions, nationalities and social classes' (Who is Hussain 2019). The focus on transforming Shi'ism into an activist ideology focused on social justice is, of course, not isolated to the United States or Western countries. Lara Deeb (2006) outlines in detail the turn towards social engagement in Shi'a Lebanon, in particular women's community service and social organisations in Al-Dahiyya.
17. Masjid-e-Ali is also the most frequent site of Ammar Nakshawani's lectures in the region, and he played a significant role in helping the board raise funds for the multimillion-dollar project. He also lends his voice to the introductory video on the site, stating that it boasts 'leadership not just of the elders, but of youth alike. Youth provide the energy, the elders provide the guidance. The youth provide insight, the elders provide a long term vision as well as experience' (Masjid-e-Ali 2015).
18. Fieldwork notes, interview with senior member of the board of Masjid-e-Ali, 22 November 2015, Masjid-e-Ali, New Jersey. In the introductory video (Masjid-e-Ali 2015), the centre's resident *alim* (scholar), Rizwan Tilmiz reiterates that MFI (its common abbreviation) is a mosque and functions as such, which means the daily recitation of prayer in *jamat* form, read by an imam or *'alim*.
19. According to Fischer, the paradigm 'provides models for living and a mnemonic for thinking about how to live' (1980: 21).
20. The limits of Iranian influence are not a new theme, one that harkens back to the limits that the Islamic Republic faced in 'exporting' the Iranian Revolution. According to Nasr (2006), 'since 2003, Sunni leaders in Egypt, Jordan, and Saudi Arabia have repeatedly blamed Iran for the chaos in Iraq and warned that Iran would wield considerable influence in the region if Iraqi Shi'ites came to hold the reins of power in Baghdad. The Egyptian president, Hosni Mubarak, sounded the alarm last April [2005]: "Shiites are mostly always loyal to Iran and not the countries where they live."' Yet, time and again, this sense of Shi'ites as a 'fifth column' or intrinsically loyal to Iran has been repeatedly debunked (see Shaery-Eisenlohr 2008). Scholars of Shi'ism have at times distinguished

between more tribal Iraqi Shi'ism versus Iranian ritualism, which has roots in Sufi orders (Nakash 2003: 177). Nakash argues that the roots of Iraqi Shi'ism were in part an attempt to settle nomadic tribes, appealing to 'Abbas ibn 'Ali as a model that captured the masculine ethos of tribal culture.

21. For further discussion of the role of English as a tool that can transcend racist social exclusion, see Modood 2005.
22. The group often employs multiple scholars to manage its growing size, including Mohammad Al-Hilli, as part of the concentric circles of these new scholars.
23. Fieldwork notes, interview with Grand Ayatollah Mohammad Sa'id Al-Hakim, 4 October 2017, Najaf.
24. Fieldwork observations, group visit with Grand Ayatollah Sayyid 'Ali Al-Sistani, 5 October 2016, Najaf.
25. Fieldwork, interview with author, 1 November 2014, Masjid-e-Ali.
26. Fieldwork, interview with author, 10 November, Mehfil-e-Shah-e-Khorasan.
27. Fieldnotes, interview with author, 28 December 2015, University of Pennsylvania.
28. Fieldnotes, interview with senior cleric, 4 December 2017, Najaf.
29. In particular, young people with limited time for *ziyarat* trips are choosing tours where they can elect to go to Iraq and skip Iranian portions of the itinerary. Few expressed a clear desire to visit Iran, despite the massive growth in pilgrimage to Mashhad in the years before Saddam Hussein's fall. I argue this is part of this emphasis on Iraq, or as Shaery-Eisenlohr argues, 'how claims to religious authenticity in the Shi'ite world draw on perceived national differences in justifying the alleged superiority of some Shi'ite practices and visions of "correct" Shi'ism over others' (2007: 17).
30. Ammar Nakshawani's much-discussed 2014 lecture on ISIS acknowledges that Muslims have to be concerned with the affairs of Muslims around the world. Based on a saying of the Prophet Muhammad, Nakshawani (2014) argues, 'when I hear Muslims being killed in Syria, I have to be concerned for them. When I hear about Muslims being killed in Bahrain, I have to be concerned for them. When I hear about Muslims being killed in the Hejaz, I have to be concerned for them. When I hear about Muslims being killed in Iraq, I have to be concerned.' Nakshawani (2014) discusses this in the context of the broader *umma*, for Muslims to be politically active and politically involved. In the context of this lecture on ISIS, however, respondents mentioned that this was a further call to action to them to focus on the targeting of Shi'ites in the Arab world, as they argue that the victims and targets of ISIS have been Shi'ites.

31. In the narrative of Karbala, Zaynab bint 'Ali and the women of Husayn's family were taken prisoner after the massacre of the tenth of Muharram. They were paraded to *al-sham*, present day Damascus, humiliated throughout the journey and in the court of the Caliph Yazid, and kept as prisoners for a year.
32. Fieldwork observations, 23 October 2015, Bayt-ul Qaim, New Jersey.
33. Fieldwork, interview with author, 29 October 2017, New Jersey.
34. Fieldwork, interview with author, 17 October 2016, Queens, New York.

Chapter 8

1. Some scholars try to avoid the negative connotation of 'extreme'/'extremist' and use other terms instead. Olsson (1998: 199 and *passim*) speaks of 'Ali-oriented Religions', During (1998: 105) prefers the expression 'hyper-Shia groups', but also uses 'Ahl-e Haqqism' (1998: 111 and *passim*). During (1998: 109) remarks that during his long stay in Iran he 'became familiar with Ahl-e Haqq culture . . . This experience led me to write a general account of the Ahl-e Haqq with specific references to music' (see as well as other works mentioned on Ostad Elahi (2016)). According to Mir-Hosseini (1997: 191), During is 'a leading supporter' of the reformist branch of the AH. For excerpts of one of his publications on 'Ostad Elahi', see Ostad Elahi (2016). His publications can be described as a blend of science and epigonism or propaganda. – Originally, the term *ghulat* was used by Shi'a heresiographers to designate those 'dissidents' (or, better to say, those who proclaimed this belief in public) who exaggerate the status of the Imams in an undue manner by attributing to them divine qualities. As Al-Qāḍī (2003) has outlined, the term had different connotations over the first three centuries in the Shi'a context. On this term, see also Hodgson (1965) and Halm (2001). For foundational texts on the *Ghulat*-traditions (German translation and comments), see Halm (1982).
2. I adapt the term used by Ziba Mir-Hosseini. For her articles on this branch, see the references.
3. Much more research has been done on Iranian AH than on Iraqi AH. As these remarks are confined to a little basic information, see for greater detail, the following publications: van Bruinessen (2013), Halm (1984), Hamzeh'ee (2009a), Moosa (1988: 185–254, and 168–84, on the 'Sarliyya-Kakaiyya'). For the Kaka'is see also Leezenberg (1997) and the bibliography therein.
4. Lit. 'friends (of the Truth)'.
5. Lit. 'brothers (of the true path)' – accurate numbers on the AH are not available; academic estimations vary from several hundreds of thousands to over two mil-

lion. See Delshad (2013: 18 – table on the alleged number of adherents to AH 'families' in and outside Iran, based on a variety of sources).
6. On the assumed relations to Zoroastrianism and older Iranian traditions, see, above all, Hamzeh'ee (2009b: 324, 326, 328) and, in greater detail, Hamzeh'ee (1990).
7. Islamic speculation on transmigration of souls has its origins in gnostic cosmological myths, exclusively found in extreme Shi'a groups. There are two forms of *tanasukh* – the temporal for the elect, the eternal for the damned. Some Mu'tazilites and philosophical/esoteric mystics were also influenced by these ideas.
8. The reformist branch is sometimes seen as a new *khandan* (Mir-Hosseini 1994b: 220).
9. For the *jam'* (gathering) and important rituals, such us the offerings, see, in addition, van Bruinessen (2013), Moosa (1988: 231–44) and During (1997).
10. See Raei (2009: 351–4) and Hamzeh'ee (2009b: 324) on similarities between the *Khaksar*, one of the main Iranian Dervish orders, and the AH. For the different categorisations, see, for example, Hamzeh'ee (1997: 102–4).
11. These reformulations can also be interpreted as a subjugation of the traditional religious ideas to the dominant religion/religious trends of the society in which their respective adherents are living; see Hamzeh'ee (1997: 112). See also Olsson (1998: 201–2) for the three phases, and Mir-Hosseini (1997) with greater details.
12. As mentioned in the analysis of *Forqan al-akhbar* by Minorsky (1960).
13. For an analysis of the works, see Mir-Hosseini (1997: 183–5) and Minorsky (1960). The efforts of Ne'matollah coincide with alternative reformist steps (doctrinal reformulations by Sayyid Baraka, mentioned by van Bruinessen (2013); support of the Iranian constitution of 1906 by another major figure of the AH in Western Iran, mentioned by Mokri (1997), and Mir-Hosseini's remarks on the case of the dervish Taymur in the mid-nineteenth century (1994a: 272–4) and with reports on successful missionary work among AH (Stead 1932: 189, for Christian missionary work; Minorsky 1921: 269–70, for the sympathy between Babis and AH as well as conversions to Baha'ism).
14. See the detailed analysis by Weightman (1964). A copy in Persian is available on the official website of Ostad Elahi – *Borhan al-haqq* is more concerned with the exoteric aspects than the following work in Persian. It is intended to offer a standardised narrative of the history, origins, beliefs, principles and rites of the AH as a mystical order within the framework of Shi'a Islam. The author claims that the AH – despite misunderstandings and distortions by some

people – observe the principles of Shi'a Islam; in addition, they follow other principles, among them general moral and ethical principles, and specific rites and ceremonies according to their specific Sufi path. Apart from his father's teachings and his own interpretations and classifications, the book uses material from AH sources (*kalams*) and Islamic (foremost Shi'a) traditions.

15. See, for instance, German translation with an introduction by Delshad (2013) – the book focuses on the esoteric aspects and describes his ideas on the soul's gradual process of maturation and perfection. It is more influenced by the Shi'a mystical and esoteric tradition.
16. Like his father, he is said to have experienced a kind of spiritual rebirth ('return from the dead, infused with a new soul' – Algar (1998)). In addition, he is depicted as a genius, having mastered the lute at the age of nine years and having completed his legal studies in a 'preternaturally short time' (Algar 1998). His stupendous juridical career can probably be explained by the shortage of lawyers and judges at the beginning of the judicial reforms implemented under Reza Shah. For details, see Floor (2009).
17. On his activities (until mid-1990s), see Mir-Hosseini (1997: 188–92).
18. *Foundations of Natural Spirituality: A Scientific Approach to the Nature of the Spiritual Self* (1997), *Spirituality is a Science* (1999), *Medicine of the Soul: Foundations of Natural Spirituality* (2005) (as mentioned on Ostad Elahi (2016)). See also Fondation Ostad Elahi (2016b).
19. The exhibition had the title 'The Life and Work of Ostad Elahi'. For further information, including photos, see Ostad Elahi (2016).
20. Morris is known as a specialist in Ibn 'Arabi (1165–1240).
21. It is noteworthy that Minou Elahi is the only permanent member of the board on whom no further information is given on the website of the Foundation. This fact indicates a rather traditional gender concept.
22. Pierre-Henri Imbert, born 1945, Professor Emeritus of Political Science and Public Law.
23. Bernard Bourgeois, Professor Emeritus of Philosophy.
24. The website of the Foundation mentions (for mid-June 2012) 623 foundations that are recognised as public interest organisations (without corporate foundations and endowments administered by the 'Fondation de France') and about 2,000 associations that are recognised as public interest organisations; for 2015 see the numbers given by France, Council of Foundations (2015): approximately 1,500 public utility foundations – also without the aforementioned two other categories (in 1995 there were less than 500) – and about 1,500,000

registered associations; the number of associations that are recognised as public interest organisations is not mentioned. All foundations in France must serve a public benefit purpose. Private foundations need to be approved by the state. For further information on the diverse forms of foundations and associations, on the specific legal regulations, and on the provisions on tax exemptions, etc., see France, Council of Foundations (2015).

25. See UN-ECOSOC (2016c), for statements between 2010 and 2015.
26. See below for an example of an implicit reference to AH tenets of belief (perfection of the soul, even after physical death, an allusion to metempsychosis and reincarnation although these principles were re-interpreted in Ostad Elahi's books in Persian).
27. For extra information, see under 'life/biography/the-early-years' and go to 'Ahl-e Haqq' in the text (inverted in red colour).
28. See, for instance, its promotion of gender equality.
29. This judgement does not necessarily apply to the professionalisation of their outer appearance, for instance on the website.
30. See, in particular, Ostad Elahi's blind sister Malak Jan Nemati (1906–93), who after the death of her brother functioned as a 'medium' between him and his followers. She died in Paris and was buried in a small French village where a glass shrine was erected on her grave ('Saint Jani Memorial'). Further links are to be found on Ostad Elahi (2016).
31. His 'World Ethos Foundation Tübingen' received financial support from the Karl Schlecht Foundation (KSF) and finally, with the funding of KSF, the 'World/Global Ethics Institute' was established at the University of Tübingen in 2011. See Karl Schlecht Foundation (2015). Küng wrote several books on his project (1990, 2002, 2012) – although I am not a Muslim, I was asked to contribute to one of Küng's workshops in 1992; my paper on the 'Possible contribution of Islam to the Global Ethics Project' remained unpublished.
32. Morris (1996: 9) quotes the following saying by Nur Ali Elahi: 'Ce que tu aimes pour toi-même, il faut l'aimer pour les autres, et ce que tu n'aimes pas pour toi-même, ne le souhaite pas pour les autres: c'est le principe essentiel de la religion'. In English: 'The religion of the Truth is One . . . and all the religions (and prophets) have said it: that you should love and do for others what you wish for yourself . . . That is the ultimate principle of religion'.

Chapter 9

1. This chapter is based on research undertaken in 2012 and 2015, supported by the American Institute for Sri Lankan Studies. The community's vulnerable position makes it imperative to conceal the identities of focal subjects and the specific locations of community sites. Detailed information can be used to identify, monitor and persecute the subjects of this study. If the quality of description at this exploratory stage of research is vague, it is only as a precautionary measure. Subsequent studies shall present more evidence of the claims made here. I am deeply indebted to the subjects of this study for their generosity in sharing access to the community with me.
2. An old community of Shi'a Bohras have achieved exceptional commercial prosperity in Sri Lanka, and their long-standing presence has also served to mute overt condemnation of the Shi'ites.
3. This pertains to the Sunni communities of South India, which also exported teachers to Sri Lanka. For an overview of the latter, see Asad (1993: 35–45).
4. Based on private communication with A. R. Ottathingal, Leiden University.
5. Al-Mustafa International University has undergone several transformations between its establishment in 1979, consolidation in 1993 and reinvention under the present name in 2007. Based in Qom, it currently has chapters and affiliates in Iran and throughout the world. See Sakurai (2015: 41–72).
6. The slur *rafidi* used by Sunnis against the Shi'ites for rejecting the caliphate of Abu Bakr and Umar is pejoratively applied with the connotation of heretic.
7. For a carefully documented account of recent anti-Muslim rhetoric and violence in the Western Province, see Haniffa (2016: 164–93).
8. There is an extensive literature on the history of Shi'a clerical quietism and activism. A good overview of origins with regard to modern Iran is Algar (1969).
9. This critical approach has not been used to analyse Islamic education, but can be a useful framework. See Fasenfest (2010: 483–7).

Chapter 10

1. Available at: at https://www.bertelsmann-stiftung.de/fileadmin/files/BSt/Publikationen/GrauePublikationen/GP_Religionsmonitor_verstehen_was_verbindet_Religioesitaet_und_Zusammenhalt_in_Deutschland.pdf, last accessed 12 January 2017.
2. I conducted fieldwork among different Shi'a communities in Germany in a research group on Shi'ism in Germany, directed by Robert Langer, between

2015 and 2017. This fieldwork mostly consisted of (semi-)structured interviews and participant observation in ritual practices and festivities, such as *ghadir khumm*. The project was, and still is funded by the Federal Ministry of Education and Research (*Bundeministerium für Bildung und Forschung*) and located at the Department for Religious Studies at Bayreuth University. I thank Robert Langer for sharing his findings within this research group with me.

3. The term 'other Shi'ites' was coined by Monsutti, Naef and Sabahi for those Shi'ites who live outside Iran and thus focus on contexts in which Shi'ism is in a minority (Monsutti *et al.* 2007: 7).
4. The term is frequently used with reference to Marshall Hodgson, who usually speaks of "Alid loyalism' in order to grasp piety and practice surrounding the loyalty to 'Ali ibn Abi Talib and his and Fatima's offspring (Hodgson 1974: 260).
5. *Ghadir khumm* is the one location where, according to the Shi'a narrative, the Prophet Muhammad designated his cousin and son-in-law 'Ali ibn Abi Talib as his successor in 632 CE. The divergent interpretation of this episode between Sunnis and Shi'ites is the point where different understandings of the legitimacy of Muhammad's successors separate Sunnis and Shi'ites.
6. See Bernheimer (2013) for a general work on the 'Alids, seyyids and sharifs in medieval Islamic history.
7. According to official data of the asylum seekers that registered in Germany in 2014 and 2015 by the *Bundesamt für Migration und Flüchtlinge*, 432,000 were Muslims (REMID 2016). Assuming again a ratio of 9 per cent of them being Shi'ites would result in 38,880 persons. As there are many refugees coming from Afghanistan, a considerable number of them being Shi'a Hazaras, one can assume a higher percentage of Shi'ites among these asylum seekers. The total number of Shi'ites living in Germany in 2017 may consequently amount to over 400,000.
8. Germans who converted in the aftermath of the Islamic Revolution are also among Esra Özyürek's interlocutors in her study on conversion to Islam in Germany (Özyürek 2015: 1).
9. Querstraße 18, 30519 Hannover.
10. 'Islamischer Rat der Ahl al-Bayt Gemeinschaften in Deutschland', founded by the Grand-Ayatollah Seyed Reza Hosseini Nassab, who acted as the director of the Islamic Centre in Hamburg between 1999–2003 (Nassab 2017).
11. Unstructured interview with the interlocutor (name changed) by Robert Langer (7 January 2015) and myself (27 October 2017, Berlin, Germany). Robert Langer granted me sight of his unpublished notes.

12. 'Ehlibeytin yolunda yürümek için, gercek anlamıyla Alevi olmak için, gercek anlamıyla Hüseyini olmak için, Caferi olmak için, ehlibeytin helalini helal, haramını haram bilmek zorundayiz' (Yeral 2014).
13. Note that there are also other etymological interpretations around the term. For example, Aksünger derives the meaning of Alevi from the compound of the name Ali and the Turkish word for house, *ev*, so that Alevi is a compound from *ali evi* – 'Ali's house' (Aksünger 2015: 29).
14. Ja'fari is also the name given to the legal school established by the sixth Imam Ja'far Al-Sadiq. Shi'a jurisprudence is therefore referred to as *ja'fari fiqh* and its followers hence as *ja'fari* to distinguish them from followers of the other *madhahib* in Sunni Islam.
15. 10 October 2015, Nuremberg, Bavaria, Germany.
16. While Shanneik (2015: 90) emphasises the aspect of how a specifically Shi'a sectarian identity is constructed through collective memory, here, the aspects of undoing such sectarian borders within the 'Alid field is given primary importance.

Chapter 11

1. Unless otherwise mentioned, the following notes result from a long-term ethnographic collaboration with Chams in Cambodia since 2000. The themes of Shi'a 'conversions', journeys to Iran, and *sayyids*, while already part of my work then, have become the focus of my research conducted since 2013 between Cambodia and Iran.
2. The Muslims of Cambodia are mainly composed of Chams, originally from the former kingdom of Champa, in what is today central Vietnam. They represent barely 5 per cent of the total Cambodian population, which is largely Khmer Buddhist. While mainly dwelling in provinces in the plains and around the main rivers, Chams are spread out all over the country. In contemporary scholarship – as much as in popular imagination among both Cambodians and outsiders – Chams are often seen as a compact community ethnically, religiously, and linguistically distinct from the majority. Yet, those networks of 'being Cham' vary across space and time and are never entirely settled. For an ethnographic overview of Chams in Cambodia, see Ner (1941) and Collins (2009).
3. In this entwinement of ethnographic observation and more 'historical' sources, I do not mean that the former, by embracing contradictions, belongs to the opaque, while the latter would act as a clarifying explanation. Rather, as any historical anthropologist, I see both domains filled with an uncertainty full of

potentials rather than holes to be sealed, and use them interchangeably in this chapter.

4. The *ahl al-bayt* expression, found in the Qur'an 33.33, is usually translated as 'people of the house', and stands for the extended family of the Prophet Muhammad. The Prophet's immediate family (his daughter Fatima and her husband 'Ali, and their children Hasan and Husayn) is also referred to as 'people of the cloak' as they are found united under the cloak of the Prophet.

5. In this chapter, I will refer to 'Saeths' when I emphasise *sayyids* within the Cham/Cambodian context, and to '*sayyids*' when I refer to the trans-local networks of the descendants of the prophet Muhammad in general, and of his daughter Fatima and son-in-law 'Ali in particular.

6. Cham studies have always asserted that Chams in Cambodia are all Muslim Sunnis, and vastly Shafi'is. However, next to this label, the scholarship has always been eager to describe forms of Islam considered heterodox and often essentialised as uniquely Cham, and anxious to find 'Shi'a traces' in those manifestations (Aymonier 1890; Cabaton 1906: 16, 1907: 4; Collins 2009; Durand 1907: 337; Fatimi 1963; Manguin 1979; Schafer 1967; Setudeh-Nejad 2000).

7. I am echoing here a narrative that takes linear continuity as granted: this is indeed a reification of the different dynamics of Shi'itisation in and outside of Cambodia. I am aware of alternative life-stories that would be precious to inform those narratives with quite a different take. For lack of space, I will for now focus on the *sayyid*/Cousin-Hidden-Imam perspective and the historical angle.

8. In this chapter, I will not use the term 'sharif'. While often used to categorise *sayyids*' descendants through a female line, the word is unknown to Chams who just speak of *sayyids*' descendants in variable levels of being 'Saeths' or 'non-Saeths'.

9. While the concept of being descendants of the Prophet and his family is nothing new for Saeths, it should be noted that the usage of the term *ahl al-bayt* was hardly ever heard of a few years ago but is now routine, probably something to link to the recent quest of Shi'itisation as a genealogical *sayyid* claim.

10. 'Ali as the first Islamiser is a recurrent trope in Muslim Southeast Asia even – or mainly – among Sunnis (Daneshgar *et al.* 2013; Ricci 2015).

11. In his detailed study of Chinese records related to Southeast Asia's early Islamisation, Wade finds that the most prominent Muslim communities in the region notably resided or traded out of Champa (Wade 2010: 369), and that

most of the envoys from the region sent to the court of China and named 'Li' in the tenth century were from Champa.
12. An alternative version can be found in Collins (2009: 72–3).
13. 'Hasan-Hosen' can refer at times to Hasan and Husayn as two different individuals and at other times to an ideal double, melting the two in one.
14. The hiding of yet-to-be heroes and saviours in mountains and/or caves as a preliminary to humanity's renewal is common to both Shi'a narratives of messianism and tropes of Muslim sainthood in Cambodia and other areas of Southeast Asia.
15. The example I draw from here – in which a *sayyid* can be 'Alid without being Famitid – is not an isolated one. The recognition of non-Fatimid 'Alids as full descendants of the *ahl al-bayt* and *sayyids* is a recurrent one in Islam, and has found many different answers across various parts of the Muslim world. Some examples of those discussions can be found in Hodgson (1955), Ho (2006) and Morimoto (2012).
16. Due to lack of space, I have chosen to only focus here on the Cham version of 'Ali Hanaphiah, which could have been inspired by that of Muhammad Hanafiyya, found in Indonesia and Malaysia – just as the reverse could be true (the Cham version could have been of inspiration to the Indonesian and Malaysian ones). I will not summarise the narrative – which has been found to be of Iranian origins – well studied by Baried (1976), Brakel (Brakel and Brakel 1977; Brakel *et al.* 1988) and Wieringa (1996 and 2000). Some key differences and similarities of interest though, are as follows: 'Ali Hanaphiah is Cham while Muhammad Hanafiyya remains a foreigner in the archipelagic sources; 'Ali Hanaphiah is the son of a non-Muslim Cham princess and Muhammad Hanafiyya is the son of Khawla bint Ja'far, a former slave of the non-Muslim Hanafi tribe; 'Ali Hanaphiah mother is local – a Cham – while Muhammad Hanafiyya's mother is an outsider – she is not from Indonesia or Malaysia. In other words, while the Muhammad Hanafiyya story is a re-appropriation of an outsider myth, the 'Ali Hanaphiah story complicates notions of outsider/insider by folding the categories together.
17. The quest for 'Shi'a traces' – or 'Shi'a character' – is far from being limited to Chams. Just as an example, Birchok writes (in reference to Indonesia): 'Scholarship . . . has often failed to recognise the ways in which it is complicit in affirming a particular notion of orthodoxy within an Islamic tradition, where disagreement over such orthodoxy is simultaneously a vexing problem and inextricably constitutive of the tradition itself. Such approaches tend to see

"Shi'a character"... as both remnants of a bygone era and sub-orthodox Sunni practice, or simply beyond the pale of Islam altogether' (Birchok 2015: 167).

18. Wade notes that in 968 CE 'the viceroy of Champa was named in Chinese sources as Li Nou which would be 'Ali Nur'' (Wade 2010: 369). Could this have been short for an 'Ali Nosavan?

19. Nosavan therefore contributes to a dissociation of Iranian and Shi'a influences long conflated in the scholarship of Southeast Asia's Islamisation, and recently revisited (Andaya 1999; Guillot 2004; Lombard-Salmon 2004; Marcinkowski 2008, 2015; Petrů 2016; Wade 2010; along with the earlier works of Cowan 1940; Marrison 1955; Wyatt 1974). As Feener and Formichi remind us: 'Persians had been a presence in Southeast Asia's maritime trade networks since at least the dawn of Islamic history. It should be remembered, however, that these earliest Persians in the Indonesian archipelago were not even Muslims' (2015: 6).

20. Among the list of Cham envoys to the court of China, 'Li' and 'Pu' – 'Ali and Abu – are the most prominent surnames, which Wade reads as 'origins and genealogies' rather than whole families (Wade 2010: 370–1). I believe this can be furthered into the hypothesis that this is already a trace of the Cham elites in place as indissociably Saeth ('Ali/Li) and Po (Pu/Abu).

21. The title of 'Tuon' is the one used among Chams in particular and among Southeast Asian Muslims in general to describe either a religious leader or a *sayyid*. Among Cambodian Saeths, it is notably women who often inherit the title of Tuon while men carry the title of Sayyid.

22. While the mention of 'Ja'far' can seem surprising, it should be noted that Ja'far Al-Sadiq is known not only as 'a major link in most Sunni chains of Sufi legitimation' but also that he 'as a figure of religious authority for both Shi'īs and Sunnīs points to the complexities involved in understanding how phenomena that have been labelled by modern scholars as "Shi'ī" might have carried other meanings for Muslims living in earlier historical contexts' (Feener and Formichi 2015: 5).

23. The Wali Sango can be found in the *Badad Tanah Jawi* ('History of the Land of Jawa'), which 'ascribe[s] the first Javanese conversions to the work of the nine saints, but the name and relationships among these nine differ in various texts' (Ricklefs 1993: 9). As Ricklefs further emphasises, 'it is impossible to reduce these variations to a list of nine persons upon which all texts would agree' (Ricklefs 1993: 9).

24. While I admit that this summary may seem selective and arbitrary, I am trying to

facilitate the reading of a potential lineage that would make sense, somehow, of the contemporary Saeth narratives which are themselves fragmentary.

25. In Ricklefs (1993), Maulana Ishak becomes Molana Usalam.
26. On a side note, Chams have long been represented in Khmer popular culture today, or in the Cambodian royal chronicles, as talented sorcerers to be feared.
27. The shrine of Po Kabrah, in today's central Vietnam, is still visited by Chams (Shine 2009). I am grateful to Nicolas Weber for bringing this reference to my attention.
28. The passage also mentions an encounter between Ishak and another Muslim who had spent time at Angkor and who reports on how Arabs were well-treated and accepted by the Khmer king. We can infer then, that potential *sayyid* lineages may have been active and even common at the royal court of Cambodia as early as the ninth century. Saeths often take pride in the role played by their ancestors in the Khmer royal palace, as much as they grieve the repressions conducted against them repetitively by the many kings and throne contenders (may those be Khmers or Chams). None of those Saeth repressions can be read in the Khmer and Cham royal chronicles if we look for an outward 'Sayyid' title, but some of the names of the protagonists can be identified as Saeths. As I have worked here with lineages themselves, women have disappeared from my narrative if we strictly look for names and genealogies. One should not conclude, however, that they are absent from the transfer of knowledge of the lineages themselves; on the contrary, but this is something that I have not touched upon here for lack of space and develop elsewhere in my work.
29. We could also note that our Hadrami Al Idrus (Al-Aydarus) also reconnects us to the Iranian/Cham line, as van Bruinessen shows, through a common lineage to Kubro: Jamaluddin Husain Al-Akbar. His genealogy connects him to Ja'far al-Sadiq and to Cambodia, where he is said to have travelled (van Bruinessen 1994: 325). In addition, his son Ibrahim Zain Al-Akbar married a Cambodian princess with whom he will have two sons: Maulana Ishaq and Rahmatullah/Sunan Ampel (van Bruinessen 1994: 325), names that are now getting very close to our previous Wali Songa lineages of Cham and Persian descent.
30. FULRO: United Front for the Liberation of Oppressed Races (from the French: *Front Unifié de Lutte des Races Opprimées*) was, during the American Vietnam war, a movement mainly operating from Cambodia and uniting Chams and other highland minority groups from both Vietnam and Cambodia with a common goal of regaining the lands towards an independent Champa.
31. In his study of seventeenth- to twentieth-century edifying stories and dream

accounts prescribing proper attitudes towards the descendants of the *ahl al-bayt*, Morimoto shows that most of the Shiʻa sources he uses take inspiration in Sunni texts, an example of how the boundary generally separating the two major sects blurs when it comes to the status of the *sayyids* and sharifs (Morimoto 2012: 16).

32. For this reason, but also due to a lack of space, I have not spoken here of the many traces of ʻAlid piety generally interpreted as 'Shiʻa traces' in literary and ritual traditions of some non-*sayyid* Cham groups often considered as traditionalists, such as the Imam San group in Cambodia or the Cham Bani in Vietnam. Those traditions are too often solely seen as limited to groups that we conveniently 'frame' as 'traditionalists' in a way that reasserts Shiʻa as something on the margins of a mainstream 'general' and transnational Islam. It also relocates those groups at the margin of the same idealised Islam, as if they were only its passive receivers and never fully engaged actors.

Chapter 12

1. Journalists have also contacted me out of interest in tracing financial flows from Lebanese in West Africa presumed to finance Hizbollah whose activities are categorised in the United States as terrorism. The historical fact that Lebanese Shiʻites began to settle in West Africa one century before the Iranian Revolution of 1979 and the establishment of Hizbollah in Lebanon in 1982 is unfortunately not the story journalists want to publish. Many of the second- and third-generation Lebanese born and raised in West Africa have never been to Lebanon.
2. See also Leichtman and Schulz (2012).
3. For recent debates in African Studies about cosmopolitanism, see Mbembe (2017) and the various reactions his essay elicited.
4. This can also have religious consequences. See Ahmad (2017) on the conversion of South Asian domestic workers.
5. I was also recently invited to Karbala, Iraq, for a religious conference and festival, hosted by the holy Shiʻa shrines.
6. I was once even asked, in all earnestness, by a US government employee if Senegal was a 'satellite' of Iran.
7. Appiah (2006) also argues that Islam was 'counter-cosmopolitan'.
8. See Leichtman and Alrebh (2018) in addition to some of the chapters in this volume.

INDEX

Abu 'Abd Allah Muhammad bin Ishaq, 248
Abu Bakr, 213
Abu Fadl 'Abbas ibn 'Ali, 145, 149, 297n.20
Academy of World Religions, Hamburg, 216
actor-network theory (ANT), 130, 135–8
Afghan diaspora, 186, 197, 198–9, 214
Afghanistan, 37, 85
African traditional religions, 270, 271
Aga Khan III, 6
agency, 76, 99, 111–12, 258, 260
ahl al-bayt
    connection to Sri Lankan cultural practices, 189
    as designated successors of Muhammad, 4
    genealogical and spiritual lineages to, 6, 23, 35, 227–51, 268, 274–5
    and narratives of oppression, 186
    possession of divine knowledge, 6
    refuge at Qom, 198
    religious authority, 6
    veneration of *see* 'Alid piety
ahl al-kisa', 229
Ahl-e Haqq
    elements of Sufism, 165, 166, 168
    esoteric roots, 17, 21–2, 163, 164, 268
    as *ghulat* group, 5, 163, 164–5, 267–8
    historical background, 165–6

not referenced on Ostad Elahi Foundation website, 172
    oral transmission of religious tenets, 163, 164, 165, 268
    organisational structure, 166
    Ostad Elahi Foundation *see* Ostad Elahi Foundation
    reconciliation of doctrines with Twelver Shi'ism, 163, 167, 173, 268
    reformist branch, 21–2, 163, 164–5, 166–9, 176, 268
    rituals and doctrines, 165–6, 167
    and universalism, 17, 18, 21–2, 163, 175–6
    writing down of religious tenets, 163, 167
Ahle-Sunnat Wal Jama'at, 197
Ahlulbayt Societies (ABSocs), 113
Ahlul-Bayt TV, 153
Al-e Ahmad, Jalal, 76, 187
Ahmadis, 44, 197
Al-Akbar, Ibrahim Zain, 308n.29
Al-Akbar, Jamaluddin Husain, 308n.29
Al Al-Bayt Foundation, 136
Al-Al-Bayt Global Information Centre, 136
Alawis *see* Nusayri-Alawis
Albania, 74, 75, 77, 78–80, 81, 82, 85, 267; *see also* Balkans
Alevi Islam, 5, 8, 22–3, 74, 75–6, 164, 209–24, 273

Ali, Mohsen, 64
Ali, Mustafa, 213
'Ali Hanaphiah, 234, 235–8, 239, 247, 274, 306n.16
'Ali ibn Abi Talib, 4, 6, 17, 132, 154–6, 166, 196, 206, 212, 217, 220–1, 229–40, 251, 268, 274, 303n.5
'Ali ibn al-Husayn *see* Zayn Al- 'Abidin
'Alid piety, 6, 9, 12, 19, 22, 25, 33, 35–6, 38, 43, 62, 73, 196, 209–24, 228–38, 249–51, 272–5
All Ceylon Salaf Council, (ACSC), 202
Al-Amin, Muhsin, 159
Anderson, Benedict, 128, 130, 284n.6
anti-imperialism, 15, 17, 19, 61–2, 65–6, 195, 267
anti-Semitism, 63
anti-Zionism, 61
Anurshivan the Just *see* Khosrow I
Appadurai, Arjun, 12, 15–16, 125, 128, 130
Appiah, Kwame Anthony, 259–60, 309n.7
Arab Alliance Cultural, Social and Charitable Association, 53
Arab Countries' Culture Week (Buenos Aires), 56, 61
Arab Gaucho, 49
Arab identity, 49, 51–2, 56–7, 267
Arabic language, 34, 38, 53, 54, 56, 59, 66, 128, 191, 192–3, 195, 199–200, 204, 227
Arabic press, 51, 54
Arabisation, 202
Arba'in, 107, 112, 143, 144, 149, 150, 156, 263
Argentina
  AMIA bombing, 55, 59–60, 63, 64
  anti-imperialism, 15, 17, 19, 61–2, 65–6, 267
  Arabic press, 51, 54
  'Ashura' rituals, 66–7, 68
  At-Tauhid Mosque, 50, 52, 54, 56, 58–9, 61, 62, 63–4, 66, 288n.36
  Catholicism, 46–8, 58, 266
  changing religious demographics, 19, 46–8
  'Colourful Revolution', 58, 65, 286n.24
  Constitution, 48, 57
  conversions to Shi'ism, 58–9
  diasporic identity formation, 49–68, 267
  diasporic politics, 55–67, 267
  discourses of autochthony, 17
  educational institutions, 53–4
  Floresta Shi'a community, 50, 52–68
  framings of the Islamic Revolution, 17, 19, 52, 57–8, 61–2, 65–6, 267
  influence of Iran, 54, 57–60
  Islamic organisations and institutions, 50, 52–5, 60–6
  Islamic cemeteries, 53
  Judaism, 51, 55, 59–60, 64
  Kirchnerist administration, 63, 64–5
  localisation of Shi'ism, 15, 19, 57, 267
  Memorandum of Understanding with Iran, 60, 63, 64
  military dictatorship, 52
  Muslim immigration, 19, 50–1
  Nakba commemorations, 56–7, 61, 62–3
  National Register of Religions, 47
  leftist politics, 15, 61–2
  Perón administration, 47
  religious pluralism, 46–8
  religious tolerance, 48, 267
  return to democracy, 19, 48, 267
  revivalism, 52, 267
  secularism, 47, 48
  Twelver Shi'ism, 19, 50, 52–68
  wearing of the hijab, 57, 60–1, 62, 66
Argentine Arab Young Persons' Social and Cultural Club, 53
Argentine Institute of Islamic Culture (IACI), 54
Argentine Islamic Arab Association (AAIA), 50, 52–3
Argentine Islamic Arab Cultural, Social, Sporting and Charitable Association, 53
Argentine Islamic Arab Institute, 53–4
Argentine Islamic Organisation, 52, 61, 62, 288n.36
Argentine Israelite Mutual Association (AMIA), 55, 59–60, 63, 64
Argentine Muslim Women's Union (UMMA), 54, 57, 60–1, 66
Asad, Talal, 144
asceticism, 137, 168
'Ashura', 5, 14, 20, 40, 42, 50, 66–8, 74, 103, 112–13, 151
Al-'Askari shrine, 21, 146
Al-Asr Foundation, 107
Al-Assad, Bashar, 159–60
Assad de Paz, Masuma, 54, 287n.29
assimilation, 18, 151, 153, 270
asylum seekers, 186, 197, 198–9, 205, 214
At-Tauhid Mosque, 50, 52, 54, 56, 58–9, 61, 62, 63–4, 66, 288n.36
Austro-Hungarian Empire, 85–6
authenticity, 9, 144, 150, 152, 156, 159
authoritarianism, 12
authority *see* clerical authority; political authority; religious authority
autochthony, discourses of, 12, 16–18, 23, 76, 81–2, 189
Al-Aydarus, Abdullah, 242
Al-Aydarus, Abu Bakr, 242
Al-Aydarus, Zayn Al-'Abidin, 231, 239, 242–3
Al-Ayn Foundation, 96, 292n.1
Azerbaijan, 6, 165

Ba 'Alawiyya, 35, 242
Baath regime, 8, 102, 114, 129, 142, 146, 264, 293n.6, 293n.11
Badr Brigades, 109
Baghdad, 103, 142, 198
Bahrain, 6, 7, 16
Balkans
  Bektashi Islam, 6, 17, 18, 19–20, 73–90, 267
  Bektashi–Sunni relations, 80–1
  discourses of autochthony, 17, 18, 81–2
  European integration, 19–20, 77–8, 81–4, 87–8, 90, 267
  fall of Communism, 19–20
  foreign influence discourses, 82–5
  genocide, 78
  history of Islam, 77, 78, 87
  nationalism, 77
  radical Islam, 81, 82, 84–5
  social class, 88–9, 269
  socialist period, 82–3, 88–9
  wars, 78, 84
Bandung, 37–9
Bangalore, 187, 191, 200
Al-Banna, Hasan, 38
Baragbah, Ustadz Sayyid Ahmad, 34–5, 37
Beheshti, Muhammad Husayn, 187, 199
Beirut, 129
Bektashi Islam
  in the Balkans, 6, 17, 18, 19–20, 73–90, 267
  as bridging Islam and Christianity, 75
  decolonial approaches to, 20, 76–7, 78, 86–90, 267
  differentiation from radical Islam, 17, 20, 75, 78–85
  as European Islam, 17, 18, 20, 76, 77–8, 79–86, 90, 267
  as 'good' Muslims, 20, 80–1
  links to Twelver Shi'ism, 20, 73
  as moderate Islam, 17, 20, 75, 77–86, 267
  Ottoman roots, 19
  persecution, 74, 81, 267
  practice of *taqiyya*, 74, 267
  relations with Sunni Islam, 80–1
  veneration of *ahl al-bayt*, 6, 73
Belgium, 8
belonging, 16, 18, 20, 82, 97, 104, 106, 147–50, 157, 210, 215, 264
Bengkulu, 33, 41–3
Bergman, Rabbi Sergio, 64
Berlin, 213–14, 216–19, 222
Berlin Alevi Toplumu (Berlin Alevi Community), 216
Bertelsmann Foundation, 209, 214
Bhabha, Homi, 124, 127, 134, 139
Bize, Gustavo C., 54
Bodu Bala Sena (BBS), 203

bordering processes, 78, 80, 82–3, 85, 87–8, 90
Bosnia, 74, 78; *see also* Balkans
Bowen, John R., 13–14
Brah, Avtar, 145
Brahimaj, Edmond, 79–80
Brahmanism, 240
Britain
  'Ashura' rituals, 20, 103, 112–13
  charities based in, 20, 96–7, 105–6, 108–9, 263
  collection of *khums* and *zakat*, 106
  colonialism, 165
  diasporic identity formation, 97–8, 100–5, 263
  diasporic politics, 20, 97–8, 103–15, 263
  Imam Hussain Conference, 97, 108, 113
  Iranian diaspora, 102
  Iraqi civil society institutions, 101, 103
  Iraqi diaspora, 8, 18, 20, 96–115, 262–3
  Iraqi embassy, 100
  multiculturalism, 18, 105
  Pakistani diaspora, 8, 106–7
  pilgrimage industry, 106–7
  sectarianism, 20, 97–8, 104
  Shi'a religious centres (*husayniyyat*), 101–3, 104
Buddhism, 202, 203, 227, 268
Buenos Aires, 19, 50–68, 266–7
Buenos Aires University, 54
bulava (spiritual invitation for *ziyarat*), 147
Bulgaria, 74; *see also* Balkans
Burhanuddin, Shaykh, 42
Butler, Judith, 98, 99

Caferis, 214, 219, 220–1; *see also* Ja'fari *fiqh*
Cambiemos alliance, 65, 286n.24
Cambodia
  'Alid piety, 228–38, 249–51, 274–5
  Buddhism, 227, 268
  Cham Muslims, 9, 17, 23, 227–51, 268, 274–5
  conversions to Shi'ism, 8–9, 11, 23, 227–35, 249, 251
  genealogical lineages to *ahl al-bayt*, 17, 23, 227–51, 265, 274–5
  influence of Iran, 227–8, 230, 268
  Islamisation, 23, 228, 235, 240, 275
  localisation of Shi'ism, 15, 17, 23, 237–8
  *sayyid*s, 17, 23, 227–51, 268, 274–5
capitalism, 59, 76
Catholicism, 46–8, 58, 79–80, 81, 175, 266
Çelebi, Katip, 213
cemeteries, 53, 132, 203
Cham Muslims, 9, 17, 23, 227–51, 268, 274–5
charisma, 6, 59, 132, 211, 232–3, 273
charitable donations, 105–6; *see also khums*; *zakat*
charities
  donations to, 105–6
  funding of development projects, 262

funding of educational institutions, 41, 136
humanitarian aid provision, 84–5
London-based, 20, 96–7, 105–6, 108–9, 263
role in fostering sectarianism, 20, 97, 105–6, 108–9, 263
and transnational networks, 105–6, 108–9
see also humanitarian organisations
Chávez, Hugo, 61
Christianity, 8, 13, 44, 46–7, 51, 58, 66, 75, 79–81, 175, 197, 216, 266, 269, 271, 284n.11
citation politics, 89
citizenship, 111–12
clash of civilisations discourses, 78, 85
clerical authority, 6–7, 9, 13, 15, 20–1, 114, 127–39, 152, 190; *see also* religious authority; senior clerics
clerical leaders *see* senior clerics
clerical networks, 6–7, 13, 15, 106, 107, 114, 127–8, 134, 135
clientelism, 104, 113–14
Cold War, 76, 84
collective memory, 5, 14–15, 49–50, 53, 62, 67, 77, 87, 144–5, 148, 154, 157
Colombo, 187, 189, 192, 196–9, 200, 202
colonialism, 76, 85–90, 164, 165, 258, 269–70; *see also* decolonial approaches; anti-imperialism
'Colourful Revolution', 58, 65, 286n.24
Communism, 19, 37, 59; *see also* socialism
conservatism, 40, 44
conversion
 from African traditional religions, 270, 271
 in Argentina, 58–9
 in Cambodia, 9, 11, 23, 227–35, 249, 251
 from Christianity, 8, 58
 to Christianity, 271
 forced conversion, 77
 in Germany, 214
 in Indonesia, 11, 19, 34–6
 and the Islamic Revolution, 8–9, 11, 19, 34, 36, 188, 214
 persecution of converts, 12, 206–7
 as rediscovery of Shi'a roots, 8–9, 17, 23, 24, 35–6, 227–8, 232, 249
 as re-orientation rather than rupture, 9, 23, 24–5, 205–7, 269–73
 and sectarianism, 12–13, 206–7
 in Senegal, 13, 270–2
 in Sri Lanka, 9, 11, 22, 188, 195–6, 205–7, 272–3
 from Sunni Islam, 8–9, 11, 13, 22, 24–5, 34–5, 188, 195–6, 205–6, 214–15, 227–35, 249, 251, 269, 272–3
 terminologies for, 269–75
 without renouncing former beliefs, 272

cosmopolitanism, 17, 23, 153, 258–60, 275–6
cultural flows, 125
cultural hybridity, 127, 134, 139

Dabashi, Hamid, 73, 77
Daesh *see* ISIS
Damascus, 146, 157–60, 264
dance, 43, 56, 267
Dar al-'Ilm, 198
Darul Islam Islamic State movement, 37
da'wa (proselytising), 37–8, 200, 259
debt, 201–2
decolonial approaches, 20, 76–7, 78, 86–90, 267
democracy, 19, 48, 133, 267
dervishes, 73, 74, 166, 212, 217; *see also* Sufism
de-territorialisation, 13, 153
'Dialogue Among Civilizations' project, 176
diasporas
 collective memory, 5, 14–15, 49–50, 53, 62, 67, 144–5, 154–5, 157
 the diasporic subject, 98–100, 103–5, 114–15
 displacement of native languages, 150–1, 268–9
 establishment of Islamic cemeteries, 53
 ideational aspects, 14
 identity formation, 49–68, 97–105, 209–11, 214–15, 221, 222–3, 258, 263, 267, 273
 institutional affiliations, 55
 mosque-building, 52–3, 54, 151–2
 narratives of origin, 49, 50, 51, 67
 networks with homelands, 13, 23, 102–3, 105–10, 114, 262–3
 and politics, 13, 20, 55–67, 97–8, 103–15, 258, 263, 267
 religious remittances, 105–6, 108, 114, 205, 263
 see also migration; *and diasporas of individual nations*
digital media *see* Internet; social media
divine incarnations, 165–6, 167
divine knowledge, 6
double minority status, 15–18, 20, 22, 25, 75, 78–85, 111, 185–6, 195, 266–9
Druze, 5
Dünya Ehlibeyt Vakfi (World Ahl al-Bayt Foundation), 218

educational institutions
 affiliated with Iran, 10, 19, 41, 202, 203–4
 Arabic colleges, 192–4
 in Argentina, 53–4
 curricula, 34, 53, 186–7, 191
 female attendance, 190
 funding, 41, 136, 201–4, 262
 in India, 186–7
 in Indonesia, 19, 33–41, 261

educational institutions (*cont.*)
  in Iran, 10–11, 33–5, 39, 135–6, 185, 187, 189, 192–4, 197, 227–8, 233, 261, 268
  in Iraq, 101, 132, 192
  madrasas, 151, 186–7, 192–4, 197, 202–3, 261
  seminaries, 7, 10–11, 34–5, 39, 101, 132–3, 135–6, 185–94, 197, 227–8, 233, 261, 268
  in Sri Lanka, 185, 186, 192–4, 197, 201–4, 261
  transnational networks, 10, 19, 41, 202, 203–4, 205
Egypt, 37, 38, 233, 296n.20
Ehlibeyt Kultur- und Kunst Verein (Ehilbeyt Cultural and Art Organisation), 219–21
Ehl-i Beyt Kültür ve Dayanişma Vakfı (Ehlibeyt Culture and Solidarity Foundation), 218–19
Eid Al-Fitr, 64, 196, 198, 200
Elahi, Bahram, 21, 163, 168–9, 170, 175
Elahi, Chakhrokh, 170
Elahi, Minou, 170
Elahi, Nur Ali, 21, 163, 167–8, 169, 172, 173, 174–5, 268
Elía, Ricardo H. S., 54
embassies
  in Britain, 100
  cultural functions, 10, 41, 42, 198
  in Indonesia, 39, 41, 42
  Iranian, 10, 39, 41, 42, 188, 198, 262
  Iraqi, 100, 262
  Israeli, 62
  in Senegal, 262
  in Sri Lanka, 188, 198
emulation, 7, 101, 133, 137, 154, 206
English language, 143–4, 151, 152–3, 156, 168, 169–71, 195, 199, 264, 268–9
Enveri, 213
esotericism, 5, 17, 21–2, 163–4, 168, 174, 175, 266, 268
Esteche, Fernando, 63, 64, 288n.38
ethics, 75, 163, 168, 170, 171, 173–6, 259–60
ethnoscapes, 125, 131
Europe (generally)
  Bektashi Islam constructed as European Islam, 17, 18, 20, 76, 77–8, 79–86, 90, 267
  bordering processes, 78, 80, 82–3, 85, 87–8, 90
  colonialism, 85–6, 165
  conversions to Shi'ism, 8
  diasporic politics, 13
  discourses of autochthony, 18, 76
  Eurocentric geopolitics, 76, 80–6, 87, 88
  Eurocentric scholarship, 88, 89–90
  integration of Balkan states, 19–20, 77–8, 81–4, 87–8, 90, 267
  Iranian diaspora, 8
  Iraqi diaspora, 8
  Muslim immigration, 8, 258
  New Age spiritualism, 79
  securitisation, 84–5
  see also European Union; *and individual countries*
European Union (EU), 19–20, 76, 77–8, 82–3, 85, 88, 90, 267
Evita Movement, 63

Fadlallah, Muhammad Husayn, 131, 138
Al-Fadschr, 210
fasting, 108
Fatima, 4, 61, 73, 229, 235, 236–7, 268, 274–5
Fatima Hanaphiah, 235–7, 274–5
Al-Fayad, Muhammad Ishaq, 132–4
Federation of Arab American Entities (FEARAB), 62, 285n.20
Federation of Islamic Entities of the Argentine Republic (FEIRA), 62, 288n.36
Feener, Michael, 11, 213, 228, 249, 274, 307n.19
Festival Tabot, 41–3
finanscapes, 125, 129
fiqh (jurisprudence), 35, 38, 39, 41, 133, 187, 188, 191, 233, 259
Fischer, Heinz, 81
folklore traditions, 19, 36, 212
Formichi, Chiara, 11, 213, 228, 249, 274, 307n.19
Foucault, Michel, 98, 99, 104
France, 17, 18, 21, 86, 163, 169, 266, 268, 270
Frashëri, Naim, 291n.1
French language, 163, 168, 169–71
Front for Victory party, 65
fundamentalism *see* radical Islam
fundraising, 52–3, 131, 134, 265–6

Gadjah Mada University, 33, 34, 37
genealogies, 6, 23, 35, 227–51, 268, 272, 273, 274–5
Georgia, 137
Germany
  Afghan diaspora, 214
  Alevi Islam, 8, 22–3, 209–24, 273
  'Alid piety, 209–24, 273
  asylum seekers, 214
  conversions to Shi'ism, 214
  cooperation between Shi'a groups, 22–3, 211, 220–1
  diasporic identity formation, 209–11, 214–15, 221, 222–3, 273
  ghadir khumm festivities, 211, 219–22
  Iranian diaspora, 214
  Iraqi diaspora, 214
  Islamic centres, 210, 215
  Islamic organisations, 213–14, 215–21
  Lebanese diaspora, 214

Muslim immigration, 214
Nusayri-Alawis, 210–11, 216, 220–4, 273
Pakistani diaspora, 214
ritual practices, 211, 214, 219–22
Turkish diaspora, 8, 22–3, 209–24, 273
Twelver Shi'ism, 22–3, 210–11, 216–17, 219–24, 273
Geschiere, Peter, 12, 16
ghadir khumm, 211, 219–22
gharbzadegi (Westoxification), 76
ghulat groups, 5, 163, 164–5, 219, 267–8
globalisation, 16, 49, 57, 125, 130, 259
Gök, Cevat, 220–2
'good' Muslim/'bad' Muslim discourses, 18, 20, 80–1
Greece, 74; *see also* Balkans
Green Movement, 286n.24
Gulf War (1991), 8

Al-Habshi, Sayyid Husayn, 35
hacking, 124
Al-Hadi *pesantren*, 33, 34–5
hadith, 137, 167, 191, 192, 196, 206, 212, 266
Hadramawt, 35, 187, 231, 243, 261, 275, 242–4, 261, 275
Hadrami lineages, 240, 242–4, 275
Hafizović, Rešid, 82
hajj, 107, 135, 144, 154–5, 263
Al-Hakim, Muhammad Sa'id, 132–4, 154
Halbwachs, Maurice, 284n.8
Hallar, Ibrahim, 283n.5
Hamburg, 210, 215
Hamburg University, 216
Hanafi *madhhab*, 84
Harabati Baba Teke, 81
Hasan ibn 'Ali, 4, 41, 239
Hatay, 216, 218, 220
hate speech, 197
Hatibi, Ervin, 77, 79
hawzat see seminaries
Haxhi-Bektash Veli, 74, 217
hegemony, 10, 24, 66, 83, 114, 138, 176, 223, 267, 275
Hezbollah, 10, 16, 34, 64, 112, 265, 309n.1
hijab, 57, 60–1, 62, 66, 150
Hilla, 106
Al-Hilli, Mohammad, 152
Hindi, 151
historical time, 56, 67
Hizb Al-Da'wa, 7
Hodgson, Marshall, 36, 212, 228, 229, 249, 250, 303n.4
homelands
 diasporic remittances to, 105–6, 108, 114, 205, 263
 Husayn as homeland, 14–15

networks with diasporas, 13, 23, 102–3, 105–10, 114, 262–3
spiritual homelands, 14–15, 21, 23, 144, 145, 149–50, 152–4, 157, 263–4
homing desire, 14, 23, 145, 149–50, 153–4, 157
human rights, 59, 65, 160
humanitarian organisations, 84–5, 106, 259, 263; *see also* charities
Husayn ibn 'Ali
 commemoration of, 5, 14, 41–3, 50, 66–8, 107, 112–13, 142–5, 263
 and genealogical lineages, 236, 239, 240–1, 246
 as homeland, 14–15
 martyrdom, 5, 14, 50, 67–8, 110, 125, 142, 144, 158, 221, 265
 revolt, 4–5, 15, 158
 shrine at Karbala, 14, 107, 142–60, 263
 succession to Imamate, 4
 as symbol of resistance, 66, 267
 as symbol of victimisation, 111
husayniyyat (Shi'a religious centres), 101–3, 104, 197–9
Hussein, Saddam, 11, 21, 102, 114, 129, 132, 142, 263–4, 293n.6, 293n.11
hybridised identity, 98, 100, 103–5, 108–10, 114
Hyderabad, 187

Ibn 'Abd Al-Wahhab, Muhammad, 155–6
Ibn Al-Qayyim Al-Jawziyya, 155
Ibn Qulawayh, 294n.4
Ibn Rusta, 248
Ibn Sa'ud, 36
Ibn Taymiyya, 155
identity *see* Arab identity; diasporas: identity formation; hybridised identity; Iraqi identity; Islamic identity; national identity; political identities; Shi'a identity
ideoscapes, 125, 133
Al Idrus *see* Al-Aydarus, Zayn Al-'Abidin
Iğdir, 214, 216, 220
IJABI (All-Indonesia Assembly of Ahlul Bait Associations), 38–9, 40, 42, 281n.5
imagined communities, 128, 130
Imam Hussain Blood Donation Campaign, 97, 292n.1
Imam Hussain Conference, 97, 108, 113
Imam Hussain Slam Poetry Competition, 113
*imambargah*s (congregational spaces), 151–2
India, 42, 149, 186–7, 191, 200, 204, 205, 261, 264
Indian diaspora, 194, 264
indigeneity *see* autochthony, discourses of
Indonesia
 'Alid piety, 19, 33, 35, 36, 38, 43
 anti-colonial struggle, 39

Indonesia (cont.)
  British rule, 42
  conversions to Shi'ism, 11, 19, 34–6
  Darul Islam Islamic State movement, 37
  educational institutions, 19, 33–41, 261
  folklore traditions, 19, 36
  founding principles, 39
  genealogical lineages to *ahl al-bayt*, 239–40, 242–8
  influence of Iran, 19, 33–44, 261
  Iranian Embassy, 39, 41, 42
  Islamisation, 244–8
  localisation of Shi'ism, 15, 19, 42–3
  Muharram rituals, 34, 41–3
  reformism, 37
  religious demographics, 281n.5
  religious extremism, 44
  revivalism, 37–9
  *sayyid*s, 35–6, 239–40, 242–8
  secularism, 39, 42
  Suharto regime, 37, 39, 42
  traditional arts, 39–40
  Twelver Shi'ism, 19, 35
  Wali Songo, 244–8
  youth culture, 40
Institute for Technology in Bandung (ITB), 37, 38
interfaith dialogue, 79–80, 152, 176, 269
Interfaith Network of Young People of the City of Buenos Aires (RIJBA), 63–4
internally displaced people (IDPs), 199
International Al-Quds Day, 62, 63
International Hijab Day, 61
International Organisation for Migration (IOM), 100
Internet
  and constituency-building, 20–1, 131, 265
  hacking, 124
  and knowledge transmission, 21, 124–5, 131, 133, 136–7, 191–2, 265–6
  Oniki İmam Yolu website, 217–18
  online access to texts, 137, 191–2
  online *ziyarat* guides, 144
  Ostad Elahi Foundation website, 168–75, 266
  and raising and distribution of funds, 131, 133, 135–8, 265–6
  and religious authority, 15, 20, 124–5, 128–9, 130–9, 265–6
  senior clerics' websites, 15, 20–1, 124–5, 131–5, 136–8, 265
  social media, 113, 134, 138, 188, 192, 195, 202, 265
  and transnational networks, 15, 20–1, 128–9, 130–9, 191–2, 265–6
invented traditions, 86

Iran
  Al Al-Bayt Global Information Centre local websites, 137
  competition for religious authority, 129
  cultural organisations, 187
  embassies, 10, 39, 41, 42, 188, 198, 262
  establishment of Islamic Republic, 36, 165
  European and US interference, 165
  and genealogical lineages to *ahl al-bayt*, 230, 234–5, 239–48, 275
  Green Movement, 286n.24
  and hegemony, 10, 24, 223, 275
  influence of, 10, 15, 16, 19, 24, 33–44, 54, 57–60, 152, 159, 185, 187–9, 193–4, 196, 198, 202–4, 207, 227–8, 230, 257–62, 268
  Islamic Culture and Relations Organisation, 42
  khums collection and redistribution, 135–8
  media, 187
  media representations of, 59–60
  Memorandum of Understanding with Argentina, 60, 63, 64
  Al-Mustafa International University, 10, 33, 41, 188, 198
  nationalism, 129
  networks of affiliated educational institutions, 10, 19, 41, 202, 203–4
  new religions, 165
  Pahlavi dynasty, 165
  pilgrimage to, 106, 264, 297n.29
  proxy wars with Saudi Arabia, 11
  relations with Syria, 10
  Revolution *see* Islamic Revolution
  Revolutionary Guards, 146, 159
  seminaries, 10–11, 34–5, 39, 135–6, 185, 187, 190, 192–4, 197, 227–8, 233, 261, 268
  shrine cities, 7, 106, 129, 264
  social movements, 165
  and soft power, 10–11
  sponsorship of mosque-building, 151
  state interference in *khums* collection and redistribution, 135–6, 137
  status of women, 58, 59–60
  Twelver Shi'ism, 6, 9–11, 275
Iran–Iraq War, 102, 188, 262
Iranian diaspora, 8, 102, 214
Iranian Revolution *see* Islamic Revolution
Iraq
  Al Al-Bayt Global Information Centre local websites, 136–7
  Baath regime, 8, 102, 114, 129, 132, 142, 146, 264, 293n.6, 293n.11
  charities working in, 20, 96–7
  clientelism, 113–14
  competition for religious authority, 129
  destruction or threatened destruction of shrines, 21, 146, 155

diasporic remittances, 105–6, 108, 114, 263
elections, 134, 157
embassies, 100, 262
fall of Saddam Hussein, 11, 21, 142–3, 263–4
ISIS, 20, 21, 61, 108–10, 112, 146, 155–6, 265
nationalism, 103–4, 129, 157, 263
pilgrimage to, 21, 106–8, 142–60, 263–5, 265, 268–9
Popular Mobilisation Forces (PMF), 108–10
resource distribution, 113–14, 263
sectarianism, 8, 11, 20, 97–8, 105–10, 146, 157, 263, 265
seminaries, 101, 132, 192
Shi'a Islamist parties, 7
Shi'a militias, 106, 108–10
Shi'a uprising, 8
shrine cities, 7, 15, 21, 101, 106–8, 129, 132–5, 142–57, 192, 263–5
as spiritual homeland, 15, 21, 23, 144, 145, 149–50, 152–4, 157, 263–4
US invasion, 110, 132, 133–4, 142–3
US sanctions, 293n.11
Iraq War, 110, 264
Iraqi Children's Aid and Repair Endeavour (ICARE), 96–7, 108–9
Iraqi diaspora, 8, 18, 20, 96–115, 214, 262–3
Iraqi identity, 98, 100–5, 108–10, 114, 157, 263
Iraqi Shi'a Cultural Organisation, 220
ISIS, 20, 21, 61, 67, 108–10, 112, 146, 153, 155–6, 158, 159–60, 265
Islamic cemeteries, 53, 132, 203
Islamic Centre, Colombo, 196–9, 201
Islamic Centre, Hamburg, 210, 215
Islamic Centre, Hannover, 215
Islamic Centre of England, 102
Islamic Centre of the Argentine Republic (CIRA), 64
Islamic College, Jakarta, 40, 41, 42
Islamic College, London, 41
Islamic Community of North Macedonia, 81
Islamic Community of Shi'ite Congregations in Germany, 214, 215–16, 218
Islamic Council of the *Ahl al-Bayt* Communities in Germany, 215
Islamic Cultural Centre (ICC), 40–1, 42, 62
Islamic Culture and Relations Organisation, 42
Islamic identity, 12, 17, 20, 23, 49–50, 52–68, 76, 209–11, 215, 222–3, 267; *see also* Shi'a identity
Islamic Propagation Organisation (IPO), 187
Islamic Revolution
 anti-imperialist constructions of, 17, 19, 52, 61–2, 65–6, 267
 Argentinian framings of, 17, 19, 52, 57–8, 61–2, 65–6, 267

and awareness of Shi'ism, 8–9, 19, 36–7, 52, 58
as cause of migration, 8
and conversion, 8–9, 11, 19, 34, 36, 188, 214
and establishment of the Islamic Republic, 36, 165
and Iran's global influence, 9–10, 36–7, 185
and reformism, 24, 187–8
support for in Sri Lanka, 187–8, 205, 262
transformations of political message, 259
women's participation, 61
Islamic Unity Society, 97, 107
Islamisation, 23, 37, 77, 84, 229, 235, 240, 242–8, 250, 270, 275
Islamophobia, 17, 77, 90, 152, 295n.14
Ismail Safavi, Shah, 217
Ismailis, 5
Israel, 16, 34, 61, 62, 265
Istanbul, 220

Ja'far Al-Sadiq, 35, 239, 243–4, 246, 308n.29
Ja'fari *fiqh*, 35, 36, 188, 304n.14; *see also* Caferis
Jakarta, 33, 39, 40–1
Jamath-e Islami (JI) Sri Lanka, 187, 188
Java *see* Indonesia
Jordan, 296n.20
José Ingenieros Assocation, 64, 288n.8
Judaism, 51, 55, 59–60, 64, 81
Jumadil Kubra, 246
jurisprudence *see fiqh*
Justicialist Party, 65

Kadhimiyya, 106
Kaka'is *see* Ahl-e Haqq
kalam, 165, 166, 191
Karachi, 137, 147
Karbala, 5, 14, 73, 106, 107, 110, 129, 136, 142–60, 221, 233, 240, 263–5
Karbala paradigm, 152, 158
Kerala, 187
Khamenei, 'Ali, 10, 135–6, 137, 217, 272
Khamenei, Muhammad, 40
Al-Khoei Foundation, 102, 106, 292n.5, 294n.4
Khomeini, Ruhollah, 9, 17, 36, 57–8, 129, 135, 187, 199, 259, 288n.37
Khosrow I, 240–1, 246
khums (religious tithes), 7, 105–6, 127–8, 129, 134, 135–8, 266
Kirazli, Ali, 218
Kirchner, Cristina Fernández de, 63, 64–5, 287n.26, 289n.41
Kirchner, Néstor, 65
knowledge
 academic agendas of, 86–90
 and citation politics, 89
 decolonising, 86–90

knowledge (cont.)
  divine knowledge, 6
  and economic exchange, 204–5
  Eurocentric scholarship, 88, 89–90
  and the Internet, 21, 124–5, 131, 133, 136–7, 191–2, 265–6
  online access to texts, 137, 191–2
  and pilgrimage, 195, 261
  production of, 77, 83, 86–90, 131, 186, 190, 201–5, 265
  and religious authority, 21, 124–5, 127, 131, 133, 265–6
  respect for search for knowledge, 192–3
  and social class, 88–9
  translation of texts, 38, 59, 168–9, 186, 187, 191, 199–201
  transmission of, 21, 22, 77, 124–5, 127, 131, 133, 136–7, 185–207, 261, 265–6
  and transnational networks, 21, 22, 43, 131, 133, 185–207, 261, 265–6
Kosovo, 74, 84–5; see also Balkans
Al-Kubra, Najmuddin see Jumadil Kubra
Kubrawiyya, 246
Kufa, 154
Küng, Hans, 175–6
Kurdish language, 174
Kurdistan, 112, 165
Kurds, 12, 219
Kuwait, 6, 7, 34, 64, 261, 262

labour migration, 8, 187, 202, 214, 261
Lacan, Jacques, 99
Lahore, 137, 197
Lashkar-e Jhangvi, 197
Latour, Bruno, 130, 138
Lebanon, 7, 16, 61, 64, 261, 264, 265
Lebanon War, 259
Lebanese diaspora, 8, 51, 214, 259, 262, 264, 309n.1
legitimacy, 36–7, 43, 47, 48, 82, 84, 98, 131, 133, 261
Lescano, Raúl, 289n.38
lieux de mémoire (sites of memory), 144, 154, 157
localisation, 15, 18–19, 22, 23, 25, 42–3, 57, 189, 237–8, 259, 262
logic, 191, 206
London, 18, 20, 41, 96–115, 169, 263
loyalty, 16, 82, 90, 136, 149, 157
Lucknow, 187

McChesney, Robert, 212–13, 224, 273
Macri, Mauricio, 65, 286n.24, 287n.26, 289n.41
Madras, 187, 191
madrasas, 151, 186–7, 192–4, 197, 202–3, 261
Mahdi, 5, 56
Maher, Bill, 124

Al-Majlisi, Mohammad Baqir, 294n.4
Makdum Brahim Asmara see Maulana Malik Brahim
Malaysia, 38, 233, 239, 240, 242–3
Maldives, 187, 204, 205
Al-Maliki, Nouri, 114
marginalisation, 6, 17–18, 25, 111, 114, 205, 267–8
marja' al-taqlid see clerical authority; senior clerics
Maronite Christianity, 284n.11
marriage, 60, 166, 205
martyrdom, 5, 14, 50, 67–8, 110, 125, 142, 144, 156, 158, 221, 265
Marxism, 289n.38
Mashhad, 39, 106, 129, 137, 297n.29
Masjid-e-Ali centre, 151–2, 153
Maulana Ibrahim, 246–7, 248
Maulana Ishak, 246, 247, 248
Mawdudi, Abu Al-A'la, 38
Mazar-e Sharif, 212
Mecca, 107, 135, 154–5, 233, 235, 263, 264
media
  American, 143
  discourses of 'good' and 'bad' Muslims, 80–1
  Iranian, 187
  minority rights discourses, 113
  negative representations of Islam, 55, 59–60
  representations of Iran, 59–60
  representations of Muslim women, 59–60
  see also social media
mediascapes, 125–7, 133, 138
mediation, 123–4, 126
mediatisation, 55, 125–7, 134–5, 138–9
Mehdi Army, 109
memory, 5, 14–15, 49–50, 53, 62, 67, 77, 87, 144–5, 148, 154, 157
metempsychosis, 166, 167, 173
migration, 8, 13, 19, 50–1, 186, 187, 197, 198–9, 202, 214, 220, 258, 261; see also diasporas
Millennium Development Goals, 171–2
Millennium World Peace Summit, 176
minorities within minorities see double minority status
minority rights discourses, 97, 98, 111–14, 263, 265
Misbah Yazdi, Taqi, 197
Al-Modarresi, Mahdi, 152, 153
Al-Modarresi, Mohammad Taqi, 153
moderate Islam, 17, 20, 25, 75, 77–86, 267
modesty, 60–1, 74, 267
Mohagheghi, Hamideh, 214, 215
Montanaro-Jankovski, Lucia, 83
Montoneros, 63
Morales, Evo, 61
Morimoto, Kazuo, 228, 233–4, 250, 274

Morocco, 86
Moroccan diaspora, 8
mosque-building, 52–3, 54, 151–2
Mossadegh, Mohammad, 57
Mosul, 110
Motahhari, Mortaza, 38, 187, 199
Mubarak, Hosni, 296n.20
Muedini, Fait, 75
Mughal dynasty, 186, 261
Al-Muhajir, Ahmad b. Isa, 35–6
Muhammad, Prophet, 4–5, 35, 58, 155, 235, 236, 268, 303n.5
   descendants of *see sayyids*
   family of *see ahl al-bayt*
Muhammad Hanafiyya, 230, 237, 306n.16
Muhammad ibn Hasan, 5
Muharram, 5, 34, 40, 41–3, 107, 112–13, 142, 144, 147, 150–2, 198, 268–9
mujtahids see senior clerics
Mulla Sadra, 187
multiculturalism, 18, 105
multilocality, 14, 25
Munich, 220
music, 56, 65
Muslim Brotherhood, 38, 203, 262
Muslim identity *see* Islamic identity; Shi'a identity
Muslims Forward, 65–6
Al-Mustafa International University, 10, 33, 41, 188, 198
Mutahhari, Murtada *see* Motahhari, Mortaza
Mutahhari School, Bandung, 38
'My homeland is Husayn (*watani al-husayn*)', 14
mysticism, 11, 40, 41, 156, 169, 172, 190, 267
mythico-religious time, 56, 67

Najaf, 7, 21, 35, 101, 106, 107, 129, 132–5, 136, 146, 154, 156, 192, 263–5
Al-Najafi, Bashir, 132–4
Nakba (Palestinian exodus), 56–7, 61, 62–3
Nakshawani, Ammar, 149, 152, 153, 155–6, 296n.17, 297n.30
Al-Nashed, Hussain, 152
National Solidarity Fund, 136
national identity, 17, 18, 49–50, 57, 79, 157, 215, 221
National Register of Religions (Argentina), 47
nationalism, 7, 77, 87, 103–4, 128, 129, 157, 202, 203, 207, 263
Ne'matollah Jayhunabadi, 21, 167, 172
neo-Kabbalah, 175
neo-Sufism, 175
Netherlands, 8, 42
networks *see* clerical networks; political networks; transnational networks
neoliberalism, 75, 76
New Age spiritualism, 74, 79

New Jersey, 151–2, 153
new media *see* Internet; social media
New York, 147, 151–2, 155, 169, 174
Niai Gede Pinateh, 247
Ni'matullahis, 6
Nimr, Sheikh, 62
9/11 attacks, 18, 171
Nizari-Ismailis, 5
Nora, Pierre, 144
North Macedonia, 74, 81, 84; *see also* Balkans
Nosavan *see* Khosrow I
Nour Foundation, 174
Nuremburg, 219–21, 222
Nusayri-Alawis, 5, 10, 22, 62, 64, 164, 210–11, 216, 219, 220–4, 273

Oliveri, Guillermo, 64
Oniki İmam Yolu (The Way of the Twelve Imams), 213–14, 216–19, 222
oral transmission, 123, 163, 164, 165, 268
Organisation to Support the Islamic Revolution in Iran (OSIRI), 188
Orientalism, 20, 76, 77, 291n.1
origin narratives, 49, 50, 51, 67
Orthodox Christianity, 81, 284n.11
Ostad Elahi Foundation
   advisory body, 170
   board of directors, 170
   conferences, 170
   'Days of Human Solidarity', 170–1
   establishment, 21–2, 163, 168–9
   and ethics, 163, 168, 170, 171, 173–6
   French state endorsement, 17, 21, 169, 266
   funding, 172–3
   headquarters located in Paris, 18, 21, 163, 266
   research and education activities, 171, 173–4
   special consultative status with ECOSOC, 163, 169, 171–2, 173, 266
   study days, 170–1
   and universalism, 21–2, 163, 175–6
   website, 168–75, 266
   see also Ahl-e Haqq
otherness, 17–18, 49, 56, 67, 87, 90
Ottoman Empire, 19–20, 74, 75, 77, 83, 86, 267

Pahlavi dynasty, 165
Pakistan, 37, 137, 157, 197
Pakistani diaspora, 8, 15, 21, 106–7, 143–60, 186, 194, 197, 198–9, 214, 263–4
Palestine, 51, 61, 288n.37; *see also* Nakba
Pallavinci, Maria Camilla, 170
pantheism, 75, 291n.1
Paramadina University, 41
Paris, 18, 21, 80, 163, 168, 266, 268
Parliament of the World's Religions, 176

patronage, 97, 105–7, 113, 127, 136, 137, 186, 201–5, 207, 261–2
Paz, Abdul Karim, 54, 64
Pekalongan, 33, 34–7
Péron, Juan, 47, 290n.50
Peronism, 64–5, 289n.38, 290n.50
persecution, 8, 12, 74, 81, 113, 114, 266, 267
Persian language, 40, 43, 167, 174, 191, 194, 195, 199, 204, 227
Pérsico, Emilio, 63, 64
philosophy, 11, 39, 40, 41, 169, 172, 186–7, 190, 197, 261
pilgrimage (*ziyara*)
  Arba'in pilgrimage, 107, 143, 144, 149, 156, 263
  and collective memory, 144–5, 148, 154, 157
  competition among pilgrimage sites, 129
  and formation of friendships, 107, 147–9
  hajj, 107, 135, 144, 154–5, 263
  to Iran, 106, 264, 297n.29
  to Iraq, 21, 106–8, 142–60, 263–5, 268–9
  to Karbala, 14, 107, 142–60
  and knowledge transmission, 195, 261
  to Mecca, 107, 154–5, 263, 264
  and meeting senior clerics, 154
  as performance of Shi'a identity, 107–8, 144–5, 153–4
  pilgrimage industry, 21, 106–7, 143, 145, 147, 148, 263–4, 268
  to shrine cities, 14, 21, 106–8, 142–60, 263–5
  to shrines of the *ahl al-bayt*, 21
  and social class, 148, 268–9
  spiritual invitation for (*bulava*), 147
  to Syria, 146, 157–60, 264
  and transnational networks, 21, 106–8
  youth pilgrimages, 107
  ziyarat manuals, 144
Pir Sultan Abdal, 217
Po Kabrah, 248
political authority, 9, 135, 137, 190
political identities, 11, 49, 56–7, 209–10, 222–3, 267
political networks, 7, 13
polytheism, 164, 207, 268
Popular Mobilisation Forces (PMF), 108–10
power relations, 12, 99–100, 114–15, 260
prag (threshold), 74
prayer, 80, 81, 108, 148, 149, 198, 200–1, 217, 218
printing, 123, 200
private sphere, 48, 51, 52, 67, 74, 151
proselytism, 37–8, 74, 200, 259
Protestant Reformation, 123
proxy wars, 11
psychoanalysis, 99

public sphere, 14, 48, 54, 56, 59, 67, 74, 151–2
publishing, 34, 40, 134, 136, 144, 171, 188, 191, 202
Putri Cempa legend, 244–8

Al-Qaeda, 146
Qatar, 64
Qom, 7, 10–11, 19, 33–5, 39, 41–2, 106, 129, 135–6, 168, 185, 188, 190, 192–3, 197–8, 227, 233, 261
Quebracho, 62
Qur'an, 58, 137, 151, 155, 167, 191, 192, 206, 213, 233, 270
Qutb, Sayyid, 38

Raden Paku *see* Sunan Giri
Raden Rahmat *see* Sunan Ampel
radical Islam, 17, 18, 20, 25, 44, 75, 78–85, 108–10, 146, 158, 261, 269
radicalisation, 75, 82, 83, 84–5
Raffles, Thomas Stamford, 41, 247
Rakhmat, Jalaluddin, 38–9, 281n.5
Ramadan, 64, 150, 153, 195, 196, 198, 200, 203
reformism, 19, 20, 21, 24, 37, 163, 164, 166–9, 187–8, 202–3, 207, 268, 270
refugees, 186, 197, 198–9, 205, 214
religious authority
  of the *ahl al-bayt*, 6
  competition for, 124, 129, 131, 132–5, 265
  diversity of authorities, 124–5
  and the Internet, 15, 20–1, 124–5, 128–9, 130–9, 265–6
  and knowledge transmission, 21, 124–5, 127, 131, 133, 265–6
  leadership succession, 129–30
  and legitimacy, 131, 133
  localised authority, 127–8
  and political authority, 9, 135, 137
  of senior clerics *see* clerical authority
  Shi'a authority structures, 6–7, 13, 127–30
  and transnational networks, 6–7, 13, 15, 20, 97–8, 105, 114, 127–39, 265–6
religious extremism *see* radical Islam
religious iconography, 125, 128, 132–3, 134, 138
religious pluralism, 46–8
religious tithes *see* khums
religious tolerance, 48, 267, 272
remittances, 105–6, 108, 114, 205, 263
Republican Proposal party (PRO), 64, 65
resource distribution, 113–14, 263
re-territorialisation, 13
revivalism, 37–9, 52, 267
Revolutionary Guards, 146, 159
ritual performance
  Ahl-e Haqq rituals, 165–6
  in America, 151, 268

Arba'in rituals, 107, 112, 143, 144, 149, 150, 156, 263
in Argentina, 66–7, 68
'Ashura' rituals, 14, 20, 42, 50, 66–8, 74, 103, 112–13, 151
in Britain, 20, 103, 112–13
and collective memory, 14–15, 144–5, 148, 154
folk traditions, 19, 36, 212
in Germany, 211, 214, 219–22
ghadir khumm festivities, 211, 219–22
in India, 42
in Indonesia, 34, 41–3, 261
Muharram rituals, 34, 41–3, 107, 112–13, 142, 144, 151–2, 198, 268–9
shared ritual practices, 211, 273
and Shi'a identity, 107–8, 144–5
in Sri Lanka, 198
see also fasting; pilgrimage; prayer
Ruqayyah bint Husayn, 146
Russia, 165; *see also* Soviet Union
Rutgers University, 152

Sadat, Anwar, 37
Al-Sadiq Foundation, 35
Al-Sadr, Muhammad Baqir, 134
Al-Sadr, Muhammad Sadiq, 134
Al-Sadr, Muqtada, 109, 134–5
Al-Sadr, Musa, 7–8
Safavid architecture, 151, 159
Safavid dynasty, 6, 186, 217, 261
Al-Sahifa al-Sajjadiyya, 191, 199–201
Salafism, 12, 22, 84–5, 124, 146, 153, 156, 188–9, 194, 196, 202–3, 207, 262, 273; *see also* Wahhabism
Samarra, 21, 106, 146
Sassanid dynasty, 240–1
Saudi Arabia
  discourses of autochthony, 16
  execution of Sheikh Nimr, 62
  influence of, 81, 85, 156, 188–9, 202, 203, 207, 257, 262
  foreign policy, 61–2
  proxy wars with Iran, 11
  Shi'a Islamist parties, 7
  sponsorship of mosque-building, 151
  Wahhabism, 81, 85, 155–6
Sayyid, Salman, 76–7, 86
Sayyida Zaynab shrine, 21, 146, 157–60, 264
*sayyid*s (descendents of Muhammad), 17, 23, 35–6, 216, 227–51, 268, 274–5
sectarianism
  academic discourses on, 11–12, 209–11, 222–3
  in America, 21, 147, 151–7
  and arbitration by neutral nation states, 17, 269
  and authoritarianism, 12

in Britain, 20, 97–8, 104
charities' role in fostering, 20, 97, 105–6, 108–9, 263
and conversion, 12–13, 206–7
in Iraq, 8, 11, 20, 97–8, 105–10, 146, 157, 263, 265
and minority rights discourses, 111–14, 263, 265
in Pakistan, 157, 197
politicisation of, 4, 11–13, 210–11, 222–3
porosity of sectarian boundaries, 22–3, 24, 211, 218–22, 227–33, 250, 273–4
in Sri Lanka, 12, 17, 22, 197, 202–4, 206–7, 261, 269
in Syria, 146
secularism, 6, 8, 10, 39, 42, 47, 48, 67, 76, 83, 164
securitisation, 18, 84–5, 159, 264
Seinol Abidin *see* Al-Aydarus, Zayn Al-'Abidin; Zayn Al-'Abidin
seminaries (*hawzat*), 7, 10–11, 34–5, 39, 101, 132–3, 135–6, 185–94, 197, 227–8, 233, 261, 268
Senegal
  conversions to Shi'ism, 13, 270–2
  economic development, 259, 272
  French colonisation, 270
  influence of Iran, 259, 261–2
  influence of Islamic Revolution, 259
  Iranian embassy, 262
  Islamisation, 270
  Lebanese diaspora, 259, 262, 264, 309n.1
  localisation of Shi'ism, 262
  religious tolerance, 272
senior clerics
  based in shrine cities, 7, 127, 129, 132–5, 154
  emulation of, 6–7, 101, 133, 137, 154, 206
  as heads of state, 9
  khums collection, 7, 105–6, 127–8, 129, 134, 135–8, 265
  khums redistribution, 127, 134, 135–8
  leadership succession, 129–30
  meeting with pilgrims, 154
  networks of representatives, 7, 21, 105–6, 107, 114, 127–8, 134, 135, 136, 137, 266, 272
  online biographies, 133
  political intervention, 133–4
  responses to followers' queries, 133
  and Shi'a authority structures, 6–7, 127–30
  and Shi'a Islamist parties, 7
  websites, 15, 20–1, 124–5, 131–5, 136–8, 265
  wilayat al-faqih, 9, 10, 135, 137, 157, 190
  writings, 133
  see also clerical authority
*sepoy*s, 42
sermons (*khutba*), 56, 59

sexuality, 59, 60
Shafi'i *madhhab*, 36, 187, 188, 192, 203, 261
Shahr Banu, 240–1, 246
Shahrestani, Jawad, 136, 137
shari'a (Islamic law), 59, 167, 192
Shari'ati, 'Ali, 38, 40, 76, 88–9, 158, 187, 199
Shi'a identity, 12, 17, 20, 23, 97, 100–14, 144–5, 153–7, 186, 209–11, 215, 263, 269–75; *see also* Islamic identity
Shi'a Islamist parties, 7, 13
Shi'i International, 15, 16, 192
Shi'a militias, 106, 108–10
Shi'a religious centres (*husayniyyat*), 101–3, 104, 197–9
Shi'a rights movement, 111–14
shrine cities
  Iran, 7, 106, 129, 264
  Iraq, 7, 15, 21, 23, 101, 106–8, 129, 132–5, 142–57, 192, 263–5
  pilgrimage to, 14, 21, 106–8, 142–60, 263–5
  seminaries, 7, 34–5, 39, 101, 132, 135–6
  senior clerics based in, 7, 127, 129, 132–5, 154
  as spiritual homelands, 15, 21, 23, 144, 145, 149–50, 152–4, 157, 263–4
  Syria, 15, 146, 157–60, 264
  see also individual cities
shrines
  destruction or threat of destruction, 21, 146, 155, 157–60, 203, 264
  featured on senior clerics' websites, 132, 134
  pilgrimage to, 14, 21, 142–60, 263–5
  see also individual shrines
Singapore, 242
silsila (spiritual genealogies), 6
Al-Sistani, 'Ali, 7, 101, 108, 110, 124, 132–4, 135–8, 154, 217, 265, 292n.1, 292n.5
Six-Day War, 37
social class, 88–9, 100, 148, 258, 266, 268–9
social justice, 56, 62, 66, 67, 111–14, 267, 296n.16
social media, 113, 134, 138, 188, 192, 195, 202, 265
socialism, 76, 82–3, 84, 88–9, 269; *see also* Communism
'Sociology, History and Thought of the Muslim World' seminar, 54
soft power, 10–11, 135
Sorbonne University, 169, 170
Soviet Union, 37, 76, 85; *see also* Russia
Spanish language, 56, 59, 267
spiritual homelands, 14–15, 21, 23, 144, 145, 149–50, 152–4, 157, 263–4
Sri Lanka
  anti-imperialism, 195
  Arabic colleges, 192–4

asylum seekers, 186, 197, 198–9, 205
Buddhism, 202, 203
civil war, 185, 193–4, 261
conversions to Shi'ism, 9, 11, 22, 188, 195–6, 205–7, 272–3
debt, 201–2
destruction of shrines, 203
diasporic remittances, 205
discourses of autochthony, 189
influence of Iran, 15, 185, 187–9, 193–4, 196, 198, 202, 203–4, 207
influence of Saudi Arabia, 188–9, 202, 203, 207
intellectuals, 194–6
internally displaced people, 199
Iranian cultural organisations, 198
Iranian embassy, 188, 198
Islamic centres, 185, 196–9, 201, 202
localisation of Shi'ism, 22, 189
madrasas, 186, 192–4, 197, 202–3, 261
nationalism, 202, 203, 207
patronage, 201–5, 207
practice of *taqiyya*, 22, 186, 194, 200, 203
reformism, 202–3, 207
Salafism, 12, 22, 188–9, 194, 196, 202–3, 207, 262, 273
sectarianism, 12, 17, 22, 185–6, 188–9, 195–6, 197, 202–4, 206–7, 261, 269
support for the Islamic Revolution, 187–8, 205, 262
transmission of religious knowledge, 22, 185–207, 261
Twelver Shi'ism, 22, 185–207, 261
visiting scholars, 196–7, 200–1, 205
Sri Lanka Muslim Students Federation (SLMSF), 188
subject-positions, 99–100
subjectivity, 98–100
Sufism, 6, 12–13, 22, 74–5, 79, 165–6, 168, 196, 202–3, 207, 212, 242, 270, 272; *see also* Bektashi Islam; dervishes
Suharto, 37, 39, 42
Sukarno, 39
Sultan Sehak, 166, 167–8
Sunan Ampel, 244–8
Sunan Giri, 246–8
Sunan Gunung Jati *see* Jumadil Kubra
Supreme Islamic Shi'a Council, 7
Syekh Jumadil Kubro *see* Jumadil Kubra
Syria
  Assad regime, 10, 159–60
  civil war, 146, 157–60, 264
  destruction or threatened destruction of shrines, 21, 146, 157–60, 264
  French mandate, 159
  ISIS, 21, 61, 146, 156, 158, 159–60

Nusayri-Alawis, 10, 219
  pilgrimage to, 146, 157–60, 264
  relations with Iran, 10
  resistance movements, 61
  sectarianism, 146
  secularism, 10
  shrine cities, 15, 146, 157–60, 264
Syrian diaspora, 51

Tabligh Jamaat, 203, 262
takfir (declaring a Muslim an unbeliever), 38, 197, 203
Tamil language, 188, 191, 196, 199–201
taqiyya (pious dissimulation), 22, 74, 186, 194, 200, 203, 267
tarbiya movement, 38–9
technoscapes, 125, 128, 131, 133, 138
Tehran, 129, 137, 168, 188, 192
Tehran University, 33, 39, 168, 194, 197
Tehrik-e Taliban, 197
television, 153
temporary marriage (*mut'a*), 60
Terengganu, 243
terrorism, 18, 55, 61–2, 112, 171
Thailand, 233
Timerman, Héctor, 64
traditional arts, 39
translation, 38, 59, 168–9, 186, 187, 191, 199–201
transmigration of souls, 166, 167, 173
transnational networks
  and 'Alid piety, 218–23
  between diaspora and homeland, 13, 23, 102–3, 105–10, 114, 262–3
  charitable networks, 105–6, 108–9
  clerical networks, 6–7, 13, 15, 106, 107, 114, 127–8, 134, 135
  of educational institutions, 10, 19, 41, 202, 203–4, 205
  and the Internet, 15, 20–1, 128–9, 130–9, 191–2, 265–6
  and *khums* collection and redistribution, 135–8, 266
  and knowledge transmission, 21, 22, 43, 131, 133, 185–207, 261, 265–6
  and pilgrimage, 21, 106–8
  political networks, 7, 13
  and religious authority, 6–7, 13, 15, 20–1, 97–8, 105, 114, 127–39, 265–6
transnationalism
  compared with cosmopolitanism, 258–9
  definitions, 13
  as field of discourse and debate, 13–14
  limitations as an approach, 258
Trump, Donald, 159, 264
Tunisia, 136

Turkey, 5, 74, 75–6, 137, 151, 214, 216, 217, 218, 219, 220, 267
Turkish diaspora, 8, 22–3, 209–24, 273
Turkish identity, 221
Turner, Victor, 145, 259, 294n.7
Twelver Shi'ism
  Ahl-e Haqq reconciles doctrines with, 163, 167, 173, 268
  in America, 143–57
  in Argentina, 19, 50, 52–68
  Bektashi links to, 20, 73
  beliefs about the *mahdi*, 56
  beliefs about Muhammad's succession, 5
  clerical networks, 6–7, 13
  in Germany, 22–3, 210–11, 216–17, 219–24, 273
  in Indonesia, 19, 35
  in Iran, 6, 9–11, 275
  religious authority structures, 6–7, 13, 127–30
  in Sri Lanka, 22, 185–207, 261

'Umar, 213
Umayyad dynasty, 4–5, 15, 265
United Arab Emirates, 151
United Kingdom *see* Britain
United Nations
  designates Sri Lanka a sub-regional sanctuary country, 198–9
  Economic and Social Council (ECOSOC), 163, 169, 171–2, 173, 174, 266
  High Commissioner for Refugees (UNHCR), 199
  Millennium Development Goals, 171–2
  Millennium World Peace Summit, 176
United States
  'Ashura' rituals, 151
  conversions to Shi'ism, 8
  depicted as Yazid, 265
  diasporic politics, 13
  Euro-American geopolitics, 76, 80–1, 87, 88
  Euro-American scholarship, 88, 89–90
  foreign policy, 57, 61–2, 160
  Iranian diaspora, 8
  Iraqi diaspora, 8
  Islamic centres, 151–2, 153
  interference in Iran, 165
  invasion of Iraq, 110, 132, 133–4, 142–3
  media, 143
  mosque-building, 151–2
  Muslim immigration, 8, 258
  New Age spiritualism, 79
  Pakistani diaspora, 15, 21, 143–60, 263–4
  pilgrimage industry, 143, 145, 147, 148, 263–4, 268
  sanctions against Iraq, 293n.11
  sectarianism, 21, 147, 151–7

United States (*cont.*)
  travel restrictions, 159, 264
  Trump administration, 159, 264
  Twelver Shi'ism, 143–57
universalism, 17, 18, 21–2, 148, 163, 175–6, 259–60, 276
Urdu, 150, 151, 153, 187, 194, 264
usra movement, 38

Vatican, 79–80
Venezuela, 17
Vertovec, Steven, 13
victimisation discourses, 18, 20, 80–1, 84–5, 110, 111–14, 265
visibility, 48–9, 50, 54, 56, 89, 111–13, 164, 166, 204, 261
voice, 86, 89–90, 113

Wadi Al-Salam cemetery, 132
Al-Wafa Pesantren, 35
Wahhabism, 37, 81, 84–5, 153, 155–6, 196, 202, 207; *see also* Salafism
Wali Songo, 244–8
Werbner, Pnina, 152, 160
Westoxification (*gharbzadegi*), 76
WhatsApp, 192, 266
'Who is Hussain?' campaign, 97, 151, 268
wilaya (authority), 190
wilayat al-faqih (guardianship of the jurisconsult), 9, 10, 135, 137, 157, 190
Williams, Raymond, 127
women
  hawza education, 190
  and the Islamic Revolution, 61
  media representations of, 59–60
  and modesty, 60–1
  organisations and associations, 54, 60–1
  performance of narratives of collective memory, 62
  segregation of, 81
  and sexuality, 60
  status of, 58, 59–60
  wearing of the hijab, 57, 60–1, 62, 66, 150
Women of Monotheistic Faith, 61
World Council of Religious Leaders, 176
'World Ethos' project, 175–6
World Organisation for Islamic Services (WOFIS), 187

Yaresan *see* Ahl-e Haqq
Yayasan Pesantren Islam (YAPI), 35
Yazid, 112, 158, 221, 265
Yemen, 6, 36, 187, 239, 240, 242, 261, 275
Yeral, Ali, 218–19, 220–2
Yogyakarta, 33, 34, 39–40
youth culture, 40
Yugoslavia *see* Balkans; Bosnia; Kosovo; North Macedonia

zakat (charitable donation), 105–6
Zaydis, 5
Zayn Al-'Abidin, 5, 199, 230, 239–44, 246, 275
Zaynab bint 'Ali, 61, 146, 157–60
Zia-ul-Haqq, Muhammad, 37
ziyara see pilgrimage
ziyarat manuals, 144
Zoroastrianism, 165

EU representative:
Easy Access System Europe
Mustamäe tee 50, 10621 Tallinn, Estonia
Gpsr.requests@easproject.com

www.ingramcontent.com/pod-product-compliance
Lightning Source LLC
Chambersburg PA
CBHW071827230426
43672CB00013B/2779